A good education consists in giving to the body and to the soul all the beauty and all the perfection of which they are capable.

Plato

Grandest
of Enterprises

Illinois State Normal University

1857-1957

BY HELEN E. MARSHALL

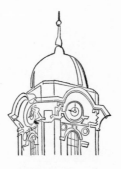

Normal, Illinois · December 1956

For the children of the free,
and their teachers

"The education of the children of the state
is the grandest of enterprises,"

—*Richard Edwards,* 1867

First, A Few Words

ALMOST a hundred years ago young Justin Richardson of Bloomington wrote in his diary that he had on Tuesday, September 29, 1857, attended the laying of the cornerstone of the State Normal University. The speakers, he wrote, seemed to gather inspiration from the "transcendent importance of the occasion." He was elated that he, only a boy barely out of his teens, had been asked to write out in his firm long hand the names of the county officials, and of those persons who had made donations for the construction of the building, so that they might be placed in the cornerstone.

Reminiscent of the oratory of the afternoon, he mused at length upon "the untold influence for good the institution might exert in years to come."

"Its powerful and salutary influence," he prophesied, "shall be more enduring than the granite foundation, it shall be perpetuated from one generation to another. . . ."

He envisaged the great building of brick and stone that would presently rise above the cornfields and dominate the landscape. "May this proud structure be but the emblem of its own proud eminence among many similar institutions. It overlooks the surrounding prairie spread out in all its beauty and loveliness. . . . May coming generations rise up and call us blessed for establishing such an institution."

Today Illinois State Normal University, a teachers college granting both bachelor's and master's degrees, is the rich fulfillment of the dreams of Daniel Wilkins, Jonathan Turner, Simeon Wright, George Bunsen, Jesse Fell, Newton Bateman, Charles Hovey, and other men of action who called it into being. From a single building high on a lonely prairie, the school has grown into a beautiful tree-shaded campus with many buildings, a faculty of nearly three hundred, and a student body of thirty-four hundred. Its alumni are numbered in thousands; its graduates are teaching throughout the world.

Great teachers such as Thomas Metcalf, Charles DeGarmo, Charles McMurry, Frank McMurry, Henry McCormick, Orson L. Manchester, Lida Brown McMurry, June Rose Colby, and such able administrators as Richard Edwards, John W. Cook, David Felmley and Raymond W. Fairchild have implemented the ideals of the founders, and have kept Illinois State Normal University what it was intended to be—a training school for teachers.

At intervals of twenty-five years commemorative volumes have recorded the progress of Normal University. James V. McHugh and John Williston Cook, later president, published the history of the first quarter-century in 1892. The *Semi-centennial History* published in 1907 was a cooperative faculty enterprise under the direction of John A. H. Keith. In 1935 the publication of *The Development of the Teachers College in the United States with Special Reference to Illinois State Normal University* by Charles A. Harper marked the anniversary of the first graduating class. The last pages of this centennial history were written with a deep sense of obligation, not only to those who in the past have written so succinctly and understandingly, but toward those who cherished and kept old programs, clippings, letters, diaries, and scrapbooks.

I am especially grateful to Ellen Edwards who preserved the voluminous papers of her father, President Richard Edwards, in the hope that they might someday become the property of Normal University, and to her brother, the late Owen Edwards, who executed this trust; to Mrs. Agnes Gale who gave me access to her collection of materials relating to her father, President John W. Cook; to Mrs. Laura Hayes Pricer of the English department and Mrs. Florence Sample Fleming, alumna, who supplied rich anecdotal material; to Dr. Robert Guy Buzzard, President of Eastern Illinois Teachers College, who read several chapters and made valuable suggestions; and to the late Dr. Raymond W. Fairchild, President of Illinois State Normal University, at whose request I undertook the writing of this volume. His confidence and encouragement were ever heart-warming and inspiring. Miss Eleanor Welch, Director of Libraries; Mrs. Inez Dunn, McLean County Historical Society; Miss Elizabeth Abraham, Withers Library; and the late Dr. Harry Pratt of the Illinois Historical Library, helped greatly in locating material and facilitating research. Dr. Gertrude

Hall, Director of Publicity, secured many of the illustrations for the earlier years, and Mr. Nelson R. Smith, University photographer, has given unstintingly of his talents and time in procuring photographs of the later period. Dr. Esther Vinson, professor of English, has read the entire manuscript and made suggestions as to style; Mr. Harry J. Owens, alumnus, and various of his professional associates, have assisted with matters of content, illustration, and format. To Mr. Paul Cary, my secretary, and to Mrs. Dorothy King, who typed the final draft, I am likewise indebted.

What a privilege it is to serve in the training of teachers, to help young men and young women comprehend the magnitude of their calling and the trust that reposes in the schools of America.

HELEN E. MARSHALL

Normal, Illinois
September 22, 1956

Table of Contents

Illustrations

Grandest of Enterprises

CHAPTER I

For the Common Schools

JESSE FELL looked up from the cubic yard of earth he had turned, toward the setting sun. Before another day dawned, it could be announced that work on the new State Normal University had actually begun. That morning, Saturday, August 22, 1857, the contractors, Soper and Mortimer of Chicago, their wives, along with some Bloomington business men, some members of the State Board of Education, and the architect, G. P. Randall, of Chicago, had ridden out north of town and selected the site. It was near the middle of the tract donated by Meshack Pike.[1] In the afternoon Daniel Wilkins and other members of the Board had staked out the lines for excavation and later Jesse Fell had returned alone and set shovel to the ground. In a few weeks the contractors would have workmen with picks and shovels swarming all over the place, but the project was dear to Jesse Fell's heart and he was quietly indulging himself in the satisfaction of having turned the first spadeful of earth. As long as he lived he would take pride in the role he had played in founding the school.[2] Sometimes as he had gone from door to door with subscription lists, he wondered if he were not the only person seriously interested in the normal school. In the end local business men had subscribed handsomely, the McLean County Commissioners had voted a generous donation of swamp lands, and Bloomington had secured the location.[3]

It was a splendid site. The architect's plan called for a great three-story building with a tower and dome a hundred and fifty feet above the ground. From the crest of the beautiful swell of land where Fell stood, the ground sloped gently in all directions. The

[1] *Daily Pantagraph* (Bloomington), August 24, 1857.
[2] Frances Milton I. Morehouse, *Life of Jesse Fell* ("University of Illinois Studies," Vol. V, No. 42; Urbana: University of Illinois, 1916), pp. 4–45.
[3] On September 28, 1850, the United States government gave to the state all swamp and overflowed lands. John H. Burnham, *History of McLean County, Illinois* (Chicago: William LeBaron, 1879), p. 116; *Weekly Pantagraph* (Bloomington), May 13, 1857; *Illinois State Journal* (Springfield), February 2, 1857.

3

building would be in direct line with that of Illinois Wesleyan University, a mile to the south, and would command a fine view of the surrounding country, including several miles of both railroads.[4] To the south and east beyond the cornfield, the hazel brush along the slough, and the railroad tracks, on another rise of ground could be seen Fell's own new home, just completed that summer. It was a large square wooden structure with a cupola atop and verandas on three sides.[5] It stood on a knoll in the center of a triangular park-like tract. A few spindly trees had been planted to mark the streets so ambitiously laid out two years before. On the whole North Bloomington presented a new and barren look. The only other house in the area was that of William McCambridge, station agent at the Junction.[6]

Jesse Fell had a keen interest in education. For a brief time before he became successively a lawyer, editor, farmer, nurseryman, real estate promoter, and land speculator, he had been a teacher. One of the things about the new country that had concerned him was its lack of schools and its need of good teachers.[7] It was estimated in 1840 that there were at least 100,000 children in Illinois who were not in school and over 28,000 adults who were illiterate.[8] When Fell laid out lots for sales in his first addition to the town of North Bloomington, he set aside the block opposite his home and designated it as Seminary Block. He considered establishing a school and had corresponded with Horace Mann of Massachusetts, whose work he had so heartily approved, to inquire his ideas as to the "constitution" of such a school, its scope and curriculum.[9] Fell

[4] *Weekly Pantagraph*, August 26, 1857.

[5] Morehouse, *op. cit.*, p. 34.

[6] About thirty lots in North Bloomington were sold by W. F. Arny and Company, June 15, 1854. Prices ranged from thirty to fifty dollars. In 1855 a company composed of Jesse Fell, R. R. Landon, L. R. Case, C. W. Holder, and L. C. Blakesly began another development. Later Fell bought out his partners. An ardent temperance man, and intent on bringing to his neighborhood a desirable class of residents, he provided in all deeds to lots in North Bloomington that intoxicating liquors should never be sold on the premises. Burnham, *History of McLean County*, pp. 426–427.

[7] Thomas Campbell, Secretary of State and ex-officio Superintendent of Schools reported January 21, 1847, that in fifty-seven counties there were 1,592 schools and 1,535 teachers. Of 155,715 persons under twenty years of age, only 46,814 were enrolled in school.
    John Williston Cook, *Educational History of Illinois* (Chicago: Henry O. Shepard, 1912), p. 108.

[8] Theodore Calvin Pease, *The Frontier State*, 1814–1848, Vol. II of *The Centennial History of Illinois*, ed. C. W. Alvord (5 vols.; Springfield: Centennial Commission, 1919), p. 431.

[9] Morehouse, *op. cit.*, p. 46.

regarded Mann as having a sound philosophy, high ideals, and vision, and had hoped that the State Board of Education would select him to direct the new normal school.

Although the building was not yet begun and not a single class had met, the school had already had a dramatic and exciting history. Several factors contributed to the realization of the need for more adequate preparation of teachers in the state. The rapid growth in the population from 1840 to 1850 had been inevitably accompanied by a dearth of teachers, and prior to 1850 anyone who could read and write and had an elementary knowledge of the so-called common branches might secure a position as a teacher. Although the School Law of 1841 had required that all teachers be examined and certified to draw public funds,[10] the scarcity of qualified persons and the lack of educational experiences on the part of the examining officers mitigated against the thoroughness of the examination. In response to the demand for improvement in the schools, the 1855 General Assembly created the elective office of State Superintendent of Public Instruction and provided for a school commissioner to visit schools and examine prospective teachers.

The low salaries paid to teachers tended to discourage the liberal arts graduate from staying long in the profession, if indeed he entered it at all. For ministers and lawyers, teaching was often a side-line, not a real vocation. The meager returns from teaching sustained many a young lawyer while struggling to build up a clientele or before turning, as Jesse Fell had done, to the more lucrative and exciting business of land speculation and practical politics. The brief teaching experience of these college trained men—physicians, farmers, lawyers, and editors—did make them sympathetic and alert to the needs of schools and teachers, however, and in the press and legislative halls they valiantly championed the cause of education.[11]

---

[10] The Public School Law of 1841 had 109 sections.

Cook, *Educational History of Illinois*, p. 109; Arthur Charles Cole, *The Era of the Civil War, 1848-1870*, Vol. III of *The Centennial History of Illinois*, ed. C. W. Alvord (5 vols.; Springfield: Centennial Commission, 1919), p. 230.

[11] William H. Powell, State Superintendent, reported December 15, 1858, that salaries in Illinois were as low as five dollars for women and nine dollars for men, and as high as $150 for men and sixty dollars for women. In 1859 the highest paid to men was $200 and sixty dollars to women. Cook, *Educational History of Illinois*, p. 82.

The Common School Law of 1825 had provided that as soon as there were fifteen families settled in a Congressional township a common school free to persons between ages of five and twenty-one could be started. Such schools were to be maintained at least three months of each year, and a popular teacher might arrange a teaching schedule so he could teach three or four short terms in as many districts. Frequently literate farmers obtained teaching employment in the slack seasons between fall harvesting and spring planting. The law provided taxation not in excess of five mills, and no one, however affluent, could be assessed more than ten dollars per year for the support of schools. In addition two dollars out of every hundred received by the state was set aside as a school fund, and five-sixths of the interest was to be divided among the counties of the state in proportion to the number of white children under twenty-one. The law of 1825 was rendered futile two years later when the power to enforce the collection of taxes was taken away.[12]

The situation was typical of the new West. The scarcity of trained, devoted teachers was invariably noted by visitors. Occasionally public spirited persons such as Catherine Beecher [13] and former-Governor William Slade of Vermont set about with true evangelistic zeal to recruit well-trained young women who would go west and teach in common schools or found seminaries. As agent of the National Educational Society, Slade secured the co-operation of the Illinois Educational Society, a volunteer organization of editors, ministers, and civic-minded persons, and through it arranged for the placement of his proteges. He made regular visits to the state beginning in 1847. In that year he brought sixteen young women to the state and in the following year eighteen. The fourteenth group was sent west in September 1853, and the recruitment continued for the rest of the decade.

The western "friends of education" complained that the young

[12] *Ibid.*, pp. 32–34; W. L. Pillsbury, "Illinois State Normal University," *Seventeenth Biennial Report of the Superintendent of Public Instruction*, July 1, 1886–June 30, 1888 (Springfield: State of Illinois, 1889), pp. LXXVII–LXXVIII.

[13] Catherine Beecher (1800–1878), daughter of Reverend Lyman Beecher, and sister of Edward, first president of Illinois College, and of Harriet Beecher Stowe, helped organize the "Ladies Society for Promoting Education in the West," and was responsible for founding female colleges at Quincy, Illinois, Burlington, Iowa, and Milwaukee, Wisconsin. The latter has survived as Milwaukee-Downer College for Women. *DAB*, Vol. II, p. 125.

women were not brought west fast enough. Too it was discovered that the eastern teachers made excellent wives and mothers, and in less than five years, two-thirds had been lured from the classroom into domestic life. In some localities suspicion was voiced that these imported eastern teachers were the "selected emissaries of abolitionism" bent on converting Illinois youth into a likeness of "New England caste and demogoguery." [14] By 1850 Illinois had at least fourteen private colleges or schools above seminary rank, mostly denominational, which were drawn upon heavily for teachers but their graduates were not especially trained for teaching and the supply was never equal to the demand. Too, the traditional denominational college curriculum with its emphasis on theology, Latin, and Greek drew the ire of certain practical farmers who were advocating scientific studies in horticulture, botany, physiology, and the causes and cure for animal diseases.[15]

Through Congressional foresight the state had come into the possession of certain lands and funds to be used as subsidies for public education but in the late 1820's when the taxable property of the state did not provide sufficient revenue to carry out the grandiose schemes for public improvements projected by the politicians of the state, legislation was passed authorizing the sale of these lands, and empowering the governor to borrow the proceeds at six percent, the interest being added to the respective funds. As an aid to the public schools, interest on the so-called seminary fund was loaned to the school fund for annual distribution. The seminary lands brought only $55,000, and as a result no great backlog of funds was available when the friends of education began to agitate for state-supported teacher training schools.[16]

To Jesse Fell, leaning on his spade that August afternoon, this seemed the late fulfillment of a long dream—a dream shared in common. In Jacksonville the year after Fell came to Illinois, the Ladies Association for Educating Females launched its program

---

[14] Stephen A. Douglas, a Vermont teacher-emigrant, later joined in this political cry. *Belleville Advocate*, February 18, 1857; *Ottawa Free Trader*, March 15, 1851, quoted in Cole, *op. cit.*, p. 235.

[15] Mary Turner Carriel, *The Life of Jonathan Baldwin Turner* (Jacksonville, 1911), p. 95; Lloyd Lewis, *John S. Wright: Prophet of the Prairies* (Chicago: Prairie Farm Publishing Co., 1941), p. 167.

[16] Cook, *Educational History of Illinois*, pp. 71–77.

to "encourage and assist young ladies to qualify themselves for teachers." Four years later the Reverend John F. Brooks opened a teachers' seminary in Waverly, but since it was not successful, he moved to Springfield in 1840 and contented himself with opening an academy with special attention given to the educating of teachers. Neither the college nor the academy with emphasis on teacher training was the answer to Illinois' problem. Latin and Greek, calculus, and higher mathematics were not essential. Statistics on illiteracy showed the real need for teachers who could teach boys and girls to read and write and perform the simple mathematical operations that would help them as farmers, storekeepers and housewives.

Educational meetings at Vandalia in 1833 and in 1834 had considered the incompetency as well as scarcity of teachers. In February 1835 William J. Gatewood, Senator from Gallatin County, introduced a bill for a uniform system of common schools and county seminaries throughout the state, and proposed memorializing Congress for liberal appropriations for the support of teachers' seminaries. The bill failed, but, undaunted, he introduced it again at the special session of the legislature in 1836.

If the legislators were not convinced of the ripeness of the time or the feasibility of the program, the sponsors did not despair. They eagerly followed the work of James Carter and Charles Brooks in Massachusetts and the creation of the Massachusetts State Board of Education. They read the Reverend Calvin Stowe's *Report on Elementary Public Instruction* "made to the General Assembly of Ohio, calling attention to the normal schools of Prussia." They were intrigued when the offer of Edmund Dwight of Boston to give $10,000 to the state for the education of teachers, provided the State of Massachusetts would appropriate an equal sum, was accepted. Soon Massachusetts had not one but three normal schools.[17]

Illinois was hard hit by the panic of 1837. On the eve of the great depression the state had embarked on a system of public improvements, highways, canals and railroads. The stock of the state bank fell to thirty-seven cents on the dollar, and by 1842 its credit had dropped to forty-four. It was forced to liquidate. The

[17] Pillsbury, *op. cit., pp.* LXXVIII—LXXX.

Old Bank of Illinois, which had been reactivated in the more prosperous era, likewise collapsed. The paralyzing effect of the panic on private and public finance was far reaching. Men like Jesse Fell and his friend Asahel Gridley had seen their fortunes swept away. Governor Thomas Ford estimated the debt of the State of Illinois, excluding interest, to be $15,157,348.71.[18] Repudiation was neither moral nor desirable.

Public schools and teacher training were among the projects that suffered, but men like John Wright, a commission merchant who had built Chicago's first school building at his own expense, would not permit the ideas to perish. Wright, who lost his fortune in the panic, now offered his time and talents to organizing progressive farmers into a society to work for the betterment of schools. In January 1839, he headed a delegation to the State Capital at Vandalia to petition the Legislature to charter the Union Agricultural Society, for the "sole purpose of instruction and science and improvements in scientific and practical agriculture and the mechanical arts in the counties of LaSalle, Will, Cook, McHenry and Kane." On February 19 the act of incorporation was passed, and six months later Wright was made secretary of the $10,000 non-profit organization. In order to sell stock, Wright insisted that the society establish a newspaper, arguing that a farm paper could awaken readers to needs that the general paper did not. Wright, who had never worked a day on a farm or written a line for publication, became the editor and publisher for the *Union Agriculturalist,* a monthly magazine.[19]

When the first issue appeared in October 1839 the most controversial article related to schools. Having discovered that the College and Seminary funds had been borrowed by the state he proposed that the $122,000 in the fund under the original terms of the grants by Congress be used to endow a normal school or teachers' seminary. In December 1840 he attended the organization meeting of the Illinois State Education Society, a voluntary organization of ministers, lawyers, doctors, teachers and others interested in education, in Springfield. He also talked over his plan with members of the Legislature in January 1841. In a vig-

---

[18] Pease, *op. cit.,* pp. 317–324.
[19] The name of the *Union Agriculturist* was changed to *Prairie Farmer* in January 1843.

orous editorial in the March 1842 number of the *Union Agriculturalist* Wright declared that in order to create a system of common school instruction adequate to the needs of the state it was absolutely essential that the state have a competent superintendent and that it establish a teachers' seminary.[20]

In 1844 Wright issued a call in the *Prairie Farmer* for an educational convention to be held in Peoria in October. Here it was resolved that interest on the Seminary and College funds ought to be applied to those seminaries in the state that would establish a teachers' department.[21]

At a convention in Jacksonville in 1845, the teachers themselves discussed the plan for state aid to colleges and seminaries in training teachers, along with such academic matters as vocational education, and differences in the education of the sexes.[22] In October 1846 at a convention and institute in Chicago, the first held in Illinois, Henry Barnard was the principal speaker. As superintendent of schools in Connecticut, he was vigorously agitating for a teachers' seminary in his home state. The Legislature the following term asked the Committee on Schools to inquire into the expediency of using a portion of the school College and Seminary funds to support a teachers' seminary.

When the Constitutional Convention met in 1847, George Bunsen of St. Clair County, a German immigrant farmer and former teacher trained by Pestalozzi, proposed a detailed system of organization for schools and teachers' seminaries, but nothing came of it. Although disappointed, friends of education were not rebuffed.

In an appeal in behalf of the common schools issued in April 1848, Horace S. Cooley, Secretary of State and *ex-officio* superintendent of the common schools of Illinois, declared: "We should not be unmindful of our paramount duty to secure the thorough qualification of our own citizens, male and female, in the art of teaching." [23] As a result the Illinois Education Society meeting in Springfield in January 1849 discussed the matter of teacher train-

[20] Quoted from the *Union Agriculturist* in Pillsbury, *op. cit.*, p. LXXX.
[21] When Reverend D. J. Pinckney of Mt. Morris introduced the resolution he probably had in mind subsidizing the denominational colleges of the state. Pease, *op. cit.*, p. 434.
[22] *Ibid.*, p. 432.
[23] Pillsbury, *op. cit.*, p. LXXXIV.

ing on four successive evenings. The secretary reported that C. B. Denio, Colonel William H. Bissell, later governor, and Richard Yates were among those who spoke eloquently in behalf of the proposition. David Gregg, *ex-officio* superintendent of public instruction, in his report for 1857 urged that the interest on the College and Seminary funds, which had been loaned since 1837 to the school fund and distributed with the income of the school fund to the counties, be diverted no longer from its original purpose but be used to educate teachers in the colleges of the state. Accordingly Newton Cloud, Senator from Morgan County, introduced a bill which if passed would have endowed colleges already existing in the state.[24]

But since the income and equipment of these colleges were inadequate, they were unable to compete with Eastern colleges in securing students from wealthier families of the West. Friends of these colleges were greatly impressed by Cloud's bill. The bill passed the Senate, but its opponents succeeded in having it held up and later laid on the table.[25]

Jonathan Turner, graduate of Yale and former professor at Illinois College, had another plan. In his presidential address at the annual meeting of the Illinois Teachers Institute at Griggsville, May 13, 1850, he proposed not only the founding of a state university for the agricultural and general industrial classes of Illinois, but a system whereby all the states of the Union would be closely affiliated with the Smithsonian Institution in Washington.[26]

On November 18, 1851 he spoke at a farmers' convention at Granville, Putnam County, which had been called to consider measures for establishing an agricultural school. Turner's plan met with approval and was widely publicized in the *Prairie Farmer, Valley Farmer* of St. Louis, the *Bloomington Intelligencer, Morgan Journal, Peoria Banner* and other newspapers of

[24] *Ibid.*, p. LXXXVI.
[25] Carriel, *op. cit.*, p. 95.
[26] Jonathan Baldwin Turner had been Professor of Belle Lettres, Latin and Greek at Illinois College and had taught everything in the curriculum except chemistry. On the side he carried on investments in land. His advanced ideas on abolition and religion were investigated by the Presbyterian Synod of Illinois and he resigned in 1848, turning his attention to horticulture, especially the development of the Osage orange. *Ibid.*, p. 61, pp. 74–94.

the state. It led to the formation of the Illinois Industrial League, chartered by the Legislature, February 8, 1853, to develop ways and means for securing adequate educational institutions for industrial classes.[27] Turner's plan, in addition to agricultural and mechanical departments, envisaged liberal arts, and a normal school which would furnish annually a corps of skillful teachers and lecturers who would go through all the towns and counties, creating, establishing, and instructing lyceums, high schools, and common schools of all sorts.[28] It proposed memorializing Congress to appropriate to each state an amount of public land not less than $500,000 in value "for the liberal endowment of a system of state universities, to cooperate with each other, and the Smithsonian Institute, for the more liberal and practical education of the industrial classes and their teachers . . . ."

It was 1854 before the matter was formally brought before Congress. Meanwhile Turner lectured far and wide but the idea did not take hold elsewhere as it had in Illinois. It was often assailed from pulpit and press as "Turner's folly." Visionary and absurd cartoons appeared, showing professors in tall silk hats and kid gloves awkwardly holding plow handles and teaching students the rudiments of farming.[29]

In Washington on March 20, 1854, Elihu Washburne introduced the resolution relative to the industrial university in the House of Representatives and James Shields presented it in the Senate.[30] A year before Horace Greeley, in The New York *Tribune* had editorialized on the Illinois plan, as "a step to hasten the coming of scientific and practical education for all who desire and are willing to work for it. It cannot come too soon." Representative Richard Yates asked Turner to draft a bill, but by the time it reached Washington a strong wave of disapproval of the government's overlavish land grants of the early fifties was being felt, and as Senator Trumbull later wrote Turner, the idea was a "grand one" but the hour was not propitious. He wisely suggested that it might be well if the bill were presented by a representative from an old state rather than a new state which had already

[27] *Ibid.*, p. 138.
[28] *Ibid.*, pp. 121-127.
[29] *Ibid.*, p. 144.
[30] *Ibid.*, p. 153.

benefited from large grants for schools. Accordingly the bill was entrusted to the new representative from Vermont, Justin S. Morrill.[31]

While Turner was busy agitating his university among farmers and mechanics, principals of schools devised plans. In the fall of 1853 Harry H. Lee, Principal of the Garden City Institute of Chicago, James A. Hawley of Dixon, an agent for an eastern book publisher, and Daniel Wilkins, President of the Central Female Institute, Bloomington, happened to meet in Bloomington. They talked over school matters and decided to request Alexander Starne, *ex-officio* superintendent of common schools, to call an educational convention. Secretary Starnes would not issue the call himself but agreed to head a call if issued by the educational men of the state. Thirty-two educators endorsed the plan, and Starne sent out notice of the convention to be held in Bloomington. Teachers, superintendents, school commissioners and friends of education were invited.[32]

The session began at six o'clock Monday evening, December 26, 1853, in the Methodist Church in Bloomington. A permanent organization to be known as the State Teachers' Institute of Illinois was effected, a constitution drawn up, and a program for action agreed upon.[33] These were serious men, intent on implementing resolutions, not merely making them; they were determined to make the new organization truly professional and announced that as soon as possible all offices would be filled with practical teachers.[34] Resolved to raise the standard of teaching and to promote the greatest diffusion of knowledge, the association promptly began agitating the creation of an independent office of superintendent of public instruction, the enactment of a free school law,

[31] *Ibid.*, p. 159.

[32] The signers of the call for the Bloomington Convention of 1853 included the presidents of Shurtleff College, Illinois Wesleyan, Knox College, and Central Illinois Female Institute, six seminary principals, six ministers, one physician, two county superintendents, seven college professors, one teachers' institute principal, principal of the Peoria Classical Institute, an agent of the American Sabbath Union, and the president of the Peoria County Educational Society. Irving F. Pearson, *History of the Illinois Education Association* (Springfield: Illinois Education Association, 1953), p. 3.

[33] *Illinois State Journal* (Springfield) December 29, 1853.

On December 26, 1855, the name "Illinois State Teachers Association" was officially adopted. It was changed to "Illinois Education Association" in 1936. Pearson, *op. cit.*, p. 5.

[34] The constitution provided for a president, three vice-presidents, a secretary, an assistant secretary, a treasurer, an executive committee, and committees on books and libraries, school government, and exercises. Memberships were one dollar annually.

and the establishment of a normal school. A committee appointed
to memorialize the Legislature on school matters was instructed
"to ask that honorable body to make conditional ventures in the
way of aiding in erecting suitable buildings and furnishing a
permanent endowment to citizens of any town or towns who may
be desirous of having a normal school erected in their midst.[35]
Bronson Murry, who attended the meeting as a representative
of the Industrial League, was hopeful that the schoolmen would
go along with the plan for an industrial university with a normal
department.

At the meeting of schoolmen in Peoria in December 1854 Professor Turner and Dr. R. C. Rutherford spoke in behalf of the
Industrial University. State Superintendent Ninian W. Edwards
advocated a separate institution. The schoolmen concluded the
latter would more quickly answer their need. When the bill for
the Industrial University was pending in 1855, they were influential in getting the bill amended so that the normal school
would have to be put into operation before other departments
could be annexed. The Industrial League was favorable to common school education and the normal department, but it had no
desire to have the agricultural, mechanical, literary and scientific
departments take subordinate place and so the bill was allowed
to die in the committee.

When the State Teachers' Institute met in Springfield in December 1855, the schoolmen solemnly resolved that they "did
not wish to discuss any university question, but to occupy themselves with the interests of common schools and normal schools."
By this time the public school teachers controlled the votes of the
Institute. Charles E. Hovey, who had migrated the year before
from Massachusetts to be principal of the Peoria Boys Stock
School,[36] was chosen president of the Institute, and also editor of
the *Illinois Teacher* which had been started the preceding February.[37] The president and vice-presidents of the Institute set up
a committee known as the State Board of Education whose busi-

[35] Pillsbury, *op. cit.*, pp. LXXXVII–LXXXVIII.

[36] Ernest E. East, "C. E. Hovey, Educator and Soldier, Aided Public School System
Here," *Peoria Journal Transcript*, March 4, 1937; Harriette Hovey to Manfred Holmes,
January 28, 1913. Holmes Papers.

[37] The first school journal in Illinois was the *Common School Advocate*, an eight page

ness it was to supervise the general school interests throughout the state. It was authorized to employ an agent to travel throughout the state, to give lectures, and everywhere to advance the cause of a normal school.[38] Newton Bateman, principal of West Jacksonville District School, was chosen to lead the crusade, and for three years he spent as much time as he could lecturing and conducting institutes. In 1857 he resigned, and Simeon Wright, a teacher from Lee County, was appointed.

Meanwhile action taken to meet the crucial need for teachers in the rising city of Chicago was to influence the normal school movement. The ordinance in January 1855 establishing a high school, stipulated that it "should have a department expressly for the qualification of young ladies to teach." Graduates of the department, "all other things being equal," were to be preferred in the appointment of teachers for the primary and grammar schools. Ira Moore, from the State Normal School at Bridgewater, Massachusetts, became head of the department and opened the high school. A year later a city normal school was opened, with William H. Wells, former principal of the Westfield, Massachusetts, Normal School, in charge.[39]

The program of the Chicago meeting December 1856 was slanted toward the normal school movement. Professor Charles Hovey of Peoria presided. The morning and afternoon sessions were given over to reports and recommendations, and the evening sessions were devoted to inspirational addresses. The first evening Principal Wells of the Chicago Schools spoke on "The Science of Teaching," and the second evening Dr. Henry Barnard, who had helped establish the Connecticut State Normal School at New Britain five years before, addressed the three hundred or more

---

quarto, published monthly at Jacksonville by Calvin Gowdy and his brother, Ensley Gowdy. Faculty of Illinois College, notably Dr. Theron Baldwin, supplied articles. The paper, begun in January 1837, lasted only a year. From May 1841 to September 1841, Edmund R. Wiley of Springfield issued the *Illinois Common School Advocate,* a thirty-two octavo monthly magazine, as the official organ of the Illinois State Education Society. The *Union Agriculturist and Prairie Farmer,* established in 1841 and edited by John Wright, was both a farm and a school paper in its earlier years. Until the *Illinois Teacher* appeared, *Prairie Farmer* was the great exponent and recorder of public education. Cook, *Educational History of Illinois,* pp. 515–517.

[38] Newton Bateman was employed as agent of State Teachers Institute at a salary of $1200 per year. He resigned when his pay was not forthcoming and Simeon Wright was made agent at the Decatur meeting in 1857. *Ibid.,* p. 531.

[39] Pillsbury, *op. cit.,* p. LXXXIX.

persons present on "The Duty of the State in Regard to Education." The next morning a resolution was proposed[40] urging that Illinois no longer delay "the immediate establishment of a state normal school for the education of teachers." While the members were discussing the recommendation that the Legislature make an annual appropriation for the next five years sufficient to support such an institution of learning, Newton Bateman rose to his feet and presented a letter from Jonathan Turner addressed to the Illinois Teachers Institute assembled at Chicago.

After noting the use that the state had made of the educational funds in the past, Professor Turner reiterated that it had always been his opinion and that of the Industrial League that a normal school with an agricultural department would be more strongly bound to the interests of the people at large, and more prosperous than if it stood alone. However if this were not agreeable to the teachers of the state or friends of the normal school he now wished them to arrange it as they thought best. He pledged that the friends of the League would cooperate on any plan the Teachers' Institute might devise, provided that the school was "effectually separated from such partisan political control as would make it a curse instead of a blessing to the State.

"It is high time, my friends," he magnanimously concluded, "that you had your normal school whether we ever get an agricultural department to it or not. Let us all take hold and obtain it, in such form as you on the whole think best."[41] No longer would the League and the Institute be working at cross purposes. The cooperation so imperative to the success of the normal school was assured. The concession gave over to the normal not only the Seminary fund, to which it had good claim, but also the College fund, which the university men might have justifiably insisted be left unappropriated until they could obtain a charter.

With enthusiasm, the association moved a committee be appointed to secure the necessary legislation. Simeon Wright, President-elect of the Association, Charles E. Hovey, and Daniel Wilkins, Principal of the Female Institute, Bloomington, were

[40] Alexander Wilder, "Annual Meeting, Illinois State Teachers Association," *Illinois Teacher*, Vol. III (January 1857), p. 1.

[41] Jonathan B. Turner to Chicago Teachers' Institute, December 20, 1856. Pillsbury, *op. cit.*, p. LX.

immediately named. They were to be assisted by William H. Powell, the newly elected state superintendent.

The sessions ended on a note of gayety and achievement. Over five hundred persons attended the banquet at the Tremont House. Chicago's popular superintendent, William Wells, presided and the toastmasters, E. D. Osband of Chicago and Charles Hovey sat at opposite ends of the long speakers' table. There was wit, good humor, and fellowship. There were toasts to the "Old-Fashioned School," "Graded Schools," "The Press," "The Railroads," "Boarding Round," The Ladies of the State Teachers Association," and such worthy personages as Simeon Wright, newly elected president, and Charles Hovey, and to the *Illinois Teacher* now starting its third year, and lastly to "Our Future Normal School— the Crowning Act of Our Next Legislature." [42]

When the Legislature assembled the next week in Springfield, the Hon. Samuel W. Moulton, who had drafted the bills creating the independent office of Superintendent of Public Instruction at the special session in 1854 and the free schools in 1855, took over the management of the bill in the House, and Captain J. S. Post of Decatur introduced it in the Senate. Zealous support was given by members long known as "friends of education," among them Wesley Sloan of Golconda, C. B. Denio of Jo Daviess County, and Dr. Calvin Gowdy of Taylorville, who with his brother at Jacksonville, for some twenty years had published *The Common School Advocate*. They assured the economy-minded legislators that the training school for teachers would not cost the taxpayers a cent, that the building would be constructed from the subscriptions raised by the city which was successful in the competition for the location, and that revenue from the Seminary and College fund would be adequate for maintenance.[43] The press came to the aid of the cause. The *Illinois State Journal* on its editorial page carried a letter entitled "Friend of the Public Schools" in which a correspondent declared, "Instruction in the normal school fits the mind for the specific duties of the teacher. . . . It is as important to a teacher as theology to a preacher." Appealing to civic pride it further queried, "Will

[42] Wilder, *op. cit.*, pp. 1–42.

[43] The interest on the College and Seminary funds in 1856 amounted to approximately $900. *Illinois State Journal*, January 30, 1857.

Illinois be behind in the encouragement of learning? Will she neglect this crowning act in the liberal system she has just established?" [44]

The bill easily passed the Senate, sixteen to four, but it met opposition in the House and there the vote was thirty-nine to twenty-five which was only one vote to spare, thirty-eight being the constitutional majority then required to pass a bill in the House. On February 18, 1857, Governor William Bissell, who had long favored the creation of a normal school signed the bill and the first milestone was reached.

The act named C. B. Denio of Jo Daviess County, Simeon Wright of Lee County, Daniel Wilkins of McLean County, C. E. Hovey of Peoria County, George P. Rex of Pike County, Samuel W. Moulton of Shelby County, John Gillispie of Jasper County, George Bunsen of St. Clair County, Wesley Sloan of Pope County, Ninian Edwards of Sangamon County, William H. Wells of Cook County, John Eden of Moultrie County, Flavel Moseley of Cook County, and Albert Shannon of White County, together with the *ex-officio* State Superintendent of Public Instruction, to constitute a corporate body known as "The Board of Education of the State of Illinois" empowered to contract, to acquire and hold property, to have a common seal, to make and establish by-laws for the government of the normal university. [45]

Superintendent Powell explained that the name "Normal University" was designated in the bill because it permitted the institution to be readily "swelled into the full proportions of a university, should the people of the State and the Legislature desire it." [46] The name too may have been something of a gesture toward the die-hards in the Industrial League, and, as Hovey often remarked, the school did receive its income from a fund earmarked for a university. [47]

[44] *Ibid.,* January 31, 1857.
[45] The term of the members of the Board was ordinarily for six years. At the first meeting lots were drawn so that one-third would hold office for six years, one-third for four years, and one-third for two years. There was no compensation, only traveling expenses. *Daily Pantagraph,* March 28, 1857.
[46] William H. Powell, *Second Biennial Report of the Superintendent of Public Instruction* of the State of Illinois, 1857–1858. (Springfield: State of Illinois, 1859), p. 54.
[47] John Williston Cook credits Dr. Alexander Wilder, Associate Editor of the *American Journal of Education and College Review* who was visiting in Springfield at the time the bill was being drafted, as the originator of the somewhat misleading name "Normal University." Wilder contributed frequently to the *Illinois Teacher* during Hovey's editor-

The newly constituted Board met in Superintendent Powell's office on March 26, and committees were set up to attend to the matters of location, course of study, buildings and officers of the school. Much of the success of the enterprise would depend upon its location and the man chosen to head its faculty. On the eve of the meeting Hovey had editorialized in the *Illinois Teacher* under the heading "Who Shall Be Principal of the Normal University?"

We can not answer this question but we can say what manner of man he ought to be. He ought to be a resident of Illinois, acquainted with her people and her schools; he ought to be a thorough scholar, an accomplished teacher, of large experience, good common sense, gentlemanly bearing, great executive ability, a shrewd judge of human nature, a skillful disciplinarian, of tireless enthusiasm, great directness and oneness of purpose, and in him should be wrapped a great big soul.[48]

In approximately fifty words Editor Hovey had given an admirable self-portrait, although he was not ready to avow himself as a candidate.

Hovey was a member of the Committee on Location and if possible he wanted to secure the school for Peoria. While the bill was being debated he had adroitly remarked, "If Peoria can furnish a better building and better schools for model schools than her sister cities she expects it, if not," he thoughtfully added, "most likely Springfield, Bloomington, and Jacksonville would also compete for it." [49] If a city had something to offer a school, so a school had something to bring to a city. Midwest cities spoke with pride of the cultural advantages their seminaries and colleges afforded their communities. Jesse Fell, Daniel Wilkins, Kersey Fell, David Davis, Edwin Bakewell, W. H. Allin, and other business men were quick to see advantages of having the school located in Bloomington.[50] For a time Fell considered offering Seminary Block but concluded it would be better not to link his activities with a specific site. The bill incorporating the Normal

---

ship. Cook, *Educational History of Illinois*, p. 94; John W. Cook to David Felmley 1908.

Charles Hovey, Editor of the *Illinois Teacher*, devoted the July 1857 issue to normal schools. He explained the derivation of "normal" from the Latin word originally being a "square" or rule used by carpenters; as applied to schools, it means a pattern, model, or example. "A normal school signifies a school where the principles of teaching are taught, and where the art of teaching is exemplified in practice." *Illinois Teacher*, July 1857, p. 233.

[48] *Ibid.*, March 1857, p. 107.

[49] *Ibid.*, February 1857, p. 67.

[50] These Bloomington business men donated from $200 in cash to $10,000 in land.

University stipulated that the permanent location would be in the place which offered the most favorable inducements.

As Fell went about soliciting subscriptions for the school in both cash and land, he spoke casually of his hope that Horace Mann could be induced to come to Illinois as principal of the school. Privately Fell's good friend John F. Eberhart, a guest at the time in his home, was already corresponding with Mann. All was not going well at Antioch and Mann expressed a definite interest in the position if it would pay as much as $2500. It was not known how much the Board would pay and on the first day of May a subscription list was circulated in Bloomington for material aid to bring the salary up to Mann's figure of $2500. Ten business men pledged $750.[51]

On May 4 the Board met in Springfield and heard the report of the Committee on Location. Sealed bids had been received from Peoria, Bloomington, and Washington. It was decided not to open the bids until another inspection was made of the proposed sites. Previously George Bunsen, George Rex, Daniel Wilkins, and Charles Hovey had visited these cities as well as Decatur, which had made no bid. Simeon Wright, who had been the agent of the Illinois Teachers Association in publicizing the school, was made the agent of the Board to arrange for an immediate junket of the sites, and a recess meeting was called for three o'clock in Peoria May seventh to make final decision on the site.[52]

It was a late wet spring. On Monday there had been a hard rain, and although the downpour stopped on Wednesday before the morning train bringing the Committee from Springfield arrived, the weather was unpleasant, raw and cold. Water still stood in puddles and the mud was ankle deep. The editor of the *Daily Pantagraph* was at the station, along with other citizens, to greet the visitors and to expound the cultural and healthful advantages of Bloomington.[53] Six tracts of land were offered as possible sites for the school.

It was decided to inspect the sites east of town first. The streets had been muddy but the roads were worse. Crossing a slough

[51] Morehouse, *op. cit.*, p. 46.
[52] *Proceedings of the Board of Education* (Springfield), May 4–6, 1857, pp. 5–7.
[53] *Daily Pantagraph*, May 5, 1857.

about two and a half miles east of town, one of the carriages became bogged down in the mud. The driver cracked his whip; the horses plunged, tugged, and slipped. Another final effort, and a singletree was broken; as the horses struggled to free themselves, the tongue plunged into the wet ground and snapped in two. The occupants waded out into mud up to their boot tops and crowded into the other carriages. The members of the visiting Committee were not complimentary of what Bloomington had to offer.[54]

After a late lunch at the Pike House, the Committee again set out, this time for the Junction north of town. Many of the cash subscriptions as well as offers of land had been contingent upon the location of the site within a mile or half mile of The Junction. Although Jesse Fell had offered any ten acres of land that he owned for a site if the Committee desired, he believed that the tract offered by Meshack Pike and Joseph Payne, a part of the old Parkinson farm, was perhaps the most desirable. It stood high above the slough and the railroad, and the land sloped gently in all directions. Fell was aware that the bare prairie about Bloomington appeared like a hopeless swamp at this time of year, so the afternoon before the Committee's visit he went very carefully over the ground, located every mudhole and dry ridge, and worked out a course that would minimize the dangers of being mired down in a sea of Illinois mud. He wanted no broken axles, no shaken nerves. On the ridge that seemed to him to be the ideal spot he planted a flag atop a tall pole.

When the visitors left the Pike House, Fell was careful to ride in the first carriage so as to direct the driver over the uncharted soggy ground. On "threat of life and wages" the drivers of the other carriages had been ordered to follow undeviatingly the course of the first, and on no account were the horses to be allowed to mire down.[55]

Local boosters pointed with pride to Wesleyan College's lone building a mile or more to the south, the cultural advantages of a normal school in a college town, and the easy access to the Illinois Central and the Chicago and Alton railroads.

[54] *Ibid.*, May 9, 1857.
[55] Morehouse, *op. cit.*, p. 44.

The land south of the tracks had been platted into town lots in 1854 and offered for a sale of lots on June 15 of that year, but aside from Jesse Fell's new home, Greenwood, little building had been done. The location of the school, however, would probably set off a veritable building boom. This new development referred to as "North Bloomington" would be made an addition to the city of Bloomington or it might be incorporated into a separate town.

Despite the shivering cold, the visitors conceded it was a pleasant view, with the soft rolling prairie, the wandering ribbons of railroad track, the brush swamp and the clumps of hazel, sumac, and willow. In the distance the Wesleyan building and the spires of Bloomington churches could be seen above tree-lined avenues. "None better," thought Jesse Fell, as he gazed off in the direction of the field of experimental sugar cane that had just been planted and envisaged the neat rows of trees that would presently outline the streets of North Bloomington.

The next morning the Committee and a party of townspeople, including Jesse Fell, Leonard Swett, attorney, and Editor E. J. Lewis of the *Pantagraph,* who was to keep his subscribers informed of exactly what took place on the memorable journey, set off for Peoria. They took the Illinois Central from Bloomington as far as Peoria Junction, where they boarded the Peoria Oquawka Eastern Extension passing through Secor, Cruger, Eureka, and Washington. From the train could be seen the Academy Building which Washington offered to the state for the new school. It was noon when they reached Peoria and were taken to the Peoria House for lunch. The editors of the Peoria newspapers, *The Statesman, The Republican,* and *The Transcript,* confident and gracious, were on hand to extol the virtues of Peoria.[56] Editor Lewis was quite impressed with the good fellowship.

Eleven of the fifteen members of the Board were present when the meeting began at three o'clock in the Peoria County Court House. Ninian Edwards took the chair. W. H. Powell, Secretary *ex-officio,* took his seat. Simeon Wright presented the bids. The first bid was that of Batavia. The city offered $15,000 in cash, 20 to 22 A of land, and a three-story building 70 by 50 feet. The citizens pledged to raise $25,000 of which $10,000 was to lift the debt on

[56] *Daily Pantagraph,* May 11, 1857.

the building. The total bid amounted to $45,000. Washington's bid in cash, land, and buildings amounted to $20,000. The city and county of Peoria offered cash and land estimated to be worth $80,000. The city of Bloomington and McLean County offered cash and land amounting to $141,000.[57]

The offer was astounding. Charles Hovey could scarcely believe Bloomington's bid exceeded Peoria's bid by $61,000. Daniel Wilkins grinned broadly and wished that Jesse Fell and John Eberhart had been in the room to see consternation on the faces of the Board members who were so confident that one of the Peoria locations would be selected.[58] John Eberhart had been in Peoria the week previous, and in talking with a teacher learned how much Peoria had raised. Eberhart disliked Peoria. To him it was a "river town and a whisky town," and he did not want to see the normal school located there. Back in Bloomington he held council with Fell. It was decided Eberhart should go to Chicago to interview the Board members there relative to the Bloomington location and meanwhile Fell would try to raise more funds. Fell hitched Old Tom to the buggy, took Eberhart to the station, and started for Peoria. He covered the forty-five miles in time to attend a citizen's meeting. Hovey recognized him but was unsuspecting. There was no secret about the Peoria bid and the citizens were confident that no other county would equal their $80,000 pledge.

Fell hurried home that night. Time was precious. McLean County citizens had already pledged $50,000 in cash and lands, and the County Commissioners, A. J. Merriman of Bloomington, Milton Smith of Pleasant Hill, and Hiram Buck of Leroy, pledged that they would appropriate from the swamp lands funds an amount equal to that subscribed by individuals. This brought the total to $100,000. Fell believed an additional $25,000 should be raised by private subscription, and that when this sum was matched by the County Commissioners, the normal school would be assured. He raised his own cash subscription to $2,000 and pledged an equivalent of $7,500 in Jackson County lands, worth about five dollars per acre. His enthusiasm was contagious; others

[57] *Proceedings of the Board of Education* (Peoria) May 7, 1857.
[58] Editor Lewis credits Daniel Wilkins, Jesse Fell, and Captain Post for arousing the people in McLean County. *Daily Pantagraph*, May 12, 1857.

added to their pledges until the total in private subscriptions was $71,000. The Commissioners risked their popularity and tenure in office and brought the McLean County total to $141,000.[59]

Puzzled looks were exchanged when the Bloomington bid was read. After a few minutes Wesley Sloan of Golconda rose to his feet and proposed "that the Normal University be located in County of McLean, near Bloomington on the 160 acres of land which is to be granted for the construction of the school," but he specified that the location should not be final until the total amount of the bid was fully secured and delivered. Charles Hovey proposed an amendment by which the location would be awarded to Peoria if the citizens of Bloomington did not guarantee the precarious county subscriptions within sixty days.

Dr. George Rex of Perry and Charles Hovey were appointed to visit various normal and high schools in the East and to report at the June meeting in Bloomington, on buildings, courses of study, finances, and matters relative to the general management of a normal school. At that meeting the new principal would be selected.

Editor Lewis hurried from the Peoria Court House to telegraph to the *Pantagraph* the good news: "Normal University located at Bloomington by unanimous choice." [60] Attorney Leonard Swett, who accompanied the Bloomington delegation, hastened to assure the Board that the title to the swamp lands was *bona fide*.

Bloomington was elated, and when Wilkins, Swett, Fell, and Lewis returned they had no difficulty securing guarantors. A week later, on May 15, 1857, Abraham Lincoln, Esq., acting as attorney for the Board, drew up the bond guaranteeing that citizens of Bloomington would pay to the Board $14,000 on the first day of August 1857, $14,000 on the first day of November 1857, $14,000 on the first day of February 1858, $14,000 on the first day of May 1858, and $14,000 on the first day of August 1858, to assure the erection of the building of the Normal University on the McLean County subscription. Eighty-five Bloomington citizens

[59] The Board of Supervisors which replaced the Commissioners ratified the latter's action the following May. J. H. Burnham, "How the Normal was Located," *Transactions of the McLean County Historical Society* (Bloomington, 1903) II, 171; Morehouse, *op. cit.,* pp. 42–44.
[60] *Daily Pantagraph,* May 8, 1857.

pledged from five hundred dollars to five thousand dollars, and in the event of any actual default, they agreed to share the loss, *pro rata* according to the sums set opposite their names.[61]

Jesse Fell continued his efforts to secure Horace Mann as principal of the school. He and Eberhart personally interviewed over half the members of the Board and found them agreeable. Mann had insisted that there be harmony in the Board and that the call be unanimous as he was too old to fight. About a week before the meeting to be held in Bloomington protests against Mann were heard.

A member of the Peoria faction came to Eberhart and warned him that it was a matter of political necessity that an Illinoisan be named to the position. "If you elect Mann, we'll kill him," he threatened. He further intimated that Bloomington got the school and that Peoria should name the principal. There were mutterings about Mann's being a "damned abolitionist." Pro-slavery advocates recalled how Mann had assailed Daniel Webster and the Compromise of 1850. The Methodists, very powerful in Illinois, questioned Mann's religious views and even branded him as a dangerous person to be leading the young. When informed of the situation, Mann wired Eberhart, asking that he be no longer considered.

After Mann withdrew, Charles Hovey was considered the best available man for the position. John Eberhart, graduate of Allegheny College, former editor of the *Dixon Transcript,* and popular lecturer at teachers' institutes, refused to let his name be presented.[62]

Those on the committee who advocated an out-of-state person and one who had had actual experience in the administration of a normal school favored William F. Phelps, Principal of the New Jersey State Normal School, which had opened two years before. Phelps had been most helpful to Rex and Hovey on their recent survey of Eastern schools. The salary about to be proposed for the principal of the new school was five hundred dollars more

[61] The total amount subscribed by the guarantors was $214,000. Their guaranty was never enforced. Some of the swamp lands were sold for cash, others on credit and the proceeds used in the construction of the building. John W. Cook and James V. McHugh, *History of the Illinois State Normal University* (Normal, 1882), pp. 21–22.

[62] John Eberhart to Manfred J. Holmes (Undated) Holmes Papers; Morehouse, *op. cit.,* p. 46; Cook, *Educational History of Illinois,* pp. 599–602.

than Phelps was receiving, an increase thought to be sufficient to induce him to come west. In the end the committee deferred to those who favored a local man, and only the majority report recommending Charles Hovey was presented to the Board. The name of William Phelps was brought up again during its deliberations, however, and when the vote was taken he had five votes and Hovey six. As a gracious gesture toward their fellow member and future principal the vote was made unanimous.

Late that afternoon Professor Hovey informed the Board he would accept the office of Principal.[63]

[63] *Proceedings of the Board of Education* (Bloomington), June 23, 1857, p. 12.

CHAPTER II

Major's Hall

THE NEW principal took up his work with high hopes and determination. In the report on the eastern schools which he and Dr. Rex had visited, he had already outlined something of the philosophy which he thought should underlie the operations of a school for training teachers. The July issue of the *Illinois Teacher,* much of which was already written and in the press, was to set forth more of his ideas. "A normal school," he wrote, "signifies a school where the principles of teaching are taught, and where the art of teaching is exemplified in practice." He continued with his conception of the responsibilities of the teacher:

When we consider the excellence of the material the teacher works upon, —the undying mind, and the susceptibilities of that mind to good or evil influences; when we consider the different results to which that mind is brought, even if we do not look beyond the termination of its earthly career; and when we consider the multitude and variety of the influences that may be brought to bear upon it from the most elevating to the most debasing; from heaven-aspiring tendencies that would carry it upward along the ascending scale of virtue and piety, to all those downward proclivities through which, one after another it may sweep to utter perdition, do we not discover some reason, maybe a sovereign reason why the guide and counselor of this mind, why the trainer and educator of these immortal susceptibilities and faculties should himself be a workman that needeth to be ashamed; and for this purpose that he should possess all the information, in relation to his art, possible to be obtained; that is, that he himself should be taught. . . .

Education must be moral as well as physical or intellectual. The heart must be cared for as well as the mind and the body.[1]

Principal Hovey was conversant with the development of the normal school idea from Pomerania through France, Ireland, Belgium, Scotland, and Britain. He had read the reports of Dr. Alex-

[1] Charles E. Hovey, "Normal Schools," *Illinois Teacher,* July 1857, pp. 233–239.

ander Bache, the Reverend Calvin Stowe, Henry Barnard, Dr. Samuel Gridley Howe, and others. He had personally visited normal schools in Massachusetts, New Jersey, New York, Pennsylvania, and Rhode Island. He sat in their classrooms, observed their model schools, took notes on their equipment, and critically studied their courses of study. Their good features he wished to see emulated, their weak ones avoided. He was prepared to advance a three-year curriculum.

In the three years that Charles Hovey had been in Illinois he had earned a reputation as a teacher, an administrator, and an editor, to which some of his contemporaries would have added politician. When Hovey accepted the principalship, he had just turned thirty, was striking in appearance, tall and handsome, with wavy dark chestnut hair, and quick, piercing eyes. He spoke with ease and he made friends readily.

Charles Hovey was born in the town of Thetford, Vermont, April 26, 1827, the son of Alfred and Abigail Howard Hovey. He was one of eleven children, four daughters, and seven sons. The father was a farmer. He sent his children to the district schools when they were open. Young Charles developed an amazing gift of solving arithmetical puzzles, reading fluently, and spelling hard words, and when he was fifteen the school committee waived the matter of age and offered him a school, for which he was to receive nine and a half dollars a month and board.

He soon advanced to a village school where he received twenty dollars a month and board. During the Millerite frenzy of the 1840's, he left the classroom and followed the trade of a lumberjack for a time before he took up teaching again. While a student at Dartmouth College, he paid his expenses by teaching school three or four months each year.

Hovey had graduated from Dartmouth College in 1852. He had thought of studying law but had turned to teaching instead. For two years he was principal of the Framingham Academy and High School, Framingham, Massachusetts.

Hovey's experience in Framingham was a happy one. He found the people "highly cultivated" and the students of the academy and high school "wonderfully intelligent." Some twenty years later, he affectionately described the Academy's preceptress, Miss

Harriette Farnham Spofford, as a "paragon of the graces."[2]

The West beckoned to youth in the 1850's. One heard it proclaimed the land of opportunity from Greeley's *Tribune* to brochures from Eli Thayer's New England Emigrant Aid Society. Westward thousands came bringing their hopes, their ideals, their convictions, and their prejudices. Some were cultured, well-educated seeking for their offspring the opportunities they themselves had had; others, unlettered and untutored, seeking for their children, those that they had not had. They came by wagon and by boat, and by the new steam trains. Some came on horseback, and a few walked, as Jesse Fell had done a generation before.[3]

Gradually the prairies were broken. New towns sprang up along the railroads and waterways and old ones saw new growth and vigor. Peoria was such a town. It had a population of 5,095 in 1850, but within a decade it would exceed 14,000.[4]

The only schools before 1850 were sporadic dame schools held in a spare room in a home, in a church, or on the second floor of a store building. They lacked continuity and equipment, and the teachers were more willing than competent. Now and then a lawyer or doctor just beginning to practice augmented his slender income from professional services by taking pupils. A few teachers disdained taking pupils at large and for slightly higher tuition rates conducted "select schools." After 1849 in the Krim or lower part of the city where many Germans had settled, private schoolmasters taught their schools in the German language. Little teaching was done above the elementary level.

In 1850 a group of citizens interested in better schooling for their daughters organized the Female School Association and opened what came to be known as The Girls Stock School. It proved not only to be a successful school but a paying investment.[5] Three years later the same citizens began to agitate for a similar school for boys.

[2] Charles E. Hovey, "Autobiography of General C. E. Hovey," reprinted from *The Schoolmaster* (1889) in Cook and McHugh, *op. cit.*, pp. 28–30.
[3] The Seventh U. S. Census (1850) reported 41,283 adults in Illinois who could neither read nor write. Morehouse, *op. cit.*, p. 15.
[4] The Seventh U. S. Census (1850) listed the population of Peoria as 5,095 including 84 free colored. The Eighth Census (1860) reported 14,045 persons.
[5] H. W. Wells, *Schools and the Early Teachers of Peoria* (Peoria: Jaquin and Co., 1900), pp. 19–103.

Inquiries were made throughout the East for a capable man to head the school. The name of Charles Hovey was presented. Here was opportunity, the West, and a school to be organized and operated along lines that were untrammeled and unfettered by tradition. Hovey accepted. On October 9, 1854, he was married to the "preceptress" of Framingham's Academy, and together they started to their new home in Peoria.[6]

The Boys Stock School opened November 27, 1854, with 119 students the first term. Besides Mrs. Hovey, who taught classes in grammar, there were two other regular teachers, two assistants, and special teachers of German and music. Hovey was interested in the new community, and above all its schools. He was outspoken. The one public school was held in a long narrow crumbling brick structure located in a stagnant, swampy section of town. Hovey thought a wrong was being perpetrated upon the school children of Peoria and that the situation was deplorable for a city so rich and populous. The head of the public school resented Hovey's interest. Hovey's school was in turn envied, epitheted and compared. "It was a rich man's school, the aristocrat's school; relied on show and clothes."

The month after Hovey arrived the second meeting of State Teachers Association was held in Peoria. He attended, and met the educational leaders of the state, teachers like Simeon Wright, Newton Bateman, John F. Brooks, Daniel Wilkins, and former teachers who had been lured into political or more lucrative pursuits but who retained their interest in education, among them Jonathan Turner, W. H. Powell, John F. Eberhart, Bronson Murray, W. F. N. Arny, as well as a galaxy of publishers and school supply men angling for contracts. He was quite intrigued by "grand strategy of some of the latter" in trying to get hold of the convention. His heart went out to the reformers, the men with vision. He listened, as Turner expounded the merits of an industrial university, and observed how the old college men from Shurtleff, Knox, McKendree, and Wesleyan were working to get the College and Seminary funds distributed among the colleges as maintenance for normal departments. He was present when the monthly organ of the Teachers Association, *The Illinois Teacher*,

[6] Cook and McHugh, *op. cit.*, pp. 30–31.

was read. It was just the sort of publication he longed to edit, but he was a new man in the state and for the time being he had to be just an interested onlooker. A year later when the Association decided to continue the organ but wished to disavow financial responsibility, the editorship was gladly handed over to Hovey.

The dream of a system of free public schools so captivated Hovey that he could not let the matter rest. The academy had barely had its legal status approved before he approached Judge Onslow Peters, Judge Jacob Gale, A. P. Bartlett, and others prominent in the Stock Association that employed him. It was decided to put through the Legislature quietly, a bill that would amend the city's charter and enable the citizens of Peoria to elect a School Board and establish a system of free public schools.[7] Meanwhile he lobbied in the Legislature for statewide free public schools. The Peoria bill was passed almost before people realized what it was all about.

Within a year the private school buildings were purchased by the Board. The building formerly occupied by the Female Association Girls Stock School became the high school and that of the Boys Stock School, a grammar school.[8] Mrs. Hovey organized the grammar school and Hovey became principal of the high school and superintendent of all the schools.

There was much to be done. Schoolhouses had to be built, courses of study planned, the teachers selected. Hovey worked hard and the Board stood back of him. Word traveled over the state that Charles Hovey was a man of action, he got things done.

At the December 1855 meeting in Springfield he was elected president of the State Teachers Association and given the somewhat dubious *carte blanche* editorship of the *Illinois Teacher*. If subscriptions came in as the schoolmen promised and the *Illinois Teacher* succeeded, the profits would be Hovey's; if it failed the loss would also be his.[9] The former publisher was pessimistic: "If Hovey has fifteen hundred dollars to throw away, he has now an excellent opportunity to do so." While Hovey busied himself with copy, making arrangements for printing in Peoria and

[7] Hovey's Stock School showed a profit of $307.86 the first year it was in operation. C. Ballance, *History of Peoria, Illinois* (Peoria: N. C. Nason, 1870), p. 89.
[8] Wells, *op. cit., pp.* 102–105.
[9] Cook and McHugh, *op. cit.,* p. 34.

assuring himself that forthcoming issues would be on better paper, in clearer type, and freer of typographical errors, Mrs. Hovey took over the matter of subscriptions, mailing lists, and accounts.

The first issue under the new editorship revealed not only promise but great improvement. Hovey's friends were true to their word and the subscriptions poured in, fifteen hundred of them,—five times that of the first year. It was a proud and happy editor who presided over the meeting of the State Teachers Association in Chicago in 1856; the budget was balanced, there was a profit, and as a matter of record, over a hundred of its 1500 subscribers were outside the state.

When Hovey was made principal of the new state Normal University he resigned from all other positions except that of editor of the *Illinois Teacher*. He gave notice that he would resign that upon the election of a successor.[10]

As soon as the Hoveys could pack up their belongings and take care of business, they took up their residence in Bloomington, where they received for the most part a gracious welcome.[11]

There was no time to be lost. At its June meeting the Board had authorized the Building Committee to make arrangements for temporary housing and to announce the commencement of the first term and to take the necessary steps for securing the appointment of students from the various counties. According to section 7 of the enabling act, each county within the state was entitled to gratuitous instruction for one pupil in the University, and each representative district was entitled to as many scholarships as there were representatives in the district. If each county and district were to use its full quota of scholarships accommodations for around 175 students would be needed. That was hardly to be expected. It was a goal that might not be realized ever unless there were amendments to the law; in fact, the Board might have to exercise its discretionary powers and admit more local students

[10] The circulation of the *Illinois Teacher* when Hovey retired as editor in December, 1857, was 2,070. It boasted subscribers in twenty-three states, eighteen in Massachusetts, twenty in Indiana, and others as far away as California, Alabama, and Vermont.

[11] The most outspoken objection to Hovey's appointment was an open letter to the *Pantagraph* signed "Punctum." The writer protested that Hovey was a member of the Board, had no out-of-state reputation, and that for $2,500 the Board should have commanded a truly great educator.

in lieu of failure of counties and districts to avail themselves of their quotas.

County school commissioners over the state were circularized as to the manner of appointments and the qualifications of candidates. Males not less than seventeen years of age and women not less than sixteen were eligible, provided they could produce certificates of good moral character, would sign a declaration of intention to "devote themselves to school teaching" in Illinois, and could pass satisfactory examinations before the proper officers, in reading, spelling, writing, arithmetic, geography, and the elements of English grammar.[12]

Hovey soon learned that the individual members of the Board, however remote their residence, were loath to surrender authority to the principal except on the more trivial or annoying details of administration. There was a wide difference of opinion on the curriculum and how much there should be of content and how much of theory. George Bunsen, learned as he was in German pedagogy, would emphasize primary education. To him it was the alpha and omega of normal training. At one point he was so annoyed at Hovey's lack of sympathy that he proposed that the Board inquire into the advisability of his removal. Ninian Edwards, the ambitious son of the former governor, looked to liberal arts colleges as a model. Hovey always regarded him as pompous and a "little at sea."

A member of the Board who liked to dabble in drawing presented a set of plans for a building at the very first meeting of the Board. "Utterly impossible" was Hovey's private verdict. He hastened to propose the survey of school architecture that had taken him and Dr. Rex on their tour through the East. Dr. Rex had returned so enamored of the New Jersey Normal, its curriculum and its architecture, that if Hovey would have concurred he would have moved the exact duplication of the Trenton plan.

There were times when Hovey secretly rejoiced in having some members of the Board so distant and preoccupied that they did not interfere. Flavel Moseley, President of the Board of Education of the City of Chicago, was quite content to let Hovey struggle alone with the curriculum but artfully reminded him from time

[12] W. H. Powell, *op. cit.*, pp. 387–391.

to time that it was he who proposed the very liberal salary for the principal.

In order to fulfill the terms of the location and make the collection of pledges easier, it was imperative that the building be started as soon as possible. Hovey looked at the problem realistically. "Given," he said, "five hundred adult students: required to find how to construct an edifice wherein they could be comfortably accommodated and assembled in one room and separated therefrom into several rooms and vice versa, in the least possible time and confusion." A normal, he insisted, was not to be organized as a college where students studied in their rooms and could conveniently go from one place to recitation and to another for "prayers." Except for some minor changes to conform with local taste, the drawings presented by G. P. Randall, architect of Chicago were accepted at a July 14 meeting of the Building Committee of the Board in Bloomington.[13] On August 18 the bids were opened and contracts awarded to T. H. Soper and Mortimer and Loburg of Chicago,[14] who assured the Committee that the building could be finished within a year.

Temporary quarters were engaged in Major's Hall, on the third floor over a general store on the corner of Front and East Streets in Bloomington. That building was fairly new and the large hall which had been completed just before the State Republican Convention, the year before, would serve nicely as an assembly room. Adjacent rooms could be used for classes.[15] Advertisements in the *Pantagraph* appealed for boarding houses for thirty or forty students "at as low a price as can be afforded." Circulars were sent to prospective students, county commissioners of education, and newspapers, announcing the opening date, Monday, October 5, and advising that board could be obtained for three dollars a week.[16] The Board empowered the principal to spend the sum of

[13] *Proceedings of the Board of Education* (Bloomington), August 18, 1857, p. 13.

[14] C. B. Denio, Board member from Galena, entered a bid of $100,000. T. H. Soper bid $80,000 and Mortimer and Loburg $81,000.

[15] In Major's Hall, May 29, 1856, Abraham Lincoln of Springfield, delivered his famous "Lost Speech," the address by which he considered himself formally identified with the Republican Party.

[16] *Daily Pantagraph*, August 24, 1857, and October 1, 1857.

At the end of the first year Hovey reported that students could obtain board and room for $2.50 to $3.00 a week exclusive of wood, lights, and laundry. W. H. Powell, *op. cit.*, p. 291.

$1,000 donated by the Merriam Publishing Company of Boston, for desks, recitation benches, globes, maps, books, and other necessary equipment. He was also given a free hand in the employing of teachers, but on the matter of textbooks the Board retained full authority.[17]

In selecting his faculty Hovey chose from the Chicago normal department, Ira Moore who had graduated from the Bridgewater Normal and had for a time attended Yale. On his inspection of eastern normals Hovey had been impressed most by the Bridgewater school. In bringing Moore to Illinois State Normal University, he hoped to bring something of the passion for thoroughness, accuracy, and truth that Nicholas Tillinghast had given the Massachusetts Normal. Since Hovey's budget for teachers was limited, he decided to employ one outstanding educator and hire part-time instruction as it was needed for such courses as music, drawing, and mathematics.

Although the model schools in the East were not as enthusiastically supported as they were earlier, Hovey was convinced that the Model School, with a master teacher in charge was one of the most significant contributions that a normal school could bring to teacher training. For the Model School, which was to open November 2, Hovey selected Miss Mary Brooks, a teacher in the Peoria Public Schools.[18]

Shortly after Hovey came to Illinois, a timid young woman, thin and large boned but with a most sincere and attractive face presented herself at his schoolroom in the Boys Stock School. She was Mary Brooks from Brimfield. A few years before she had come west with her family from Vermont. She wanted to be a teacher and asked if she might "pursue some preparatory studies" under his tutelage. She developed rapidly, serving first as a pupil-teacher and then as a full-time teacher. Children loved her at sight. She seemed to have an "intuitive knowledge of a child's mind at different stages of development, and was a genius for inventing methods to aid its growth." [19] Mary Brooks was loyal. Charles and Harriette Hovey became her best friends. How proud

---

[17] For many years the Board retained its prerogative of selecting textbooks. If a teacher preferred another text, he might petition the Board and present his reasons in writing.
[18] *National Flag* (Bloomington), October 30, 1857.
[19] Cook and McHugh, *op. cit.,* p. 227.

she had been at the teachers' meeting at the Tremont in Chicago when her principal, Charles Hovey, had presided. She was proud to be one of his teachers, one of the first that he had trained. When he asked her to open the Model School he had not been able to offer anything positive in the way of salary, only opportunity. At first the Model School might not pay as well as the public schools in Peoria but in time it should do as well. Teacher training was a "cause" in an age when causes were sacred. Mary Brooks decided to cast her lot with the Hoveys and teacher education.[20] Hovey worked frantically getting things in order. With the help of his wife he wrote hundreds of letters to school superintendents, newspapers, and prospective students. During the long hot days he hurried back and forth between the Junction where construction had begun and the temporary headquarters in Major's Hall where the odor of strong soap suds, wallpaper and paint told of preparations being made for opening day. The furniture had been ordered promptly because freight from Boston was often delayed in transit and the Board was anxious that everything be in readiness by the first week in October.

Hovey was delighted with the progress the builders were making. The excavation was completed in record time and soon the foundation of Joliet stone began to rise from the broad concrete footings. Local townspeople were assisting with the plans for the laying of the cornerstone. Two o'clock, Tuesday, September 29, was the date set. More and more the community was coming to realize the possibilities of the school. On July fourth, as orator of the day, Leonard S. Swett had taken as his subject "The Normal University." In commenting on its name, he had said "school" was not big enough for the prairies. "University" was better. He praised the county court for donating the land. Dr. E. R. Roe who spoke later reiterated Swett's predictions. Bloomington was to be the "educational head of the state."[21] The laying of the cornerstone was to savor of celebration over the successful location of the school and also to be a forecast of a greater one to come, a prelude to the dedication ceremony which according to

[20] Illinois had 11,000 teachers in 1857 and 13,000 in 1858. Salaries were as low as five dollars a month for women and nine dollars for men, and ranged as high as $150 for men and $54 for women. Cook, *Educational History of Illinois*, p. 82.
[21] *Daily Pantagraph*, July 7, 1857.

Hovey's schedule would take place in September one year later.

The Honorable Samuel W. Moulton of Shelbyville, Member of the House of Representatives, chairman of the Committee on Education, and also chairman of the Board's Committee on Buildings, was asked to make the address. Governor Bissell and former governor Matteson were invited to attend and participate in the exercises.

A welcoming committee drove to the station to meet the distinguished visitors. The trains were late. When the *Pantagraph* went to press it carried a note to the effect that the speakers had not yet arrived but assured the readers that hand bills would be printed and circulated if the morning trains arrived in time to have the exercises as scheduled. About noon the crowd began to disperse. The local committee held council. With or without distinguished guests the laying of the cornerstone must go on. The masons must not be kept from their work. The townspeople would have to make the speeches. Around two o'clock twenty or thirty carriages bearing leading citizens and their wives, together with a goodly company of children and adults on foot, made their way to North Bloomington.

At three o'clock Dr. George Rex of the Board of Education called the meeting to order as the people gathered about a large block of Joliet stone on the southeast corner. The stone had been hollowed sufficiently to hold a tin box twelve inches square and six inches deep. The Reverend H. J. Eddy of the Baptist Church invoked Divine Blessing upon the enterprise. Dr. Rex apologized for the unexpected absence of Moulton and introduced the persons who had been selected to deposit items in the cornerstone. The Reverend Alfred Eddy of the Second Presbyterian Church deposited a copy of the Scriptures as testimony that "Christianity of the Bible was the foundation of this edifice and the foundation of the education to be given here." State Superintendent of Public Instruction, W. H. Powell, deposited a copy of the School Laws of Illinois and his latest report and prophesied that here Illinois would have such an institution as no other state possessed. A letter from former governor Matteson was read, and then Jesse Fell placed a list of contributors to the institution in the little tin box. He remarked upon the importance of popular education, and said that the great need of the state was educators. He hoped to see it develop into an institution of wider scope than an ordinary normal school, a real university with an agricultural school and a model farm.

Principal Hovey deposited lithographic views of the building as it would look when completed and copies of the *Illinois Teacher* containing proceedings of the State Board in reference to the institution. He then traced the history of the school since the teachers meeting in Bloomington three years before, and properly praised teachers, legislators, and townspeople who had a part in its establishment.

Dr. Roe, editor of the *Illinois Baptist,* deposited copies of the daily and weekly newspaper of Bloomington, Springfield, Chicago, Alton, and Peoria. According to the *Pantagraph,* he made a "humorous and eloquent speech." The press and the schoolhouse were the two great engines of education, he hardly knew which to put first. John Deitrich then soldered the box and Dr. Rex solemnly placed it in the cavity. Mr. Loburg of the contracting firm filled the remainder of the cavity with dry sand, a good bed of cement was spread on the lower stone, and then Judge Merriman of the County Court laid the upper stone in its place. The Reverend Taylor of the Congregational Church pronounced the benediction.[22] There was hand-shaking and happy leave-taking as the masons resumed their work.

Jesse Fell looked again toward Greenwood and smiled. Only a few weeks before he had turned the first earth. The Hoveys, beaming and happy, drove back to Bloomington. The cornerstone had been laid and in less than a week classes would begin.

* * *

By seven o'clock on the morning of October fifth Principal Hovey and his assistant, Ira Moore, were at Major's Hall to await the coming of the students. They looked to see that everything was in order in the large hall and the six small rooms that were to serve as assembly room, offices, and classrooms. The desks and chairs that had been ordered from Boston had not arrived. Backless benches had been improvised from rough oak and a few tables and chairs had been borrowed. The "generous owners of

[22] *Daily Pantagraph,* September 30, 1857; *National Flag,* September 30, 1857.

nearby church property supplied other essential requisites." [23]

There was no way of knowing how many students would be enrolling. On Friday the *Pantagraph* had carried a list of 102 bank failures. Eastern papers were beginning to print long stories about unemployment. The nation was in the grip of a financial panic.[24]

The first student to arrive was Enoch A. Gastman, Jr., from Hudson. He was twenty-three, tall, and well-built. A few years before he had injured his foot with an axe and walked with a limp. He had already taught school at Saybrook and Kappa and between teaching jobs had spent a semester at Wesleyan and a term at Eureka College. He was alert, interested, determined.[25] Hovey and Moore were pleased with the first arrival. Surely it augured well for the school. In a short time Joseph G. Howell from White County, John Hull from Marion County, and Sallie Dunn from Bloomington arrived. During the morning nineteen students enrolled, six men and thirteen young women. More came in the afternoon. By the following morning the number had risen to twenty-nine. When the last student enrolled for the first term eight days later the total number was forty-three.[26]

There were no spectators and no fanfare attending the opening of school. Each student brought with him a letter testifying as to his moral character, and if a scholarship student, a certificate of appointment. Each signed a pledge to teach and agreed that for three years after leaving the University each June and December he would write the principal and tell where he had been and how he was employed. Although textbooks were to be provided for students, they were advised to bring along any books which they had at home. As it later developed textbooks furnished by the school were to be used in classroom only and the student who wished to study at his room had to provide his own. The Text-

[23] W. H. Powell, *op. cit.*, pp. 388–389.

[24] *Daily Pantagraph*, October 2, 1857. It was reported that in Chicago 20,000 were unemployed. There was not enough work on Chicago streets at seventy-five cents a day for two days a week to meet the demand for jobs, so wages were cut to fifty cents and one-third more men given the benefits of employment.

[25] Mildred Tschlabach, "Enoch Gastman." MS., Illinois State Normal University; Cook, *Educational History of Illinois*, p. 503.

[26] No other normal school in America had opened with such an auspicious number of students. The average age of students admitted the first term was twenty years and two months.

book Committee of the Board had presented its report on August 18. The list contained many of the time-honored classics in American educational history: McGuffy and Sanders' *Revised Spellers* and *Readers,* Davies, Ray and Thompson's series of *Arithmetics,* Cornell and Warren's *Geographies,* Cowderies' *Moral Lessons,* Wells' *Science of Common Things,* Quackenboss' *Composition and Rhetoric,* and Webster's *Dictionaries.*[27]

Principal Hovey reserved for himself classes in metaphysics, history and pedagogy and assigned the teaching of the other subjects to his assistant, Ira Moore. With the increasing enrollment and supervision of the building construction Hovey found it necessary to hire a second assistant, Charlton Lewis, and to turn much of his own work over to Moore.[28]

The Model School opened on November second in one of the rooms on the second floor of Major's Hall. There were only seven pupils, one of whom could not pay the fifty cents a week tuition, but Mary Brooks accepted him gratuitously. She hoped the reputation of her school would be favorable and that by the end of the ten weeks' term it would not only be self-sustaining but remunerative. Board and room in Bloomington, fortunately, was not high.[29]

Principal Hovey believed the Model School to be the true heart of the normal school and Mary Brooks was a master teacher. When Editor Edward J. Lewis of the *Pantagraph* made a visit to the Model School the second week after it started, he was moved to write an editorial on the Normal University. The seats and desks from Ross' in Boston had just been installed. He spent considerable time in the primary department, where he was deeply impressed by the "kind and familiar but efficient manner" of Miss Brooks and by the "interest and docility of her little pupils." [30] When Board member Dr. George Bunsen, a Pestalozzian who maintained his own little private school for training teachers in

---

[27] *Proceedings of the Board of Education* (Bloomington), August 18, 1857, p. 14.

[28] *Daily Pantagraph,* January 18, 1858. Charlton Lewis, lawyer and classicist, taught mathematics at Normal University for one term. He was later prominent as an insurance actuary and classical scholar, lecturing at Harvard, Columbia, and Cornell, *DAB.*

[29] Rates at the city's finest hotel, The Pike House, were only $3.50 a week. In the private home where Mary Brooks lived it was much less. Wood, candles, and laundry were extra.

[30] *Daily Pantagraph,* November 14, 1857.

St. Clair County, visited the Model School, he was amazed and delighted. He had always placed great emphasis on number work, phonics, and object lessons. "From the known to the unknown," he was constantly repeating. To him Mary Brooks was the kind of teacher from whom not only children but adults could learn.[31] Years later Hovey recalled how Bunsen would "sit for hours, sometimes whole days watching Mary's work as pleased as any of the children, and apparently unconscious of the lapse of time."[32]

The fame of Mary Brooks spread. The second term opened with ten pupils and closed with fourteen. When the third term opened over fifty who applied had to be turned away for lack of room. Section A began observations in earnest, and a few privileged students were employed as part-time teacher assistants. Principal Hovey proudly reported to the Board that receipts for the Model School during the first year amounted to $439.50 and the sum applied wholly for the payment of Miss Brooks and her assistants.[33]

On Friday evening after the opening of school the men students, led by Charles Irons and Harvey Dutton, met in one of the small classrooms, lighted by a single sputtering tallow candle. The meeting was called to discuss the formation of a debating club. It was believed that such a society would extend social relations, elevate moral character and intellectual attainments. On this high note a committee was appointed to draft a constitution and to present it the following evening. The completed document in less than a hundred and fifty words committed the signers to attend regularly, to appear on programs and perform such other duties as the society imposed. It threatened with expulsion any member who should move dissolution of the society. The constitution provided for nine officers; in addition to the usual ones, the Normal Debating Society, as it was decided for the time being to call the organization, provided for a marshal, a student critic, editress and chorister. Terms of office were short. It was expected that there would be sufficient rotation that all members would have the privilege, and discipline of office-holding. To discourage

[31] Minnie Niess, "George Bunsen." MS., *Felmley Papers.*
[32] Cook and McHugh, *op. cit.,* p. 227.
[33] W. H. Powell, *op. cit.,* p. 393.

tardiness, a twenty-five cent fine was assessed late-comers. All of the fifteen men currently enrolled, except one, were present and signed the document. Charles Irons was elected president; Justin L. Spaulding, vice-president; Harvey Dutton, secretary, and John Hull, treasurer. For a debate at the regular meeting the following Wednesday, the subject chosen was, "Is a lawyer justified in defending a bad case?" Five speakers were selected for the affirmative and five for the negative.

Charter members of the society were men but the ratio of two women to one man, could not long be ignored. It is not known just when women students were admitted to membership but it must have been quite early in the first term. The *Pantagraph* relates that on Friday evening, January 15, 1858, at the conclusion of Dr. Roe's lecture on "Respiratory Organs" the Lyceum recently organized by the students convened. On behalf of the students Matilda Reisinger presented Professor Charlton Lewis, who was giving up teaching because of his health, a "magnificently bound copy of Mrs. Cowden Clarke's *World-Noted Women.*" Following a debate in which all the men students took part, the *Ladies Garland,* a manuscript periodical prepared by two of the women students was read.[34] In the years to come there would be many stirring debates, a few near disastrous clashes but withal fierce loyalty and an ever-widening horizon of activity. The debating society, begun so inauspiciously by the light of a single candle, was to cast its beam across the life of the University for ninety years.

The masons continued their work and from time to time the editor of the *Pantagraph* reported on the progress that was being made. However the panic which had swept across the nation struck Bloomington and McLean County. Lands took a drop in price, the market for farm commodities struck an all-time low, and there was no market for the swamp lands donated by the county. Subscriptions so enthusiastically made in May failed to come in. When the Board met in December 1857, the treasurer, John McClum, reported that he had received only $311.25 and

[34] *Daily Pantagraph,* January 18, 1858. Prior to this meeting the *Ladies Garland* was a manuscript periodical known simply as *The Garland.* In early society history debate was the province of men; editing of the society paper was given to the women. Cook and McHugh, *op. cit.,* pp. 102–103.

that he had already paid out $1,141, making the Board his debtor by $879.25. He reported however that most of the subscriptions had been converted into notes and if the Board wished, it might by law force collection. Bonds had been taken for deeds of the lands donated by Judge Davis, E. W. Bakewell, Meshack Pike, and Joseph Payne.[35] It was certain that construction could not go on without funds. The chairman of the Building Committee, C. B. Denio of Galva, proposed that the guarantors of the county's subscription of swamp lands be required to pay $14,000 by February first and that if the money were not forthcoming, the Board's attorney, Abraham Lincoln, should be instructed to bring suit. To Hovey this was a severe measure. He did not want to see friends of the school treated so harshly. Better, he thought, to cover the materials that had been delivered and suspend construction temporarily than ruin men who had pledged their support in good faith.[36]

As the Building Committee pondered ways and means, the first term drew to a close. The *Pantagraph* carried an announcement of the final examinations, to which the public was invited.

All twelve members of the Board of Education and a number of townspeople, including Editor Lewis of the *Pantagraph* attended the public examinations, which concluded the term. The students were examined and drilled in reading, arithmetic, grammar, and geography. Sentences were analyzed and maps were drawn freehand and from memory on the blackboard. There were exercises in mental arithmetic which greatly impressed the *Pantagraph* reporter.

The teacher would say for instance, "Add 7 and 9 together, subtract 4, divide by 3, multiply by 6, add 9, multiply by 2, extract the square root, divide by 3, add 7, and what is the result." He would talk as fast as he could and we thought for a time that none of the scholars could keep even with him, but whenever he stopped, several hands would be raised as signs that they knew the correct answer.[37]

After the teacher drilled and questioned the class for a time, members of the class were called to question the group. Now and then

---

[35] *Proceedings of the Board of Education* (Bloomington), December 23, 1857, pp. 18–19.
[36] Cook and McHugh, *op. cit.*, pp. 42–43.
[37] *Daily Pantagraph,* December 23, 1857.

Board members and other visitors propounded questions. Samuel Moulton, President of the Board, asked a question which he thought most provocative. Slowly he began, "At Cairo, where I reside we get the white pine lumber of New York and yellow pine lumber of Mississippi all the way by water; and none if it comes up stream. How does it come? and by what route?" To his amazement one of the young women promptly raised her hand. The answer was correct.[38]

Principal Hovey moved quietly in and out anxiously, listening to questions and answers. He watched the expressions on the faces of the Board members. He smiled encouragingly at the students. At last the examinations were over, and Board members Denio, Moulton, and Sloan made speeches approving the work of the school.[39]

When the second term opened after the Christmas recess, work on the building had stopped. But there were six more students in the normal department, and the Model School, which had gotten off to a slow start, now had twice the enrollment of the first term. At the moment Principal Hovey was not greatly disconcerted that building operations had been suspended. In a short time he thought normal business conditions would be restored, the donors would redeem their pledges, and there would be a market for the McLean County lands. Most of the lands designated as swamp were far from being swamps; in fact most of McLean County was fertile productive prairie with here and there a rich grove of oak or walnut.

Hovey felt indeed fortunate that he had been able to secure the services of Chauncey Cady of Chicago as part time teacher of music. Professor Cady was editor of the *Chicago Musical Review,* a composer of local note, and conductor of the Chicago Musical Union.[40]

Hovey enjoyed music for itself and regarded it "as a means of giving expression to the highest and holiest emotions of the soul" . . . "capable of exerting an important influence upon human character and progress." He believed the young could be taught

[38] *Ibid.,* December 29, 1857.
[39] *Ibid.,* December 24, 1857.
[40] Hovey was so impressed with Professor Cady's address before the state teachers meeting that he asked to have it published. *Illinois Teacher,* April 1857, pp. 146–151.

to sing as well as to read and write and saw no reason "why vocal music should not enter into every elementary course of study and take its place beside the essential branches."

As principal he was concerned about the social life of the students. He wanted them to be happy and to have rich friendships. For the time being the students were dependent on the churches and their own devices for entertainmnt. Repertory stock companies frequently stopped in Bloomington and played to capacity audiences in College Hall or at the National Theatre, but few students could afford fifty cents for admission. The week following the opening of school in October the Henderson Stock Company, "starring Miss Etta Henderson" presented "Star of the North," "The Queen's Own," "Uncle Tom's Cabin," and "The Hunchback." [41] Hovey hoped when he built his home in North Bloomington that it would be a center for student gatherings.

The second term had barely begun when trouble arose from an unexpected quarter—the Debating Society. Enoch Gastman was just beginning his term as fourth president of the society. A rule of the society made it the duty of the presiding officer to fine any member who left the room without his permission. An exciting debate prolonged the meeting. C. D. Irons, Harvey Dutton, and Justin Spaulding asked permission to leave. As the meeting was almost over, President Gastman asked the gentlemen to remain until adjournment. The three members promptly left the room, and the somewhat disgruntled officer ordered a fine of twenty-five cents assessed each of the refractory gentlemen. The following afternoon a special meeting was called. The society resolved itself into a committee of the whole. Irons, Dutton, and Spaulding appealed to the house from the decision of the chair in the matter of the fine. There was much wrangling. Some one called for the question. Gastman stated it swiftly, "Will the society sustain the President?" The vote was in the affirmative. Henry Pope moved that the fines be expunged from the record. The motion carried. The matter was not solved. Spaulding, Dutton, and Irons felt they had been mistreated. Two factions developed. John Hull rushed to the aid of his friend Enoch Gastman. A week later when

[41] The southern element in Bloomington was not favorable to a second performance of "Uncle Tom's Cabin," and the Hendersons tacitly substituted "The Hunchback." *National Flag*, October 13, 1857.

Spaulding, Dutton, and Irons turned in the resignations Hull moved that Irons be expelled. The majority concurred, but a special meeting engineered by Irons' friends was called the next day and his resignation accepted. Agitation continued until Irons and his friends obtained "honorable discharges."

Irons and his friends were not content without the cultural and social contacts that the literary society afforded. They were annoyed when told that the original society has changed its name to Philadelphian, since without Irons, Dutton, and Spaulding, the members worked together harmoniously, in a "spirit of brotherly love." When the D and E sections entered in the spring term, with twenty new men and sixteen women the time seemed ripe for the organization of another literary society. The second day after the term opened, the new students were invited to a meeting in one of the classrooms. The principal speakers were students who had been or were members of the existing society. Some of the remarks made were in poor taste and registered so much of personal bias that some one suggested that before any action was taken, it might be well for the new students first to attend a meeting of the present society and later decide whether they cared to organize a new and rival society.

Meanwhile some of the new students took a Saturday hike to look at the foundation of the new building. From a copy of the architect's drawings, they noted on the third floor provisions for two society halls. The meeting of the old society to which new students had been invited turned out to be such a poor exhibition of literary ability that it required little effort to convince the majority that the D and E sections could organize and carry on a society, the equal of the one in existence.

Principal Hovey was not favorable to the idea but after talking it over with Ira Moore, who was definitely opposed to the new society, and with Board member, Simeon Wright, who was kindly disposed toward it, he decided to let the rival be organized as a temporary expedient. He warned that the time might soon come when both societies might be broken up and new institutions organized along a different basis.

The Philadelphians believed their organization was permanent and superior. It was given a choice of evenings for using the hall for its meetings. The new society demonstrated great zeal and pride in its performance. Simeon Wright was especially pleased with the new society. He counseled its members as to the work that it could accomplish for the school. He had been impressed with society libraries in other colleges and suggested this to the D and E Society. Meanwhile the organization found its name inconvenient. The members wished to devise a name that would surpass that of the Philadelphians. Their knowledge of Greek and Latin was too limited to construct an original word, but they fell back on first principles and declared that their society required an expressive name of English origin. Someone suggested that the society be named for Simeon Wright, who had not only been one of the founders of the school but had more recently prevailed upon the principal to give the new society his approval "as an experiment." [42] Eleven of the seventeen votes cast favored the change in name, and Vice-President John Burnham, who was presiding, solemnly ruled that that eleven was two-thirds of seventeen, the majority required to amend the constitution. The six who opposed the name appealed from the decision of the chairman. The discussion waxed loud and spirited. Burnham tried to think of a parliamentary device by which his ruling could be sustained. Simple majorities were required on all other questions. He now asked for a vote to sustain the decision of the chair. By a bare majority the decision was sustained and by a somewhat questionable ruling, Wrightonia became the name of the University's second literary society.

After a few weeks students settled down, and the only reports from the societies that came to Principal Hovey were those enthusiastic over the programs which by this time were being widened to include not only debates but essays, musical numbers, and a society newspaper. Simeon Wright secured for each of the societies the donation of one of Moore's district school libraries, of over one hundred volumes each, with five library cases. To his namesake, he personally donated a number of valuable books.

As the school year drew to a close in July, Principal Hovey began to think of some suitable ways of entertaining the public. There would be no graduating class until 1860, but it seemed fit-

[42] Cook and McHugh, *op. cit.*, pp. 102–129.

ting and proper that more cognizance should be taken of the closing of the school than the usual drills and examinations. Many persons in Bloomington interested in the two societies had formed a habit of coming to Major's Hall on Friday and Saturday nights and listening to the students' programs. Favorites developed. Why not celebrate the conclusion of the first school year by an intersociety contest?

In an address of welcome as principal, he might bring townspeople, parents, and friends up to date on the progress of the school. The examinations and the debate, the music and the literary offerings could speak for themselves, but there were other things Hovey wanted the public to know. The record was good. Eighty-eight different students had been enrolled in the normal department. No Eastern normal could boast as many for its first year. There were three regular teachers and Miss Brooks in the Model School. Professor Cady gave lessons in music twice a week and Dr. E. R. Roe, Bloomington physician, gave a weekly lecture in physiology. True, construction on the building had halted, but as soon as crops were harvested and subscriptions began to come in, work would resume. Just this past June, some of the leading naturalists in the state had organized a society for diffusing information on the natural history of Illinois, and voted to locate their museum in the Normal University, thus making the society auxiliary to the normal school.[43] Jesse Fell had been asked by the Board to consult with experts relative to the landscaping of the campus, and William Saunders, landscape gardener of Philadelphia, who lately had drawn up a plan for Mr. Fell's estate, Greenwood, had made a similar one for the Normal University. With trees, flowers, shrubs, and lawn and the magnificent building of red brick topped with a white tower and dome, the campus would be a joy to behold.

The Philadelphian and Wrightonian societies quickly fell in with the plan. The debate especially appealed to them. Budding orators were trying to improve their style. When court was in session they frequently dropped in to listen to the local bar, Leonard Swett, Ward Lamon, and David Davis.

The topic selected for the debate, the only part of the program

[43] W. H. Powell, *op. cit.*, p. 392.

on which the judges were to render a decision, was "Resolved that Compulsory Attendance is Beneficial." Peter Harper and James Ridlon upheld the affirmative for the Philadelphian Society and Peleg Walker and John Burnham, the negative for the Wrightonian Society.

A manuscript periodical prepared by four young women of the school was read and then came the debate. The discussion was as exciting as the subject and the honor of the two societies would permit. While the judges deliberated, Board member Charles Denio talked of the past, present, and future of the school, the building situation, and the role that Normal University was destined to play in educating teachers for the schools of Illinois.

The judges came quietly back into the room. Anxiously the audience waited the decision. Denio sat down, and after a hurried conference with the judges, the chairman made the fateful announcement.

Wrightonia had won.[44]

[44] *Daily Pantagraph,* July 3, 1858.

CHAPTER III

The Noblest Building

EVENTS OF 1858 proved Hovey's optimism ill-founded. Despite a consistent rising enrollment, there was dissatisfaction throughout the state. Since Bloomington and McLean County had defaulted in the matter of subscriptions there was talk of moving the location. Some unsympathetic persons were even advising that the project be abandoned. The situation called for action. If only there were buyers for the swamp lands! These tracts were good land with black, rich soil but local speculators were already up to their necks in debt and dared not buy more.

By this time Hovey liked Bloomington. He admired men like Charles Ames, Jesse Fell and his brother Kersey, Daniel Wilkins, Dr. Henry Schroeder, John McClun, and dozens of others who had given generously of themselves as well as of their means that the Normal University might be located at Bloomington. He was quite in sympathy with Jesse Fell's idea of platting all North Bloomington and having it set aside as a separate town, with a separate charter. Fell wanted the charter to contain a clause prohibiting the sale of intoxicating liquors and restricting the operation of billiard parlors, and public dancehalls. Whenever Fell sold lots he stipulated in the deed that no intoxicating liquors were ever to be sold on the premises.[1] Bloomington had been a prohibition town in 1854 and 1855, but by the time the Normal University was founded, the *National Flag* was lamenting that "perhaps there is no town where drinking is carried to such an extent for the number of inhabitants as Bloomington. Innumerable are its doggeries, places of resort for drinking, gambling, crime of all descriptions."[2] Perhaps the same thing could have been said for Peoria or Springfield or Urbana. Hovey realized if the location were changed, the whole educational system would be retarded.

[1] Morehouse, *op. cit.*, p. 73.
[2] *National Flag*, November 25, 1857.

Jesse Fell, friend of the School for over thirty years, was directly responsible for its location in McLean County.

Charles Hovey, principal, 1857–1862, rose from Colonel in the Illinois Thirty-third Volunteer Infantry to the rank of Brevet Major General in 1863.

Mary Brooks, first teacher in the Model School, taught from 1857 to 1860.

Thomas Metcalf, training school teacher, member of the faculty, 1862–1894.

Richard Edwards, who was second president of Normal University 1862 to 1876, described teaching as the grandest of enterprises.

Edwin C. Hewett joined the faculty in 1858 and as president, 1876–1890, carried on the Bridgewater tradition.

"Uncle" Simeon Wright, defender of the D and E Society.

Miss Emma Dryer, 1863–1870. An early Preceptress.

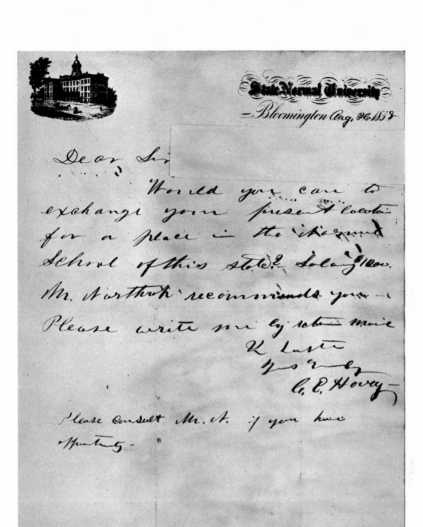

State Normal University
— Bloomington Aug. 26 1858

Dear Sir

Would you care to
exchange your present location
for a place in the *Grammar*
School of this state? Salary $1000.
Mr. Northrop recommends you —
Please write me by return mail
& later
Yours truly
C. E. Hovey —

Please consult Mr. N. if you have
opportunity —

Hewett comes to Normal, 1858.

Major's Hall, Bloomington, scene of Lincoln's "Lost Speech," where first Normal classes met, October 5, 1857.

Graduating class of 1860.

Normal pioneered in audio-visual aids.

Normal Hall, third floor of Old Main, where all auditorium events were held until 1909.

President Hewett and faculty.

The office and reception room when Hewett was president, 1889.

Old Main in the 1860's.

Old Main loses her crowning glory, May, 1946.

Drawing was once required of every elementary student teacher.

The Charles Hovey home, built in 1863, is now an apartment house.

A year and a half went by. The enrollment increased but the coffers did not. Some of the donors who subscribed lands had refused to deed them until the building should be completed. Hovey never forgave Judge David Davis for the example he set by withholding the deed to the forty acres he had subscribed. Every one knew that in the end the state would pay the necessary bills, but the immediate need was prompt payment of the subscription on faith of which the Board had located the Normal University in McLean County.[3]

The county subscription of seventy thousand dollars, which would go a long way toward completing the building, was payable out of the proceeds from the sale of her swamp lands, but by law these could not be sold for less than their appraised value. The Board did not think it should go to the Legislature and ask for funds inasmuch as one of the considerations that prompted the passage of the Normal University Act was the provision that the building would be constructed by local subscription and that it would not cost the state a cent.

If the location were changed, the materials already purchased and the work already paid for would be lost. There seemed but one way out of the awkward situation, and it might not work. It was possible that the McLean County subscription could be used as collateral on which to borrow money. The Legislature would not meet again until January 1861, so there was no chance of any aid coming from that quarter. Neither could the location be changed for eighteen months!

The Board had conferred what amounted to dictatorial powers on the Building Committee. As resident member of the Committee, Charles Hovey was left very much with the job. As Hovey said later no man ever had "worse means, or better backing." Superintendent W. H. Powell, Samuel Moulton, Simeon Wright, Charles Denio, and Dr. George Rex would leave their own business at any time on call and come to Normal.

The Board further authorized the sending of an agent east to sell the county lands. It was intended that James Miller, State Treasurer and a resident of Bloomington who was familiar with the land and its value, should be the agent. Although he was

[3] Cook and McHugh, *op. cit.*, p. 40.

neither a donor nor a guarantor, it was believed that his knowledge, wealth, and prestige as a state officer would afford him enough influence that he would find a purchaser. He refused this somewhat dubious honor. When other rich and influential men refused to assist, Hovey turned to his faculty.

One of these was Chauncey Cady, instructor in vocal music, a man of pluck and tact, and as Hovey later related, "not afflicted with a serious tenderness about investing his skill in an attempt to negotiate the sale of the county lands." With a list and description of the lands he set off for New York, where he seems to have made something of a stir in the real estate world but Cady needed more than a list of the lands. He could do nothing without bonds for deeds which could be transferred by a simple endorsement and although Cady had a buyer, he had to have authority or bonds before the transaction could be cleared.

Hovey immediately asked the county authorities for bonds for the lands, but they would not enter into any kind of a transaction except a direct sale. The only way that he could get deeds for Cady was to buy the lands himself, paying for them by a small cash advance and the balance in time notes. Accordingly he bought seven or eight thousand acres of land at a cost of twenty-five or thirty thousand dollars.[4] On the assumption that the Board would take over the titles and provide bond for the deeds required by Cady, Hovey had borrowed money and purchased the swamp land. But the deal with the County had been made without the Board's sanction and it refused to take over the transaction. Hovey then realized that he had exceeded his authority both as principal and as member of the Building Committee, and that he must shoulder this tremendous financial responsibility alone. The county authorities turned over to the Board his personal notes to the amount of approximately $25,000, and the Building Committee paid them out to various contractors for labor and materials.

As soon as Hovey obtained the bonds he notified Cady but the parties with whom the latter was negotiating failed, the deal fell through, and he was unable to find another purchaser. Those were hectic days for Charles and Harriette Hovey. The Board

---

[4] Hovey's account of the transaction was told years later and the exact amount of his purchases is not known.

held Hovey's notes. If he did not meet them promptly or if he could not pay them at all, he was at its mercy. In June, George Bunsen moved that the Board appoint a committee of three to determine whether all necessary steps had been taken in the administration of the school to secure the results called for in Paragraph 4 of the Statute concerning Illinois State Normal University and to report at the next meeting. This was a shocking proposal and was promptly defeated; however when it was later introduced by Superintendent Powell, it carried. Bunsen, Simeon Wright, and Powell made up the investigating committee. When Bunsen saw his proposal was regarded as a personal attack on Hovey, he resigned from the Board. He later told Bateman that to his mind "the institution was giving a . . . purely academic training and that it could hardly be distinguished from any other academic institution" and that Principal Hovey, "while a man of unimpeachable integrity of character and genuine piety, was a practical man of the world, who by means of real estate transactions managed to add annually five hundred to fifteen hundred dollars to his income and that he lacked zealous devotion to the cause . . . the first requisite in the head of a training school for teachers." [5] Hovey's honor was involved. Then his beloved little son, Charles Edward, died suddenly of diphtheria.[6] After this tragic blow Hovey seemed for weeks not to sleep. He scarcely spoke to any one about the house and seldom mentioned the child's name. Harriette, away at the time, was deeply stunned, but her "brighter nature rallied" and she sought to console her husband for whose sanity she feared.[7]

Somehow the news got circulated that over $25,000 worth of swamp lands had been purchased by one party but the county authorities divulged no names. The story spread, and in the telling the amount of the transaction grew. Hovey took care to have it suggested that all the swamp lands would soon be sold. Through the efforts of Superintendent Powell, McLean County swamp lands were purchased by state officers in Springfield, Auditor Jesse K. Dubois, Treasurer James Miller, and Secretary

[5] Minnie Niess, "George Bunsen." MS., *Felmley Papers.*
[6] Letter, Agnes Cook Gale, to Helen Marshall, Chicago. February 17, 1955. *Marshall Papers.*
[7] *Ibid.*

of State Ozias M. Hatch. Hovey and Powell were careful to see that wide publicity was given the investments of these men. Others took heart, bought land, and soon there were sufficient funds in the treasury to resume construction.

The original contractors for the masonry, Mortimer and Loberg, were paid off and their contract was surrendered. Of the $17,845.60 account, $844.65 had already been paid. The remaining $9400 the Board agreed to pay within two years with ten percent interest. A first lien was awarded the firm.[8] Soper, who had the contract for the carpentry work, decided to retain his contract and take his chances on being paid. It was difficult to find a mason who would be willing to undertake construction of the walls, with subscriptions as the only evidence of payment. Bloomington masons were wary of the job, but by dint of much talk, appeals to local pride, and the confidence that sales of the county lands generated, Samuel D. Rounds was prevailed upon to take the contract in April.[9]

On May 18, 1859, the *Pantagraph* proudly announced that

Mr. Rounds after prospecting carefully all over the neighborhood of Normal University, without success, has at last struck upon a bed of it, (clay) seven feet thick and of excellent quality at the very summit of the hill, and just as near the site of the building as he would have wished it, had the depositing of it been left at his discretion. The bed is not extensive but abundantly enough for the purpose.

The reporter then thoughtfully added

Was there ever a more opportune discovery? Had it been made while the location of the institution was still in dispute, wouldn't it have looked as if the finger of Providence was in it? Doesn't it look so as it is? [10]

Rounds was to have the brick work completed on or before the first of October 1859. He was to receive "$14 per 1000 brick in the wall." The stone work was to cost $22 per cord. When Rounds provided the stone he was to receive $40 per cord.[11] He erected a kiln for firing the brick about a hundred yards from the clay pit and about twice the distance from the building.[12] When a *Panta-*

[8] *Proceedings of the Board of Education* (Bloomington), July 1, 1859, p. 5.
[9] *Illinois State Journal*, April 27, 1859; Cook and McHugh, *op. cit.*, p. 45.
[10] *Weekly Pantagraph*, May 18, 1859.
[11] *Proceedings of the Board of Education* (Bloomington), July 1, 1859, p. 5.
[12] The clay pit was near the site of the present Baptist Church and the kiln stood where the Normal Central School is now located.

graph reporter visited the University in mid-August, he reported that the window frames had been set for first story above the basement and that the joists were in for the second floor. Sixteen bricklayers, their hodmen, and four or five carpenters were on the job.[13] To Hovey the construction seemed to be going at a snail's pace, and some weeks it did not progress at all. After Rounds took the cream of the subscriptions, there was little left to pay carpenters, painters, plumbers, and plasterers.

Once more the point was reached where work could not go on without funds. It was evident that money could not be obtained on the credit of the Board, nor could it come from private notes based on the assets of the Board. Hovey saw but one way: once more friends of the institution must either loan it money or give it credit. Moulton and Hovey borrowed a few thousand dollars, but it did not last long. Jesse Fell and Charles Holder volunteered to help and put their names to a paper on which Hovey and Moulton obtained more money. In this way from time to time, funds were secured. Hovey often said that without the help of the Fells and the Holders construction could not have gone on.

Hovey told merchants of Bloomington that he would be personally responsible, and that they would be paid out of the first money the Board received for building supplies if they would supply Soper with the materials he needed, hardware, paints, oils, glass, lumber, groceries, clothing, and other provisions for his family and workmen. The Legislature was to meet the following January and Hovey assured the merchants it would appropriate funds for any deficiency in the building funds, and that they would be paid out of this appropriation. It was a daring piece of financiering but it worked. The materials Soper needed were provided and the building proceeded.

On Saturday, November 4, the last brick was laid. The men drew lots for the honor of putting this last brick on the north wall of the third story. W. H. Powell, representing the Board of Education, passed out slips of paper. S. D. Rounds who held the contract then laid the last brick, with his son serving as hodman. There were loud cheers from the townsmen gathered below. The workmen climbed down from the scaffolding and gathered around a

[13] *Weekly Pantagraph*, August 17, 1859.

table that had been set with refreshments. Colonel Asahel Gridley, one of Round's heaviest creditors, made a brief speech congratulating him. Judge John McClun spoke in behalf of the Board, and then everyone present was invited to enjoy the free lunch of bread, cheese, and lager beer.[14]

Much remained to be done, but Hovey and the Board hoped that the building would be completed in time for the first graduating class to have had classes in it for a short time at least. Again there were delays. At last assurance came from the contractors that the two central halls on the second and third stories would be floored and in shape for commencement but it would be late summer before the classrooms would be finished. Plans were made accordingly. Parents and friends must see the building which was already being extravagantly described as "the finest building of its kind in all America." Examinations would be held in Major's Hall, but the graduating exercises and the grand collation to follow would be held at the building in North Bloomington.

The last week in June was an eventful one. As Mrs. David Davis wrote her sister, Fanny Williams, in Stockbridge, Massachusetts, "This is the week of the meetings, agricultural, horticultural, historical, and last but not least meeting of the Friends of the Normal School. I hear 1,000 invitations were given to friends abroad." [15] Chicago and local papers styled it Anniversary Week and both the *Chicago Times* and the *Chicago Press and Tribune* had special reporters to cover the events. On Tuesday the Ilinois Natural History Society, organized two years before, held its annual three-day meeting in Phoenix Hall. It had as one of its major projects the developing of a museum to be located at the State Normal School building, and the collecting and mounting of every species of plants, birds, shells, fishes, insects, quadrupeds, minerals and fossils in Illinois and conducting exchange of specimens with similar societies throughout the nation and other parts of the world. Many of its members stayed over for the joint meeting of the State Agricultural and Horticultural Society, which

---

[14] *Ibid.*, November 9, 1859. This is probably the only time that beer has been served at an official function on the campus of Illinois State Normal University!

[15] Mrs. David (Sarah Walker) Davis to her sister, Fanny Williams, Bloomington, June 28, 1860. Davis Papers, Williams College.

opened its session in Phoenix Hall on Wednesday afternoon. The convention concerned itself with agricultural education. All of the delegates and friends were invited to the festivities of commencement on Friday as well as the examinations on Thursday and the special society program on Thursday night.[16]

Despite a heavy rain on Thursday the examinations were well attended. Among the spectators who sat on the platform at Major's Hall and observed the examinations were Governor John Wood, State Auditor Jesse K. Dubois, Newton Bateman, late of Jacksonville, who succeeded Hovey as editor of the *Illinois Teacher* and was now the State Superintendent of Public Instruction, all twelve members of the Board of Education, Captain J. N. Brown, Lewis Ellsworth, and a large number of well-known and prominent citizens of Illinois.

At nine o'clock Principal Hovey opened the exercises with a devotional service. A chapter of the New Testament was read responsively, with the principal and the students alternating verses. This was followed by the repetition of the Lord's Prayer.

Professor Leander H. Potter examined the students in selections taken at random from the first two books of the *Aeneid*. The students then assumed the teacher's place and questioned each other. "No chance for collusion," or "benefit from any cramming process, and there seemed to be need of none," commented the reporter.

Professor Ira Moore examined his students in mathematics, and Professor Edwin Hewett in geography and history and Professor Sewall in botany and chemistry. Twice during the forenoon Professor Cady led the entire school in singing.

Several times the sound of childish voices from the floor below lured the *Press and Tribune* reporter to visit the Model School. He found thirty children gathering about their teacher, Mary Brooks, "forming altogether one of the happiest and most united little communities imaginable." He saw nothing of the "straight-jacket" about the Model School. "Each child apparently was as

---

[16] Press clippings of the Agricultural Convention, the Annual Meeting of the Illinois Natural History Society, the Commencement Exercises of the State Normal University, and a concluding paper descriptive of the course of study, faculty, and prospects of the Normal University were published in a pamphlet entitled, "Anniversary Week in Bloomington." This was distributed to friends of the school and to prospective students.

responsive to their teacher's voice and look as organ keys to the touch of a skillful player." Later when these bright-faced and happy children filed upstairs and took their places on the platform and gave their exhibit of proficiency, reading and singing in concert, he was reminded of a "tree full of canaries." There was deep emotion when tiny Fanny Graves in a neat little faltering speech presented Mary Brooks, now resigning to be married, a writing desk as a gift from her pupils. Mary Brooks smiled and hesitated, but tears not words came. Principal Hovey stepped forward and acknowledged the gift for her.[17]

On Thursday evening the Reverend Thomas Hill, who had succeeded Horace Mann as President of Antioch College, spoke before a joint and open session of the Wrightonian and Philadelphian Societies. The day closed with heavy showers and as a consequence the audience was small, but Commencement morning rose bright and clear. The dust that clogged the roads and covered the cornfields was laid and the fields glistened fresh and bright in the sunshine. The students arrived early to finish the last touches of cedar boughs and flowers that were to decorate the two halls. Soon families began to arrive with well-filled baskets, dishes, and carefully labeled silverware to be used at the dinner which would follow the graduating exercises. There was excitement in the air. "By nine o'clock the road from town toward the University was a busy scene," the reporter wrote, "with vehicles of all classes and numerous pedestrians." [18]

Seats had been improvised and chairs brought out from Bloomington and long before nine o'clock the room was filled with parents, townspeople, and friends. The muddy roads caused some of the distinguished visitors to be late in arriving. Professor Cady rose to the occasion and led the company in group singing.

At last the Board, state officers, and graduates filed in. Principal Hovey took his place and announced the Lord's Prayer. Quietly, clearly, reverently, and solemnly the words were repeated. Hovey then announced that the special subjects on which the graduates would speak or read compositions had been assigned but that none of the finished papers had ever been read by any teacher

[17] *Anniversary Week at Bloomington* (Chicago), July 1860, pp. 46–49.
[18] *Ibid.*, p. 52.

and the faculty as well as the audience was in complete ignorance of what was to be heard.

Enoch Gastman from Hudson, who had been the first to enroll, was given first place on the program. He had a further distinction of never having been absent from classes. His subject was "Horace Mann." Mary Washburn read a paper on "The Fine Arts in the Classroom," and Edwin Philbrook presented his graduating essay on "The Agriculturalist." Then there was the chorus from *Masoneillo,* "Away, Away, the Morning Freshly Breaking" by Auber. Silas Hays next spoke on "What Poverty Has Done." Elizabeth Mitchell read her composition, "The Worship of the Past," and Peter Harper read his on "Amusements." A male chorus directed by Professor Cady lustily sang "The Ship of Union."

> Sail on, O ship of State
> Sail on O Union, strong and great
> Humanity with all its fears
> With all the hopes of future years
> Is hanging breathless on fate.[19]

John Hull spoke feelingly of "Our Calling" and Frances Peterson, "The Wealth of a Nation Is in Its Men." Again there was a musical break, a four-part song, "Never Forget the Dear Ones." Sarah Dunn spoke on "Hereditary Opinions" and Joseph Howell delivered the last of the class speeches on "Positive and Negative Men."

The class rose and sang its graduating song which Professor Cady arranged. It began

> We walked, the morning seen beneath
> Glad wand'ring side
> Our hopes entwined, a pleasant wreath
> Bright friendship's smile our guide . . .

And ended two stanzas later,

> Oh, may we to our God, the Light
> Uplift our gaze afar
> Beholding through the darksome night
> The bright and morning star.

[19] "The Ship of Union" is an excerpt from Henry Wadsworth Longfellow's long poem "The Building of the Ship." It was set to music by George F. Root, who was Chauncey Cady's partner in the music publishing business in Chicago.

And finally that climactic moment came toward which they had ordered their lives for the past three years. Samuel Moulton, President of the Board, spoke briefly and appropriately and then stepped to the be-ribboned rolls of parchment that Principal Hovey had brought forward. "Enoch Gastman, McLean County." It was Principal Hovey's voice. Enoch limped forward, took his diploma and shook hands. Illinois State Normal University had graduated its first student. There was loud applause. There were four more graduates from McLean County and one each from Fayette, Peoria, Lee, Marion, and White Counties. After the last round of applause, the Reverend Alfred Eddy of the Second Presbyterian Church, Bloomington, came forward, and pronounced the benediction.[20]

Friends pressed forward to congratulate the graduates and Principal Hovey. Some members of the class could wait no longer. Off from the diplomas came the bows and streamers. Proudly they were unrolled, read, and displayed.

The collation beckoned those who had not been too excited to become hungry. Those fortunate enough to have received one of the invitations sent out by a committee of the graduating class pressed toward the stairs. All during the exercises the occasional rattle of dishes, and the rustle of starched skirts going up and down the stairs gave rich promise of good things to come. Earlier in the week editorially the *Pantagraph* had commented,

We trust our citizens will do themselves honor this week in extending hospitality to those who will visit us. Unless our friends have reflected upon this subject they are not prepared to realize its importance. Let liberal donations to the collation on Friday make it a handsome thing and one to which all participated therein shall hereafter recur with pleasure.[21]

The long tables with their white cloths decorated with bouquets and laden with great platters of cold roast, fried chicken, pressed veal, baked beans, potato salad, cole slaw, pickled beets, deviled eggs, cottage cheese, pickles, jellies, jams, freshly churned butter, home-baked bread, pies, cakes, lemonade and iced tea bespoke the generous response of Bloomington housewives.

[20] *Anniversary Week,* pp. 53–55.
[21] *Weekly Pantagraph,* June 27, 1860.

It was a gay and happy occasion. It was certainly well-planned, thought Mrs. Jesse Fell, as she surveyed the company. Even Professor Ira Moore, who was often unpopular with the class and the butt of some of their harsh jokes, seemed to have mellowed as he and Professors Hewett and Potter greeted the visitors. Principal Hovey, beaming on the graduates, found it difficult to decide which of the four girls was loveliest in the specially designed dresses, with tight basque, long full skirts, and carefully brushed hair. Some of the boys appeared ill-at-ease, in their long-tailed coats, starched shirts and bowstring ties, but after all such clothes were the marks of the profession. Soon they would become accustomed to them as well as to being addressed as "professor." Substantial farmers from various sections of the state had remained after the close of the Agricultural Convention to be present at the Commencement and collation. The Bloomington clergy seemed to have turned out in full force, and well they might. Every member of the graduating class was a member of a church, and the majority of them had made their affiliation since coming to the Normal University.[22] The governor did not stay over for the Commencement, but the presence of other state officials gave an air of importance to the scene.

The first toast on the printed program was appropriately addressed to the hosts and donors of the building. "The citizens of Bloomington, in this splendid structure have given proof of their noble devotion to learning, it will be fitly associated in pleasant memories by the graceful hospitality of today." Bloomington's finest orator, Leonard Swett, responded and paid high tribute to donors and predicted a glorious future for the school. The Reverend Thomas Hill, President of Antioch, who had given the societies' address the evening before, responded to the toast to "Our Higher Institutions." "The Desk," "The State Board of Education," "The Ferule," "The Plow," "The Bar" were among the other toasts. C. B. Wilber, President of the State Natural History Society, replied to the toast, "Rocks, Sermons in Stones," and told of plans for the museum. Jesse Fell, long patron and friend of the school, responded to the toast "Planting of Trees." He envisaged

[22] Baptist, Methodist, Presbyterian (Old and New), Congregational, and Christian churches were represented in the graduating class. *Anniversary Week,* p. 64.

a campus with a carriage road winding among the trees of every known variety that would grow in Illinois—birches, magnolias, beeches, oak, walnut, ash, elm, tulip, chestnut, larch, gum, pine, balsam, hemlock, fir, willow as well as shrubs and flowers. It was reminiscent of the plan which William Saunders had drawn up three years before. Fell was proud that already some of the trees had been planted. A few were already as large as an inch in diameter and tall as a man's head. After thirteen formal toasts, there were numerous voluntary ones and responses. Someone remembered the role of Charles Hovey and paid high tribute to his labors and sacrifices. Another remembered the contractors, who were the Board's creditors by several thousands of dollars. Another proposed the mechanics. Through it all Mary Brooks sat entranced, her face slightly flushed. She had resigned and soon she would be leaving. "The Model School," someone was saying. "These rivulets hitherto fed by the beautiful and intellectual Brooks, may they speedily become rivers of intelligence." A burst of loud applause. Blushing, she bowed. In three years Mary Brooks had set a standard for the Model School that was not to be forgotten.[23]

The Hoveys drove slowly back to Bloomington. It would be eleven weeks before school reopened. Harriette hoped that her husband would take a good rest. He was especially concerned about building the house on the lot he had bought over on Mulberry Street not far from the school. During the panic, when his funds had been tied up in the swamp lands, all he had been able to do was to plant a hedge and set out a few trees.[24] Now he was particularly anxious to get the house finished. One of the advantages of having classes in Bloomington had been the availability of room and board. With classes in the new building so far from town there was the problem of housing students. Plans for his own home were such that he could take care of sixteen young ladies in addition to his own family. He encouraged his faculty to build houses and take in students. The Hewetts were projecting quite a large house, and he hoped other houses would soon be built. His own home was so nearly a reality that he had included

[23] *Weekly Pantagraph*, July 4, 1860.
[24] Edwin C. Hewett's description of his first visit to The Junction, 1858. *Index* 1901, p. 14.

in the Anniversary Week souvenir the statement "The social gatherings of the students are expected to be hereafter at the residence of the Principal, at such times and so often as the officers of the Institution shall deem expedient."

For the time being Hovey dismissed the mile and a half that the large portion of students would have to walk from their boarding houses to the school as affording "regular and sufficient exercise." [25] Always planning! Harriette Hovey marveled at her husband's ambitions. She thought he was looking better, not rested but less harassed. She would never forget the agony of those anxious months before his equity in the swamp lands was sold and while he was undergoing shock of the loss of their first-born son.

But now the building was up. Commencement and a grand collation had taken place beneath its roof; by September classrooms would be finished. Heavy debts hung over the school and there was a mortgage on the very building. Thousands of dollars' worth of subscriptions made in good faith could never be paid. There was only one thing to do, Hovey had told the Board, and that was to go before the Legislature in January and ask for an appropriation to lift the school's indebtedness. He was confident that Anniversary Week had demonstrated the school a going concern and one that was rendering a real service to the state.

It was a beautiful building, everyone agreed. It seemed to rise out of the prairie in red and white grandeur. Someday above that silvery dome a flag would float and a bell ring out.

[25] *Anniversary Week*, p. 64.

CHAPTER IV

The Roll of Drums

BEFORE THE Legislature met in January 1861, Principal Hovey and his friends made careful plans. The Board went on record as approving the appeal for funds. Samuel Moulton, President of the Board, reported that the building now completed, with its fixtures, had cost approximately $145,000. This, together with one hundred and sixty acres of land and unpaid collectable subscriptions, represented the property holdings of the corporation of $200,000. The Board had collected all but $76,000, and liabilities amounted to $65,000. "The encumbrances," said Moulton, "must be discharged or the whole of it will have to be abandoned to the rapacity of the creditors."

If the legislators saw the school, they would surely appreciate the work being done and lift the burden of debt. At its December meeting in Bloomington the Board concurred in a plan to bring the entire Legislature to visit the school on the occasion of the dedication of the building on January 24.[1] Hovey conferred with his good friends, Jesse Fell and C. W. Holder. A community's honor was involved and the Legislature's visit should be a community responsibility. The City Council appointed a local committee with Hamilton Spencer as chairman and Editor Lewis as secretary. Spencer was public spirited and a good fund raiser, and Lewis was needed to give the blessing of the press. Mayor H. S. Herr and other leading citizens were adroitly given roles to play. The St. Louis, Alton and Chicago Railroad, ever-anxious to ingratiate itself with the law-makers, agreed to provide a special train from Springfield to Bloomington and return. Transportation would be free to members of the Legislature, their wives, sons or daughters, or anyone invited by the local committee.

There would be a grand tour of the building, a cold collation in Normal Hall, and to show the school in operation there would be

[1] *Proceedings of the Board of Education* (Bloomington), December 20, 1860, p. 1.

64

a demonstration in music and exercises in geography and mental arithmetic. After this there would be the dedicatory program, and at night a banquet in Royce's Hall and a grand ball at Phoenix Hall.[2] Mrs. Jesse Fell and her cousin, Mrs. C. W. Holder, arranged with Gray of Gray's Hotel to serve the meal at the school, and with the well-known caterer Smith to have charge of the evening banquet at Royce's.[3] This time Bloomington businessmen, not their wives, were providing the hospitality. Even hotel accommodations were free to the special invited guests.[4]

The day was very cold but clear. After a gay two-hour trip, enlivened by occasional music from a Springfield band, the special train arrived at the Junction about eleven-thirty. Members of the delegation buttoned their coats tightly and walked over the corn stalks, across the slough and on to the building. Governor Richard Yates failed to make the special train, but the local committee was assured that he would be along on the next train and that the festivities should proceed without him.

Soon between four and five hundred persons were traipsing up and down the stairs, marveling at the beautiful walnut balustrade and nodding approvingly at the highly polished brass cuspidors that lined the lower halls. The building was just as the architect described it. Visitors entered from the south and on passing the vestibule found the public reception room on the right side, soon to be enhanced by a Brussels carpet.[5] They saw two halls, ten feet wide, running quite through the building, crossing each other at right angles and terminating in the middle of the sides and ends with vestibules and outside doors. The students, the visitors were told, entered at the east and west ends, near the dressing rooms. These, too, were a noticeable feature of the building. They were large, fitted with wash bowls, hat-hooks, mirrors, and boxes for rubbers and slippers, and near the entrance so that in wet weather the students could take off their boots and put on slippers before they had gone far enough into the building to soil the floors. On the north side of the building ranged side by side were four Model School rooms, primary, intermediate, grammar, and high school.

[2] *The Illinois Teacher,* February 1861, p. 78.
[3] Morehouse, *op. cit.,* p. 48.
[4] *Weekly Pantagraph,* January 23, 1861.
[5] *Proceedings of the Board of Education* (Bloomington), December 20, 1860, p. 14.

If one proceeded to the basement he found it largely above ground. Here were the janitor's quarters of four rooms, the chemical lecture and laboratory rooms, the water closets, the coal furnace and boiler room.

The second story was the Normal School floor. In the center was a large hall, 70 by 80 feet, with a high ceiling and lighted from north and south by many windows. It was approached by two flights of stairs. Across the wide halls at the opposite ends of the great study hall were four large classrooms. This grouping of the classrooms around the assembly or study room with "ample means of ingress and egress at separate doors," Principal Hovey pointed out, "enabled a school of three hundred pupils to be shifted from room to room without confusion in the same length of time that a single class could be moved. The double stairways, on either side of the main hall, one for ladies and one for gentlemen, furnish ample means of escape in case of accident or fire."

The third floor was the students' pride. Directly above the assembly room was Normal Hall, high, airy, and described as one of the finest auditoriums in the state. Nearby were the rooms of the Philadelphian and Wrightonian Societies, the Gallery of Art and the Museum of the Illinois Natural History Society. Large locked bookcases in the hall were opened several times each week for use of students interested in consulting the atlases and government documents with which their shelves abounded. The literary societies had the largest collections of books for circulation. Books from their libraries could be checked out during the hour preceding the regular meeting. Although textbooks were furnished by the state, students were encouraged to purchase books for their personal use outside the classroom.

Some of the younger visitors ascended the narrower stairs past the attic water cisterns and on to the belfry and the observatory. The view of the city of Bloomington and the adjacent prairies, they reported, was well worth the climb.[6]

The collation over, the visitors were directed into the school-hall where the pupils were anxiously waiting to begin their exercises. Principal Hovey talked briefly on the history of the school and its

[6] *Catalogue of the State Normal University* for the Academic Year ending June 29, 1860. Description of building in preface.

service to the state. The pupils gave a demonstration of what they had learned in singing. Professor Hewett conducted an exercise in geography, and an essay on Normal Schools, designed to bring the audience up to date on the progress of modern education, was read by a pupil. By January 1861 the secession of South Carolina and the position of Major Anderson's garrison at Fort Sumter was uppermost in men's minds, and a special exercise was devoted to a description of Fort Sumter and the principles of fortification illustrated in its structure. The students then lustily sang Longfellow's "Ship of State" which Professor Cady had taught them for the past Commencement. Professor Moore put the students through a quick drill in mental arithmetic. Amazing feats were performed in the addition, division, and multiplication of numbers of several digits, all without recourse to pencil and paper.

Governor Yates had not arrived by three o'clock, but President Moulton, representing the Board, nevertheless took the chair. He congratulated the state, the community, the principal, the teachers, and the pupils. There was stirring music by the Springfield band. According to reports, when Governor Yates finally arrived, he spoke with his "usual felicity and eloquence, placing the permanence of our glorious institution upon the intelligence and virtue of the whole people, referring to our schoolhouses and our churches as the stronghold of our country and as the sure indices of a happy and invincible people, and urged all present to contribute their share in making our beloved state the center of the great union." [7]

Judge Underwood, Senator from St. Clair County, "stirred the audience to experience the same noble and patriotic emotions which swayed his heart," while Senator Richard Oglesby "with wit, humor, and practical sense kept the audience in a roar of laughter."

After a brief speech by Speaker of the House Cullom of Springfield, came the culminating feature of the afternoon's program, the singing of the "Dedication Ode" written by Henry B. Norton, a member of the next year's graduating class, and set to music by Chauncey M. Cady, now of Chicago.

[7] *Weekly Pantagraph,* January 30, 1861.

Copies of the Ode were available to all who wished them.[8]

> The ancient Night is almost gone;
> Deep answers to awakening deep;
> As ever westward, ever on,
> The banners of the morning sweep
> New thought from out the chaos starts
> New powers are struggling into birth
> The crisis call for kingly hearts
> To guide the progress of the earth.
>
> The opening era points the way,
> And makes that mission work sublime
> Which moulds the infants of today
> To giants of the coming time
> And joyfully we gather here
> To consecrate with solemn praise
> A fame which honest men may rear
> For such a work in future days.
>
> By all the progress and the might
> Which other ages shall enfold
> By all the prophecies that light
> The Future's skies of morning gold;
> By all which sheds a cheering ray
> Upon the path the past has trod
> We dedicate its walls today
> To Truth, Humanity, and God.

Despite the bitter cold a thousand persons crowded into the building to listen to the dedicatory program and at seven, three hundred persons attended the banquet in Royce's Hall. The editor of the *Illinois Teacher* reported the meal as a "sumptuous dinner" Jesse Fell, as toastmaster, made the evening a gala affair. Hester Fell was very proud of her husband that night. There was so much laughter that one wondered if the high sentiments enunciated during the afternoon were alone the motivating force of the evening. Such a multiplicity of toasts. No one seemed to be forgotten. There were toasts to the University, the Common Schools, the Railroads, and the members of the Legislature. It became slightly wearisome to those who had gone through the inspection

---

[8] *Illinois Teacher*, February 1861, p. 78. Chauncey Cady had become associated with George F. Root in the music publishing business.

tour, the examinations, the dedicatory ceremonies, and two heavy meals; still there were so many young and energetic persons in attendance that the ball from nine to midnight at Phoenix Hall was well patronized. The legislators returned to Springfield in a convivial if not convinced state of mind. The *Illinois Teacher* regretted the "noisy carousal" that marked the end of the day. Some of the legislators were so imbued with Bloomington hospitality that they failed to make the mid-night special and remained to take the trains next day.[9]

To Hovey the whole affair was one of deepest tension. So much hung in the balance. The governor and the legislators with whom he had talked privately were reassuring. For the next two weeks he anxiously waited news from Springfield. The Board had granted him two months' leave beginning March first to again visit normal schools in the East and Canada. Dire threats to the nation might make it impossible for him to go. Secession by South Carolina, the calling of a meeting in Montgomery, Alabama, on February 4, the proposal of the State of Virginia that the various states appoint commissioners to meet in Washington on the same date and consider peaceable means of settling difficulties between the states, and the preoccupation of the Legislature with federal affairs, made Hovey wonder if the Normal School Bill might be lost in the many caucuses being held in Springfield. President-elect Abraham Lincoln, standing firm against any concessions to the South, advised that Illinois take no action and that Governor Yates appoint no commissioners. It was reported that Lincoln had said he "would rather be hung by the neck till he was dead on the steps of the Capitol before he would beg or buy a peaceful inauguration."[10]

On February 12 the amended act "to refund interest on the University Fund and to appropriate same to use of the Illinois State Normal University" was reported back from the House. Two days later it was law. Perhaps now the University could move forward free of debt and financial embarrassment.[11]

Events on the national scene were very close to the students at Illinois State Normal University. The Dred Scott decision was

[9] *Ibid.*
[10] Cole, *op. cit.,* pp. 257–258.
[11] *Proceedings of the Board of Education* (Bloomington), December 20, 1860, p. 101.

still a topic of conversation when the school opened in 1857. They avidly followed the campaign of Lincoln and Douglas in 1858. John Brown's raid on Harper's Ferry, his trial, and execution roused their emotions. Some of the students were especially attracted to the Reverend Charles Ames, pastor of the newly established Free Congregational Church in Bloomington.[12] He announced that if the telegraph brought news of John Brown's execution, he would preach his funeral sermon on the following Sunday. An immense crowd gave rapt attention. A week later members of the church paid to have it printed verbatim in the *Pantagraph*.[13]

The students and faculty had carefully followed the political campaign of 1860. They had heard Douglas and Lincoln speak and knew what they stood for. After the election when Lincoln passed through Bloomington on his trip to Chicago to confer with Hannibal Hamlin, Normal University students were in the crowd that gathered at the railway station to hear him speak his appreciation of the voters of McLean County. They pressed forward to shake his hand and get a better look at Mrs. Lincoln, enroute to the city to buy a wardrobe for the inaugural.[14] Through the newspapers students and faculty had followed the progress of Lincoln's trip east and anxiously awaited the inaugural. What action would Lincoln take? What of the forts that had been occupied? What of Major Anderson whose provisions were dwindling at Sumter? Buchanan had vacillated. The *Star of the West*, with reinforcements, had been fired upon in January. Was that incident not an act of war? Why had Lincoln refused to meet with delegations? What of the Minute Men organizations that were springing up over the country? How long would it be before Bloomington men would be drilling?

Then came the news by telegraph on Friday, April 12—"Fort Sumter fired upon!" The *Powhatan* had been unable to land reinforcements. On Sunday people on their way to church were

---

[12] The Free Congregational Church which later became identified with the Unitarian movement, was organized in Bloomington, August 14, 1859. Among its early members were Jesse Fell, Kersey Fell, Cyrenius Wakefield, F. K. Phoenix, E. M. Prince, C. P. Merriman, and Meshack Pike. The first pastor was the Reverend Charles G. Ames. Burnham, *History of McLean County, Illinois*, p. 358.

[13] *Weekly Pantagraph*, November 14, 1859.

[14] Lincoln passed through Bloomington enroute to Chicago on November 20, 1860.

startled by a man on horseback, who had just come from the tele-graph office shouting, "Anderson surrenders, to march out at one o'clock."

The next morning President Lincoln called for 75,000 three-months volunteers. The word spread like wild-fire. That night a crowd gathered at the court house. The flag had been fired upon. The Union, consecrated by the blood of patriots through two wars, had been attacked. That all this would mean fratricide made it more dramatic. William H. Harvey, a veteran of the Mexican War, respected for high character and courage, opened the south window on the west side of the court house and called for volun-teers, announcing that he would go with them. Young men pressed forward to sign their names to an enlistment paper. The evening's muster roll when completed bore the names of one hundred and thirteen men, among them five from the Normal University: Joseph G. Howell, a graduate of the Class of 1860, now a member of the faculty, and students, Henry C. Prevost, Charles M. Clark, Hiram W. Johnson, and Justin L. Spaulding.[15]

On Tuesday morning Jesse Fell hurriedly called together a group of the leading men of Bloomington in an upper room on Washington Street. He had prepared some resolutions in which all of the men except D. J. Snow, editor of the Bloomington *Times,* concurred. Snow sympathized with the secessionists and was outspoken on the subject. The local union leaders turned their attention to building up sentiment. Handbills announcing the mass meeting to be held in Phoenix Hall that night were printed and distributed. The group decided upon a long program of speakers upon whose sentiments they could rely. They deter-mined to leave no time for dissenting volunteers to come from the audience. Bloomington's most respected lawyer, the vener-able Hamilton Spencer, presided, and first one prominent citizen and then another spoke: James S. Ewing, Colonel W. Boyd, Dr. E. R. Roe, the Reverend C. G. Ames, Harvey Hogg, and E. M. Prince. Professor Messer, the new teacher of music at Normal University, led the audience in the spirited singing of the *Marseillaise* and similar stirring songs. A great flag draped across the platform proclaimed its message of loyalty. The Reverend Mr.

[15] *Weekly Pantagraph,* April 24, 1861.

Ames read the resolutions calling for allegiance to the government of the United States and avowing the President's authority as granted in the Constitution. He asked that all "who in their hearts swore to the sentiments therein expressed" raise their right hands. According to one present, "A response like thunder came up from the densely packed audience and a thousand hands flashed in the light above the sea of heads, like the drawing of myriad swords." [16]

Next day when Governor Yates issued a call for six regiments, the Bloomington Company was promptly tendered. Thursday the volunteers met at Royce's Hall and elected officers. The veteran, William H. Harvey, who had offered the electrifying challenge on Monday night, was chosen Captain, and Henry Prevost of the Normal University was elected one of the company's four sergeants.

On Friday night the company paraded by torch light to music by the German Band. A beautiful silk flag was presented by the Prairie Bird Engine and Hose Company, Number One. W. W. Orme asked that it be defended "to the bitter end." Asahel Gridley pledged the honor of the company as he proclaimed the word that Governor Yates had accepted the Bloomington Company and that the men were to obtain undress uniforms if possible and to come to Springfield at once. Following a brief speech by Captain Harvey a subscription was started to buy Colt's revolvers for the local volunteers. One citizen subscribed fifty dollars. "This," said the *Pantagraph,* "is a holy war in defense of the best government that ever blest the earth." [17] On Monday, April 23, the company entrained for Springfield, where they were to make camp at the State Fair Grounds until called into action.

As Principal Hovey and Ira Moore wondered about the effect upon the Normal School, they pondered their own roles in the months to come. Lincoln had called for volunteers for three months only. If he had expected it would take longer to settle the problem, he would surely have asked for longer enlistments. The spring term had just begun and Hovey did not want to see

[16] The Bloomington mass meeting was one of the first to be held in Illinois. Jesse Fell moved that the Bloomington resolutions be sent to the leading newspapers throughout the state. Morehouse, *op. cit.,* pp. 65–66. *Weekly Pantagraph,* April 24, 1861.
[17] *Ibid.*

the school disrupted. The need for teachers was critical. Those who stood behind the desk served the nation as well as those who took up arms.

But the men were restless; they missed Howell and Spaulding and Johnson and Clark and Prevost, and wondered if they were shirking their duty to remain in school. As they ate their cold lunches at noon, they talked of nothing else. They discussed enlistment with the women students. They wrote home to their parents. Hovey talked with them in class, in the corridors, and wherever he saw little groups talking together. He counseled against immediate enlistment. He knew if war truly came, they should all be needed. He proposed that while the men remained in school they should prepare for the day when they might be called. Then he would go with them. John W. White was hired as drillmaster. The yard where the brick kilns stood was cleared away. The girls of the school lined up beside the Parade Grounds as the old brick yard came to be called and watched the men at their daily drill. A few men had guns, but most of them had only drilled with make-believe guns sawed and whittled from cast-off wood. Left, right! Forward, march! Left! Right! Left!

As spring wore on into summer, it became inevitable that the "Normal Rifles," as the students chose to call their company, would be needed. The drillmaster was encouraging. The men were beginning to march more like soldiers, less like "clod-hoppers." They could keep step. They could go through the manual of arms. They stood straighter, walked more briskly.

When Joseph G. Howell, a captain, came home on furlough after re-enlisting, it was as the return of a conquering hero. The faculty and students gathered around the man who had been the youngest and conceded to be the most brilliant member of the first graduating class. His former pupils admired his trim blue uniform and filled his soldier's cap with flowers.

The women of the school quickly fell into the spirit of the times. They collected old linen, scraped lint and rolled bandages and talked over how they could help. Some one suggested a banner for the Rifles, another a ceremony of dedication. A beautiful flag was carefully designed and made, and June 5 set aside for the presentation. The school was aflutter with expectancy as students and townspeople gathered in Normal Hall once more. Professor George F. Root's new song, "The First Gun is Fired," was sung by the young women of the school. Sophie Crist, a member of the graduating class was chosen to make the presentation. Long and hard she had labored over her speech. One detected deep emotion as she spoke:

Captain Hovey and the Normal Rifles, the ladies of the University have conferred upon me the honor of addressing you today in their behalf. Hitherto we have known you only as teachers and as schoolmates.

There was a moment of hesitation; then she launched into a tribute to Charles Hovey, an appreciation of his work, and an expression of the love and affection which they had for their principal. Turning again to the flag, she continued:

We cannot say, 'go forth to danger,' and it may be to death but if go you must, take with you this banner, which is to all the nation the emblem of our common freedom. Let its colors inspire you on the battlefield, and in the stillness of the night, when the campfire dimly burns, and the bayonet is at rest, when heaven's glittering canopy shall be your only shelter, it shall proudly float above you to the breeze and as the mellowing moonlight falls upon it, ever and anon its stars of beauty will peep from beneath its silken folds as talisman of your holy mission, and too in that sacred hour, will oft time pour out from the depths of memory, the scenes in which you have mingled here.

Now and then, we, your pupils, your sisters shall come in fancy to remind you of the high positions, the social pleasures you have sacrificed upon your country's altar, and the manly tears, will steal forth all unbidden, but you will not falter for the sweet invisible power that shall bring us to you, will return to us laden with kindly memories of you, and warm sympathy and prayers shall encircle you, and you shall gather strength on each succeeding day. Trust in the living God.[18]

On July 2 the term ended, the Rifles disbanded, and the silken banner was folded away until the company should be called to duty. Hovey promised his students that if their services were needed, he would organize a Schoolmaster's regiment. In company of Jesse Fell he set off for Washington to talk the matter over with Secretary of War Simon Cameron and President Lincoln. The ninety-day enlistment period for the April volunteers

[18] *Weekly Pantagraph*, June 5, 1861.

was soon to expire. By the time Hovey and Fell arrived at the Capitol, there were loud cries for action. What was McDowell doing? The public was impatient and the volunteers were becoming restive. Congress authorized the President on July 5 to accept services of 500,000 volunteers for three years.[19] On every hand was heard the cry "On to Richmond! On to Richmond!"

In Washington, it was predicted that there would be an engagement on Sunday, July 21, between McDowell's forces, then bivouaced at Centreville, and Beauregard's, stationed not far away on Manassas Creek. Visitors were under no military restraint: they brought their own supplies, passed to and fro among the troops as they pleased, and gave the scene the appearance of a great military picnic. Senators and representatives with whom Hovey and Fell talked felt that an attack was imminent. Since it was known that a number of carriages were going over on Sunday, Hovey and Fell arranged to go along. The Battle of Bull Run proved to be more than a skirmish. It was a rout. By four o'clock the raw troops that had fought so well in the beginning were demoralized; dead and dying men lay everywhere. The Union men began to drop back with the Confederates in close pursuit. They fired upon supply wagons and Congressmen's carriages. There was terrific panic, and the bridge over Cub Run was impassable with the jam of pleasure carriages, gun carriages, and ammunition wagons.

When the smoke of battle cleared away, Hovey and Fell, who had been observing from a safe distance in the rear, moved forward and surveyed the scene. Hovey looked over the field while Fell busied himself giving what aid he could to the wounded and helping about the improvised hospitals.[20]

Immediately after Bull Run, Lincoln acted upon Hovey's petition, commissioned him a colonel, and authorized the formation of the Schoolmaster's Regiment as Hovey chose to call it. He hurried home to recruit his men, and call back the Rifles who had left school, pledging that if needed they would enlist as a body.

Headquarters for the Normal Regiment were set up on the second floor at 7 Front Street west of the McLean County Bank.

[19] James Ford Rhodes, *History of the Civil War* (New York: Macmillan Co., 1917), p. 47.
[20] Morehouse, *op. cit.*, p. 68.

Ira Moore, Hovey's first assistant at the Normal University, helped with recruitment.[21] Students, teachers, and educational men were invited to join. Only one other western regiment had a college president as its commanding officer. It was the 42nd Ohio Regiment under Colonel James A. Garfield from Hiram College. Forty-six members of the Illinois Thirty-third Infantry had been students at Normal and twenty of these had drilled with the Normal Rifles. Not all the Rifles waited for the Schoolmaster's Regiment but had volunteered and enlisted in other regiments.

The day that Hovey received his commission as Colonel he began mustering men into service. Ninety-four men from McLean County signed on August 15, sixty on August 20, and seventeen on August 21. Within a month nine hundred men throughout the state had enlisted in the Illinois Thirty-third Infantry. The company was formally organized in Springfield early in September. Herman J. Eddy, Pastor of the Baptist Church, Bloomington, became chaplain. Normalites J. Howard Burnham became lieutenant of Company A., Henry Pope captain of Company D., Professor Ira Moore captain of Company G., Leander H. Potter captain of Company A., and Julian E. Bryant second lieutenant of Company E., Dr. George P. Rex, Board member from Perry, became regimental surgeon, and Simeon Wright, Kinmundy, another member, quartermaster.[22]

On September 20, the Schoolmaster's Regiment was moved from Camp Butler to Pilot Knob near Ironton, Missouri. Here officers and men went into serious training.

When the fall term of school began, there were only about eighty students enrolled, fifty of these were in the entering class, composed of twenty-three men and twenty-seven women. In place of Charles Hovey, there was Perkins Bass of Chicago, member of the Board, a former principal of the First Ward School in Chicago but now practicing lawyer, who agreed to serve as principal until some one could be found to substitute or Hovey should return.[23]

[21] John H. Burnham, "The School and the War," *Semi-Centennial History of Illinois State Normal University* (Bloomington, 1907), pp. 19–31. *Weekly Pantagraph,* August 21, 1861.

[22] *Adjutant General's Report Illinois (1861–1866)* revised Roster of Officers and Enlisted Men 16–35. Vol. II (Springfield, 1900), pp. 621–653.

[23] *Proceedings of the Board of Education* (December 21, 1862), pp. 68–73.

The Parade Grounds had grown over with weeds during the summer. The golden rod and the cattails along the slough were as profuse as ever. Students walking across the stubble on their way to classes exchanged the latest news from the front and shared letters and copies of *The Picket,* the little paper from the headquarters of the Thirty-third Infantry. In the life of the school, the coming of the war marked the end of one era and the beginning of another.

CHAPTER V

In the Bridgewater Tradition

PERKINS BASS believed so strongly in teacher training that he was willing to sacrifice his legal practice temporarily. He wanted to hold the school together and to continue the work that had been started. He had no great plan for developing the curriculum. Hovey had taken up that matter cautiously. The three-year course of study had been patterned after recommendations of the Board and plans in use in the best eastern schools. No detailed catalog was printed until after the first class had graduated in 1860.

The school year was forty weeks in length. The first term consisted of fifteen weeks, the second term of thirteen weeks, and the third term of twelve weeks. Hovey had classified the work under the different instructors as divisions. Bass' most significant departure was to group "divisions" as much as possible around subject matter.[1]

When Bass took up his duties as acting principal in September 1861, only four members of the regular faculty of the previous spring remained. Edwin C. Hewett, a graduate of Bridgewater Normal School who came in 1858 and was to remain for thirty-two years spending the last fourteen years as president, was the very thorough and exacting instructor in geography and history. Joseph A. Sewall,[2] instructor in natural sciences, who had studied at Yale and Harvard, had come to Normal University only the year before. Frances A. Peterson, a graduate of 1860, taught mathematics and Latin. B. S. Messer now took over the teaching of

---

[1] *Catalogs,* Years ending July 3, 1861; June 27, 1862; and June 26, 1863.

[2] In 1858 Joseph Addison Sewall, druggist and physician from Tonica, Illinois, called to see his old New England friend, Principal Hovey. The latter was looking for a science teacher. Sewall had an M.D. from Harvard and asked how much training would be required to qualify. He returned to Cambridge for scientific studies under Gray and Agassiz. In the fall of 1860 he was appointed Professor of Natural Sciences at Illinois State Normal University. He left Normal in 1878 and later became President of the University of Colorado. Cook and McHugh, *op. cit.,* p. 48.

drawing in addition to music. Henry Norton, who had graduated in the spring and had assisted in the Model School, became principal of the Model School with two women teachers as his assistants.

Bass took over the classes in "mental science" and "laws," and John Hull, a graduate of 1860, was employed to teach Ira Moore's classes in mathematics.[3] Margaret Osband became instructress in grammar, taking over the classes formerly taught by Leander Potter. The museum of the State Laboratory of Natural History was now being established on the third floor and arrangements were made to have Charles D. Wilber, general agent for the Society, teach courses in geology.

In 1860 an arrangement was made whereby Public School District No. 2 was merged with the Model School and all the children in the area of the Junction would attend classes in the Normal University building or in other buildings that might be constructed as the need arose. Already a program was evolving by which upper class students might be given an opportunity to teach in the Model School or "practice teach" as some were beginning to speak of it.

Perkins Bass did not find his task an easy one, but some of the decisions that he made respecting the selection of faculty were to leave a deep imprint on the University. At the end of the first term, Henry B. Norton, who was in charge of the Model School, left to take a better position in Warsaw schools and his assistants also resigned.[4] Charles F. Childs, who had been principal of Franklin School in St. Louis, was elected principal of the Model School, with Livonia Ketcham as teacher in the primary department. Childs, who was about thirty-two years old, had graduated from Antioch while Horace Mann was its president and was a teacher of considerable experience.[5] Almost immediately he began to make plans for developing a high school along with the Model School.

[3] John Hull resigned in 1862 to become principal of the Bloomington High School. He was later superintendent of McLean County Schools, and editor of the *Illinois Schoolmaster*. In 1875 he joined the staff of Southern Illinois Normal at Carbondale.
[4] Report of Principal Richard Edwards to the Board of Education, *Fourth Biennial Report of the Superintendent of Public Instruction, 1861–1862*, pp. 62–63.
[5] Charles F. Childs returned to St. Louis in June 1863 to become principal of the high school. He died in 1866. Cook and McHugh, *op. cit.*, p. 225.

When John Hull announced that he was resigning at the end of the second term to become principal of the Bloomington High School, and that a teacher of mathematics would need to be employed, Childs recommended his friend Richard Edwards, principal of the St. Louis Normal and High School, an institution in sad straits financially.

Edwards had attended the Illinois State Teachers Association in Springfield in December 1861 and was known to Superintendent Bateman, W. H. Wells, Simeon Wright, and Bass. His salary of $1200 was quite inadequate for him and his wife and their growing family of six children, and since payment depended on tuition collected, his salary was often in arrears, and he was looking desperately for another position. Although Edwards was considering a position in Washington University when the vacancy at Normal University occurred, he had even thought of giving up teaching and going into business.[6]

Although Hovey had not resigned, Bass assured Edwards that he could feel reasonably safe in coming to Normal University on the assumption that he would be made principal and his connection with the school would be permanent if he chose to remain. On February 22, 1862, Edwards completed arrangements to come to Normal University as teacher of mathematics. His tried and trusted friend, Thomas Metcalf, also a Bridgewater graduate, succeeded him as principal of the normal and high school at St. Louis.

On April 15, 1862, Hovey replied to a letter from Edwards saying he was glad that he had come to Normal and that he would like to see him remain as principal. Bass, who was anxious to get back to his law practice in Chicago, assured Edwards that the Board would support him. At the annual meeting at the Pike House in Bloomington a letter from Hovey was read:

> Headquarters, Second Brigade
> First Division A S W
> Camp near Batesville Arkansas
> June 16, 1862

Pres. Moulton

Dear Sir: It will be entirely impossible, with my plans for the future for

[6] Burt Weed Loomis, *The Educational Influence of Richard Edwards*. (Nashville: George Peabody College for Teachers, 1932), pp. 60–61.

me to again assume duties in the Normal University; I beg you tender to the Board over which you preside, my grateful acknowledgments of the thousand kindnesses which they extended to the first Principal of the University. I am very truly

Your obedient servant
C. E. Hovey

Bass announced he was returning to Chicago and that the principalship was vacant.[7] The Board resolved thanks for the energetic and successful manner in which Bass had conducted the school and the "judicious and able manner in which he managed the finances and business matters" and then proceeded to elect Richard Edwards principal by a unanimous vote. The following morning Dr. Calvin Gowdy of Taylorville, was appointed to notify Edwards. At three that afternoon he read Edwards' reply.

Bloomington, June 26, 1862

Dr. Gowdy—

Dear Sir: In reply to your note of today, I answer that I cheerfully accept the appointment you have done me the honor to tender me; and I invoke the cooperation of the Board, in my attempts, feeble though they may be, to make this school what it ought to be, the best normal school on the continent.

Very respectfully
Richard Edwards [8]

A week later Perkins Bass returned to Chicago and resumed his practice of law.[9]

The appointment of Richard Edwards was a fortunate one. He was well-known to educators throughout the state. He was a provocative and forceful speaker. Almost immediately upon his arrival in St. Louis in 1857, he was asked to address educational meetings and institutes in Illinois. He spoke on "Normal Schools" at the Illinois State Teachers Association in Chicago, December 30, 1857.[10] Two years later he addressed the first annual convention of the American Normal School Association meeting in Trenton, New Jersey, on "The Course of Study Best Suited to the American Normal Schools." [11]

[7] *Proceedings of the Board of Education* (Bloomington), June 25, 1862, p. 3.
[8] *Ibid.*, p. 7.
[9] *Weekly Pantagraph*, July 9, 1862.
[10] *The Illinois Teacher*, 1858 III, 2–3.
[11] *Proceedings of the First Annual Convention of American Norman School Association*, August 19–20, 1859, p. 73.

Edwards had discussed courses of study in great detail with Hovey and Moore and there was marked similarity between the Normal University's first printed catalog in 1860 and the one that Edwards had issued earlier at the St. Louis Normal. Both bore testimony to the genius of Nicholas Tillinghast and the Bridgewater Normal.

The background of Richard Edwards was unique among the early normal school men. He was a Welshman, born in Cardiganshire, South Wales, on December 23, 1822. He was the eldest son of Richard Hugh Edwards, a stone-mason, and his wife, Anne Jones, the daughter of a thrifty farmer.[12] The family lived in a small thatch-roofed, one-room earthen house with a single window to provide light and ventilation. The father had worked hard at his trade but wages were low. His wife and children helped to till a ten acre farm which provided vegetables for their table and a small surplus to market in the nearby village.

The Edwards family belonged to the Calvinistic Methodist Church while their gentry neighbors were mostly Anglican. Like other members of the congregation, the Edwardses were very loyal to their church and the Welsh language. Religious instruction was given in Welsh, the Bible was diligently studied in the home, and the children regularly attended Sunday School.

English was spoken in the day school, but the instruction was crude and Welsh-speaking people were wont to pronounce words according to their own taste and convenience. The poverty of the family precluded extensive schooling for their children. Richard was sent to a "loud school" where the tuition was low. Instruction was limited to the three R's and the pupils shouted as they read their lessons from their seats. In this noisy and sing-song manner he learned the English Catechism, the multiplication tables, and the essense of good manners.

When Richard Edwards was ten, his parents emigrated to the Western Reserve in Ohio. John Jones, an uncle who had come to America earlier, had written such favorable reports to his sister, that she and her family were led to follow his example. They sailed by brig from Liverpool to Quebec and thence by steamer to Montreal, via Lake Champlain and Schenectady and Utica,

---

[12] Ellen Edwards "Life of Richard Edwards," MS., Illinois State Normal University.

where they enjoyed the hospitality of their countrymen. After purchasing a wagon and team, they drove the remaining four hundred miles to the home of John Jones in Palmyra. Their total resources were by this time only a little more than a hundred dollars, most of which was soon used to make the initial payment on fifty acres of land.

Although much of young Edwards' time was spent helping his father on the farm or carrying hod for him when on a masonry job, he did manage to go part time to the district school taught by a farmer who augmented his income by teaching during slack seasons on the farm. Here as in Wales the curriculum was limited to the barest essentials.

At sixteen Richard Edwards was apprenticed to a joiner and carpenter at Ravenna, Ohio. He advanced to "boss carpenter" and thence to foreman and junior contractor, but he was more interested in reading the books in his employer's library relating to Greece and Rome than those on architecture.

His daily work brought him in contact with men of prominence in the community. He became very much excited over the campaign of 1840. He regretted that he was not old enough to vote for William Henry Harrison, but he joined heartily in the songs and yells of the log cabin and hard cider campaign. "Tippecanoe" was a champion of the working class, and it had been to enjoy the privileges and opportunities of this class that his father and Uncle John had migrated to America. Edwards' democracy would give suffrage to the laborer, education for the deaf and blind, and freedom for the slaves.

In the fall of 1843, he gave up farming and carpentry to teach a district school near Ravenna at a salary of eleven dollars and "board 'round." In a debating society organized for mutual improvement, Edwards met Henry Hudson, a Harvard theological student, who was conducting a private school in Akron. Hudson saw that Edwards had unusual ability, began tutoring him at night, and urged that he go east for further study.

After the district school term ended, Edwards took up carpentry in Akron. He met Samuel S. Greeley, who had succeeded Henry Hudson as principal of the private school. Greeley tutored Edwards and insisted that he go to Massachusetts and enter a normal school. He loaned Edwards some money and gave him two letters of introduction, one to the Reverend Samuel J. May, principal of the Lexington Normal School, and the other to Horace Mann, Secretary of the Board of Education.

With thirty dollars in his pocket Edwards set off for Massachusetts on October 27, 1844. He traveled by stage, canal, and on foot. It was twelve days before he reached the home of Samuel May in Lexington. The normal school had meanwhile been moved from Lexington to West Newton, and May was no longer principal. West Newton was receiving only women students, so May advised that Edwards enter Bridgewater Normal rather than the recently re-activated normal at Westfield. After conferring with Cyrus Pierce at West Newton, Edwards thought it advisable to teach a term of school and earn some money. He walked twenty-seven miles one day, only to find the vacancy filled; however, he continued on to Hingham, where he received appointment for a six months' term at twenty-five dollars a month. He read all that he could on normal schools and education in general.

One day shortly after his school opened he walked in high enthusiasm the eighteen miles from Hingham to Bridgewater to talk with Nicholas Tillinghast about his plans for entering Bridgewater Normal. Nicholas Tillinghast, a former West Point instructor, appeared neither interested nor cordial, and had it not been for May's encouragement and counsel Edwards might have given up the idea of attending Bridgewater. When his school was out, Edwards again took up carpentry, studying Latin and Algebra at night. After paying his debts, he was able to spend a term at Bridgewater.

Edwards' work with Nicholas Tillinghast began on July 30, 1845. His mind was "awakened into a new consciousness."

Heretofore Edwards had read by instinct and fancy. Tillinghast was constantly asking "Why? Why?" His students had to have reasons; they had to know the facts. They made no generalizations without supporting evidence.

When Edwards entered Bridgewater Normal, Horace Mann's *Seventh and Eighth Annual Reports to the Board of Education* were being widely discussed, as were the issues over which Mann and the schoolmasters in nearby Boston were disputing. Fully in sympathy with Mann, Edwards debated the questions of corporal punishment and methods of teaching before the Bridgewater Lyceum.

In November 1845 Edwards resumed his teaching at Hingham and continued until April 1846. He returned to carpentry until it was time for Bridgewater Normal to open again. This time he was able to stay through two consecutive terms and graduated on November 6, 1846. Meanwhile Edwards had made the personal acquaintance of Mann and was ever to be his friend and co-champion of free public education and normal schools.

Edwards' next teaching position was a difficult school in nearby Waltham at forty dollars a month, and despite his convictions as to corporal punishment, he occasionally resorted to the switch.

While at the Tarpelo School in Waltham, he was made president of the Bridgewater Normal Association, an organization of the alumni and faculty dedicated to bringing about a professional attitude toward teaching. They assisted Mann in arguing in behalf of normal schools at institutes and teachers' meetings.

Edwards was not content with his normal school diploma. He felt the need of perfecting himself in subject matter and in June 1847 he entered Rensselaer at Troy, New York. With financial assistance from friends, family, and odd jobs of carpentry he was able to stay in school until he completed his Bachelor of Science degree October 1, 1847. The subject of his graduating thesis was "Diatase, and Its Chemical Relation to the Feculas in Germination." An assistantship enabled him to complete a Civil Engineer's Course in March 1848. He was now equipped to do civil engineering but he preferred teaching.

He had barely begun his work as assistant engineer on the Boston Water Works when he was invited to lecture at the Bridgewater Lyceum. He called on Nicholas Tillinghast who was in ill health. A few days later Tillinghast asked him to take over his work for a term. The salary was only $300 a year but it would give Edwards opportunity to teach and to promote the cause of normal schools.

The Bridgewater appointment originally for a single term extended over five years. Six hundred dollars a year and additional remuneration from institutes and lyceums enabled him to marry

Betty Josslyn Samson of Pembroke, Massachusetts on July 5, 1849.

Edwards' work in institutes and teachers' associations brought him in close touch with educational leaders such as Barnas Sears, who had followed Horace Mann as secretary of the Massachusetts Board of Education, Louis Agassiz, Dana P. Colburn, Cyrus Pierce, and Lowell Mason.

In December 1852 Edwards was asked to come to Salem as principal of Bowditch High School, at double the Bridgewater salary. He could not afford to decline, although the school was small and he had no assistants the first term. Eleven months later he resigned to become agent for the State Board under Barnas Sears. He visited schools throughout the state, talked with school boards and with teachers on how schools could be improved. Sometimes he taught a demonstration class in order to help a teacher. He urged the abandoning of the district system.

When the Salem Normal School was opened in 1854, Richard Edwards was made its principal. He had one assistant, Martha Kingman, who had trained at Bridgewater and later assisted him in the Bowditch High School. Within two years Salem was the largest of the four Massachusetts normal schools; its course of study and methods were far in advance of the other normal schools and its students were accepting positions before finishing their course. Essex County, of which Salem was the county seat, had been the center of opposition to Horace Mann. Now the old guard Yale and Harvard graduates of the Essex County Teachers Association transferred their opposition to Edwards and the normal schools. They saw teachers who had gone to normal schools for brief periods taking positions that they might have had. They debated with Edwards, ridiculing him and his work. "Teachers are born, not taught," they contended.

Edwards carried the fight to the State Teachers Association in 1856, when he spoke on "The Necessity of a Special Preparation for the Business of Teaching." He attacked the position of the college men and pleaded for a profession of teaching. Edwards won for himself recognition, but he could not quell the scholastics and Essex County combustibles. Three years after Edwards left the state, they launched a move to abolish the state normal schools.

In the spring of 1856 William H. Wells, principal of the Westfield Normal School, accepted a position as Superintendent of Chicago Schools. In organizing the high school, he set up a department for training teachers. A few months later Horace Mann, now President of Antioch, wrote Edwards that he had been asked to find a principal for a projected normal school in St. Louis. The salary was $2500, a thousand more than Edwards was receiving at Salem. The offer was made to Edwards, but the ailing condition of Nicholas Tillinghast and his connection with the *Massachusetts Teacher* as an editor led him to defer the decision a year.[13]

The death of Tillinghast and the financial demands of his growing family made it easier to break eastern ties when he received the second offer to become head of the St. Louis Normal.[14] Enroute to St. Louis he stopped with the Manns in Antioch.

In St. Louis on October 28, 1857, twenty-three young women appeared for entrance examinations. Edwards admitted sixteen of them. To this group were added twelve students from the high school and two substitute teachers, making this an opening class of thirty. The course of study and plan of entrance examination, system of keeping diaries, reports, methods and discussions were patterned after those in use at Salem. As Edwards stated in the preface to the course of study, the St. Louis Normal was a "strictly professional school," its object being to prepare teachers for elementary and primary grades. Most of the course was concerned with professional studies. Training in academic subjects such as science and advanced mathematics could be obtained in the high school.

One of the innovations which Edwards developed in St. Louis was a program of Saturday classes for teachers who wished to improve their teaching. Thomas Metcalf, a former Bridgewater pupil who had been employed to teach English in the high school took over one of the Saturday morning classes in orthography and enunciation. In 1860 mental philosophy was added to the list of

[13] During Tillinghast's last illness, Edwards along with other former students contributed liberally to defray expenses of the beloved teacher. Edwards gave the memorial address before the Bridgewater Association. It was later read at the first meeting of the Normal Association. Loomis, *op. cit.*, p. 46.

[14] Edwards' work in the Salem schools was long remembered. When the old normal school building was torn down in 1919, and the site converted to a park, it was named in his honor, Edwards Park.

Saturday classes taught by Edwards, who for ten years or more had been following the philosophic writings of Emerson, Alcott, and other Transcendentalists. Among those stimulated by Edwards' lectures was William T. Harris, later noted as leader in the St. Louis Movement.

Just as the work of the St. Louis Normal was beginning to be recognized, the Civil War came. Business in St. Louis was at a standstill. Revenues from the state for school purposes were cut off, and only by reducing salaries to the "lowest living rate" and charging tuition could the high school and the normal be re-opened. Many of the faculty took employment elsewhere; Edwards, now the father of six young children, was in a quandary. It was at this point he had written to Wells in Chicago about the advisability of going into business.

When Richard Edwards came to Normal University as a teacher of mathematics in the spring of 1862, there were only about a dozen houses in the vicinity of the school and not over thirty in the area designated as North Bloomington. The town had been platted, and with his customary zeal Jesse Fell, along with F. K. Phoenix and other nurserymen, had set out lines of trees, many of them in double rows to shade the sidewalks of the future. Fell had planted 12,000 before a single house was built. Bloomington was already spoken of as "Evergreen City." Unsold lots near the school were utilized as branch nurseries. Their well-tended rows of seedlings, grafted fruit and shade trees, evergreens, and grapes gave a charm and certain sense of order to the community.

One day shortly after Edwards began his work at the Normal he decided to investigate why some of the young women had not reported to class. He found them drying their skirts and feet, which had become wet from walking through the mud and slush from Bloomington. Quickly Sue Pike challenged the teacher, "Give us a day off and we'll raise money enough to build a sidewalk." To her surprise he replied, "I'll do it." Sue Pike and Harriet Dunn promptly entered upon a canvass of the business men of Bloomington and in one day obtained ninety-five dollars in cash, and contributions in lumber. On Saturday following, the young men of the school aided by a few Bloomington men, completed the sidewalk. It was only two boards in width, and as much of the lumber was still green, it soon warped and buckled.[15]

Hard pressed for funds to care for the vast lawn about the building the Board instructed the principal to have the yard resurveyed and to assign each student a portion to keep in order.[16] A few trees and shrubs, donations of local nurserymen had been set out, but to Jesse Fell's disappointment most of the Saunders' landscape plan was still in the blue print stage.

Inside the building halls and classrooms had taken on the finished appearance of well-appointed schools of the period. There was ample blackboard space in all classrooms. Framed steel engravings hung midway between the blackboard and the high ceiling. The equipment was of the latest model and best quality. The teachers' desks stood on an elevated dais at the front. The desk was of soundest walnut supported by slender iron stanchions, and was equipped with a book rail and a cloth-covered, hinged writing board formed a slanting cover to a deep hold where registers and purloined articles were stored. A narrow drawer in front provided space for pencils and pens while a larger drawer on either side held other supplies. A few feet from the dais in front of the teacher's desk were the recitation benches or "pupils' settees." Beyond these were the neat rows of carefully bolted down desks and chairs. The pupils' desks were simple, shallow oak troughs with cloth-covered, hinged covers, likewise supported by iron stanchions. Some of the desks were single but most were double. The double desks took up less space and afforded easy exchange of textbooks. Cupboards afforded storage for maps and charts, globes, wooden spheres, cubes, rulers, yard sticks, and measuring equipment, which facilitated teaching. A set of raised or relief maps, imported from France, was a prized possession of the school and never failed to excite comment from visitors.[17]

The museum of the State Laboratory of Natural History on the east end of the third floor, with its growing collection of stuffed owls, eagles, grasses, and rocks was another object of pride, but it was the society halls that claimed the first affection of the stu-

[15] Elmer Warren Cavins, "Student Life in the Town," *Semi-Centennial History of Illinois State Normal University,* pp. 165–166.
[16] *Proceedings of the Board of Education* (Bloomington), June 26, 1862, p. 8.
[17] *Weekly Pantagraph,* July 6, 1859.

dents. On the west side Philadelphia occupied the south hall,[18] and Wrightonia, with its motto *sapere aude* (dare to be wise) boldly painted over the transom, occupied the north hall. Professor Ira Moore, who had no love for Wrightonia, had, to the delight of Philadelphians, once translated the inscription to mean "sapheads and adders," a thrust that Wrightonians were never willing to forgive.[19] The Board granted the halls to the societies, but the elaborate furnishings, carpets, drapes, chandeliers, pictures, and pianos had to be financed by the members. Faculty members were equally divided among the two societies and assigned by the principal, but student members were assigned alternately and alphabetically. Dues, fines, gifts, and sundry money-making schemes were used to obtain funds.

In 1861, the Philadelphian Society contrived to surprise its rival at Commencement by displaying a new red and white Brussels carpet costing two hundred and fifty dollars, the gift of Professors Hewett, Moore, and Hovey, and a few other members of the society. The secret was not well kept, however, and the Wrightonians by almost superhuman effort obtained pledges for two hundred twenty-five dollars and ordered a carpet from New York by telegraph, to be sent by express to Bloomington. To the chagrin of the Philadelphians, the Wrightonian carpet arrived first. It was several years before either society could afford a piano. A small piano could be taken upstairs alternately by the societies on condition that it be carried down after the meeting. Few musical numbers were worth the effort, and more often the societies sang a capella or to the accompaniment of a harmonica, jewsharp, or comb.

Once each year the Wrights and Phils laid aside their rivalries, joined forces and presented a public lecture during Commencement week to which the entire school and townspeople were invited. Bayard Taylor, editor of the *Chicago Evening Journal,* had given the first of these annual lectures in 1859.

In June 1862 Richard Edwards, who was expected to be the new principal, was invited to give the lecture. Edwards selected as his

[18] The Philadelphian Society secured the most desirable location by assisting Professor Ira Moore through the transom and taking possession of the room for the society. In later years Philadelphia occupied rooms vacated by the museum.

[19] Cook and McHugh, *op. cit.,* p. 109.

subject "The Heritage of Culture." In an eloquent address he traced the great achievements of history through the character and precepts of great men. "Culture has consisted," said Edwards, "in the effort on the part of students to master the thoughts of some great mind, worthy disciples of whom it is the height of their ambition to become."

From a vast knowledge and understanding of the historic past he traced the evolution of the modern heritage. From Ancient Greece, Rome, Israel, China, the great religions, philosophers, prophets and saints he marshaled illustration after illustration, precious gifts laid at the feet of humanity by Zoroaster, Pythagoras, Socrates, Plato, Elisha, the Christian marytrs. "History," declared Edwards, "teaches us the lesson of a Divine Intelligence presiding over the affairs of men; of a consistent plan in the development of human society." "Culture," he asserted, "is no less than the history of human thought in its highest and noblest efforts. It is the spur of our youth and the solace of our age. It kindles our aspirations and refines our souls. It establishes a bond between us and our kind through all time. It exalts our conception of humanity by keeping before us the noblest results it has achieved." He cited the humanitarian movements of the nineteenth century, man's concern for man, the unfortunate, the erring, the sick and the insane, concluding that "inasmuch as moral greatness is more than intellectual we have here an element of greatness more glorious than anything of which the ancient world can boast." He concluded:

If fortune is to frown upon us at all, we bid her take our outward prosperity, our houses, our railways, our shipping . . . ; if dire necessity comes, let her take from us even the institutions that have protected our infancy and nourished our manhood; but let her not rob us of that which underlies our institutions, and is of more value than all our wealth, and is the best part of our life,—the heritage of knowledge and culture which has descended from the good and great of bygone times.

The address given following Edwards' formal acceptance of the principalship set forth a manifesto of truths. The Board members who had been the special guests of the societies that evening, listened attentively to the earnest young teacher. The next day they voted the "interesting and elegant" address well worthy of preservation among the archives of the University: and offered to help defray the cost of publication.[20]

Edwards began his administration with his usual energy and precision. He saw great possibilities in the institution intrusted to him. His influence on the curriculum had long been felt through his association with Charles Hovey and Ira Moore. He sought to implement the program by bringing to the staff instructors that were tried and true, and turned quite naturally to the protegées of Nicholas Tillinghast.

For his own position in mathematics he secured Thomas Metcalf, who had followed him as head of the St. Louis Normal and High School.[21] Metcalf was a scholar and a gentleman, meticulous in dress and precise in speech. Years later Charles DeGarmo said that to Metcalf "a false pronunciation, a slip in grammar, a mistake in spelling or calculation, was a kind of sin, a departure from the true and right." Metcalf was the kind of man Edwards would naturally turn to, for he too was meticulous in speech. Once after Edwards had given an address, John Cook, later to be president of the University, raised his hand to ask a question. Edwards looked over his glasses, and said, "Yes, Mr. Cook." Cook rose and said, "I did not get the i'dea." To which Edwards laconically replied, "When you get it, accent the second syllable." [22]

Albert Stetson, high school principal of Provincetown, Massachusetts, a student an Antioch preparatory in the days of Horace Mann, and graduate of Harvard, Class of 1861, was employed to teach language. Margaret Osband, relieved of some of the work in language, now taught drawing in addition to grammar. Only two of Hovey's faculty remained: Edwin C. Hewett, a former pupil of Edwards at Bridgewater who taught geography, and Joseph Addison Sewall, who was to have complete charge of science, the Board having voted to dispense with the lectures in Natural History.[23] Charles F. Childs was in charge of the high school and Livonia Ketcham, formerly of the Foster School of Chicago, the primary department.

[20] Richard Edwards "The Heritage of Culture," an address delivered before the Literary Societies of the State Normal University at Bloomington, Illinois, June 26, 1862. (Pamphlet)
[21] E. C. Hewett, "Thomas Metcalf," *The Index* 1895, p. 20; Loomis, *op. cit.*, p. 61.
[22] Interview with C. W. Whitten, Class of 1900, July 5, 1953.
[23] *Proceedings of the Board of Education* (Bloomington), June 26, 1862, p. 5.

The Model School was Edwards' particular pride. He concurred with Hovey on its importance and regretted that it had not been emphasized at Bridgewater. The difficulties under which he labored in St. Louis had allowed no opportunity for developing a unique system of observation and practice. He regarded a strong model school as essential in guiding students in the method and discipline of their own schools and insisted that it be placed under instructors "whose methods and skills in teaching and in governing" might be held before the uninitiated as the best known. When students were required to teach in the school and have their work observed and criticised by teachers of both the normal and model schools, he felt there was "an opportunity for improvement in the art of teaching such as offered by no other instrumentality." [24]

The course of study in the Model School embraced every grade from primary through high school. At the beginning of each term the principal designated those students in the upper classes that he felt were qualified for practice in the Model School. One class for one hour a day was assigned to each student for a term, and the "pupil teacher" was held responsible for the progress of his class. He was observed by the principal and other teachers, who gave suggestions for improvement. From time to time the class, under its teacher would be called upon to go through an exercise before the faculty and the other pupil teachers. After the pupils were dismissed, the manner and methods of the instructor were freely discussed by all present and merits and defects noted. Principles of pedogogy were set forth, illustrated, and fixed in the minds of the students. The community liked the Model School, and by the fall of 1862 enrollment had increased from 80 to 153 pupils, 109 of whom were in the high and grammar departments and 44 in the primary and intermediate departments. There were 138 in the normal department.

Although Edwards was ever alert and receptive to new ideas in education, he carefully evaluated the new before discarding the old. When Edward Austin Sheldon became secretary of the Oswego (New York) Board of Education, he developed a model school in which considerable experimental teaching was done.

[24] *Proceedings of the Board of Education* (Normal), December 17, 1862, p. 77.

Edwards followed the Oswego plan with interest. On a visit to Toronto, Sheldon had come across some new and remarkable apparatus, charts, pictures, and educational manuals published in London by the Society for the Promotion of Knowledge, and began corresponding with the society and in May 1861 brought Miss Margaret E. M. Jones from the English Home and Colonial Infant Society to take charge of the teachers' department in the public schools of Oswego.[25] The Pestalozzian methods which she introduced were well-received, and in the spring of 1862 the Board of Education of the City of Oswego proudly issued an invitation to American educators to examine and report on the system. At the instance of Richard Edwards, Livonia Ketcham at her own expense made the trip to Oswego to observe Miss Jones and the Oswego Model School. Miss Ketcham resigned however the following spring and it is not known how much of Pestalozzi via London and Oswego reached into Normal University's Model School in its formative years.

Richard Edwards believed that teachers functioned by example as well as precept, and to that end he insisted on rigid discipline of both faculty and student body. Restraint should be sufficient to ward off temptations too strong for the feeblest to resist. He tolerated no practices bearing the slightest appearance of evil. He believed a student strong in good purposes would respect rules because he saw the propriety of them and that a person of feeble moral power owed them his support because they could provide him with the precise aid that he needed. A regulation, he said, should never be announced until consideration was given all circumstances bearing upon it, and once made, obedience should be inexorably and impartially insisted upon; but always a student should be approached in a kind and courteous manner.

From the time that the school moved to the campus there had been some kind of physical exercise but with the Edwards regime came a new improvement, "free gymnastics" accompanied by music. He dwelt enthusiastically upon the matter in his first Report to the Board. The musical accompaniment had the advantages of giving precision to movement, relaxing the mind, and

[25] Charles A. Harper, *A Century of Teacher Education* (Washington, D.C.: National Education Association, 1939), p. 48.

adding to the interest and enjoyment of the exercises. He wondered if the general vigor and good health throughout the school might not be attributed in part to this system of exercises.[26]

Edwards soon saw that the war had made its impact on Illinois as well as Missouri. No battles had been fought in Illinois; business had not been paralyzed nor schools closed, but there were heavy demands for men and for taxes. Expenditures were questioned and teacher training came under scrutiny. Was the Normal University accomplishing the objects for which it was established? Carefully Edwards marshaled his facts. He set out to show that a sufficient number of persons had been recipients of instruction to justify the expense. To date, 228 men and 278 women had attended the school, a total of 506 students from eighty-one counties. Twenty-six of these had been granted diplomas at the end of the three-year course. Edwards pointed out that the influence of the school was not to be measured at the moment by either the number or the character of its graduates. Many of the students who remained but a year were among the best and most serious-minded "scholars." Often young men and women with superior preparation and some teaching experience were the ones whose circumstances did not permit them to stay in school long enough to graduate. However, there were those who after one year's connection with the school by virtue of their maturity and previous experience, carried away from the school more of its spirit and its good training than others might after staying twice as long.[27]

Of the 506 students who had enrolled prior to the winter term of 1862, only 52 remained to graduate. The proportion of men to women was 228 to 278 entering; and of those graduating, 19 to 23. The war deeply affected the enrollment and the number of students who remained to graduate. Young men who were potential schoolmasters entered the army, and young women often took no more courses than were necessary to qualify them to teach in schools that were literally crying for teachers.

The stress and tension of war was seen in classrooms and in the faces of students waiting for news from the front. The Normal Rifles, as some still referred to the Normal University contingent

[26] *Proceedings of the Board of Education* (Normal), December 17, 1862, p. 71.
[27] *Ibid.*, p. 75.

in the Illinois Thirty-third Regiment, saw their first engagement at Fredericktown, Missouri. Shortly before Richard Edwards came to Normal University, word had come of the first casualty. Lieutenant Joseph G. Howell, Company K, 8th Illinois Infantry, member of the first graduating class and former teacher in the Model School, was shot off his horse in the Battle of Fort Donelson, February 15, 1862.[28]

Through the newspapers and letters students and teachers followed the progress of the Illinois Regiments. Colonel Charles Hovey was promoted for distinguished conduct under fire, at Bayou Cache in July 1862. When five hundred Confederates suddenly attacked, he dashed from the rear at the first sound of battle and desperately tried to rally his men. Buckshot ripped through his clothing and pierced his chest. The pain was intense, and for an instant he staggered. Then he tore open his shirt to feel of his wound. Quickly drawing out two or three buckshot with his hand, he reassured his men: "It is nothing but a flesh wound, and some buckshot. I am not hurt." He again threw himself in the battle and reorganized his soldiers for a desperate defense. Other troops arrived and the Texas regiment dispersed.

In their spare time young women knitted for the Soldiers Aid Society, scraped lint, and rolled old sheets into bandages and wrote cheering letters to their soldier friends. Over their lunch pails, they exchanged news and rumors. Once in the summer of 1862, the students were almost paralyzed with fear when word spread that a Confederate army had invaded Springfield. Later they learned that the dispatch referred to Springfield, Missouri. There were tales of escaped slaves and whispered activities of the underground. It was well known that certain Bloomington citizens aided and abetted escaping Negroes. No one doubted where Richard Edwards stood on the matter of abolition.

Edwards was happy to be away from the tensions in St. Louis. Shortly after Hovey had gone away with the Schoolmaster's Regiment in 1861, Edwards had applied for the position. He wrote his wife, who was visiting relatives in Wisconsin, that he had applied for the position although he was not sure it was vacant. He

[28] Letter, C. M. Clark, Camp Lyon, Missouri, February 19, 1862 to E. C. Hewett. Hewett-Reeder Papers. Howell's body was returned to Illinois and school, community joined in a memorial service honoring the hero.

thought Bloomington "a pleasanter place to live," [29] and set about a long range campaign to secure the position. He missed no opportunities to speak in Illinois Institutes and teachers' meetings, and to make friends with Illinois educators.

Edwards did not move his family to Illinois when he accepted the temporary appointment in mathematics, which he was assured would lead to a permanent assignment as president. He took a room with the Hewetts, who were still living in Bloomington and boarded with them for three dollars a week.[30] Of the students he wrote his wife, "They seem on the whole to get their lessons very well. Their chief deficiency is in quickness and promptness." Of the Caesar class, consisting of only three students, two of whom were from the Model School, he said "I pile the work on the students, you may be assured, and they seem to like it on the whole.[31] For Perkins Bass, who was substituting in Hovey's absence, Edwards had great respect. He had brought order out of confusion, and reduced the school to a "very wholesome state of discipline." The difficulty, he confided to Betsey, had stemmed largely from Hovey's practice of allowing the affairs of school "to be managed to a great extent by the students and the people of the neighborhood. Mr. Bass had partially dispelled that illusion." He concluded that it was really fortunate that he had not been "so lucky" as to have come in the fall. The students were "very respectful" to him, and he was confident he would have no trouble in managing the school. He took it as a matter of course that "in places of this size everybody knows or tries to know everybody's business."

Mindful of his wife's concern for the health of the family, he wrote reassuringly "the climate here seems on the whole very healthy. The young women in school are fat and rosy, far different from St. Louis girls or even Massachusetts girls." [32] A handkerchief that he carried for a week looked cleaner than it would in St. Louis for one day of wear.

[29] Letter, Richard Edwards to his wife in Wisconsin, St. Louis, September 16, 1861. *Edwards MS.*
[30] Letter, Richard Edwards to his wife in St. Louis, Bloomington, March 22, 1862. *Edwards MS.*
[31] Letter, Richard Edwards to his wife in St. Louis, Bloomington, April 11, 1862. *Edwards MS.*
[32] Richard Edwards to his wife, Bloomington, April 1, 1862. *Edwards MS.*

Without currying favors or lowering his standards, Edwards sought the good will of the students. "They have two societies here like the Bridgewater Lyceum," he wrote his wife, "and each has a weekly meeting and a paper and one of my woes is that they want an article apiece from me every week. . . . I write these articles because I want to do so much to secure popularity, inasmuch as I do nothing else that looks that way at all. . . . They wish me to join one of the societies but I think it is not best at present." [33]

There were times when Edwards was skeptical of the future. In January 1861 the Legislature had appropriated $65,000 to clear up indebtedness on the building, but a new crop of claims amounting to between twenty and thirty thousand dollars arose; some of the creditors proceeded to bring suit and threatened to close the school. It did not appear likely that the Legislature would be willing to grant additional relief. In desperation Edwards wrote to Samuel Moulton, President of the Board, for a clear statement of exactly how things stood with the school; at the same time he dispatched a letter to Dr. William Greenleaf Eliot, St. Louis, inquiring about the possibility of employment in Washington University. The fact that Dr. Eliot could offer but $1500 made Edwards all the more concerned about the appointment at Illinois State Normal University.[34]

Earlier he had written his wife, "If I ever get comfortably settled down in a decent place like this, catch me moving if you can." [35] Although no formal offer of the principalship had been made, he was led to expect that it would be given him. In April Hovey had written that he did not expect to return and that, if necessary, he or Wright "would come up and set matters right" about the appointment.[36] But Hovey's resignation had been slow in coming through. It was in this state of "glorious uncertainty" that he wrote his memorable *Heritage of Culture,* setting forth all the wisdom he had gleaned from the classics, Tillinghast, Bridgewater, Mann, Salem, and St. Louis.

With the appointment signed, sealed, and delivered, Edwards

---

[33] Richard Edwards to his wife, Bloomington, April 11, 1862. *Edwards MS.*
[34] Richard Edwards to his wife, Bloomington, May 24, 1862. *Edwards MS.*
[35] Richard Edwards to his wife, Bloomington, May 10, 1862. *Edwards MS.*
[36] Richard Edwards to his wife, Bloomington, April 26, 1862. *Edwards MS.*

seemed to breathe more easily. The Hewetts were going East for the summer and had offered Edwards and his family the use of their home. He wrote his wife that they should accept the offer: "The situation is healthy, the garden is abundantly stocked with all manner of vegetables . . . a horse and buggy in the stable, all of which we can use, . . . also a cow that gives an abundance of milk." [37]

With the curriculum built so closely after Edwards' own ideas, he had no changes to suggest; nor was it altered materially during the fourteen years of his administration. Science courses, reading, and criticism were given greater emphasis. The three year course concentrated on a review of elementary subjects and the methods of teaching and administering schools.

The subjects comprising the course at Normal University in 1860–1876 were grouped in six categories:

(1) metaphysics, didactics, history and methods of education, school laws of Illinois, constitution of the United States and of Illinois, and teaching
(2) reading, spelling, grammar, rhetoric criticism, and English literature
(3) arithmetic, bookkeeping, algebra, geometry, trigonometry, and higher mathematics
(4) natural philosophy, astronomy, geography, botany, physiology, zoology, chemistry, and general history
(5) writing, drawing, and vocal music
(6) optional studies: Latin, French, and higher mathematics

Edwards explained to the Board in December 1862,

True scholarship and proper mental culture are much better promoted by a few studies well taught than by a superficial acquaintance with an extensive course. More valuable mental acquisitions will be secured by a thorough conquest of one or two provinces in the realm of knowledge, than by skirmishing on the frontiers of a hundred. The man who has thoroughly and philosophically mastered a few sciences, or even principles, is prepared to go on by himself. . . . All knowledge is, in a sense, within his reach.[38]

Edwards made it clear that he considered discipline and proper behavior of students at all times essential to the "great moral pur-

[37] Richard Edwards to his wife, Bloomington, May 31, 1862. *Edwards MS.*
[38] Richard Edwards, Report to the Board of Education, *Fourth Biennial Report of the Superintendent,* 1861–1862, p. 72.

poses of the school." "Every teacher," he said, "is continually surrounded by a multitude ready to note any deviation from rectitude
which he may exhibit. . . . A single false step may cost him all
his reputation."

He was fully aware of "temptations lying in wait" for virtuous
young people away from parental restraints for the first time, for
the well-intentioned who lacked pertinacity of purpose, and for
those who were ignorant of what constituted proper conduct or
unable to perceive the "immutable but delicately shaded and
illusive line that divides the realms of virtue from those of vice."
Always the students should be under the influence of good example and positive precepts. Rules were established regulating the
hours students were to keep. Edwards, having convinced himself that a regulation was desirable and within his power to
execute, impartially demanded full, honest obedience.[39]

Young men and young women, during the first years of the
school, roomed at the same house, sat on the same porch and
studied under the same harvest moon; but they were expected to
be in their own rooms at 7 p.m. in winter and at 7:30 p.m. during
other seasons, except on weekends. Saturday curfew was at 10 p.m.
and Sunday at 9 p.m. There were no extra-curricular activities at
night except the literary societies on Saturday nights; students
were expected to do their studying at home. A student who vio-
lated the rules was asked to explain the matter to the president.
Edwards had a desk in the assembly hall, and here he held a little
court, calling up one at a time those who for one reason or another
had been reported by the faculty. Henry McCormick recalled
that Monday morning brought the most students to the president's desk. Sunday night's curfew was the hardest.[40]

There were rules for conduct at school as well as in the rooming
houses. Men students were required to change from shoes to
slippers upon entering the building, in order to reduce the noise
and at the same time keep mud off the floor. Only for reasons of
health were men allowed to wear their shoes in classrooms. Men
from the faculty were posted at the student entrances, to see that
no mud was carried into the building. Not until sidewalks were

[39] *Ibid.*, p. 71.
[40] Henry McCormick, *The Index* 1907, pp. 27–28.

laid and scrapers installed did the faculty escape their onerous turn as "mud-guards." During school hours all students when not in classes were expected to be in the library or Normal Hall. They could not go to their rooms between recitations or visit on the stairs or in the halls. Never were they to be seen on the streets during school hours.

Of student opinion, Henry McCormick wrote years later, "Dr. Edwards was so enthusiastic himself that every one of his pupils felt 'Woe is me, if I do not teach.' In his masterly way he so pointed out the great possibilities for bettering humanity that were open to the teacher that the matter of salary seemed a secondary affair, ..." [41]

In a similar vein John Calvin Hanna reminisced, "Who can forget the impression of massive intellect and power embodied in President Richard Edwards as he twirled his glasses and came down on his heels in his brief and pungent morning addresses." [42]

"A teacher," he said, "must be animated by a higher motive than a mercenary one. He must teach because he loves to teach; because he looks upon teaching as a noble, . . . a holy employment." [43]

Nor were Edwards' services to education unheralded and unsung. In the spring of 1863 his good friend, W. H. Wells, wrote Edwards he had been recommended by President Hill as a possibility for an honorary master's degree at Harvard. In reply Edwards wrote a prompt, modest, but very detailed and convincing list of his attainments, citing his teaching experience, his academic training at Bridgewater and Rensselaer. He was careful not to overlook his knowledge of Latin, Greek, French, and German but added that he was self-taught or tutored in those fields and was currently "rusty." He suggested Governor Boutwell of Massachusetts and Professor Crosby as desirable persons to consult relative to his fitness. He prefaced his letter by saying that although the honor would be very agreeable to him personally that it might also be of some use to the Normal to have its

[41] *Ibid.*, p. 26.
[42] John Calvin Hanna, "Early Days at Normal." MS Milner Library.
[43] Richard Edwards, Report to the Board of Education, December 14, 1864. *Fifth Biennial Report of Superintendent of Public Instruction*, (Springfield, 1865), p. 44.

president receive a degree from Harvard, or other college of similar grade.[44]

On July 15 Edwards received a letter from his old friend Thomas Hill, whom he had known during his early teaching years at the Tarpelo School in Waltham. It read:

I take pleasure in informing you that the Government of this University have this day conferred upon you the degree of Master of Arts in recognition of your long, valuable, and successful labors in the cause of education, and in recognition also of your own personal worth of character.

The diploma will be forwarded by mail in a few days.[45]

Later Hill wrote informally that he had been heartily glad that the very first honorary degree that he had conferred in Harvard College had been upon one he had known and honored so long. He remembered how he urged in vain that the School Committee employ Edwards permanently in Waltham.[46] Instead, Richard Edwards had chosen teacher training. He had pioneered at Salem and in St. Louis; he had matured at Normal University. Two other colleges were to confer honorary degrees upon him: Shurtleff College, Alton, Illinois, the degree of LL. D. in 1866, and Blackburn College at Carlinville, Illinois, the degree of Doctor of Divinity in 1891.

[44] Letter, Richard Edwards to W. H. Wells, Esq., Bloomington, May 30, 1863. *Edwards MS.*

[45] Letter, Thomas Hill to Richard Edwards, Cambridge, Massachusetts, July 15, 1863. *Edwards MS.*

[46] Letter, Thomas Hill to Richard Edwards, Cambridge, Massachusetts, July 23, 1863. *Edwards MS.*

CHAPTER VI

Grandest of Enterprises

WHEN RICHARD EDWARDS came to the Normal University in 1862, he had the advantage of coming to a school already familiar with the philosophy in which he had been trained. Because of the demands on Hovey in supervising the construction of the building and in raising funds, much of the teaching and direction of the school had fallen to his assistant, Ira Moore, a graduate of Bridgewater.[1] Edwin Crawford Hewett, who had joined the staff in its second year as teacher of geography and history, had graduated from Bridgewater while Edwards was acting as principal during Tillinghast's illness. Edwards' early appointments were likewise Bridgewater men. His first appointment was his old friend and former associate in the St. Louis High School, the meticulous and gentle Thomas Metcalf, one of Tillinghast's most devoted students. He was induced to give up a position paying $2,000 for one which paid only $1,300. Metcalf was employed to take over Edwards' position in mathematics, but he later took over the training department and remained on the staff for thirty-two years.[2] Albert Stetson, who came in the fall of 1862 to teach grammar and literature, was a former pupil of Edwards at Bridgewater. He had taught under Horace Mann at Antioch.[3]

[1] Ira Moore was a thorough teacher but not always popular. The Board voted not to re-employ him after his sojourn in the army. He went to Minnesota, taught in the University and became president of the normal school at St. Cloud. Later he was president of the State Normal School, San Jose, California. He died October 28, 1897.

[2] Thomas Metcalf was born in West Wrentham, Norfolk County, Massachusetts in 1826. He attended rural schools in winter, worked on his father's farm, and during off hours braided straw for bonnets. At sixteen he substituted eleven weeks for a homesick teacher at her regular salary of three dollars a week. When twenty-one, he spent a year at Bridgewater. After seven years as principal of a grammar school he moved to St. Louis. He taught at Illinois State Normal University for thirty-two years. He died in January 1894. Cook and McHugh, *op. cit.*, p. 47.

[3] Albert Stetson, born in Kingston, Massachusetts, in 1834, studied at Bridgewater 1852–1853. After a year in charge of a grammar school on Cape Cod, he entered the preparatory school at Antioch, Yellow Springs, Ohio. In 1858 he entered Harvard and graduated in 1861. He was a student editor of the *Harvard Magazine*. He taught Latin, rhetoric and grammar at Illinois State Normal University 1862–1887. He married Margaret

It was a noble coterie: Edwards of the sonorous voice and the great vision; Hewett, slight of build, honest, energetic and fun-loving; Stetson, polished, precise, and so highly irascible that he kept a palm leaf fan on his desk to cool his temper when his indignation had been aroused; and the handsome, immaculate Metcalf, the great training teacher "whose criticisms always closed like a church service, with a benediction." All had sat at the feet of Nicholas Tillinghast,[4] has been assistants at the Bridgewater school for at least a term, and they ascribed a large part of whatever success attended their labors to the great Tillinghast. For forty-two years, five of his Bridgewater graduates provided leadership in determining the policies and spirit of the prairie normal school, and most of its other teachers for the generation 1857–1876 were pupils of these five.[5]

The mentor of these early teachers, Nicholas Tillinghast, first principal of Bridgewater Normal School, was a graduate of the Military Academy at West Point. During an army career of twelve years in which he advanced to rank of captain, he alternated tours of duty on the western frontier with assignments to the staff at West Point. When ill health and a distaste for military life led him to resign his commission, he opened a preparatory school for young men who wished to prepare for West Point or for engineering. When a third normal school was to be opened in Massachusetts, Horace Mann, then Secretary of Education, had urged Tillinghast to become its principal. Reluctantly he agreed; and for a year he studied, prepared lectures, and observed the work in the normal schools at Barre and Lexington. In 1840 Bridgewater opened. Soon Nicholas Tillinghast began to exert a telling influence upon the public schools of the state. The Bridgewater Normal was poorly housed, meagerly equipped, and attendance small; but its influence was not to be measured statistically.

Osband, the school's first preceptress, in 1887 and migrated to California where he entered into the Cable Car business.

John W. Cook "History of the Faculty." *Semi-Centennial History of Illinois State Normal University* 1857–1907 (Normal: 1907), p. 102.

[4] W. R. Heath "Genesis of the Chicago Club," an address given before the Illinois State Normal University Club of Chicago, 1905. Printed and circulated with the club's Handbook and Directory, 1907.

[5] Charles A. Harper, *Development of the Teachers College in the United States* with special reference to the Illinois State Normal University. (Bloomington: McKnight and McKnight, 1935), p. 79.

Over his students Tillinghast had a sort of fascination, a strange power that enabled him to fill them in a great measure with his own spirit and to confer upon them his own quiet, unflinching devotion to principle. Reserved and modest, he at first seemed cold and forbidding, but when one came to know him, Tillinghast was generous and kind. His words were few, but they carried with them the force of judgment, integrity of purpose, sincerity, purity of character, and justice. His pupils seemed to surrender unconditionally to his influence; no one wished to pursue a course which he disapproved or to incur even his mildest reprimand.

A lesson taught by Tillinghast was a stimulating experience. He demanded logic, proof, accuracy, punctuality. He would not abide idleness or deception or neglect of duty. Graduates of Bridgewater became crusaders for moral values. But the course at Bridgewater left much to be desired, and Tillinghast realized it. For the first few years pupils were expected to graduate as full-fledged teachers after two terms, not necessarily consecutive; and in some instances graduation was achieved by a single term. The curriculum offered little more than an attempted mastery of the common branches and some attention to method, ethics, and discipline. Near the end of his teaching career, Tillinghast wrote to Henry Barnard:

My idea of a normal school is that it should have a term of four years; and that those studies should be pursued that shall lay a foundation upon which to build an education. The teacher should be trained to be above his textbook. Whatever has been done in teaching in all countries, different methods, the thought of the best minds on the sciences and the art of instruction should be laid before the neophyte teacher. In a proper normal school there should be departments and the ablest men should be put over them.[6]

Although Tillinghast failed to attain his goal at Bridgewater, he laid down precepts that were to guide Edwards in his efforts to make Illinois State Normal University the best normal school on the continent.[7] Other teachers at Normal University soon caught the spirit of Bridgewater and the vision of Edwards.

[6] Richard Edwards, "Memoir of Nicholas Tillinghast," an address given before the graduates of the State Normal School, Bridgewater, July 30, 1856. Reprint, *American Journal of Education* (December 1856), pp. 6–23.
[7] Harper, *Development of the Teachers College*, p. 83.

There had been a model school at Bridgewater during its first years but it was soon allowed to lapse, perhaps because of lack of public interest and financial support. At Normal University the Model or Training School was ever a prime consideration. Hovey had started it during the first term in Major's Hall, and when Edwards came he continued and expanded the program. When Childs returned to St. Louis and Miss Ketcham resigned, William L. Pillsbury, who had recently graduated from Harvard, was placed in charge of the Model School. Miss Marion Hammond of St. Louis was appointed to the primary department, and Miss Bandusia Wakefield, a student, was made assistant. Lyman B. Kellogg, another student, served as an additional instructor. In 1866 a grammar division was set up. Margaret Osband, who taught drawing and music for a short time before becoming the wife of Professor Stetson, had other duties which earned for her the title of "Preceptress."

The purpose of the Model School had been to furnish the Normal pupils an opportunity for practice in teaching, but under the act incorporating the University, the Board was not to be responsible for its operation. The only way that it could be operated was through a tuition charge. In the beginning the pupil teachers had little supervision. The principal of the University was almost as busy teaching as any of the other instructors, and the principal of the Model School had a full load as teacher of high school classes. Edwards determined to bring up the quality of teaching and arranged to have his hours vacant at the time most of the pupil teachers were teaching and then called pupil teachers after school hours to discuss their work. Each pupil teacher was required to keep a diary, with an account of every recitation, its subject matter, procedures in conduction, successes and failures. Lectures were given and conferences held. Although supervision was a full-time job, it was 1874 before the Board became convinced that a special training teacher should be employed, and Thomas Metcalf was released from teaching mathematics to take over the work.[8] An object of the high school department of the Model School during this era was the "thorough fitting of boys for the best colleges of the country."

[8] Cook and McHugh, *op. cit.,* p. 198.

Bloomington had established a high school in 1857,[9] but its teachers were not so well trained. The reputation of Professors Pillsbury, Sewall, Stetson, and Hewett led many a Bloomington youth to ride the Illinois Central to the Junction every day or walk the two miles in the hope that instruction given in the classics at the Normal's high school would enable him to enter Harvard or Yale or Princeton without embarrassing conditions.

There was no defined pattern of sequence in the high school and normal work. Some students entered the normal department directly from elementary school, others after graduating from high school. Often high school students and normal students took the same studies. Sometimes after teaching several years graduates of the normal department returned to take courses in the high school and increase their fund of subject matter. Some took special courses such as drawing and penmanship.

The first class was graduated from the high school just as the Civil War drew to its close. There were seven in the class: Gertrude Case, Jesse Fell's daughter Clara, Charles L. Capen and Robert McCart, who went on to study law; Howard Crist, who became a physician; Hosea Howard, who became an accountant for the Wabash Railway; and William McCambridge, who after twenty-six years as editor of the Bloomington *Daily Pantagraph,* became confidential secretary to the Interstate Commerce Commission.[10]

On Saturday, April 15, six weeks before Commencement, the nation had been shocked by the news of the assassination of President Lincoln. He had been attorney for the school when it was founded, and he was personally known to most of the students and faculty. The Wrightonian Society discarded the humorous program scheduled for that evening for an impromptu one appropriate to the occasion.[11] The political campaign of 1864 seemed as only yesterday—the great mass meeting in October, the morning procession, the speeches, the fireworks at night, and the torch-light parade of the young "Wide-Awakes" from the Normal. The "Union" men had kept their stores lighted and one

[9] *National Flag,* September 26, 1857; October 29, 1857.
[10] "Alumni Register," *Semi-Centennial History of Illinois State Normal University,* p. 254.
[11] Charles L. Capen, *Index* 1909, p. 145.

rarely saw a darkened window.[12] In June 1860 the Board had ruled that "since it was its policy to administer its affairs without reference to political parties, it was improper for teachers in the University to take an active part in partisan politics." They were free to vote as their consciences dictated but warned against doing anything that would prejudice the school. Consequently, they had been careful not to participate in political demonstrations, although they felt free to stand along the line of march and smile indulgently, if not encouragingly, at the students.

Now the University and the community joined in mourning. On April 19, at a memorial service in the great hall of the University President Edwards delivered the principal address on "The Life and Character of Abraham Lincoln." [13] Two weeks later when the funeral train approached the University at four forty-five in the morning, it passed under a large memorial arch erected by students and townspeople.[14] At the University a memorial evergreen was planted in front of the Normal Building just south of the carriage drive.[15] As its gift to the school the class of 1865 left a bust of Lincoln.

Alert to the needs of teachers in the common schools, Edwards organized a four-week institute to be held at the Normal University, beginning September 14, 1863. The announcement printed on a single sheet of pink paper sent out in August stated that the time would be devoted to thorough drill in the Philosophy and Methods of Teaching the Common Branches, discussion on the Duties of Teachers, Discipline and Organization of a School, Hearing Recitations, and Rights of Teachers Under the Law. The "exercises" were to be conducted by the regular instructors of the University, who would each give an hour of the day to the institute, and there would be addresses by prominent educators from other parts of the state. County Commissioners were invited to be present. Prospective members of the institute were admonished that "constant and thorough work would be required." Fifteen teachers attended.[16]

[12] *Weekly Pantagraph*, October 19, 1864.

[13] Richard Edwards "Life and Character of Abraham Lincoln," an address delivered at the Hall of the Normal University, April 19, 1865. Pamphlet. M. J. Holmes Collection.

[14] *Daily Pantagraph*, May 4, 1865.

[15] Capen, *op. cit.*, pp. 145–146.

[16] *Weekly Pantagraph*, August 19, 1863.

At its tenth annual meeting the Illinois Teachers Association went on record as favoring an institute during August, and accordingly on May 1, 1864, President Edwards [17] sent out a circular to the effect that such an institute would be held if seventy-five teachers would pledge in advance to attend.[18] More than the requisite number pledged attendance, and the institute was advertised to begin August 1, 1864. There was no tuition, and the faculty served without pay. One hundred and twenty-seven teachers came. While in attendance they organized into a permanent institute, adopted a constitution, and elected officers.

No sessions were held in 1865 and 1866, but in 1867 Edwards inserted a notice in the May *Illinois Teacher* that an institute would be held in July or August if before the next issue of the *Teacher* went to press one hundred teachers would promise to attend. Teachers institutes were taken seriously. Railroads provided reduced fares. Two sessions were held each day except Saturday. Roll was called at the beginning of each session, and the morning session opened with devotional exercises. Each day's proceedings were criticised by some one previously appointed. A Query Box was set up and fifteen minutes a day set aside to consider its contents. A literary society was organized for general discussion of questions such as "The Duties of a Principal of a Grade School," "Securing Prompt and Regular Attendance," "Promoting the Moral Growth of the Pupil," "The Best Method of Securing Good Recitations and Good Behavior," and "The Self-Reporting System."

President Edwards, always popular as a teacher, conducted classes in the theory and art of teaching, reading, and the teaching of reading, and Professor Hewett taught geography and history; Professor Metcalf, arithmetic methods, and phonics; Dr. Sewall, botany and physiology; Professor Stetson, grammar and composition; and Professor William L. Pillsbury gave instruction in etymology and the Dio Lewis system of free gymnastics. The members of the institute were so impressed with Pillsbury's work that they unanimously resolved "that physical culture ought to receive attention in all our public schools, ..." It further re-

---

[17] The title of "principal" was changed to "president" in 1862.
[18] *Weekly Pantagraph*, June 28, 1864.

solved that all children of lawful age, without regard to race or color, should be freely admitted on terms of entire equality to the public schools of the state.[19]

At the conclusion of the institute a 174 page pamphlet "containing as extended a setting-forth of the work done at the institute as it was possible for the instructors to prepare" was published at the expense of the members. The pamphlet was in such demand that the supply was soon exhausted.[20]

A fourth institute was held at the Normal University in 1868. Writing to his wife June 26, 1868, from Quincy, where he was assisting in a county meeting, Edwards implored:

Talk institute to anybody and everybody. Say that we shall be strong-handed—Hewett, Stetson, Pillsbury, Miss Johnson and . . . Tell everybody that everybody must be prompt for the machine only runs two weeks. . . . You must become skillful as a diplomat. $4,000 per annum requires a good deal of affortifying. . . . Good bye, I am more cheerful than when I left home. How long it will last I cannot say. Have drunk nothing stronger than coffee.[21]

The institute in 1868 was attended by 248 teachers from fifty counties. By this time the pattern of the Normal Institute was very well established. Examination for teachers' certificates was held the second week. In 1869 the attendance was 291 with fifty-five counties represented. The report for that year proudly states that of the twenty-three who took the examinations "nearly all passed." [22] In 1870, the enrollment was 242 and in 1871 it was 215, representing forty-four counties. At a three week session in 1872 devoted to the study of the new school law, three hundred were in attendance.[23]

Meanwhile the five-day county institutes became more general, and the services of faculty members were in great demand. Although the School Law of 1855 had provided that county commissioners and supervisors might make appropriations for teachers institutes, it was not until Newton Bateman, State Superintendent,

---

[19] *Report of the Illinois Teachers Institute,* held at the Normal University, Normal, Illinois, August 1867, (Peoria: N. C. Nason, 1867), pp. 15–19.
[20] Richard Edwards, "Decennial Address" delivered at the State Normal University, June 27, 1872, (Peoria: N. C. Nason, 1872), p. 27.
[21] Richard Edwards to his wife, Quincy, June 26, 1868. *Edwards MS.*
[22] *Report of the Illinois Teachers Institute,* Normal, Illinois, 1869, p. 14.
[23] Edwards, "Decennial Address," p. 27.

worked out a practical formula for financing that the county institute began to flourish. Faculty members enjoyed these off-campus
contacts. They were good drawing cards for their classes during
the regular year, and furthermore the instructors were paid for
their work at the county institutes but not paid for the institutes
held on campus.[24]

Of all the institute speakers none was in greater demand than
President Edwards. His diaries and letters to his family seldom
indicate a week that he did not lecture somewhere. When he was
not speaking before institutes and teachers meetings, he was
occupying pulpits. If the Governor of the state could not attend
the dedication of a building or the laying of a cornerstone, an
inspiring address by President Edwards of the Normal University
was regarded as a highly satisfactory substitute.

With the war over, President Edwards believed that the state
should give serious attention to teacher training and provide the
Normal University with some facilities it had long been needing.
When the Board met in Bloomington on June 22, 1865, Edwards
lamented the poor quarters and food available to students. The
school was a long two-mile walk from Bloomington. The immediate neighborhood had only a few rooms for rent. While
General Hovey had been away with the army, his large house on
Mulberry Street, designed to care for his family and sixteen students, had been completed. After leaving the army Hovey had
gone to Washington but his wife remained in the big house for
many months, renting rooms to students and faculty,[25] now and
then befriending Negroes in their flight to Canada.[26] President
Edwards' own home on Broadway cared for twenty-four students.
Professor Hewett had built a large house on Ash Street and
Professor Metcalf, one on the corner of North and Broadway.
The Jesse Fells and two or three other families helped by keeping
from two to twenty students. These facilities were quite inade-

[24] Cook, *Educational History of Illinois*, p. 122.
[25] From the upstairs windows of the Hovey home the girls waved to soldiers on their
way to the front. Among Mrs. Hovey's boarders were Lyman B. Kellogg, a student who
later became president of Kansas State Normal at Emporia, and E. Clarence Messer, a
teacher of art in Bloomington. He was later associated with the Corcoran Gallery in
Washington, D. C., and painted the portrait of General Hovey which was presented by
the Illinois State Normal University Club of New York in 1913. "Greeting from Lyman
B. Kellogg, '64" Program files, Milner Library.
[26] Interview with Agnes Cook Gale, July 5, 1955.

quate for the needs of a growing school and Edwards did not feel he could keep on indefinitely asking new faculty to build houses to provide student lodging. He proposed to the Board that a building capable of accommodating 150 students be erected by the state or private subscription and "furnished with most approved cooking apparatus, with sleeping, bathing, and study rooms and a gymnasium conveniently arranged, also with parlors for receiving company." He believed the cost of board could be set at a very low figure since there would be no rent to pay and on so large a scale everything could be systematized.

Another advantage, he said, was that the formation of the pupils' habits could be "guided by the faculty," and "moral forces could be brought to bear upon them" as under no other system.[27]

President Edwards again advanced the idea of a dormitory in the *Sixth Biennial Report of the Superintendent of Public Instruction*. In the *Seventh Biennial Report* he reinforced his appeal with a paper written by Miss Dryer, the preceptress. Briefly citing the high cost of living in Normal, board and room often being as much as five dollars a week, she dwelt at length on the cultural, social, and health benefits from living in a carefully supervised dormitory. She described vividly the students carrying coal up two or three flights of stairs, storing, cooking, and eating food in the same room in which they studied and slept, as many as four occupying a room furnished with odds and ends brought from home, rickety bedsteads with straw ticks, soiled bedding, inadequate lighting, ventilation, and closet space for clothing—a dismal picture but one that persisted until long past the turn of the century.[28]

No dormitory was forthcoming, but the Legislature in 1867 voted $3,000 to beautify the campus, $500 for repairs and $2,500 for the Natural History Museum. Already the building had begun to show signs of wear and the weakness of construction that was to plague it for the rest of its existence. The indoor toilets that had marked the building as so very modern when it opened in 1860 proved unsatisfactory, and the Board ruled that they should be removed from the building during the summer vacation and

[27] *Proceedings of the Board of Education* (Bloomington) June 22, 1865, pp. 6–7.
[28] *Seventh Biennial Report of the Superintendent of Public Instruction* 1867–1868, p. 349.

proper out-houses be erected under the "superintendency of the chairman of the Building Committee." [29]

High hopes of expanding the nature and function of the University came in 1867, when it was proposed that the State of Illinois avail itself of the provisions of the Morrill Act of 1862 and establish an industrial university. Jesse Fell, who had always dreamed of an ideal educational system emanating from a great university which embraced schools of liberal arts, medicine, law, teacher training, agriculture, and engineering, took up his familiar subscription lists. "Teachers," he said, "would profit by the breadth gained in coming into contact with those who were in turn training for other kinds of work; and as education was a field as dignified as that of any other calling, it was practicable to make the normal school one of the colleges of the University." Over a half million dollars was quickly subscribed, Fell's own $15,000 ranking next to Judge David Davis's, as the largest pledge. A site of 140 acres was offered.

Assuming there would be strong competition from Champaign, Logan, and Morgan counties, Fell organized a party to go to Springfield and lobby for the location at Bloomington. Urbana, especially to plead its cause, had elected to the Legislature the powerful and persuasive Clark R. Griggs. He promptly introduced a bill definitely locating the institution at Urbana, provided the offer therein listed proved *bona fide*. Competition was thus eliminated, and it was understood if the Legislature did not act at this term the state would probably lose out as a beneficiary of the land grant act. There were rumblings of discontent and rumors of bribery. Fell would have no part in anything that savored of underhandedness.[30] In the end Champaign won the location and Illinois State Normal University dedicated its future solely to the training of teachers.

In January 1869 bills for a dormitory and gymnasium were again brought before the Legislature, but the measures were de-

[29] *Proceedings of the Board of Education* (Normal), June 24, 1868, p. 5.

[30] After McLean County failed to get the land grant university, Fell labored that the university at Urbana-Champaign should be a real university with an advanced professional curriculum, not a glorified high school. He helped secure the Soldiers and Sailors Orphans Home for Normal. He wanted it to be a trade school. When it did not develop in that direction he said, "Don't call it my school, it is not what I wanted it to be." Morehouse, *op. cit.*, pp. 78–82.

feated. The new normal school at Carbondale and the state university were claiming shares of the state's educational budget. Some of the faculty blamed the local community because the citizens had not responded with a strong lobby. "They deserve it," declared the disappointed preceptress. Writing to her husband who was attending an educational meeting in Providence, Rhode Island, and telling of a students' indignation meeting, Betsey Edwards wryly commented, "They will feel better now." [31]

Shortly after the Saunders plan was submitted, Fell had transplanted many trees from his own grounds, including the row of tulip trees along the south edge of a horse shoe drive south of the building. After storms Fell would drive out to the campus and replace the tattered tulip trees and put up props to protect them. Trees and shrubs were donated by local nurserymen the first year, but after that the campus landscaping was sadly neglected. When Jesse Fell became a member of the Board in 1867, it was his avowed purpose to see that the original Saunders plan was carried out. He was instrumental in securing a legislative appropriation of $3,000 in 1867. During that summer he supervised the ploughing and subsoiling of the entire campus, and the next spring he set out 1740 trees, and the following year 107 more. He even had a small portion of the campus set aside as a nursery to provide replacements. In 1871, a length of new board fence costing $1,015.04 was set around the grounds to keep out the horses and cows which were wont to graze on the lush grass and nibble the tender saplings.[32] For over seventy-five years the campus of the Normal University was known and praised throughout the Midwest for the variety and beauty of its trees.[33]

The community was likewise being improved. Jesse Fell had come home from a visit to West Philadelphia and Germantown in 1856 convinced that a tree-planting campaign would make North Bloomington as lovely as any town in the East. Before the Normal University was established, he had planted thirteen thousand trees in the projected addition to North Bloomington. At first he planted black locust, because of its rapid growth and

[31] Betsey Edwards to Richard Edwards, Normal, January 27, 1869. *Edwards MS.*
[32] *Proceedings of the Board of Education* (Normal) December 5–6, 1871, p. 12.
[33] William Saunders who did the original landscape planning for the University charged sixty-five dollars for his services. Morehouse, *op. cit.,* p. 108.

durable wood, but when borers attacked the young locust groves he turned to hard and soft maples, ash, American and British elm, linden, catalpa, European larch, and varieties of evergreen. Within a few years a sizable village grew up around the Junction and the Normal University. Spacious homes and modest cottages sprang up along its tree-lined streets and new business was attracted to the area. A hotel, the Pennell House, was erected across from the Junction by Jesse Fell and William Pennell. It was a four-story Mansard-roofed structure with spacious rooms and wide verandas. Good hostelries were rare, and its large ballroom made it for a time the social center of the two towns.[34] Jesse Fell induced W. H. Mann, Cyrus Overman, and F. K. Phoenix to locate their nurseries in the Normal area, and so made Bloomington one of the largest nursery centers in the nation. A foundry and a grist mill operated east of the Junction for a time. In 1861, a post office was established, and like the name of the township, the village came by common consent to be known as Normal.

When in 1867 the population had grown to several hundred, the citizens took advantage of the State Law of 1865 and had the town incorporated. A unique feature of the charter stipulated that no intoxicating liquors were to be sold within its borders. Jesse Fell had previously included a clause in title deeds for lots that he sold that no liquor should ever be sold upon the premises, thus laying a foundation for a "prohibition" community. For many years parents believed that the absence of saloons and pool rooms and undesirable persons who so often frequent them made Normal a more desirable place for raising their families and sending their sons and daughters to school. President Edwards, ever a "temperance" man, joined forces with Fell, John Dodge, and William Pennell in obtaining signers to the petition to the Legislature that the prohibition clause be included in the town's charter. He secured the signatures of the students at the Normal University. Over nine hundred names appeared on the petition; it was said to have been signed by every man, woman, and child in Normal who was over the age of six.[35]

[34] The Pennell House burned in 1872 and was not rebuilt.
[35] Morehouse, *op. cit.,* p. 74; also David Felmley, "Debt of Normal University to Jesse W. Fell," *Alumni Quarterly* (August 1916), p. 4; *Daily Pantagraph,* December 19, 1866.

Churches were organized: the Methodist and the Congregational in 1865, the Baptist in 1866, the Presbyterian in 1868, and
the Christian in 1873. Soon church spires rose above the tops of
trees. Visiting pastors from Bloomington churches no longer held
Sunday afternoon services in the Assembly Hall at the University,
and students were urged to affiliate with the local church of their
choice.[36]

Normal became an even more desirable place to live when a
street railway was opened between the two towns. In 1867 a company of public-spirited men, including Jesse Fell, William Hen-
drix, William Pennell, Henry C. Fell, Norval Dixon, and Lyman
Ferre, undertook to construct a car line, not for profit but for civic
improvement. The lines were soon extended over the entire city of
Bloomington. At first Board members seriously questioned the advisability of allowing tracks to be laid across the east side of the
campus. One member feared that strange men riding on the cars
past the rooming houses where the women students lived might
attempt to engage in flirtations and distract the young ladies from
their studies. However Fell was able to convince the Board that the
car line would be more of a service than a hazard. At first the cars
were hauled by a steam dummy engine, but the panting, puffing
little engines left long trails of black smoke behind which rose to
darken laundry drying on the line and lace curtains at the windows. The shrill whistles "disturbed the scholastic quiet of the
university towns," and so many complaints were made that the
dummy engines were replaced by mules, which pulled the little
bobbing cars with ten or twelve passengers back and forth between the two towns until the lines were electrified in 1890.[37] The
small cars were bitter cold in winter and to protect the feet of
the passengers the floors were covered with heavy straw. In the
early years the cars operated on a forty-minute schedule with no
service after nine at night.[38]

[36] Burnham, *History of McLean County*, p. 450.

[37] Jacob L. Hasbrouck, *History of McLean County, Illinois* (Topeka-Indianapolis:
Historical Publishing Company, 1924), pp. 224–5: Harriet Fyffe Richardson, *Quaker
Pioneers* (Milwaukee: Gillet Company, 1940), p. 37.

[38] Although gas lighting of streets in Bloomington came with the Bloomington Gas,
Light and Coke Company in 1857, gas did not come to Normal until 1901. In addition to
passenger service, the car line did an extensive business from 1868 to 1873 hauling
wheat from the tracks of the Chicago and Alton in Normal to the Novelty Mills, Market
and East Streets in Bloomington.

For many years it was with reluctance that the state made any appropriations to assist the Normal University. The school had been chartered on the premise that it would cost the state nothing, the building being provided by private subscriptions and the expenses of operation paid from income of the University and Seminary funds. The Model School, instituted on a self-sustaining basis, had in the course of years more than paid for itself. Edwards in his report in December 1867 declared that if the Model School were discontinued the normal school could not be maintained. The State Fund yielded but $12,445.99 per year. Faculty salaries amounted to $9,900.00, leaving a balance of only $2,545.99 for janitors' fees, heating, stationery, personal expenses of members of the Board, and other contingencies. The heating alone had cost $2,300 a year, and if it had not been for the surplus from the Model School, there would have been a deficit of $3,485.07 for the school year 1866–1867.

Edwards believed that the creation of the university at Urbana cut in deeply on the appropriations that might have otherwise been granted to advance the cause of teacher education—a conviction which subsequent presidents of the Normal University have shared.[39] The enrollment in December 1867 reached an all-time high of 327. Prices had risen as a result of war-time inflation, but the salaries of staff members had remained unchanged. Discontent mounted. Hewett, Sewall, Metcalf, and Stetson in a petition to the Board said their present salaries were not equal to current family expenses, that public school teachers in small towns were better paid, and that they considered it a disgrace to work for less than others in positions involving less responsibility. The Board complimented the four professors on their valuable services and promised to raise their salaries, and that of the preceptress, as soon as possible.[40]

The following June Edwards reported that "the loyalty of some members of our faculty has been severely tried. . . . Dr. Sewall and Professor Powell, in particular, have been repeatedly urged to accept higher salaries and easier labor. But their love for the Normal, and their hope of better things to come in respect

[39] *Proceedings of the Board of Education* (Normal), June 26, 1867, p. 7.
[40] *Ibid.* (Normal), December 17, 1867, p. 7.

to salaries here, have enabled them thus far successfully to resist all appeals." Edwards warned that "either this institution must descend from the high position it now occupies, or there must be larger appropriations for it. . . . The question can not much longer remain unsettled." [41]

The Board's response was the authorization of increases in salary. President Edwards was to receive $4,000, the same as was being paid to the President of the New Illinois Industrial University. Four professors—Sewall, Metcalf, Stetson, and Pillsbury of the Model School, whose salaries had been $1,500, were to receive $2,000; Miss Dryer, the preceptress, $1,100, and Mrs. Haynie, the new language and grammar teacher, $900. A teacher to take Mr. Hewett's work while he was on leave "without pay" was to have $1,500, and the new primary teacher $700.[42] Prices had risen over a hundred percent, and the professors were grateful for small favors. They remained ever watchful of opportunities to earn a few extra dollars, speaking at farmers' meetings and teachers' institutes, and tutoring. Edwards projected a series of analytical readers and quietly began a little private speculation in Iowa lands which was to provide for him a comfortable old age.

Along with the Bridgewater coterie was another professor who was to add to the reputation of the Normal University. In March 1867 John Wesley Powell became official curator of the Illinois Natural History Collection housed in the museum on the third floor. Powell came from Illinois Wesleyan University, where as professor of natural sciences he had taught courses in botany, histology, comparative anatomy and physiology, zoology, biology, natural philosophy, the logic of natural science, geology, and mineralogy. He had fought in the Civil War and given his right arm for the Union.[43] He had studied at Wheaton, Illinois College, and Oberlin. Before the war he had been teacher of the upper grades at Hennepin on the Illinois River. Weekends and after school he had searched the region for mollusks, plants, and fossils. He became interested in the work of the Illinois Natural History Society, and in the fall of 1859 began a barnstorming tour

[41] *Ibid.* (Normal), June 24, 1868, p. 5.
[42] *Ibid.*, p. 7.
[43] William Culp Darrah, *Powell of the Colorado* (Princeton: University Press, 1951), p. 76.

of institutes and teachers' meetings, urging that science be included in the common school studies. He gathered specimens for his own collection and exchanged with others. Many were sent to the new museum at Normal.

During the war Powell met many men in the Illinois Thirty-third, Schoolmasters Regiment, who had been associated with the Normal University and were also members of the Natural History Society. While at Vicksburg in 1863 he was awarded for his contribution to the study of science an M. A. degree from Illinois Wesleyan University, receiving one of the first honorary degrees conferred by the school.[44]

In the fall of 1865 he came to Wesleyan as professor of geology at a salary of $1,000 per year. He was an inspired and inspiring teacher. He taught his students about their environment first hand. He took them to the woods to gather specimens of plants and animals, and on their return they used his microscope to study the minute structure of leaves, fruits, and insects. They made notebooks of pressed flowers, leaves, and grasses. Powell believed that the classification of knowledge was not enough. Practical use must be made of it. At the annual trustees meeting in June 1866 he was singled out for special commendation and appreciation for his labors in improving the college campus and for his contributions to the museum.[45]

Two months after coming to Wesleyan, Powell helped to organize a branch chapter of the State Natural History Society and he often visited the State Society's collections at Normal University.[46] The work of arranging and collating the specimens had been entirely voluntary. Professor C. D. Wilber, the unofficial curator of the museum, had given whatever time he could to the classification of materials. Much remained to be done to make the museum a truly functional one.

At the meeting of the Natural History Society in Bloomington on July 30, 1866, Powell moved that a committee confer with the State Board of Education to explore the possibility of an appropriation for the museum.

[44] Elmo Scott Watson, *The Illinois Wesleyan Story, 1850–1950* (Bloomington: Illinois Wesleyan University Press, 1950), p. 69.
[45] *Ibid.*, p. 74.
[46] Darrah, *op cit.*, p. 77.

Meanwhile an idea was taking shape.

Powell was a brilliant teacher but had the wanderlust in his veins. He was aware that exploring and collecting was an expensive avocation. More than anything he wanted to explore the Rockies. He talked over a plan with Emma, his wife, by which he could eat his cake and have it too. Emma was willing to go along, provided they could finance the trip without losing their home. Powell proposed to attach himself to the faculty of one of the colleges in such a way as to allow himself considerable freedom. Normal University, as headquarters of the Natural History Society, would serve his purposes better than Wesleyan.

His plan was first to suggest that he give a course of lectures in geology at Normal; after that he would press the establishment of a paid curatorship and secure the job for himself. He felt assured that Joseph Sewall, professor of natural science who was temporarily serving as curator, would welcome relief from this responsibility.

The two colleges and the Natural History Society concurred in Powell's recommendation for a state appropriation for the museum and named him as agent in Springfield. He spoke three times before the General Assembly. The Illinois Society, he said, was analogous to the Royal Societies of London, Russia, Belgium, Sweden, the Smithsonian and other government-supported institutions. He proposed a general commissioner and full-time curator whose duty would be "to superintend research and collections, take charge of the museum, carry on the exchanges, and make the contributions." He asked for an appropriation of $1,500 for the salary of the general commissioner and curator and an additional $1,000 for books, apparatus, and other supplies. The appropriation was secured and the Board of Education was made administrator of the fund. When the Board met at Normal, March 26, 1867, and unanimously chose Powell to be the general commissoner and curator, he was prepared to make a neat little speech.

He explained that he had planned to spend the summer exploring the Rockies and that since a trip to that little-known region would greatly enhance the collections of the museum he now proposed that part of the thousand-dollar appropriation be allocated to the expedition. The Board promptly set aside five hundred dollars for field expenses.[47]

The Powell expedition was the Normal University's first venture in extensive field trips. Each member of the party, student and teacher alike, was to pay his own expenses. Five hundred dollars was only a small amount of the money needed, and Powell had to look to other sources. He went to Washington to enlist the support of his old commander, General Grant, now of the War Department. He succeeded in obtaining an order on the Commissary for rations at government rates for a party of twelve and an escort of soldiers from Fort Laramie through the Bad Lands.[48]

Meanwhile Powell, who always liked to be sure of a teaching position to fall back on, secured a two years' leave of absence from Wesleyan. He quietly negotiated with the trustees of the new Industrial University at Urbana for a professorship there and obtained an appropriation of $500 from its funds by agreeing to send that university duplicates of all natural history specimens that he collected, as well as duplicates from his own cabinet previously collected. The Chicago Academy of Science advanced $100 and tools and supplies as a token for specimens that it would receive.[49] The total that he was able to obtain from the Normal University, the University at Urbana, and the Chicago Academy amounted to $1100. Powell estimated this would be about one-half the cost of the expedition. The rest he would have to supply himself.[50]

Powell solicited free transportation for his men, equipment and specimens. His appeals were as dynamic as his lectures. Various railroads responded with passes valued at more than seventeen hundred dollars, and express companies agreed to transport parcels without charge. Expensive scientific equipment required for making topographical measurements was borrowed from the Smithsonian Institution on condition that copies of the data ob-

[47] In a burst of fervor and enthusiasm, the Board authorized the curator to have printed and displayed conspicuously in the museum the scriptural text, "The visible things of God from the creation of the world are clearly seen, being understood by the things that are made." Romans 1, 20. *Proceedings of the Board of Education* (Normal), March 26, 1867, p. 10.

[48] Darrah, *op. cit.*, p. 81.

[49] Watson, *op. cit.*, p. 84.

[50] *Proceedings of the Board of Education* (Bloomington), March 30, 1867, p. 9.

tained would be deposited later with the institution in Washington.[51]

Powell had little difficulty in obtaining personnel for his expedition to the Rockies. He was vigorous and enthusiastic. Barely turned thirty-four, he was short but well built and handsome, with his thick dark reddish hair and neatly trimmed sideburns. (Presently he would grow a beard.) President Edwards caught some of his enthusiasm and reported that the museum of the school would be greatly enriched with many and rare specimens in the various fields of natural science and "that to the Normal University will belong the credit of having been among the first to explore in the interest of science, a region supposed to be very rich in the means of guiding the thoughts of scientific men." [52]

In the main Powell's party was composed of amateur naturalists, but their listings in the report to the State Society and to the Smithsonian were imposing; four of his former Wesleyan students, Martin Titterington, S. H. Kerrick, Joseph C. Hartzell, and Francis M. Bishop were listed respectively as herpetologist, mineralogist, zoologist, and assistant zoologist. T. J. Burrill, a graduate of Normal University and principal of public schools at Urbana, was designated as botanist; A. H. Thompson, superintendent of Bloomington public schools, entomologist; Edwards Spencer, Rock Island and S. H. Huse, Evanston, ornithologists. George D. Platte of Rock Island, skillful in the new science of photography as well as with pencil and brushes, was artist for the expedition. Powell, as curator of the Illinois Natural Historical Society, was listed as geologist.[53]

Leaving Illinois late in May, Powell and his party proceeded by train to Council Bluffs, where riding animals, teams, wagons, and equipment were purchased. On the long trek westward from Omaha the party began collecting vast numbers of specimens of plants, insects, mammals, birds, reptiles, fishes, and fossils. Powell had heavy commitments in regard to duplicates. He had agreed before the General Assembly to supply collections for schools over the state and had contracted to provide the Chicago Academy, the University at Urbana, the museum at Wesleyan, and Normal University with duplicate specimens in exchange for funds.

[51] Watson, *op. cit.*, p. 82.
[52] *Proceedings of the Board of Education* (Normal), June 26, 1867, p. 4.
[53] Darrah, *op. cit.*, p. 83.

A warning from the War Department that there were hostile Indians in the Dakotas deterred Powell from visiting the Bad Lands and he headed directly for Denver taking the route along the south bank of the Platte. Without mishap the party reached Denver in July and then proceeded over the Rampart Range and through Bergen Park to Pike's Peak. The party ascended the Peak on July 27, and Emma Powell claimed the distinction of being the first woman to ascend its rugged and dizzy heights. The party next explored the headwaters of the South Platte and returned to Denver by way of Central City, where Powell spent considerable time adding to his great variety of fossils and mineral specimens.

Letters written to the *Daily Pantagraph* carried descriptions of snow-crowned mountains, vast parched prairies, great forests and tremendous boulders, rock-slides, the difficult and near tragic ascent and descent of Pike's Peak, the monotony of hardtack and cold beef, but ever the enthusiasm of the indomitable Powell and the courage and endurance of his faithful Emma.

The party disbanded in late August and all except Powell and his wife returned to Illinois. They remained in Denver to assemble, sort, and pack the collections of skeletons, skins, birds, insects, reptiles, fossils, minerals, and rocks that some months later would arrive at Normal in great boxes and barrels to clutter the halls while awaiting further classification and distribution.

In December Powell appeared before the Board and presented his report on the expedition and a detailed financial statement. Exclusive of favors rendered by the railroads, express companies, Smithsonian Institution, and the War Department, it had cost $2,138.[54]

The Board was greatly impressed with the report as well as his plans for a second expedition to the West and unanimously resolved that a sum of three hundred dollars be appropriated for the purpose of paying the actual expenses incurred by Professor Powell, curator of the museum, in making his large and valuable private collection which he had placed in the museum of the University, and that a further sum of six hundred dollars be appropriated to enable him "to resume and still further prosecute his

[54] Powell estimated the donation, transportation, cartage, and escort service at $10,000.

explorations and general field work during the coming year." It authorized him to distribute duplicates among the principal schools where he thought advisable. Meanwhile the petition of Hewett, Sewall, Metcalf, and Stetson for salary increases received but a promise for serious future consideration.[55]

Powell and four assistants hired at his own expense labeled, catalogued, arranged exhibits from the collections of the past summer's expedition. By the middle of March most of the arrangements had been completed for the second expedition, which the press entitled "The Rocky Mountain Scientific Exploring Expedition." [56] Powell was much in demand for public lectures, especially the one with the delightful alliterative title, "The Peaks, the Parks and the Plains." Both Normal and Wesleyan looked with pride on the distinguished professor who was coming to be recognized as one of the nation's outstanding natural scientists. They had no way of knowing that quietly and without the fanfare that usually accompanied Powell's comings and goings, the trustees of the Industrial University at Urbana had unanimously elected him to the Professorship of Natural History, his term to commence at such time as could be agreed upon between himself and the Committee on Faculty and the Courses of Study. Neither the appointment nor the tentative acceptance was announced because at the time Powell could not easily ask a release from Normal University when he was receiving support from the Board on his impending expedition to the Colorado.

The second expedition officially began from Chicago on June 29, when the party embarked on the Union Pacific for Cheyenne, where the individual members would be provided with horse and pack mule. Once more the public-spirited railroads and express companies provided free transportation. This time there were twenty-one in the party, five of whom were students, Samuel Garman, a sophomore from Normal University and four others from Wesleyan. Two ministers from Chicago served as historians and correspondents to keep newspapers informed of the progress of the expedition. Dr. George Vasey, prominent member of the Natural History Society, was now able to accompany the

[55] *Proceedings of the Board of Education* (Normal), December 18, 1867, p. 15.
[56] *Daily Pantagraph*, March 17, 1868.

party as botanist. The Reverend W. H. Daniels, former professor of literature at Wesleyan, and Dr. Henry Wing, ailing Board member from Collinsville, paid their own expenses as did every other member of the expedition but had no official listing.

When the Board met in early June, Powell, whose resignation at Wesleyan had been accepted only the evening before, took the members on a personally conducted tour of the museum, pointing out the vast number of specimens that had resulted from the exploration of the previous summer. The field catalog showed that they had found nine hundred birds, several hundred plants, and thousands of insects. The series of rocks, minerals, fossils, reptiles, skins and skeletons of mammals was considerably smaller. It had been a most successful expedition.[57]

Dr. Wing and President Edwards were especially enthusiastic over the work that Powell was doing. Edwards asserted that Professor Powell had given to Normal University's museum, and to the subject of natural history, as pursued at the school, a national reputation.

The Board belatedly voted that an order be drawn on the Natural History Society's fund for four hundred dollars in favor of Professor Powell to enable him to purchase "philosophical" instruments as would be needed on the exploring expedition to the Colorado River and in connection with his services as curator.

Dr. Wing accompanied the party only as far as the Rocky Mountains but his association with Vasey and Powell made him such an ardent enthusiast for the study of botany that at the meeting in December 1869, he moved that the Board "in the interest of science and education" go on record as recommending that the scientific survey of the state include botany as well as geology and entomology; and that a State Botanist should be appointed who would deposit at Normal and in the Industrial University, a complete collection of the grasses and plants of the state.[58]

Powell remained in the West during the winter following his hazardous trip down the Colorado, collecting specimens and following his interest in Indian culture. President Edwards proudly

[57] Darrah, *op. cit.*, p. 91.
[58] *Proceedings of the Board of Education* (Normal), December 16, 1868, p. 13; also Wallace Stegner, *Beyond the Hundredth Meridian* (Boston: Houghton Mifflin Company, 1954), pp. 18–30.

reported that Powell had already sent back parcels of specimens totaling over half a ton "free of expenses through the liberality of the railroads transporting them." In the lot were more than five hundred birds and two hundred fifty specimens of mammals "ranging from the little chief of the Arctic regions" to four huge grizzly bears which had been captured during the past winter by residents of the mountains. He also commented on the contributions of the explorers in their extensive meteorological observations, topographical notes, and especially Powell's own observations on the geology of the mountains and parks. All of this new and rare data had unusual scientific value.

Powell's determination to continue his explorations in the West led him to resign from the post he had never filled at the Industrial University. When the story leaked out, it was disillusioning to Normal. It was evident Powell had not intended to return to the museum. Some of his colleagues recalled the special considerations he had been shown and were annoyed at the sight of the piles of unopened boxes of specimens.

When Powell came back his reputation as a scientist had skyrocketed, but after the first excited greetings by former students and faculty friends, he found he had lost considerable popularity. He was greatly in demand for lectures and he turned from the unfinished business of mounting, collating, and distributing specimens to more exciting matters of describing his adventures and the wild and little-known country that he had explored.[59]

Powell was not satisfied with the accomplishments of the 1869 trip. Parts of the notes taken were lost, some of the collection had to be cached and left behind, and many points of interest had to be passed by in the closing weeks of the expedition. The Major now planned a second canyon expedition to supplement the first. This one would probably cover two years. As in the past he would hire assistants to do work in the museum from time to time, to unpack the specimens as they were sent back, and to show the exhibits to visitors and classes. He began the rounds of getting financial assistance. None was forthcoming from the Industrial University, but he was confident of at least $1,500 of the General

[59] Powell had numerous speaking engagements throughout the fall and winter of 1869–1870. Among them were Detroit, Cincinnati, Wheaton, Chicago, Hennepin, and Bloomington.

Assembly's appropriation of $2,500 annually for the curator and maintenance of the museum, and the rest he would try to secure from the Federal Government and the railroads.

Through the efforts of Powell and friends of the Natural History Society the museum on the third floor was literally bursting at the seams. The collections were valued at $95,000. The botany collection, which numbered 100,000 specimens, was alone valued at $25,000; 15,000 fossils were valued at $20,000; and 15,000 shells were listed as worth $15,000. There were a thousand books in the library cases of the museum.[60] It was impossible to display the collections properly. There was no way for the museum to expand. Halls and passageways of the building were already being used for classrooms. Professor Agassiz, Dr. Sewall's old friend and teacher from Harvard, had examined the collections with much satisfaction but had remarked that "fire should not have so great a temptation." In December 1870 a special committee appointed to inquire into the expediency of erecting a suitable fireproof building to house the collections of the museum, reported that a fireproof building was imperative. Many valuable contributions to the museum were being withheld because the donors did not wish to place their valuable collections where the fire hazard was so great.

The committee recommended a two-story fireproof building 50 by 70 feet with a basement which would provide space for a workshop, furnace room, and three storerooms. A plan worked out by Powell, Vasey, A. H. Thompson, and Sewall, had been submitted to architect and preliminary drawings made. On the first floor there would be halls for botany, zoology, and library, and on the second floor, laboratories for geology, ethnology. The floors were to be of masonry supported by iron girders, the roof of iron and slate, and the stairways and shelves of iron. It was estimated that such a building could be built for $60,000 and fully equipped for an additional $15,000.

The Assembly was reluctant to appropriate money to house collections which the state did not own, and further question arose as to whether the state was justified in making an appropriation to assist the Natural History Society in carrying out its program

[60] *Proceedings of the Board of Education* (Normal), December 6, 1870, p. 6.

unless title in the collections was transferred to the state.[61]

The Appropriation Act which passed April 1871 was subject to the condition "that the collections, cases, and equipment of the Natural History Society, then in the museum, should be made over to the state in such a way as should be satisfactory to the governor." The transfer was effected June 22, 1871, and the Board of Education now acted as agent of the State rather than the Society.[62]

It became clear both to the Society and to the Normal University that Powell, the dynamic teacher and intrepid explorer, had no intention of returning to the laborious and unexciting job of collating specimens and arranging exhibits. It had been a steppingstone to fame, but now a wider horizon was being glimpsed. On June 28, 1872, Powell resigned, and Stephen A. Forbes was appointed curator. An inventory of the museum gave a total of 24,230 specimens, with 3,000 different species of plants, 1,200 species of fossils, and 26 species of mammals.[63]

On the first of June Powell had purchased a house at 910 M Street, Washington, D. C. He now prepared to dispose of his holdings in Normal, and packed his collections and personal effects to ship to Washington. Members of the Board who had grown tired of the sight of halls cluttered with great wooden boxes, now became apprehensive about the ownership of materials in the museum. It was well known that Powell had been a collector for years before he came to Normal and had placed some of his own materials in the museum. A question also arose about the propriety of Powell taking any of the specimens obtained on his western expeditions while in the employ of the Natural History Society, for whom the Board of Education acted as agent.

Jesse Fell, Enoch Gastman, and C. F. Noetling were appointed to "instruct the curator of the museum to prevent all persons

[61] The act chartering the Natural History Society in 1867 provided that the state's appropriation was to be expended under the Board of Education, and under its direction the curator was to be appointed.
[62] During the year 1872 Dr. George Vasey who had accompanied Powell on his first trip down the Colorado served as acting curator and added to the museum from his own herbarium several hundred items of botanical specimens, grasses, and plants indigenous to Illinois. He also sent specimens of fossils, minerals, wood, plants, shells, and geological items to twelve of the principal schools of the state. Cook and McHugh, *op. cit.,* pp. 237–238.
[63] *Ibid.,* p. 239.

from removing any of the contents of the museum except on order of the committee." All questions of doubt about legality and propriety of removal were to be referred to Fell.[64]

The fact that only a single sentence in President Edwards' Decennial Address, delivered the following day at the Commencement, referred to Powell and his work indicates he had lost favor with the administration. The new curator in his semiannual report six months later stated that, although he found much work to be done, a very good beginning had been made, and he thought it "proper to say that Drs. Sewall and Vasey have left behind them unmistakable evidences of conscientious and thorough work." He too avoided reference to Powell.

Meanwhile the Major, with his thoughts on greener pastures, dispatched great boxes of collections to the Smithsonian and his new home in Washington, paying little heed to communications from Jesse Fell in behalf of the "Committee Upon Lost Property of the Museum."

After Forbes reported the wide gaps in the exhibits in ornithology, entomology, mammals, reptiles, and fishes, the Board authorized Fell to correspond with Professor Joseph Henry of the Smithsonian and to assert the right of the Board to the Relics of the Ute Indians sent from the museum to the Smithsonian Institution.[65] Fell's request that all of Powell's materials be returned to Illinois was ignored and the claim later disallowed on grounds that Powell was in federal employ.[66] Later Powell, on his own initiative, returned specimens of Indian arts to replace those sent from the Normal museum to the Smithsonian.

In 1872 the museum took on new significance when four new sciences were introduced in the common school course in which knowledge was required for certification. Few teachers were truly qualified to teach the new courses. The museum promptly sent out circulars listing its facilities and suggesting a program of mutual exchanges. Cabinets of duplicate specimens were arranged and sent to schools where there was greatest need. A vacation school of natural history was conducted in the museum in July and August 1875. Visiting professors from Cornell and from the

---

[64] *Proceedings of the Board of Education* (Normal), June 26, 1872, p. 4.
[65] *Proceedings of the Board of Education* (Normal), December 3, 1872, pp. 13–17.
[66] Darrah, *op. cit.*, p. 186.

Illinois Industrial University as well as the state entomologist aided Dr. Sewall and Curator Forbes. So outstanding was their work that the Board concluded to send an exhibit of natural history as pursued in Illinois schools to the Centennial Exposition in Philadelphia.[67]

In addressing the graduating class in 1872, President Edwards took occasion to review the fifteen years of the school's existence. Of the thirteen classes that had graduated he had supervised all but two. Of the faculty when Edwards came in 1862, only Dr. Sewall and Professor Hewett remained although two of his first appointments, Dr. Metcalf and Professor Stetson, were still on the staff, vigorously carrying on the work of the school in the Bridgewater tradition. Admissions to the student body to 1870 had averaged $174\frac{1}{4}$ per year, but for the two years past it had averaged $266\frac{2}{3}$ pupils. The total number of admissions to the normal school was 2617 and to the Model School 2626. Two hundred had remained to take diplomas from the normal department and seventeen from the high school.

Edwards dwelt upon the Model School, its service to teacher training and to the community. From the time that the school moved to the new building in 1860 until 1868 the Model School was the only school in the village of Normal.[68] By 1863 the Model School, with its 170 pupils, occupied six large rooms of the first floor of the building. Four years later it enrolled 580 children. The income from the Model School was $5,000 a year. All children of school age in District 2 attended the Model School, which until 1866 was under the supervision of the principal of the high school. A separate grammar department was organized in 1866. The population of the village and the number of children increased so that the rooms at the University became inadequate, and a schoolhouse on the corner of Ash and School Streets was built by the district. In April 1867 the grammar and intermediate grades were moved to the new building.

[67] A second vacation school of natural history was held at the University laboratory in the summer of 1878. Both were attended by Ange. Milner, later librarian, 1890–1929. Cook and McHugh, *op. cit.,* p. 240.

[68] The first public school in the district of Normal was taught by Miss Mary Shannon in a small building erected by John Rees as a shop for the workmen while constructing Jesse Fell's residence, Greenwood. It closed in 1856 after six month's term. In 1859 a private school was maintained in the library of the Fell home. Owenetta Mildred Edwards, "Early Schools and Teachers in McLean County."

For seven years school moneys of the district had been turned over to the State Board of Education, and the University in turn had provided buildings and teachers. Objection to such an economic windfall to a community was bound to come, but the criticism against the arrangement was touched off in an unexpected manner. President Edwards saw no objection to educational opportunities for Negroes in the normal departments and had boldly stated his opinions. The test came in 1867 when a Negro child was admitted to the Model School. The storm was brief but fierce. The Chicago *Republican,* May 11, 1867, reported:

The other morning a little girl of color was found sitting in her right mind in the Model School waiting to have her idea taught to shoot. The world didn't hear of the circumstance or it would immediately have come to an end; but the one and a half Democrats of the place had a regular conniption . . . However Topsy stuck to her seat. The teachers taught her; the president treated her as he thought the Saviour would have treated her if she had come to Him to be taught. All is now quiet at Normal.[69]

However the incident rankled and President Edwards asked for a directive from the Board relative to receiving pupils in the district. Judge Green, W. H. Wells, and Jesse Fell were named to draw up a policy report. A majority report submitted by Green and Wells favored separating the schools, whereupon the Board agreed that the president of the University, with the advice and consent of the president of the Board, might make any arrangements with the Board of Education for the city of Normal that might be mutually advantageous, but that no contract should be for more than one year at a time.[70]

In December the Board voted to terminate the existing connections between the District School of the village of Normal, at the close of the scholastic year.[71] In February 1868 the Chicago *Times* took a blast at the school.

Here is an institution supported at great expense by the taxpayers of Illinois, and run in the interest of nigger-radicals, and radical niggers. Our hope is that if ever white people have a voice in controlling the affairs of Illinois again, they will blot out of existence this, and all similar

[69] Quoted, Harper, *Development of the Teachers College,* p. 111.
[70] *Proceedings of the Board of Education* (Normal), June 27, 1867, pp. 10–11.
[71] *Ibid.,* December 16, 1867.

institutions, that are carried on for the benefit of the radical party and niggers, at the expense of the people. They are of no benefit, save only as miscegenation and money-squandering establishments.[72]

The Model School continued to serve pupils from outside the district, from faculty families, and from those Normal and Bloomington homes where the parents preferred to pay tuition in order that their children might receive their training at the Normal University. Not until 1901 was tuition discontinued.[73] The Model School had always been more than self-sustaining; in fact the surplus from the Model School went a long way toward paying salaries of the professors in the Normal Department, which was largely dependent upon the $12,445 income from the Seminary Fund. It now became evident that if the Normal University were to continue properly its work for teacher education, the Legislature would have to consider substantial biennial appropriations.

The matter of Negroes attending the Normal University would come up again. President Edwards had his private opinion, but he tactfully referred the matter to the Board in December 1871: "Applications have been made by a number of colored persons for admission to the University. I respectfully ask that some order may be taken on this subject by which I may hereafter be guided." In a report signed by Newton Bateman and Enoch Gastman, the Committee on Teachers enunciated what has ever since been one of the guiding principles of the Normal University relative to admissions.

In our opinion, neither the Board nor the Faculty of the University has any right to recognize distinctions of race or color in determining who shall or who shall not be admitted to the several departments of the University, the equal rights of all the youth of the state to participate in the benefits of our system of public education, of which the Normal University is a part, being, as we think, fully established and guaranteed by the organic laws of the state.[74]

These sentiments were quite in accord with Edwards' own

[72] Chicago *Times,* February 22, 1868. Quoted, Harper, *Development of the Teachers College,* pp. 111.
[73] John W. Keith, "Development of the Model School," *Semi-Centennial History of the Illinois State Normal University,* p. 80.
[74] *Proceedings of the Board of Education* (Normal), December 5, 1871, p. 4.

principles. Years later Manfred Holmes, a professor of education at Normal University, wrote that he believed Edwards' championship of the colored pupil seeking an education after the Civil War was a handicap to him with certain educators in Indiana and Illinois. Some students left school when colored pupils were admitted.[75]

Richard Edwards always had high standards for teachers. He wanted a graduate of the Normal University to have a well-rounded education as well as training in method. He himself had not been satisfied with his Bridgewater training in subject matter and had gone on to Rensselaer. Likewise Stetson had gone to Harvard after Antioch and Bridgewater. It worried Edwards that the large percentage of persons who applied at the Normal University had little more than eighth grade schooling and consequently he had considered the high school and liberal arts subjects in the normal department as essential to developing better teachers.

Not all members of the Board agreed with Edwards' educational ideas. In his fourteen years as president, Edwards weathered many a storm. Eight times there was a threat that the school would have to change its policies or close. Notable was an attack made on the curriculum and organization of the school in June 1868. Benaiah G. Roots, Board Member from Tamaroa, recommended that the standards for qualifications for admission to the Normal University be "materially elevated" and that two types of diplomas be awarded to those who desired them, one when the applicants were qualified to organize and teach primary or common district schools and another for those qualified to become principals of grammar and high schools. He further proposed that the policy of the University be modified to enable persons qualified in all respects except in the Theory and Art of Teaching, to pursue such a course and be graduated as soon as they have completed it.

The Board delayed action and asked Roots to prepare a written report to be presented at a subsequent meeting. Roots maintained that there were now schools in every county in which pupils could acquire all the knowledge necessary to entitle them to a first grade certificate, "except for a theoretical and practical

[75] Manfred Holmes' personal notes (n.d.) *Holmes Papers,* Milner Library.

acquaintance with the complicated and responsible duties of the professional teacher." Consequently he recommended that high school and high school subjects be eliminated from the curriculum of the Normal University, that it cease to be a rival or competitor of the high schools, academies and colleges of the state, and that it operate within the province originally created for it—a professional school for teachers. He would shorten, rather than lengthen, the period spent in the professional school— the wider knowledge of subject matter which he so strongly advocated would be secured elsewhere. The resolutions that he proposed were tactfully tabled for further consideration.

From other quarters came the question, "Do students who go to Normal really teach?" Edwards marshaled his statistics. He sent out letters of inquiry to county superintendents and others of the 2084 young persons who had attended Normal University prior to September 1869, 145 of whom had graduated. Replies revealed that only twenty-nine of the graduates or seven percent were not teaching. Even thirteen of these who were now married had taught one year; six were deceased. Of the graduates Edwards found that only ten had abandoned the profession, and none without having first taught several years. He warned the Board that

Periodically it is asserted normal schools are a failure. Like discoverers of perpetual motion, these inventors of disaster reproduce the old complaints with the regularity of the decades. It matters not that they have been refuted. In each new reiteration, they find a new champion and each effort requires a new hand.

In June 1870 Edwards was proud to report that a cultured English traveler wrote in the *London Christian World* of his visit to the school:

I had the privilege lately to participate in the annual examinations and exercises of the commencement of this noble institution and can testify that it is conducted with the most honorable and happy results. The proficiency of the graduates who received their diplomas amidst the loving greetings of hundreds of fellow students and a large assembly of friends, together with the enthusiasm of all present in the noble cause of Christian Culture, afforded inspiring hope for the future of the community.[76]

[76] Quoted, Richard Edwards, "Report to the State Superintendent," *Seventh Biennial Report of the Superintendent of Public Instruction*, p. 86.

By 1873 Normal University led the nation's normal schools in enrollment and expenditures. It was eighteenth in per capita cost. Ypsilanti, Michigan, was second with an enrollment of 250 and Buffalo, New York, was third.[77] The superintendent of Boston schools in 1870 had declared the Normal University inferior to none.

As in other schools of the period the literary societies were the strongest student organizations. Every student who attended Normal became by lot either a Wrightonian or a Philadelphian.[78] Only by careful conniving in registration lines over the years, was it possible for several members of a family to belong to the same society.

The societies obtained charters from the Legislature in 1867 and, as corporate bodies, they could now borrow money, own property, sue and be sued; in the course of time each experienced the frustrations of debts and litigation. Rivalry between the two societies led to contests not only in programs but in furnishing their respective halls with expensive carpets, draperies, bookcases, books, pictures, chairs, plaster copies of Greek and Roman busts, secretary's tables and elaborate frescoing. Philadelphia boasted a red and white Brussels carpet and Wrightonia a floral. Philadelphia bought opera chairs and Wrightonia, captains' chairs. From tallow candles the societies progressed to wall lamps and elegant kerosene chandeliers. Both societies purchased grand pianos in 1864. Wrightonia chose a beautiful rosewood piano.

Heating and plumbing facilities for the large building were inadequate, and the rooms on the third floor were often so cold that meetings had to be disbanded. The societies at their own expense experimented with temperamental ventilating stoves and loyal volunteers carried kindling and buckets of coal up the three long flights of stairs. As the societies became more affluent, janitor service was hired, with the fees advancing from eighteen cents a week to a dollar and a quarter.

To pay for their luxurious furnishings, they collected dues, made pledges to be redeemed after a year's teaching, gave plays, sponsored lectures, union suppers and strawberry socials, and held

[77] Charles A. Harper, "A Century of Teacher Training." *Daily Pantagraph*, April 2, 1939.
[78] *Weekly Pantagraph*, June 27, 1864.

festivals. The proceeds from all sorts of gambling devices such as grab-bags, ring cakes, and fish ponds were divided equally. Honorary memberships were conferred upon prominent persons who were actively interested in the University, and who usually contributed from one dollar to ten or twenty dollars. During the Civil War Wrightonia voted to make Abraham Lincoln an honorary member.

The women students were quite as loyal to their respective societies as the men. They were faithful in attendance and in writing essays, in delivering dramatic recitations with gestures and costumes as occasion demanded; they played the piano, sang in the choruses, and edited the Philadelphian *Ladies Garland* and the Wrightonian *Oleastellus*. They prepared deviled eggs, ham sandwiches, potato salad, layer cake, and lemonade for picnics and spreads, but in the early decades debating and holding office above the rank and glamour of secretary taking copious notes and writing up "minutes," was regarded as the sacred province of the stronger sex.

When Susan B. Anthony, Lucy Stone, and Elizabeth Cady were campaigning across the nation for women's rights, it was inevitable that there should be echoes and repercussions on college campuses. In 1870 after a hard fight Alice Emmons, daughter of an Illinois judge, and a senior who had already had some teaching experience, was elected president of the Philadelphian Society. There was evidence of wounded pride with the election of a woman to this exalted position and there was mumbling about "collusion." A committee was appointed to canvass the election, with the result that Miss Emmons was unseated and R. Arthur Edwards, son of President Edwards, chosen to fill the vacancy.[79] The women labored not alone for Alice's election but for a noble cause. Subsequently Louise C. Allen, a member of the same class, was elected president of Wrightonia.[80]

Since the first commencement in 1860, an original essay or oration had been presented by each member of the graduating class. Under the benign influence of the Natural History Society, Dr. Henry Wing proposed and the Board enthusiastically concurred

[79] Cook and McHugh, *op. cit.,* p. 106.
[80] *Ibid.,* p. 129.

that henceforth, two months before his contemplated graduation, each candidate should present a paper "discussing either the geology, botany, or some department of the Natural History of the district in which he or she resided." While the archives accumulated theses on oaks, pines, elms, common locust, osage orange, mosses, the topography of various counties, frogs and varieties of maples, the graduation programs carried titles of essays and orations such as "Our Legacy from the Past," "Intellectual Independence," "Common Sense," "The Power of Example," "Pathfinders," "Man the Master of His Own Destiny," and "The Influence of Imagination upon Character." Salutatorians and valedictorians were appointed on the basis of scholarship, but when the classes were very large the other speakers were drawn by lot. The honor of being a commencement speaker was coveted by every serious student.

Commencements became precious memories and diplomas prized possessions. Since so many students did not complete the three-year curriculum the Board began in 1869 to award diplomas to those who had finished the first two years. The diploma certified that the possessor had the respect and confidence of the faculty and had completed a two-year study in the subjects of "Arithmetic, Geography of North and South America and Europe, History of the United States and Ancient History, Spelling, Phonic Analysis, Reading, English Grammar, Theory and Art of Teaching, Mental Philosophy, Rhetoric, English Criticism, Algebra, Geometry, Trigonometry, Drawing, Chemistry, Botany, Physical Geography," had had two terms in practice teaching and "is accordingly recommended as a teacher." Space was provided for signatures of the President of the University, the President and the Secretary of the Board of Education, and ten teachers.

In 1870 Richard Edwards took his first real vacation. For eight years he had labored at the Normal University as a teacher and administrator. He had lectured throughout Illinois and traveled as far as Rhode Island and Kansas to conduct institutes and make educational addresses. He had launched a successful campaign for a second normal school at Carbondale. He had also written textbooks, preached, and, with Jesse Fell, speculated in Iowa, Nebraska, and Missouri lands. Both Edwards and the University had prospered.[81] His reward to himself was a trip to his beloved Wales, with excursions into England and Scotland, and across the Channel to Belgium and France.[82]

His wife and their ten children ranging in age from twenty years to one week would remain in Normal.[83] The children had been trained to take responsibility about the home, and he felt no apprehension about leaving them. Arthur, the eldest son, who was attending the Institute that summer, was entrusted with looking after his father's correspondence at the University and mailing the catalogs as soon as they came from the printer. Betsey promised to keep her husband informed of local happenings, births, illnesses, and deaths, the Institute, the repairs being made at the University, and the well-being of the family, especially "the youngest juvenile" as she called the baby. In turn Edwards would keep a diary and write long letters home describing the historic places that he visited, the amusing and interesting people that he met, educational conditions, and every member of the family would receive a present upon his return. Aside from the estate which turned out to be non-existent, Edwards' vacation abroad was all that he wished it to be. His outlook was broadened and enriched, and he was able to plunge into his work with renewed vigor.

He scarcely recognized the campus. During his absence the grounds had been given some overdue improvements, the fence had been repaired, some new trees had been planted, and the building painted cream color.[84]

[81] Edwards collaborated with Russell Webb in publishing the *Analytical Series of Readers* (Chicago: George Sherwood and Company, 1866) (New York: Taintor and Company, 1866). There were six books in the series. Between 1867 and 1875 they had an annual sale of 80,000 copies. They were revised in 1880 and for years continued in demand. The illustrations were by Thomas Nast. The *Analytical Speller* (Chicago: George Sherwood and Company, 1867) was quite as popular in its field. Loomis, *op. cit.*, pp. 97–113. Edwards noted in his *Diary* April 3, 1876 the valuation of his holdings in Normal, in Chicago, and in Iowa, Missouri, and California "at low figures" to be $30,157.

[82] The upshot of Edwards going abroad at this particular time was that a relative in Wales reputed to be quite wealthy had died and he was concerned about the Edwards' interest in the estate.

[83] The Edwards children: Annie Marie (born 1850); Richard Arthur (1851); Ellen Samson (1853); Mary Caroline (1855); George Herbert (1860); Walter Allison (1862); Ralph Allen (1865, died 1869); Owen Meredith and Florence Mildred, twins (1868); and Frederick Newton (1870). *Edwards MS.*

[84] Betsey Edwards to Richard Edwards, August 21, 1870. "The University has donned a new dress, cream color. I do not like it, perhaps the more fastidious ones will." *Edwards MS.*

Edwards' reputation as an educator was becoming known throughout the world, and through his lectures, and the graduates he trained, Normal University gained stature. Edwards frequently spoke before joint meetings of the Normal School Association and the National Teachers Association, in which he held advisory offices. He was president of the National Teachers Association, 1863–1864. The subject of his presidential address was "One or More Normal Schools Should be Established at Public Expense in Each State." He was asked to repeat it before the same organization in 1865. He worked on the joint committee of the National Teachers Association and the National Association of Superintendents to secure a Federal Bureau of Education. He was present at thirteen of the first sixteen meetings of the National Education Association and had a paper read at another. He invited the Association to hold its annual meeting in 1870 in Normal but it selected Cleveland instead.[85]

In December following Edwards' return from Europe, he spoke before the Illinois State Teachers Association on "Educational Fallacies." In 1871 he gave two addresses before the National Education Association meeting in St. Louis: "The Model School in Connection with Normal Schools," and "How Much Culture Shall Be Imparted in Our Free Schools." He declined an invitation to go to Japan and organize its school system.[86]

When the Kalamazoo case was arousing considerable opinion on public tax-supported high schools in 1872, Edwards spoke boldly. Taxpayers, he pointed out to the Illinois State Teachers Association were not playing the role of benefactors or giving charity when moneys were appropriated for high school construction. The high school and university as well as common school tend to increase wealth, decrease crime, and build better citizens. "Ignorance," he asserted, "was responsible for ninety percent of the crimes committed. It was not the business of the school to furnish students with opinions but to develop their powers so they may form just opinions of their own." In a noble peroration he declared:

No limit should be set beyond which the state shall not go in educating

[85] Loomis, *op. cit.*, pp. 114–126.
[86] *Ibid.*, p. 186.

its children. Whatever there is of value in the charms of literature, in the writings of history, in the revelations of science, or in the beauty of art should be offered freely to the millions who are coming upon the stage.

Let us cling to our noble system of free education. It is the birthright of the American people, it is in keeping with our political freedom. Let it be as free as the sunshine and rain.[87]

Withal his professional demands, Edwards took an active interest in community affairs. He was a faithful member of the Presbyterian Church, a member of a literary club, and a patron of the Bloomington Library Association. He played the role of Shylock in a benefit performance of the Merchant of Venice in the new Durley Hall, December 12, 13, 1872.[88]

Edwards reorganized the training school in 1873 following some recommendations of the Board. Thomas Metcalf of the careful diction and refined manner was promoted to the position of training teacher. Edwards was granted a leave in order to visit other schools, and upon his return in order that he might give more time to classroom supervision and general affairs about the University, he was empowered to hire a bookkeeper whose services were not to exceed three hundred dollars a year. Until 1874 th president of the University had served in the capacity of bookkeeper, purchasing agent, public relations officer, registrar and recorder of grades as well as teacher and supervisor. It is understandable that Richard Edwards complained to his wife that the work was growing heavier and heavier each year. Sometimes he wondered if he should go on teaching. In January 1875 he declined the chancellorship of the University of Nebraska.[89]

The legislative session of 1873 was especially trying. When the appropriation bill for the Normal University was introduced, the opposition asserted that normal students did not teach, that the faculty was radical, and that the institution was a home for broken-down New Englanders. In 1875 the fight was even more bitter. The Chicago *Times,* which had opposed the use of the Edwards Readers and posed as a champion in exposing frauds in

[87] Proceedings of the National Educational Association 1873, p. 58.
[88] *McLean County Historical Transactions* II, 253.
[89] *Proceedings of the Board of Education* (Normal), December 10, 1873, p. 10; Richard Edwards to his wife, Princeton, Illinois, January 5, 1875.

education, came forth in a blasting editorial. The *Times* alleged that tax-supported schools had been so long protected that great abuses had grown up within the system, that the Normal University, being farthest from public scrutiny, was the worst offender, and that in its seclusion the energy and talent of those in charge at Normal had been employed in devising new methods to create a demand for new appliances, textbooks, charts, and similar teaching devices invented by its president.[90] In a sarcastic vein a legislator introduced a bill to abolish the normal schools at Normal and Carbondale, and to convert one into a refuge for the hopelessly mentally ill and the other into a home for feebleminded children. Another legislator quite as contemptuously proposed closing the school and giving the building back to McLean County.

The Normal University was prepared not only to defend itself but to launch an aggressive campaign. So effectively did Edwards and Bateman and friends of the University refute the charges made against it that never again was such a direct attack made upon it in the Legislature.[91]

After 1874 Edwards' rugged constitution began to show signs of strain. Like so many of the early normal schoolmen he was deeply religious. He began accepting speaking engagements in churches as a service that might be expected of a normal school president. After he was ordained in 1873 as a minister, there was seldom a Sunday when he was not "supplying" a pulpit. The late night hours preparing sermons, traveling great distances, arriving home and going to work without sleep, along with a variety of poorly cooked food, began to tell upon him. He loved to preach, and Illinois had need for good preaching. He talked the matter over with Betsey, who generally deferred to his judgment, especially when it involved greater protection for his health.

On December 15, 1876 Edwards presented his resignation to become effective on the first of January. The Board had not anticipated his action and asked him to reconsider. Already Edwards had thought the matter over long and prayerfully. He attributed the disturbed condition of his nervous system not so much to the

[90] Quoted, Harper, *Development of the Teachers College,* pp. 94-95.
[91] *Tenth Biennial Report of the Superintendent of Public Instruction, 1873-1874,* pp. 130-133; Richard Edwards to his wife, Princeton, Illinois, January 5, 1875.

intellectual work he was performing as to the responsibility it involved. A pastorate would afford more needed rest.

Four churches quickly called him: one at Winona in Minnesota, and others at Bloomington, Galesburg, and Princeton, in Illinois. He accepted the invitation of Owen Lovejoy's old church, the Congregational in Princeton. When his eyesight failed nine years later, he became financial agent for Knox College. He had refused to be a candidate for Congress, but in 1886 he was elected State Superintendent of Public Instruction. During his administration Illinois' forward-looking compulsory education laws were enacted. After being defeated for reelection, he served for a year as president of Blackburn College.

Bloomington-Normal was ever dear to Richard Edwards, and there he chose to retire. He often reminisced of the fourteen years he had been president of Normal University. Together he and Betsey laughed over amusing things that had happened in the days when he felt he had to keep a straight face and maintain stern decorum. He followed the progress of the students he had taught: Lyman Kellogg, who organized the first Kansas State Normal School at Emporia; Charles DeGarmo, who became president of Swarthmore; John Cook, who became president of Normal University and later president of the normal school at De Kalb; Lida Brown McMurry, and scores of others who rose to distinguished positions. He lived to see eighty books written by twenty-nine of his students. From his home on North Park Street in Bloomington, he was in easy sight of the great silver dome atop the white clock tower. On pleasant days he often wandered out to visit with his old friends, John Cook, Henry McCormick, Ange. Milner, and Clarissa Ela, and to talk with those young professors, Orson Manchester, David Felmley, and June Rose Colby. His interest in the literary societies and public speaking led to the establishing of an annual contest in oratory and poetry reading. For many years he personally awarded the gold medals to the winners. Only a week before his death, March 7, 1908, he addressed the student body.[92]

The imprint of Richard Edwards upon Normal University was deep, rich, and enduring.

---

[92] Since the death of Richard Edwards, members of his family have continued to provide medals for the winners of the annual Edwards Medal Contests.

CHAPTER VII

The Era of Transition

WHEN RICHARD EDWARDS refused to reconsider his resignation, the Board of Education turned to Professor Edwin C. Hewett, who had been a member of the staff since 1858. Too short of stature to qualify for military service, he had watched Joseph Howell and Ira Moore go away to war, and later Charles Hovey and the Normal Rifles, while he remained to serve his country in the classroom. He had been Perkins Bass's righthand man the year he had managed the affairs of the school, and Richard Edwards had taken lodging in his home when he came to Normal University in the spring of 1862.

Often they had recalled their association at Bridgewater. Hewett had been a student, and Edwards, assistant to the ailing Tillinghast. They had much in common—friendships, training, ideals, goals. Now after fourteen years Edwin Hewett was taking over Edwards' position as president.

Hewett was well-liked by the students, faculty, and townspeople. He neither courted popularity nor shrank from it. Barely five feet two inches in height and never weighing more than 120 pounds, he was not prepossessing in appearance, but he was good-natured, industrious, patient, and devoted to truth. He was fearless, willing to part company with the world and go his way alone when he believed the world was wrong and he was right.[1]

Edwin Crawford Hewett was born in Worcester County, Massachusetts, November 1, 1828, the son of Timothy and Levina Leonard Hewett. The father was a farmer, wheelwright, and plowmaker. Theirs was a thrifty, frugal, liberty-loving, God-fearing household, but it afforded little means for education. At thirteen Edwin Hewett was sent to learn the shoe-maker's trade but he longed to go to school. He managed to finish the grammar

[1] Cook, "History of the Faculty," *Semi-Centennial History of the Illinois State Normal University*, pp. 95–99.

school and later attended the local academy. At twenty-one he began teaching at thirteen dollars a month. Not content with either his salary or his meager training he entered Bridgewater in March 1851. He was there only one year, but he brought to his studies a mature, eager, and receptive mind. The rigid methods and strong character of Nicholas Tillinghast greatly appealed to the Puritan-trained youth. He was inspired by Richard Edwards' zeal for popular education. After a year as assistant in the high school at Pittsfield, Massachusetts, he was made a member of the Bridgewater staff, where he remained for four years. Meanwhile he had become engaged to Angeline N. Benton of Franklin County, Massachusetts, whose family had moved to Sublette, Illinois. The offer of a more liberal salary in a grammar school in Worcester enabled him to journey to Illinois, where he was married to Miss Benton in August 1857.

Charles Hovey, who was then organizing the staff for the new Normal University, heard of Hewett, possibly through Ira Moore, whom he had just employed as his assistant. Hovey was impressed and a year later after a short correspondence he invited Hewett to join the faculty as teacher of geography and history at a salary of $1,200 a year.[2]

Hewett liked what he had seen of Illinois the year before: the soil was rich, the school was new, and it was withal the land of opportunity. His wife longed to be near her family, and doubtless the salary would be increased as the school prospered and he proved satisfactory. After all, ten years before he had been teaching for thirteen dollars a month and he was not employed a full year.

When the Hewetts first came to Bloomington, they had taken rooms on Main Street but after classes were moved to the campus they built a house at 202 West Ash Street. The house was larger than was needed by Hewett, his wife, and the little daughter May, who was born in 1860, but Hovey had advised that he build a larger house and rent rooms to students "as an investment as well as a service to the school."

In 1858 Bloomington had a population of 7,000 and not a foot of paved streets and only a few brick or board sidewalks. Hewett

[2] C. E. Hovey to E. C. Hewett. Bloomington August 26, 1868. *Reeder-Hewett Papers.*

was not impressed with Major's Hall and its coal stoves belching forth noxious yellow smoke. The fall and winter were very rainy and, as he said years later, he had had "an impressive introduction" to Illinois mud. It tracked into the schoolroom, where it dried and was set afloat by the sweeper's brooms to settle on books and furniture. He often related how he walked out to the Junction on the first Saturday he was in Bloomington, to see how the building was coming along. The campus was only a cornfield with plenty of cornstalks but not a tree or shrub upon it. The basement was nearly finished but work was at a standstill. He remembered the first commencement in the incompleted structure in 1860, and the ill fortune that had plagued the building in these early years. The great dome when barely finished was struck by lightning, two rafters were torn out, the covering badly damaged, and one of the posts which supported the dome reduced to splinters.[3] Another time in the spring of 1876, when the roof was being repaired, a severe rain storm damaged so badly the Steinway Grand piano in the hall on the third floor that it had to be sent to New York to be renovated. The plumbing and the heating of the building were unsatisfactory, and although the lead water tanks in the attic with minor repairs lasted for fifty years, the great weight inadequately supported took heavy toll of the structure.

But in spite of misfortune and delays, in eighteen years Hewett had seen the campus transformed into a beautiful park with the finest collection of tree specimens in the West. The cow belonging to Peter Kettleson, the janitor, was still grazing on the plot northeast of the building, but before very long the janitor's quarters would be moved out of the basement and the pasture used as a playground. The shrubs and trees were now a veritable haven for birds and squirrels. Migratory birds paused, and their chatter and song inspired some of Hewett's finest poems.

Hewett had been hired to teach geography and history but over the years he had also taught classes in mathematics, literature, pedagogy, spelling, and psychology. He was thorough and exacting after the manner of Tillinghast and Edwards. In the year before Hewett came little attention had been paid to anything

[3] *Weekly Pantagraph*, July 4, 1860.

approaching a definite method of instruction in geography. He placed emphasis on definitions and map-making. No student was qualified to pass the course in geography unless he could go to the blackboard and draw freehand, to approximate scale, any of the five continents, and locate countries, states, important cities, peninsulas, mountains, and rivers. When Robert Bower of LaSalle protested that he could not draw a straight line, much less a map, Hewett was not impressed. The map was an assignment and Bower manfully shouldered his burden, became the best map-drawer in the class and eventually progressed to be head of the map publishing division of Rand, McNally and Company.[4] Students complained among themselves over his assignments, saying they were developing literal curvature of the spine from carrying around Lippincott's *Universal Gazetteer,* the chief textbook in geography.[5]

Hewett read widely. In the subjects of astronomy, science, literature, psychology, philosophy and the Scriptures he was largely self-educated. He bought good books, borrowed good books, read them and pondered over them. He delighted in discussing the ideas of other men. If Bridgewater had not provided him with a complete classical education, it had sharpened his curiosity, taught him how to think and provided him with the tools that were to make him a careful and discerning scholar.

Edwards had appreciated having on his staff men of the calibre of Hewett, Stetson, Sewall, and Metcalf and students such as Henry McCormick, Charles DeGarmo, and John Cook. He advanced them as he could and recommended them as speakers for institutes and teachers' associations. He encouraged them to attend the state and national association meetings, introduced them to his friends and used his influence to have them put on programs. They helped, he said, "put Normal University on the map." The year that Harvard conferred the Master of Arts degree on Edwards, the University of Chicago took cognizance of Hewett and awarded him a similar honorary degree, although perhaps at the time a degree from Chicago was regarded as less significant. In 1864 the *Daily Pantagraph* took note of Hewett's work. After he

[4] *Semi-Centennial History of Illinois State Normal University,* p. 201.
[5] McCormick, "Historical Sketch," *Index,* 1907, p. 29.

had conducted a week's institute for the teachers of Macoupin County, a letter signed "Traveler" praised him for a lecture he had given one evening to a full house of townspeople and teachers. "The state can not overestimate the services of such men as Mr. Hewett," the anonymous correspondent wrote, "He is quiet and unpretending but he makes himself friends wherever he goes. He is not a giant in stature but when he places his shoulder to the educational wheel, all the interests of the state are advanced." [6]

A few months later, the *Pantagraph,* commenting on the term's final examination at the Normal University, conferred on him one of the highest accolades of the times. "Hewett did not spare his pupils," the reporter wrote. For two hours he had questioned his pupils at random until the "theories of the common phenomena of nature were explained in a satisfactory manner." [7]

In the years that Hewett had been on the faculty he had grown, mellowed and ripened. He had a sense of humor that he had not hesitated to share with his students. Edwards had appeared more straight-laced and dignified, preferring to store up amusing incidents and laugh over them later with Betsey at home. Hewett often laughed with the students, sometimes he "downright joked" with them. In 1862, when there was some internal friction in the school that needed pacification, he had taken the affirmative side of a comic debate with Dr. Sewall on the subject, "Is Mother Goose to be believed when she said 'Hey, diddle, diddle, the cat and the fiddle'?" Years later he chuckled over the arguments.[8]

Hewett even enjoyed seeing Edwards squirm behind his official dignity. In an age when practical jokes were common rather than unusual, a group of students and young men about Normal who called themselves "Scribes and Pharisees" decided to play a trick. One Sunday night they stole a wagon, took it apart, climbed up a ladder, cut out a window pane with a glazier's diamond, and reassembled the wagon in the central aisle of the study hall on the second floor. Edwards learned that mischief was afoot. He waited until the culprits were safely away from the scene, and had the wagon cleared away before morning. The students who had been

[6] *Daily Pantagraph,* April 12, 1864.
[7] *Daily Pantagraph,* December 15, 1864.
[8] *Index,* 1901, p. 15.

in on the joke were surprised not to find the wagon and awaited
President Edwards' opening remarks with uncommon interest.
Professor Sewall came in just as Edwards, stern faced and solemn,
was about to begin his lecture. Sewall quickly noted an empty
bottle of Pike's Peak Whiskey on the president's desk, one which
Edwards had evidently missed while cleaning up after the Scribes
and Pharisees. Holding it up so everyone could see, he called out
in a loud voice, "Well, Mr. President, you might have left a little
for the rest of us." The students laughed loud and long. The
amazed Edwards was forced to grin, and forthwith changed the
subject of his morning's discourse.[9]

President Hewett was deeply religious, a Baptist by affiliation.
Like Edwards he had an open and receptive mind on matters of
religion. He made a special study of theology and the Bible and
taught a Bible class up to the time of his death. Each year he gave
a hundred dollars to educate young men for the ministry, and he
was himself licensed to preach by the Baptist denomination. Because of the peace and satisfaction that religion had brought into
his own life, he looked with favor upon the organization of young
men and young women on the campus into religious associations.

Since 1866 Christian associations had been springing up over
the country. In 1871 seven young men from the Normal University met in the Presbyterian Church on Linden Street and held
an informal prayer meeting. The following February, a constitution was drawn up and the organization became the first college
Young Men's Christian Association in Illinois and the fifth in the
United States. A leader in the organization was Isaac Eddy
Brown. On November 12, 1872, his sister, Lida Brown invited six
friends to come to her room in Mrs. Charlotte McMurry's home,
512 North School Street, and spend an hour in prayer and singing
hymns. The meeting was so uplifting that the young women
decided to hold meetings every Sunday afternoon.[10] Before a
week had passed every woman in school had received an invitation to join the group. So many responded that it was no longer

[9] Hanna, *op. cit.*
[10] Those present were Jennie Leonard, Ida Brown, Emma Stewart, Mrs. Charlotte
McMurry, Mrs. Harriet Lawson and Miss Hopkins. *Index,* 1896. In 1874 the name
chosen was the Young Ladies' Christian Association. In 1883 it became known as the
Y. W. C. A. During the first two winters it was recorded that 120 students professed
conversion.

possible to hold meetings in the little study bedroom and the Congregational Church offered its quarters to the devoted group of women. The first college Y. W. C. A. had been founded. After the Congregational Church burned in 1873, the organization found a temporary home in the Methodist Church. When the new Congregational Church was completed, meetings were resumed there.

The two societies carried on a very active campaign to interest their fellow students in religious activities in attending revival meetings, and in becoming affiliated with a church group. For the first three years following its organization the Women's Association held twenty-minute prayer meetings at noon in the White Room in the basement of the University building.[11]

This upsurge in religious activity came about the same time that science was being given a marked emphasis in the curriculum and when there was a number of intellectually curious young men in school. In the fall of 1874 a so-called "Liberal Club" was organized. Meetings were usually held in a small office off campus. No man could become a member who had not attended at least two meetings and been elected unanimously to membership. The "Liberals" were supposedly dedicated to impartial investigation of subjects of common interest and the opinions expressed by members on all subjects of education, politics, morals, and religion were to be treated with respect. They read and discussed the writings of Draper, Tyndall, Huxley, Darwin, Herbert Spencer, and Theodore Parker. Essays were written and criticized by the members. All the members were inclined toward liberalism in theology and they frequently were out-spoken in their opinions in the Wrightonian and Philadelphian meetings. The orthodox members, especially those who belonged to the Young Men's Christian Association, disapproved. Soon there was a clash between the fundamentalists and modernists, the readers of Genesis, and the readers of Darwin and Huxley. The controversy permeated the societies and the classrooms. After the close of the day's classes students would sit around in groups and discuss the deliverances of Huxley and Spencer with heat and vigor until the janitor's sweeping chased them out.

[11] "The Y. W. C. A. 1872–1922" (Pamphlet) (Normal, 1922).

School politics became envolved. For the presidency of the Philadelphian Society in the spring of 1875, the Y. M. C. A. advanced a candidate and the Liberals supported a rival candidate, Charles McMurry, a non-member. When McMurry was elected, there were loud cries of fraud. The die-hards called for a new election, but McMurry and his friends would not consent. The strife grew fiercer day by day until a faculty member got both factions to agree to a new election. A campaign was started to get members to pay their dues so they would be eligible to vote. Philadelphia's paid membership more than doubled, its indebtedness was cleared, and a nice reserve accumulated toward a new carpet. When McMurry won, the issue on campus died down, but it was not before it had come to the attention of the press and the Board.[12] The societies were solemnly warned that in the future they would be deprived of their rooms "if their exercises became of such nature as to be derogatory to the good name and usefulness of the University." To some of the faculty who had been quite disturbed about the affair Hewett had only remarked, "It will . . . have no permanent effects. It's like the chicken pox, they (the students) will get over it." [13]

Hewett made no promises to revolutionize the course of study. He had sat in on most of the deliberations of the Edwards regime and was content at least for the time being to let things go along as they were. Although he allowed several faculty members to recast their departments and to add new courses, there was no relaxing of standards. Each teacher tried to make his department the best in the school. In his first report to the Board, Hewett stated that students were sometimes rejected at Normal University, largely because of deficiencies in grammar, arithmetic, and geography, and since the demand for teachers was so great, good students often stayed in school only a short time.[14]

He cautioned his faculty that they must be thorough in instruction and make sure that their students were well-grounded in the rudiments of their subjects, and in the tool subjects of penmanship, arithmetic, and spelling. As a guide to self-

[12] Cook and McHugh, *op. cit.,* pp. 115, 164–166.
[13] Hanna, op. cit., Ms.; *Proceedings of the Board of Education* (Normal), June 30, 1875, pp. 25–26.
[14] *Proceedings of the Board of Education* (Normal), June 30, 1876, p. 6.

education, he insisted students must know how to use a dictionary. Spelling was an everyday occurrence. During Henry McCormick's student days the class in spelling was held following the noon recess. Rows of young men could be seen sitting in the dressing room during the intermission with a slice of bread and butter in one hand and a copy of Edwards' speller in the other, doing their daily four columns.[15]

One of Hewett's first official acts was to dispatch to the Philadelphia Exposition, about to open, an exhibit designed to give educationally-minded visitors some idea of how one midwestern state was training teachers for its common schools. Illinois State Normal University, the second oldest normal school west of the Alleghenies and the tenth in the United States, took second place to none. Statistics accompanying the exhibit indicated that the appropriation made to it by the Illinois General Assembly far exceeded that of other states, but that the large number of students reduced the per capita cost to about half what instruction was costing in other states.[16]

There were photographs of the large building standing on its prairie eminence. It looked a little less stark and barren now that trees and shrubs were growing up. There were photographs of society rooms—of Wrightonia with its rows of captains' chairs and Philadelphia with its more formal opera seats, and of classrooms showing high blackboards with careful assignments in the teacher's best Spencerian handwriting, and prim, rigid seating with a teacher's desk and recitation benches up front. There were pictures of model classrooms with teachers and pupil assistants and little children with hands upraised or firmly clasped on the desk. Some of the little girls in braids wore pinafores reaching to their shoe tops. The teacher, with high pompadour and long dark dress relieved only by a watch and chain and ruching at the top of her high collar, pointer in hand, illustrated the difference in "vulgar," proper, and improper fractions. There were pictures of young women performing wand drills, and the young men exer-

[15] *Index*, 1907, p. 28.
[16] Under a tabulation prepared by the Normal School Board of Minnesota, Illinois State Normal University ranked eighteenth in per capita cost, and the first in the number of pupils and total expenditures. *Seventh Biennial Report of the Superintendent of Public Instruction of the State of Minnesota* 1867–1868, p. 34. Quoted in Harper, *Development of the Teachers College*, p. 92.

cising with Indian clubs. Although the Normal University as yet did not have a gymnasium (and what normal school did?), it made the best of its facilities and considered body building important along with mind teaching. A large book of drawings and maps made by students in the normal department, the high school and the Model School and eight volumes of selected class exercises were evidence of the superior work being done in grammar, composition, Greek, mathematics, and other subjects. The curator of the Museum likewise sent representative materials. No funds had been appropriated for the exhibit, and as there was little money in the meager contingent fund that could be diverted to it, the students and faculty contributed $108 to pay the costs of transportation.[17]

Illinois visitors to the Fair, among them Professor and Mrs. Stetson, President and Mrs. Hewett, their daughter May, the Adlai Stevensons of Bloomington, Dr. Richard Edwards, and later his wife, Betsey—all spoke favorably and proudly of the place accorded the Normal University.[18]

Attendance in all departments decreased sharply in 1875–1876. The new president attributed this decline to the demand for teachers and the tightness of money, which kept many from attending or completing the courses already begun. All students were required to sign a pledge to teach. Only in rare cases was a student ever permitted to deviate from the printed course of study which required professional work from the start. President Hewett surmised that if the Board were to establish a "Commercial Department," a "Literary Department," a "Classical Department," a "Musical Department" and others, the school would be overrun with students. "By so doing," he said, "we should cease to be a normal school in any proper sense of the term." [19] He feared that the faculty had perhaps not been as aggressive as formerly in doing county institute work and inducing bright and capable country teachers to come to the Normal University for further training. Fewer candidates had been rejected, although standards had not been lowered.

When the Model School decreased in enrollment, practice op-

[17] *Proceedings of the Board of Education* (Normal), June 21, 1876, p. 7.
[18] Correspondence, Betsey and Richard Edwards, Summer 1876. *Edwards MS.*
[19] *Proceedings of the Board of Education* (Normal), December 18, 1878, p. 7.

portunities for pupil teachers were limited. In order to bring attendance in the training department to a point where it was practical for the needs of the normal department, President Hewett issued a circular to parents in Normal offering to eighteen pupils under the age of seven one term in the Model School without tuition. The response was good, and on a limited scale kindergarten techniques, which he highly favored, were introduced into the primary school.[20] Standards in the high school were raised to meet the requirements of Eastern colleges to which the more affluent Bloomington citizens were beginning to send their sons. It was always a matter of great pride to the faculty that University High School graduates were admitted to Yale and Harvard and Princeton. Both a general and a classical course were offered. The latter, especially designed to fit students for college, embraced three years of Greek, four years of Latin and courses in Greek and Roman history, arithmetic, physiology, English grammar, algebra, English literature, chemistry, and criticism.[21]

In February 1878 President Hewett spent three weeks visiting normal schools at Ypsilanti, Toronto, Oswego, Albany, Millersville, and Terre Haute. "On comparing our work with what I saw in these schools," he reported, "I am satisfied that we have no reason to feel ashamed of what we are doing here. I saw many things to commend in the schools I visited; in some points, I thought some of them were surpassing us. But on the whole I believe the Illinois Normal University is doing as good work as any of them." [22] Shortly thereafter the economic recession struck Illinois, and an immediate retrenchment in expenditures was ordered at Normal. Hewett was forced to lay aside any new ideas involving money. Teachers' salaries were cut back, and as a result some of the teachers resigned. President Hewett's own salary was cut from $3,500 to $3,150. Professors Metcalf, Forbes, Stetson, Cook, and McCormick were reduced from $2,000 to $1,800. The women whose salaries were normally only half that paid to the men were reduced only by a hundred dollars. Miss Wakefield, whose salary was $700, was reduced to $630. Miss Miller, the art teacher, continued to receive $600. The salary of the principal of

[20] *Ibid.* (Normal). December 13, 1876, p. 10.
[21] *Annual catalog of Normal University for year ending July 1, 1895.*
[22] *Proceedings of the Board of Education* (Normal), June 19, 1878, p. 12.

the high school was cut from $2,000 to $1,500 or $1,800 depending on the income from the Model School.[23] Three years later the cuts were restored to the women teachers, and the following year President Hewett's salary of $3,500 and those of the male professors were restored.[24] The regular school year was reduced to three terms of twelve weeks each. The third term was arranged to end early in May so that the young men could help with the harvest. Hewett also proposed a four-week summer term in August in which all faculty would teach.[25]

The first special summer term for teachers was held in August 1880. One hundred ninety-eight persons, 123 women and 75 men, attended. Some of the persons attending had taught from five to ten years, only eight had never taught, and approximately forty-five percent had at some time attended the Normal University.

By 1880 attendance was again on the upgrade at the Normal University. After salaries were restored, President Hewett took up the matter of extensive improvements which the retrenchment program had not permitted. The building was cramped for classroom space. The Board looked with some favor upon the construction of a separate fire-proof building to house its valuable museum, but the Legislature failed to share in the enthusiasm for mollusks, pressed flowers, birds' nests, and skeletons; neither did it seem interested in gymnasiums, although it had no scruples in prescribing specific courses in other departments. As other schools developed "physical culture" programs, President Hewett would repeat his recommendation for a gymnasium. Meanwhile it behooved the University to make the best of its facilities.

Since 1860 the janitor had had four rooms in the basement for his residence. If a cottage were erected for the janitor, these rooms might be used for classes. The arrangement had not been altogether happy. Peter Kettleson was a faithful employee, but his taste in food ran to highly seasoned sauerkraut, onions, and sausage, and the odor that wafted upward from his kitchen often penetrated quite incongruously the atmosphere of Greek and Roman culture that ambitious teachers were trying to recreate. The boiler and furnace rooms were in the middle of the basement

[23] *Ibid.*, pp. 28–29.
[24] *Ibid.*, May 24, 1882, pp. 20–21.
[25] *Ibid.*, June 25, 1879, pp. 11, 16

on the north side. The steam pipes were arranged horizontally around the walls. In cold weather the pipes snapped loudly and persistently, at times drowning out the voices of pupils and teachers. During the winter, entertainments in Normal Hall were almost disrupted by the noises in the steam pipes. If the heating plant and coal storage were moved outside, space might be provided for instruction in manual training, which was becoming popular throughout the cities, and for gymnastic exercises. For several years gymnastic exercises had been conducted in the large halls on the third floor, but the rhythmic movements of so many persons put too great a strain on the building. Marching exercises between the rows of seats in study hall on the second floor likewise had to be abandoned.[26]

A solution to the problem of janitor's quarters came when Peter Kettleson resigned after sixteen years. His cow no longer rested in the shade or had to be tethered in some remote corner of the campus when the boys desired to use her pasture as a baseball field. When a new janitor was employed, it was understood that he would maintain a home elsewhere and that only sleeping quarters were retained for the janitor who also served as night watchman and fireman. It was now possible to convert the two dressing rooms on the first floor into classrooms and to transform the former janitor's quarters into a classroom for primary children and dressing rooms for both men and women. Hewett was grateful that a new primary room could be outfitted for only $206.[27]

During the dry season of 1880 the water supply in the lead tanks failed and water had to be hauled from the city water works at the cost of about nine cents a barrel. To offset any further recurrences of water shortage, a university well was dug and connected with the steam pump in the basement. The lead tanks continued to be used for some years, and iron supports were installed in various parts of the building to relieve the strain in the floors and walls.

A new brick walk in 1882 replaced the old broken boards, and the campus took on an air of elegance and refinement that was a delight to the University and the townspeople.

[26] *Ibid.*, December 12, 1888, p. 8.
[27] *Ibid.*, January 17, 1883, p. 20.

More appreciated perhaps was the installation of kerosene chandeliers in the large hall and the reception room. For years an evening entertainment in Normal Hall had necessitated borrowing reflection lamps and chandeliers from the society halls and from churches about the town.[28] It seemed but another evidence of the ill fortune that plagued the building that on the first occasion the new lights were being used, one of the chandeliers, improperly installed, crashed to the floor, tearing out the ceiling plaster and throwing oil over the floor. Only the quick action of two young men averted a devastating fire.[29] Leaky gutters and roof damage and seepage from the attic cisterns constantly threatened the plaster. It fell off in little pieces, and again in great chunks. Corrugated wood ceilings had to be installed in 1885.[30]

One day in 1880 the bell in the tower, which for years had served as evening curfew and marked the time for students to go to classes and housewives to prepare and serve meals, suddenly cracked and fell apart. The town seemed very quiet and lost without the bell. President Hewett said a new one was imperative, and although the Board concurred, it was two years before the new one was installed. There was considerable copper in the old bell; its tones had been quite mellow, and the bidding for the old scrap was sharp. Vanduzen and Tift of Cincinnati cast the new bell on a low bid of twenty-seven cents a pound and nineteen cents for the scrap. The new bell was as large as could be conveniently placed in the belfry and was hung at a cost of only $139.33. The old clock which had lost so many of its parts and no longer worked, was entirely removed.[31]

The hazards of fire had always worried President Hewett, and after the state discontinued the practice of insuring its buildings, he was doubly concerned about the safety of the Normal building. Lightning rods had been put up as a precaution and fire hoses had been attached to the tanks in the attic, but there were other dangers. After the fire at Carbondale Normal School in November 1883, ten dozen Harden hand grenades were distributed about the Normal University to be used in case of fire, and doors were

[28] *Ibid.*, May 26, 1881, p. 18.
[29] *Ibid.*, June 18, 1882, p. 14.
[30] *Ibid.*, June 24, 1885, p. 18.
[31] *Ibid.*, January 17, 1883, p. 21.

changed to open outward.[32] To President Hewett's request for a telephone, the Committee on Buildings and Grounds ruled that this was "a modern improvement which can not well be dispensed with in this institution, that it is not only a convenience to the faculty and the Normal School generally but . . . . in case of fire in the building the fire department of the City of Bloomington could be notified in less than a minute." The telephone was installed in the reception room with a signal bell in the assembly room above.[33]

The General Assembly passed legislation in 1877 creating the State Museum at Springfield and converting the Illinois Natural History Museum at the Normal University into a State Laboratory. Duplicates of zoological and botanical specimens at the Normal University Museum were transferred to the new state museum in the west wing of the State House. Stephen Forbes, who had replaced Dr. George Vasey, Powell's successor, as curator of the Museum, now asked to be known as Director of the Laboratory. He asked for drawer space for taxidermist materials, microscopes, and breeding cages for the study of embryology, and a library of scientific books, all of which was granted him.[34] His work was now divided between original research and the "dessemination of knowledge." He continued to send cabinets of specimens to high schools until by 1883 seventy-five schools had been supplied.

In 1882 Forbes became State Entomologist with a staff of eight assistants. An extension program of research upon plant, animal, and insect life of the state was launched. In 1885, when Forbes resigned to go to Indiana University, Minor Lawrence Seymour, professor of science, took over the local museum and laboratory, and in a short time the surplus collections were removed to the State House in Springfield and the University at Urbana. The museum and laboratory had occupied a space 98 by 32 feet. This space was now available for classrooms.

One of Hewett's fondest hopes was a library which would

---

[32] *Ibid.*, June 8, 1884, p. 12.

[33] The telephone system was set up in Bloomington in 1880. Hasbrouck, *op. cit.*, I, 231. The cost of installing the first telephone at the University in 1880 was fifty-five dollars. The cost of operation was estimated at fifty dollars a year. *Proceedings of the Board of Education* (Normal), January 19, 1881, p. 20.

[34] *Ibid.*, June 21, 1877, pp. 17, 25.

gather in one place various collections of scientific literature, reference volumes and documents scattered about the building. The printed catalog for 1889 listed 1030 different titles. The books were widely used.[35] There was no authorized librarian. From $200 to $400 was allocated a year for the purchase of books but from time to time portions of the library fund were diverted to buy maps and scientific materials. With the advice and suggestions of faculty members, the president ordered the books, mainly reference and pedagogy, and applied to the Board for reimbursement. A student borrowing a book wrote his name in a large register and the student librarian wrote the name of the book borrowed. The chief student librarian received fifty dollars a year for his services and the three assisting student librarians were given five dollars a term.[36] Biography, history, and books of fiction were available in the libraries of the Wrightonian and Philadelphian societies which were open for half an hour before the programs and half an hour afterward. Neither faculty nor students liked the system, both favoring a general library with a paid librarian. In 1889 the two societies voted to transfer their libraries to a general library "if the Board would provide a suitable room for the library and maintain an efficient librarian." The only reservations were that the society libraries were to be kept separate and apart from the general library and that the societies were to have the privilege of adding to them.[37]

In the spring of 1890 Miss Ange. V. Milner was employed to prepare a card catalog of the books in the five libraries of the school. The reception room on the first floor, which had more recently also served as a lounge for faculty women, was designated as the room to be used and fifty dollars set aside to put it in condition. This space was quite inadequate and it was September before the new general library was set up in the old reception room.[38]

After the Board in 1885 had directed the Committee on Training to prepare a course in free gymnastics as a regular branch of instruction in the normal and model schools, the matter of place

---

[35] *Ibid.*, June 26, 1889, p. 9.
[36] *Ibid.*, June 25, 1873, p. 6.
[37] *Ibid.*, June 25, 1889, p. 10.
[38] *Ibid.*, December 10, 1890, p. 23.

in which to conduct the classes was of much concern.[39] The General Assembly was petitioned in 1889 for a new boiler house and a combination gymnasium and grammar school to cost about $12,000. The boiler house was granted, but the gymnasium-school item was voted down. Hewett was disappointed but not discouraged. The request would be repeated at the next session and again until it would eventually be granted. With the removal of the heating plant and the coal, temporary rooms could be outfitted where exercises with wands and Indian clubs, and marching and calisthenic drills could be performed without fear of endangering the building. One hundred dollars had already been spent for dumbbells and wands.[40] A room on the northeast corner of the basement was outfitted with tools and benches with $250 appropriated by the Board to try out an experiment in manual training. Professor Reeder, who was in charge of the experiment, devoted two hours a day to teaching rudimentary wood work to boys in the grammar school. He was instructed to keep very careful notes, especially on the effect this type of training had on their other subjects.

In the 1880's there was much talk of the perennial "new education." Hewett wrote in 1884:

The air is full of talk about the new education. The meaning of the term is not very clearly defined yet I am certain that it stands for some things of value. The problem to be solved is, in my opinion, to avail ourselves of all that is good in it, and still adhere to the old methods of thorough drill in the several branches sufficiently to instill fair scholarship as that term is commonly understood.[41]

In Hewett's own book, *A Treatise on Pedagogy for Young Teachers,* psychology was made the basis of educational method. He defined "education as the development of the faculties or germs of power in man, and the transforming of them into harmonious action in obedience to the laws of reason and morality." [42] "All method," he said, "must rest on principle." He briefly stated what he considered to be the four grand principles or fundamental truths of pedagogy: (1) All power under control of will may be

[39] *Ibid.*, January 21, 1885, p. 10.
[40] *Ibid.*, June 26, 1889, p. 9.
[41] *Ibid.*, June 18, 1884, p. 8.
[42] Edwin C. Hewett, *A Treatise on Pedagogy for Young Teachers* (New York: American Book Company, 1884), p. 40.

cultivated or trained. (2) These powers are trained only by wise use. (3) The wisest training will be directed to those powers that are conspicuously active at the time. (4) An indispensable pre-requisite to any profitable training is careful attention to the matter in hand.[43] It was a philosophy as modern as Dewey and the Progressives, as ageless as truth, expressed in less than fifty words, and considerably simpler than that of Rosenkranz, whose textbook had for years been evoking endless groans and frequent tears.

Hewett was quite as gifted as Edwards in his ability to discover rare teacher potential among his students and in his willingness to encourage them, and, when they were ready, to place them on his own faculty. John Cook, a graduate of 1865, was moved from principal of the grammar school to professor of mathematics, and Charles DeGarmo, a promising graduate of 1873, was made second assistant in the grammar school, under the direction of Thomas Metcalf. Bandusia Wakefield and Ellen Edwards, graduates of 1865 and 1873, were brought back as second assistants in the normal department. Lida Brown McMurry, a graduate of 1874, and her brothers-in-law Charles McMurry (1876) and Frank McMurry (1876) were later to return to the faculty and make significant contributions to education. In 1879 Edmund Janes James, who graduated from the high school in 1873 and had studied at Northwestern and Harvard and Halle, became principal of the high school.[44]

Some of these young teachers would later study at Halle and Jena, return to their alma mater and after a brief but inspired sojourn, move on to other colleges and universities to make far-reaching impacts. Charles DeGarmo would, in the course of time, be president of Swarthmore, and professor of education at Cornell; Charles McMurry and Frank McMurry would be prominent in the development of Teachers College, Columbia; John W. Cook would in turn become president of his alma mater, and when he left to become first president of Northern State Normal

[43] *Ibid.*, pp. 45–46.
[44] Edmund James had come up through the elementary department of the Model School. His mother before entering him in 1863, had gone from school to school, visiting classrooms. After she decided on the Model School, her husband bought a farm within easy walking distance of the building.

School at DeKalb, Illinois, he took with him Lida Brown Mc-
Murry, author of numerous children's books, as one of the training school teachers.[45]

When Edmund James became principal of the University High
School in 1879, he had already studied at Halle and come under
the influence of the disciples of John Frederick Herbart, the
German educator whose philosophy was later to give Normal
University an international reputation. President Hewett was
especially challenged by a circular on German Normal Schools
which had come to him from the United States Bureau of Education in 1878. From it he learned that teachers' seminaries had
been in existence in Germany for one hundred forty years, that
there were ten such schools in Prussia and that no person was
allowed to teach in a public school who did not have a diploma
from one. He compared the German curriculums with the course
of study at Normal University and with considerable satisfaction
informed the Board that "the proportion of professional to other
studies is no greater than it is with us." "This fact," he said, "is
very significant in view of the claim often urged that our normal
schools ought to do nothing but professional work." [46]

When Charles DeGarmo returned to the faculty in the fall of
1886, he was instrumental in organizing the "Faculty Club,"
which met every two weeks. Half of the meeting was devoted to
the study of some topic bearing on the philosophy of education
and the remainder in discussing the work being carried on at
Normal. Out of their deliberations came a faculty lecture to students once every four weeks.[47] A photograph of the Faculty Club
made at A. M. Marston's fashionable studio in Bloomington
shows ten men and six women grouped about a marble-topped
table. In the most honored places sat the venerable, stately
Thomas Metcalf and President Hewett, short but sitting as tall
and erect as possible, quite conscious that he was dwarfed by the
stout and stalwart Henry McCormick seated at his right. They
appear to have been a serious lot, these men in narrow-collared
dress suits, five in bearded dignity, four with moustaches and only
one smooth-shaven, and women in tightly buttoned basques and

[45] "Alumni Register," *Normal School Quarterly*, July, 1927.
[46] *Proceedings of the Board of Education* (Normal), December 18, 1878, p. 12.
[47] *Ibid.*, December 14, 1887, p. 8.

long bustle-backed skirts. They looked capable of discussing anything from Kant, Aristotle, or Froebel to calisthenics and manual training. The proportion of men and women is interesting. Upon the motion of N. E. Worthington, the Board ruled in 1874 that since the majority of students were women and since women had demonstrated their capacity to compete with men teachers at least one third of the regular professorships should be given to women as soon as possible.[48] However, for many years, Mrs. Martha D. Haynie, teacher of modern language, was the only woman to attain the rank of professor. The differential between the salary of the women and men who held the same rank was roughly $800.[49]

Nor were members of the faculty alone in their desire for self-improvement. In 1879 a group of hopeful young men, enamored of Roman history and political thought, organized a club which they called the Ciceronian. Its meetings were given over to debate, oratory, parliamentary procedures, and a study of issues, local, state, and national. A model Senate took the place of the regular program every fourth meeting night. Members took assigned seats, Republicans and Democrats sitting on opposite sides of the room. Meetings were held in the White Room in the basement until membership expanded beyond its comfortable limits. Wrightonia then graciously extended her hall to the use of the society.[50]

There was much talk about Ciceronian, the men's very select and important club. In October 1887 a number of girls decided to crash the Ciceronian Society, and learn about it for themselves. The men were expecting the impending visit, and made no effort to oust their visitors. The girls regarded it as quite a joke, and thinking they might be bored decided to take along their embroidery, tatting, and crochet. In spite of themselves they became so interested that they decided to start a similar society. After consulting the preceptress, Miss Flora Pennell, and other members of the faculty, a meeting of all women students was called. A

[48] *Ibid.*, June 24, 1874, p. 14.

[49] Mrs. Martha Haynie who taught English, French, and German for twenty years was receiving $1,200 when she resigned in June 1886. Her successor, Charles DeGarmo received $2,000. *Ibid.*, June 22, 1886, pp. 10, 16.

[50] *Index,* 1901, pp. 66–68.

Bloomington Square fifty years ago.

The old gate and the iron fence.

Mrs. Martha D. L. Haynie, teacher
of languages, 1866–1886.

Mary Hartmann, teacher of mathematics,
1882–1907.

June Rose Colby taught literature from
1892 to 1932. She served for a time as
Preceptress.

Mrs. Lida Brown McMurry, member
of the training school faculty, 1891–1900.

Charles DeGarmo, Principal of Grammar School, 1876–83; languages and reading, 1886–1890.

Frank McMurry, a graduate of Normal and a member of the faculty, studied in Germany under Dr. Rien and became a leader of the Herbartians in America.

John Williston Cook, president, 1890–1899, an alumnus of 1865, joined the faculty in 1866.

Arnold Tompkins, president, 1899–1900. In one year he wrought a revolution.

President John W. Cook and members of his faculty. By his side is Thomas Metcalf and at the extreme left, David Felmley.

President Tompkins and the devoted class of 1900.

Clarissa Ela introduced art appreciation and art history into the curriculum in the 1890's.

Normal's own bloomer girls, 1900.

Study hall, Old Main, in the 1890's.

A candle making project in the lower grades of the training school, 1900.

Altgeld's pride—gymnasium, 1897.

The old training school building, now known as North Hall, was first occupied in 1892.

Students' and architects' dream of student center, 1893.

And here it is, the Student Union, opened September, 1956.

committee was appointed to draw up by-laws for the new society. The new group chose to be known as the Sapphonian, after the Tenth Muse, Sappho, the Greek lyric poetess. The first meeting was held November 4, 1887. With enthusiasm unbounded the Sapphonians undertook a study of art, literature, travel, and music. They evolved elaborate rituals for initiation and the installation of officers. Before a year had passed they had inaugurated the pleasant custom of exchanging programs with the Ciceronians, an evening of declamations, essays, music, a social hour, and refreshments. Four years later they were beginning an annual clash of talents and wits—the Greek Muses versus the Roman Senators.[51]

If the Normal University students of the first half century were timid about standing up, speaking out and being heard, they dedicated themselves to overcoming their timidity and mastering the niceties of diction and elocution. Commencement offered the grand and final opportunity for speech-making. When the first class had graduated in 1860, each of the ten graduates had a place on the program. Each had either delivered an oration or read an essay, and each had written a paper, an essay or a "thesis," as it came to be called, to be filed in the school's archives as testimony of his ability to use language and organize ideas. At first these papers were written on professional topics, but in the seventies when natural science was becoming prominent, the essays had been on related topics. Efforts were made to publish these graduating papers in educational journals and periodicals throughout the state. With slight changes many of these could be converted into papers suitable to be read at commencement.

As the classes increased in size, it was evident that something needed to be done to shorten the graduating exercises. Various proposals were made and tried, such as having addresses by only the valedictorian and the salutatorian, or choosing speakers by casting of lots. In 1880 the members of the senior class petitioned that the custom of allowing all the members of the graduating class to participate in commencement exercises be re-established. The members of the class of 1881 likewise wanted all members to appear on the program. That year there were twenty-three grad-

[51] *Ibid.*, 1902 (n.p.).

uating from the normal department and two from the high
school. One Board member proposed that a five-minute limit be
set. A motion to amend the limit to ten minutes failed, and the
Board finally agreed to let all members of the class speak but ruled
that there should be a morning and an afternoon session, the time
being left to the faculty.[52]

On January 18, 1882, the Board voted that members of graduating classes should be allowed to speak in the graduating
exercises until ordered otherwise,[53] and in June 1882 the commencement program listed twenty-one graduates from the normal
department and one from the high school. The orations ran the
gamut from the salutatory on "Thou Art the Man" to "A Plea for
Mediocrity." There were essays on "Margins Make Life's Successes," "The Liberal Education of Women," "Silent Builders,"
and "The Small Boy." The valedictorian came down to earth
with an essay on "Reading." The exercises began at nine o'clock.
The essays and orations were interspersed with music, and midway in the program came the noon recess. The programs were
long, but the graduates and their parents did not seem to mind.
Some deemed it a right, not a privilege, to appear on the program.
Families brought well-filled picnic hampers and were prepared to
spend the day. The faculty were mildly tolerant, but soon the
Board members, who were expected to sit on the platform, made
objections. To forestall long commencement programs, William
Green in January 1883 moved that seven members of the graduating class deliver addresses at commencement, three to be selected by the class and four by the faculty. There was not a single
dissenting vote.[54]

The students, however, did not relinquish time-honored places
on the program without a murmur of protest. The class of 1884,
which numbered but twenty-six, appealed once more to have all
its members speak, but in case the Board refused, proposed the
alternative of a speech by one "lady" and one "gentleman" chosen
from the class as the Board would direct. But the Board was

[52] *Proceedings of the Board of Education* (Normal), May 20, 1880, p. 22; *Ibid.*,
January 19, 1881, p. 21.
[53] *Ibid.*, January 18, 1882, p. 19.
[54] *Ibid.*, January 17, 1883, p. 30. The printed programs for 1883 listed the full titles
of the orations and essays of the forty-five graduates of the high school and normal
departments.

adamant. There would be seven speakers. The printed programs continued to list the theses, as the original essays and orations came to be known, and it was not until 1921 the practice of requiring a graduating paper was abandoned.[55]

In 1887 the Normal University suffered the loss of its loyal friend and supporter, Jesse Fell. He died February 25, at the age of seventy-nine. He was highly regarded by the people of Bloomington and Normal and particularly by the faculty and students of Illinois Wesleyan and Normal University, the schools he had helped to found. No church was large enough for his funeral and the services were held in the Assembly Hall, on the third floor of the Normal University building. The public schools were closed, and special streetcars were run out from Bloomington. Sixteen hundred people thronged the aisles, corridors, and stairs. The minister and the choir came out from the Unitarian Church which he had also helped to found, and Richard Edwards, former president of the Normal University, and now state superintendent of public instruction, gave the eulogy. Shabby and smart vehicles alternated in the long cortege on its way to Evergreen Cemetery on the southern outskirts of Bloomington. As the last carriage left Normal University, the first reached the Court House, with its flag at half-mast, where the Bloomington school children were waiting to join the school children from Normal.[56]

At conventions of the National Education Association, state teachers' meetings, and sessions of the General Assembly, Edwin Hewett, the short little man trying to look taller in a high silk hat and a long frock coat, was a familiar figure. He always wore the fine gold watch and carried the handsome little cane that his grateful students had given him in the days before the Board had ruled against gifts being presented to teachers. His poise, affability, and sense of humor made him an entertaining companion. He was energetic but calmer than Edwards. Occasionally he appeared on programs but never so often as Edwards. Although the work of administration increased with the years he refused to retire from supervision. The Board realized his situation and allowed $200 annually for the services of a bookkeeper, and a few

[55] *Ibid.*, January 16, 1884, p. 21. Rachel Crothers, high school 1891, later a distinguished American Dramatist, wrote as her thesis, "The Proper Study of Mankind is Man."

[56] Richardson, *op. cit.*, p. 85; Morehouse, *op. cit.*, p. 116.

months before he retired voted $250 for clerical help to assist members of the faculty.

For the position of chief clerk he employed Flora Pennell Dodge, who was to remain the personal secretary for four presidents. Ever with his New England eye on the budget he carefully explained that he had selected Miss Dodge because she knew how to use the typewriter and the "multiplying pads." Typewriters were rare in the 1880's and to be able to use one was a special accomplishment. Hectographs as a device for duplicating materials were also new. "Her work," he continued, "promises to be a great help. She is receiving seven dollars a week for her services, a portion of her wage to be paid from instruction in shorthand and typewriting, which she will give so far as it is desired and as her time will allow." [57]

Although the Normal University was operating on a fairly firm foundation by the time Edwin Hewett became president and was no longer threatened with dissolution as under President Edwards, his administration was by no means free of annoyances. Especially recurring were the Bakewell claims.

Edwin W. Bakewell sought to have returned to him a forty-acre tract of land which he had donated to the University in 1857. Along with many other donors he had signed the subscription paper circulated to secure the location of the Normal University for Bloomington. He had attached the stipulation relative to the teaching of experimental agricultural chemistry. This paper had been lost or destroyed before or shortly after the first meeting of the Board on May 7, 1857. The forty acres donated by Bakewell was a part of his farm of 360 acres. He expected the other 320 to increase in value by its proximity to the Normal University. Prior to the meeting in Peoria on May 7, 1857, Jesse Fell took care to convert the existing subscriptions to legal binding form. When Bakewell put his subscription into the form of a bond for a deed, nothing was said about the teaching of agricultural chemistry. The bond valued the land at $8,000, although it was probably not worth more than $1,000.[58] When the Board on May 15, 1857,

---

[57] *Proceedings of the Board of Education* (Normal), December 12, 1888, p. 7.
[58] Bakewell was reputed as wealthy. His father-in-law, Alexander Campbell, founder of Disciples of Christ Church, was a "vocal" supporter of the proposed normal. *Ibid.*, December 18, 1893, p. 18.

demanded a guaranty that $70,000 of the Bloomington pledge should be paid at certain fixed intervals in order to secure the location, Bakewell obligated himself for $5,000. On February 5, 1858, Bakewell and his wife Julia executed a deed of warranty to the tract with only one restricting clause, "Provided, the Normal University, under the control of the Board of Education of the State of Illinois, shall forever remain where now located." On February 9, 1860, Bakewell and his wife executed another deed to the Board specifying that the foregoing provision was the only one attending the transfer of title.

From time to time the Board disposed of land which had been donated for securing the location and construction of the building. The Bakewell tract was rented to various farmers for cash from $325 to $700, or to nurseries, of which there were a large number in the area. In 1859 the Board talked of establishing an agricultural professorship, but the means of the Normal University were currently inadequate and the matter was tabled until after the new building was occupied.

Edwin Bakewell suffered severe financial losses during the depression of 1873. In 1875 he asked the Board to convey the land he had subscribed to his wife Julia A. Bakewell on the ground that no attempt had been made to carry out the conditions of the grant. The Board contended that since it had been given bonds for deeds to lands subscribed in 1857 and not the original subscription paper and that since neither the bond for the Bakewell deed nor the warranty deed contained a qualification relative to the teaching of agriculture and as a consequence was unknown to the Board, there was no contract.

In 1878 Bakewell brought an unsuccessful suit against the state. Many of the more prominent citizens supported his claim and he took the matter before two successive legislatures. The Thirty-third General Assembly in 1885 ordered the Board to reconvey the land to Bakewell. The Board refused, asserting that the Legislature had no jurisdiction.

The appropriations bill in 1887 originally carried a rider which made the release of funds contingent upon the restoration of the Bakewell land, but friends of the school intervened and the rider was removed. Bakewell took his case to the Supreme Court, which rendered the judgment that the Normal University was a private corporation protected in its charter from legislative dictation. Judge Green hastened to say that this should not bar the Legislature from making appropriations.[59] This decision again was obviously against Bakewell, but he would not be silenced for long.

In 1882 the Normal University celebrated the completion of its first twenty-five years. Despite the early struggle for existence the school had proved its worth as a "necessary auxiliary to the common schools." It had not deviated from its original purpose to prepare teachers for the schools of the state and as such was attaining recognition. When the observance of the Quarter Centennial was held on August 24, 1882, Professor Cook, to whom President Hewett had turned over the matter of statistics, was able to report that at least 968 former Normal University students were currently teaching in eighty-eight of the 102 counties of the state and that 104 were known to be teaching in seventeen other states and territories, and several had gone to foreign countries. Many of the graduates had gone on to other colleges, taken degrees, and were teaching in other normal schools. A number were county superintendents and city superintendents in Illinois and other states.

A fair number of these returned for the reunion, the early classes being well represented. Charles Hovey, first president, returned from Washington and joined former president Richard Edwards and President Hewett on the platform that first evening. One outcome of the alumni business meeting was the taking of a subscription for a monument to Joseph Howell, training school teacher and member of the class of 1860. He was one of the first six students who enrolled that first day in October 1857 and the first to enlist from Normal University when Lincoln called for volunteers and among the first from Normal University to fall in battle. The funds collected provided a marble tablet which was placed in the wall of the classroom where he taught. At this reunion "Wrights" and "Phils" renewed acquaintances and reminisced over the old contests, the old rivalries, the hay rides

[59] David Felmley to F. W. Shepardson, August 22, 1918, *Felmley Papers; Proceedings of the Board of Education* (Normal), February 1, 1887, p. 5.

and the sleigh rides, and the practical jokes. Did President Edwards ever know that a group of fellows had a duplicate of Janitor Kettleson's key to the attic made and used it to slip up to the belfry and play euchre? [60] The Wrightonians recalled "Uncle" Simeon Wright, their patron, to whom they owed their society's existence to say nothing of its library. When the members heard that he had willed their society a thousand dollars, they had gone on a spending spree, only to learn later that his estate did not cover the bequest.

A visit to the old school brought to mind many memories. There was that never-to-be-forgotten evening of March 18, 1870, when Professor Hewett had debated Miss Susan B. Anthony on the question, "Is it best for the women of America that they should vote?" Every seat in Schroeder's Opera House was occupied. Special streetcars had been necessary to bring the crowds who wanted to see the genial little professor match wits with the mighty Amazon. President Edwards had presided. Miss Anthony talked for twenty-five minutes and Hewett for thirty; then each had twenty minutes for refutation, and Miss Anthony five minutes for summary. Hewett asserted that men always gave women what they wanted. Miss Anthony boomed, "The women of Bloomington want the grog shops closed. Have the men closed them?" The sparring went on. Hewett warned, "Womanly power will not be developed by voting." Miss Anthony countered, "Voting with men will not contaminate women any more than living with them!" [61]

There was sparkle and affection in Hovey's eyes as he reviewed the founding of the school and paid tribute to those who supported him in the dark days. Richard Edwards spoke of the training school, of Childs, Metcalf, and Powell, and the other teachers who had helped to build the school. W. L. Pillsbury, who had once been in charge of the Model School, told of Childs and Mary Brooks and the coming of the high school. Hewett, whose association with the University dated from 1858, took up where the others left off and filled in the gaps. It was heart-warming and inspiring to see these three presidents together and to hear from

[60] Hanna, *op. cit.*
[61] *Daily Pantagraph,* March 19, 1870.

their own lips their dream of a great institution for teacher training.[62]

In the Hewett administration as in that of Hovey and Edwards the Board continued to direct, if not dictate, educational policies and procedures of the school. The Committee on Textbooks and Course of Study from time to time visited the school, observed classes, took notes on teaching techniques, and evaluated the work being done. Recommendations might come from the president or the faculty, but decisions and frequently curriculum changes were initiated by Board members. In January 1887 the Board recommended to the Committee on Textbooks and Course of Study that the amount of time in the training department by each pupil teacher be doubled, and that the time devoted to reading, grammar, and arithmetic be doubled, but that whenever any student could make a grade of 85 in spelling and geography he would be excused from one-half the time ordinarily allotted to those subjects. In the Hewett regime there was considerable relaxation of the standards of spelling, but when Richard Edwards was president, no student had been allowed to "pass" spelling until he had gone a term without missing a single word. Some students took spelling as many as five terms before they successfully "carried" it.

The committee modified its recommendations after talking over their findings with such teachers as Thomas Metcalf, Henry McCormick, Charles DeGarmo, Mary Hartman, President Hewett and young Rudolph Reeder, assistant training teacher.[63] Despite the seeming arbitrary rule of the Board, the right of petition, individual and collective, direct or through the president was genuinely respected. In June 1890, Clarissa Ela,[64] teacher of drawing for the past year and a half, appealed for more than two terms of drawing if teachers were to be adequately prepared for the demands of the public school. She proposed that a term in art history be added to the course of study and that more time be

---

[62] Two hundred twenty persons attended the banquet which lasted for five hours. The speeches of the Quarter Centennial are printed in Cook and McHugh, *op. cit.*, pp. 171–227.

[63] *Proceedings of the Board of Education* (Normal), June 22, 1887, p. 12; *ibid.*, December 14, 1887, p. 9.

[64] Clarissa Ela, graduate of 1884, was first employed in 1888 at fifty dollars a month for four hours a day. She had previously studied one year in Boston and had taught three years in Bloomington. *Ibid.*, December 12, 1888, p. 7.

spent on art in the Model and high schools. Music had been dropped from the curriculum in the very early years and had not been restored. When Miss Ela appealed for art, John Cook, professor of mathematics, who had an especially fine voice and thoroughly enjoyed singing, asked the Board through President Hewett, that a part time teacher of vocal music be employed to give two lessons a week and that all students completing the normal course should be qualified to give instruction in vocal music in the public schools.[65] The members listened respectfully to these pleas for the fine arts, and later made up their own minds how far they could go.

Art history was not included in the course of study, but the number of terms required in drawing was increased, and the president was allocated $200 to employ a part-time teacher in vocal music. Often a faculty member, seeking what he considered a just increase in salary used this direct approach. Student petitions varied from protests against spelling requirements and against Rosenkranz as a textbook to requests for heating for their society rooms.[66]

As the school year 1889–1890 drew to a close, President Hewett found himself a little more weary than usual. He had been in educational work for forty-one years. Of the thirty-three years that the Normal University had been in existence he had been on the faculty every year except the first. He had labored with Hovey and Edwards through the vicissitudes of early years, and he himself had been head of the school for fourteen and a half years. He had seen the faculty increase to eighteen, the enrollment of the normal school to 677, and the Model School to 503. The income had risen to $36,200. Like Hovey and Edwards he had been interested in writing, and for a time he took over the editorship of the *Illinois Teacher*. In 1871 Hewett and Aaron Gove purchased the *Chicago Schoolmaster,* and in 1873 they purchased the *Illinois Teacher* and united the two publications under the name of the *Illinois Schoolmaster*. When Gove went to Denver as superintendent of schools in 1874, his brother-in-law John W. Cook,

---

[65] *Ibid.,* June 23, 1890, p. 23.

[66] President Edwards, a stickler for spelling, decreed that failure of more than one word during a term, out of the twenty-five that were assigned for each day would mean failure of the course.

succeeded to his place as joint editor and proprietor with Hewett.[67]

After Hewett became president in 1876, Cook became sole proprietor and editor. Hewett continued to write occasional articles on educational subjects and to indulge in his hobby of writing poetry. In 1881 Edmund James and Charles DeGarmo brought out the first issue of a new educational monthly, *The Illinois School Journal*. The young editors stated that the purpose of the publication was to free their minds as to certain "definite and firm convictions" on the various subjects which they meant to discuss. For a time it was a sort of university organ wherein every faculty member might crystallize ideas and see them in print. When DeGarmo went to Germany in 1883, John Cook bought the paper and took another fling at educational journalism. Within a year he had taken in Rudolph Reeder as a partner. In 1886 Cook and Reeder sold out to George P. Brown, former president of the Indiana State Normal School at Terre Haute, who had retired because of ill health and recently moved to Bloomington.[68]

Brown published *The Illinois School Journal* for three years, then changed the name to *The Public School Journal,* and later to *School and Home Education*. Brown was a scholar and a philosopher, and a great friend of William T. Harris. The faculties of Wesleyan and Normal took him quickly to their hearts. Hewett and Brown became fast friends. Hewett began contributing to *The Public School Journal*. Before very long he again found himself a partner in a publishing enterprise. Brown had found satisfaction in this "type of retirement" from teaching. Perhaps he would too.

At the conclusion of his report to the Board on June 25, 1890, Hewett resigned "his connection with Illinois State Normal University to take effect on the first of September next or sooner if

[67] In 1859 Hewett was editor of the Illinois Teacher for one year. John Hull, McLean County Superintendent of Schools, purchased the old *Normal* begun in 1866 by E. D. Harris, and issued a new paper known as the *Chicago Schoolmaster*. Cook sold his interest in the *Illinois Schoolmaster* in December 1876 to a Chicago firm which after buying up several educational journals undertook a new publication *The Educational Weekly*. It soon failed. Aaron Gove had married Carolyn Spofford and John Cook had married Lydia Spofford; both were sisters of Harriette Spofford Hovey. *Semi-Centennial History of Illinois State Normal University,* pp. 169–170.

[68] *Ibid.*

the Board so elect." The resignation was brief but not unexpected.

The newspapers that carried the report of Hewett's resignation also carried the news of John Williston Cook's appointment as his successor.

The mantle had fallen on Hewett's beloved and respected pupil, an alumnus of the class of 1865.[69]

[69] Edwin C. Hewett died March 31, 1905. Three years after the death of his wife in 1895 he had been married to Mrs. Helen Clute Paisley. *Daily Pantagraph*, April 1, 1905.

CHAPTER VIII

The Herbartians

On July 1, 1890, John Williston Cook took up his duties as fourth president of Illinois State Normal University. He had long been associated with the school, first as a student and later as a teacher. As a young farm boy making occasional trips to Bloomington he had seen the great red brick building with its high tower and silver dome rise above the corn fields that surrounded it. As a country school pupil he had been fascinated by what he saw and heard. Someday he hoped to attend the new normal school.

He entered the Normal University in the fall of 1862 and graduated in 1865. He was a student of Richard Edwards and Edwin Hewett, had done his student teaching under Thomas Metcalf, and had come to know Charles Hovey through his marriage to Lydia Spofford, a sister of Hovey's wife. He was thoroughly indoctrinated with the educational philosophy of his three predecessors. He knew firsthand much of the tradition and history of the school. With James V. McHugh, he published in 1882 a history of the Normal University's first twenty-five years. He brought to the presidency of the school, not only the fine flower and appreciation of the past, but a positive program for its growth.

John W. Cook was born April 20, 1844, in Oneida, New York. His father, Harry Dewitt Cook, was a carpenter and a railroad bridge builder; his mother, Joanna Hall Cook, was a former school teacher. When Harry Cook heard that the General Assembly had passed legislation providing for the construction of the Illinois Central Railroad, he prepared to move his family to Illinois. They made the long trip by Conestoga wagon and settled in McLean County about nine miles north and east of Bloomington. John Cook attended the log schoolhouse near his home. Earlier he had for a time attended a private school in a basement of a hotel in Oneida. After the railroad bridges on the Illinois

Central were completed the family moved to Kappa, where the father became station master and grain dealer. During the winter the boy attended school in Kappa and in summer he worked on farms or clerked in local stores. He often drove a yoke of five oxen to plough the hard unyielding sod. The wages were small, from eight to ten dollars a month, but young Cook managed to save enough to start his normal school work at Normal University.

From his mother, John Cook had inherited a love of books and an inquiring mind. His record as a scholar was impressive; he was an alert and intelligent reader. He was active in the Wrightonian Society, representing the society in the annual contests with the Philadelphian Society in 1862 in vocal music, and in 1865 in debate.

Following graduation he taught one year in Brimfield, Illinois, where one of his most valued patrons and counselors was Mrs. James Wiley, who as Mary Brooks had been the first teacher of Normal University's Model School.

After a year President Edwards asked him to come back to Normal University as principal of the grammar department of the Model School. While Professor Hewett was on leave in 1868, Cook took over his work in geography and history. In 1869 he was made professor of reading and elocution, and when Harriet Case resigned her work in mathematics in 1876, he took over her classes. For the next fourteen years he taught mostly mathematics and physics with an occasional class in reading.[1]

Cook soon became well-known and respected among the schoolmen of the state. He participated in teachers' institutes and was a popular speaker at state and county teachers' meetings. In 1874 and again in 1883 he ventured into publishing, first *The Illinois Schoolmaster* and later *The Illinois School Journal*.[2]

Cook had no formal education beyond the diploma of Illinois State Normal University, but he read widely. Whenever a book was recommended to him, he took pains to read it, and if possible to discuss it later with the person who had suggested it. He had a keen analytical mind and a wide range of interests. The business

[1] *Proceedings of the Board of Education* (Normal), June 21, 1899, p. 9; *Daily Pantagraph*, July 17, 1922; DAB.
[2] Clipping (n.d., n.p.) *Gale MS.*

of self-education was a serious one. He was ever open-minded and he cultivated men of learning and ideas. He was active in the Faculty Club, preparing papers and taking part in discussion. George P. Brown, who had bought Cook's and Reeder's *Illinois School Journal* in 1886, became a very special friend. Through him Cook became acquainted with William Torrey Harris. He kept in close touch with his friends Edmund James, Charles DeGarmo, Frank and Charles McMurry, John Hall, John J. Wilkinson, Elmer Ellsworth Brown, and several others from Normal University who attended German universities between 1883 and 1900.[3] He could not afford to go abroad himself, but he was generous in loaning money to bright young men who desired to do advanced study either in American or foreign universities. In turn they wrote to him of the courses they were taking, the points of view, and methods of presentation. At home he read Kant and Hegel and corresponded with Dr. William Rien, under whom so many of his friends had studied in Jena. Cook sent Rien catalogs of the Normal University, institute programs, and educational addresses by Normal faculty members. He was happy when Rien wrote that he was impressed by the work being done at Normal University.

Cook's public addresses were marked by a gentle and nimble wit, clear and apt phrasing, and pertinent illustrations. In 1880 he was elected president of the State Teachers Association. Knox College recognized his leadership in education and in 1883 conferred upon him the honorary degree of Master of Arts. Later in 1892, when Richard Edwards was president of Blackburn College, he was to receive a second honorary degree, that of LL.D.[4]

When Cook came to the presidency of Illinois State Normal University the faculty was composed of seven women and twelve men. Seven, including Ruth Morris, the Preceptress, who taught English, held the title or rank of professor. Others were listed as teacher, training teacher, assistant or principal.

Cook was truly proud of his faculty. Seven held earned degrees. Charles DeGarmo, Professor of Modern Languages and Reading, had the degree of Doctor of Philosophy from Halle in Germany.

---

[3] Harper, *Development of the Teachers College,* p. 199.
[4] Clipping, *New York School Journal,* January 19, 1895. Gale MS.

He had graduated from Normal University in 1873. After three years as a principal of an Illinois grade school, he had returned to Normal University to take charge of one of the departments of the Model School. In 1883 he went to Germany to study and returned three years later to teach modern languages. At Halle he was deeply influenced by the educational philosophy of John Frederick Herbart, who was coming to be an accepted leader among prominent German educators. DeGarmo saw in Herbartianism a return to the Greek ideal of many-sided interests as the aim of education.[5] DeGarmo had been a prolific writer of educational essays and reviews ever since he and Edmund James had founded *The Illinois School Journal* in 1881. He had collaborated with Thomas Metcalf on *A System of Dictionary Work for Common Schools,* which was published in 1879. Now he was about to bring out a new book, *Essentials of Method.*[6]

Buel P. Colton, M. A., Professor of Natural Sciences since 1888, was a worthy successor to Minor Seymour and Stephen Forbes. Mary Hartmann, M. A., alert and quick-witted, assistant in mathematics, was regarded as being quite as competent in the field as Cook himself.[7] Henry McCormick, beloved and respected teacher of history and geography and the only other staff member to hold a doctor's degree, had been a member of the staff since 1869.[8] Staunch supporter of his former pupil was the venerable Thomas Metcalf, the man of careful diction, gentle voice, and gracious manners, who had been a member of the faculty since 1862. Clarissa Ela, teacher of drawing, a graduate of 1884 who had joined the faculty two years before and would remain for over forty years, was doing a commendable piece of work.[9] New to

[5] John Frederick Herbart (1776–1841) studied under Fichte, and later took Kant's chair of philosophy at Konigsburg. William von Humboldt, Commissioner of Education for Prussia, made him a member of the Commission in Charge of Higher Education. He established an experimental school. The school operated by William Rien at Jena was the outgrowth of Herbart's philosophy that the understanding of child behavior is the basis of educational method. Herbart's most distinguished work was *The Moral Revelation of the World as the Chief Function of Education.*

[6] Harper, *Development of the Teachers College,* pp. 201–203.

[7] Mary Hartmann, A. B., M.A., Lombard College, taught mathematics at Illinois State Normal University, 1882–1910.

[8] Henry McCormick obtained a Master's and a Doctor of Laws degree from Illinois Wesleyan University by examination in non-resident work. "Alumni Register" *The Normal School Quarterly,* July 1927, p. 11.

[9] Clarissa Ela graduated from the Massachusetts Normal Art School in 1888. She taught at Illinois State Normal University 1888–1931.

the faculty was David Felmley, A. B., University of Michigan, professor of mathematics who would remain forty years, ten years as a teacher and thirty as president. That same fall the school had its first full-time paid librarian, Ange. Vernon Milner, a frail little woman who remained the school's librarian for thirty-eight years.

Within the year Orson Leroy Manchester, principal of Joliet High School, who had both a Bachelor of Arts and a Master of Arts degree from Dartmouth, became principal of University High School. Professor Manchester was to remain on the faculty thirty-seven years, serving first as high school principal, then as teacher of foreign languages, next as teacher of economics, and finally as dean, meanwhile endearing himself to the community as the far-sighted and efficient mayor of Normal for ten years. When Charles DeGarmo resigned to become professor of logic, psychology, and philosophy at the University of Illinois, Frank McMurry, another alumnus and ardent Herbartian with a Ph.D. from Jena, would become "superintendent of the training work in the primary and intermediate grades." [10] Soon McMurry's sister-in-law, Lida Brown McMurry, another outstanding graduate and teacher in the Normal public schools would become training teacher in the primary department. Already she had earned a reputation as a speaker and writer of children's stories.

The Faculty Club continued its study of philosophy and educational method. Under the inspired leadership first of DeGarmo, then of Frank McMurry, Charles McMurry, and later Charles Van Liew, and the patronage of George P. Brown, who published educational essays which the faculty wrote, Illinois State Normal University became the center of the Herbartian Movement in America, a program that promised a scientific approach to education.[11]

John W. Cook stretched himself to his full height as he surveyed the Normal University, its objectives, its curriculum, its buildings, its faculty and its students. He saw himself the executor of a sacred trust, traditions of nearly thirty years standing, and the unfulfilled dreams of the three presidents who had preceded

[10] *Proceedings of the Board of Education* (Normal) June 24, 1891, p. 13.
[11] Chris A. De Young, *Introduction to American Public Education* (New York: McGraw-Hill, 1942), p. 175; Harper, *Development of the Teachers College,* pp. 170, 199–221.

him. He also had his own ideas and ambitions for the school. Where to begin? There were many changes that he wanted to see made in the curriculum. He wanted psychology, vocal and instrumental music, drawing, and physical culture to have a larger place in teacher training. However, the new president was loath to jeopardize his administration at the outset by undertaking any radical changes in such a delicate and sensitive area. He astutely turned to matters of the training school and the over-crowded building.

In his first report to the Board, December 2, 1890, he stated the case for a new training school concisely: "A normal school with-out a suitable training school is like an industrial school without proper shops for practical work." The supervising force, he said, was strong but all departments were hampered by lack of room. Thirty-nine pupil teachers were teaching in the primary room that fall. With the exception of one class there were never more than six or eight pupils to a teacher. It was impossible under such circumstances "to give any adequate training to the pupil teachers in those most difficult arts of discipline and management." In some rooms three, four or five classes were being conducted simultaneously. The din and confusion was almost beyond de-scription. By an arrangement with the normal public schools two of its departments were used for a part of the day. Thirty-seven pupil teachers were employed in other departments of the train-ing school. Twenty-three classes recited in dark, ill-ventilated basement rooms, and on cloudy days it was necessary to use coal oil lamps. The high school increased in such numbers that Her-bert J. Barton, the principal, advised that the enrollment be re-stricted from its current number of 179 students to 160, that permission be granted to drop pupils from the rolls who did not make satisfactory marks, that the tuition be increased from $32 a year to $39, and that an additional instructor be employed.

The immediate need was a training school building. The young president pleaded his case well. Upon the motion of a new mem-ber of the Board, Mrs. Ella Flagg Young of Chicago, a committee was instructed to prepare plans and specifications for a new ten-room building, two stories in height, heated by steam, and cor-responding in architecture with the present building, to cost approximately twenty-five thousand dollars, a very modest figure.[12]

A committee of seven, including former president Richard Edwards, the new state superintendent, was to present the matter to the Legislature when it met in January 1891.

The General Assembly acted favorably on the matter of a training school building but it reduced the amount appropriated to eighteen thousand dollars. The architects had to redraw the plans. President Cook, however, was not dismayed. In fact, he said, "The action of the Legislature is most encouraging. In a few months we shall bid adieu to basement dungeons that a pressing necessity has forced us to use, the halls will no longer serve the double purpose of corridor and recitation room; four classes in a room simultaneously will pass into the traditions. Let us be duly thankful." [13]

That same year the sale of two sections of Jackson County land, subscribed by Jesse Fell in 1857, yielded enough money to warrant extensive repairs on the building such as replacing plaster ceilings of several rooms with wood, painting the interior woodwork and walls, installing new blackboards, repairing the roof and heating system, putting new matting in the library rooms and carpet in the reception room.[14] Of all the improvements the most highly acclaimed was the installation of 106 electric lights. No longer would the societies have to worry over the filling of the lamps, trimming the wicks, and polishing the chimneys. It was rumored that before long there would be electric lights in the students' rooming houses.[15]

Without legislative or Board ruling, President Cook quietly disposed of the cuspidors that had been annoying him for thirty years as they lined the main corridors and served as stumbling blocks for absent-minded professors and unwary students. He looked forward to improving the campus and making it more attractive, with new shrubs, trees, and a better fence. All too long the campus had been described as the state cow pasture.[16]

---

[12] *Proceedings of the Board of Education* (Normal) December 10, 1890, pp. 10–24.
[13] *Ibid.,* June 24, 1891, p. 13.
[14] The Fell lands in Jackson County sold for $5.15 per acre.
[15] The *Vidette,* September 1892, p. 29; *Proceedings of the Board of Education* (Normal) December 21, 1892, p. 13.
[16] The janitor's cow grazing over the baseball diamond and the tennis courts was an abomination to the students. The *Vidette,* April 1891, printed a long poem written by

On their own initiative the students were attempting to relieve the cramped classroom situation. Wrightonians and Philadelphians laid plans for a Society Hall with quarters ample for the societies' rooms, a large auditorium, parlors and reception room, adequate for the six hundred persons who were presently trying to pack themselves into quarters that were crowded by half that number. Many college campuses had beautiful buildings erected through gifts of alumni and friends, quite a number of these buildings being society halls or student unions, as they were later called. Why could not Normal University have such a building? In October 1891, the two societies at Illinois State Normal University set up the joint "Philadelphian and Wrightonian Inter-Society Building Committee" to collect funds for the construction of a building. George Miller, Bloomington architect, drew plans for an elaborate structure of brick and stone, with a basement and enormous attic beneath the steep slate-covered roof that combined the gable features of a Swiss chalet and the turrets of a Turkish mosque. It fitted in well with the design of the new training school building, and the students were enthusiastic. The estimated cost was fifteen thousand dollars. Construction would begin when twelve thousand dollars had been subscribed and paid. The terms of the subscriptions uniquely stated that no part of any subscription would be due until the gross amount of bona fide pledges should reach twelve thousand dollars. When that sum was reached, all subscriptions would become due and payable after thirty days' notice from the Inter-Society Building Committee. If twelve thousand dollars were not pledged by July 1, 1893, all subscriptions would be null and void.

The response of the first few weeks was most gratifying. President Cook, Charles DeGarmo, Edmund James, Frank Gove, and three or four other generous alumni gave momentum and unqualified endorsement to the scheme by each pledging one hundred dollars. Other members of the faculty subscribed smaller

---

E. M. Wilson, deploring her Bovine Highness. The last stanza reads:
> Oh the janitor's cow, of her I am fond
> For she feeds where the flowers are fairest
> And the water she sips from the lily-brimmed pool
> Is fragrant with odors the rarest
> I love her—my love I often have boasted
> But if all were equal, I'd like her best roasted.

amounts. One volunteered to increase his pledge upon the abolition of the Inter-Society Contests that since 1858 had been the most exciting event of the school year. A cautious student made his subscription contingent upon his graduation.[17] The graduating Section A of 1892 pledged a total of $1065, and as the deadline of July 1, 1893, approached the two societies each voted to subscribe two thousand dollars while President Cook agreed to secure a donation of two thousand dollars. The student publication, the *Vidette* in June 1893, went to press with the confident assurance that "the new society hall will ere long take its place upon our campus as the home of Wrightonia and Philadelphia." [18]

The editors of the *Vidette,* engrossed in preparations for final examinations and the World's Fair in Chicago, had not taken into account certain grave portents. Early in May members of the faculty and the few students who had money deposited in W. H. Schureman's bank in Normal were horrified to learn that it had closed its doors. There were rumors that it might pay off fifty cents on the dollar, then fifteen cents, and finally only five cents. Many of the townspeople, loyal supporters of the University, lost all that they possessed.[19] July first came, and the requisite twelve thousand dollars had not been subscribed. Not a dollar for the Society Hall was ever collected. The project that had motivated every meeting of Wrightonia and Philadelphia for nearly two years collapsed.[20]

To the disappointed and heart-broken students President Cook offered a palliative. Since the days of President Edwards he too had dreamed of a gymnasium for Normal University. When the Wrights and Phils first began their campaign for funds, he had brought the matter before the Board and suggested the possibility of a combination society building and gymnasium. He thought

[17] The original pledges are in Milner Library.

[18] The *Vidette,* June 1893, p. 25.

[19] Heads of departments deposited any moneys that they collected in a fund at Schureman's bank. The principal of the grammar school had $515 deposited to his account as treasurer when the bank closed. After much deliberation the Board voted to assume the loss. *Proceedings of the Board of Education* (Normal) December 20, 1893, p. 12.

[20] The *Index* 1894 p. 9 in telling the story of the failure of the proposed Society Hall, declared the idea was "not abandoned." It was "confidently expected" that it would be realized "before many years should pass." Sixty-two years later the first earth was turned for a Student Union. Meanwhile the two societies which sponsored the first venture died of apathy and neglect.

that a room eighteen feet high and sixty feet by eighty feet could be built for ten thousand dollars. He built a strong case for a gymnasium. Heretofore all physical culture had been for girls: calisthenics and wand drills, exercises designed to improve their posture and insure better health. He felt exercise even more necessary for men. Accustomed to manual labor, they found the transition to the sedentary life of a student abrupt, even harmful. A gymnasium would aid not health alone but "the cultivation of graces of the body." Nowhere was there greater need for good carriage than in the schoolroom. It was impossible to use the great hall for exercises because of its threat to the building. A combination gymnasium and a society building was included in the budget to be presented to the General Assembly in 1895.[21]

President Cook was a strong and vigorous man. He enjoyed outdoor games, baseball, football, and tennis, and thought sports were excellent for relaxation and body-building. He was quite intrigued by reports of a new game called basketball, which could be played indoors when the weather was inclement. He was glad when the *Vidette* took cognizance of sports and devoted a special half column each month to the subject of athletics.[22]

Lawn tennis was very popular among the students. Every spring the campus broke out in a rash of tennis courts. Wherever students could find a level spot between the trees that was large enough for a tennis court, they preempted it, cleared it, and strung up a net. Even the young women seemed to prefer the new game to the less strenuous and more ladylike croquet. The fashionable shirtwaist blouse, with its wide Gibson pleat and generous sleeves, and its companion ankle-length fourteen gored skirt allowed freedom of movement for the quick running, jumping, and serving. There was seldom a sunny afternoon that one did not see at least a dozen girls on the Normal courts, with stiff sailor hats perched atop their high pompadours, running about, deftly swinging their rackets and shouting, "Love, five! Love, ten!"[23] As yet, there was no athletic association, and the school

[21] *Proceedings of the Board of Education* (Normal) June 22, 1892, p. 10.

[22] The *Vidette* first appeared as a monthly publication, March 1888. Its lone predecessor *The Ventilator* was a rowdy sheet and after one issue the editors were expelled.

[23] *Index* 1932, p. 30. One report says there were sixty lawn tennis courts on the campus in 1892.

owned no sports equipment except for a few dumbbells, wands, Indian clubs, ball bats, baseballs, and gloves. Students provided their own rackets and tennis balls and pooled their resources, bought nets, and limed the courts. When football first made its appearance on the campus in 1884, the players provided their own gear.

The year 1893 was marked not only by the panic and the defeat of the Society Hall project but by the World's Fair in Chicago, the issue of the school's second yearbook, *The Index,* and the beginning of a number of new campus organizations. Six weeks before school was out in June 1892, one of the girls received a copy of the Purdue yearbook and showed it to her fellow students. John B. Cleveland, George W. Riley, and Herbert Hicks decided that an annual should be put out for Illinois State Normal University. A local print shop estimated the cost at seven hundred dollars. Advance subscriptions were taken, and the three self-appointed editors with the blessing of the faculty, promises of photographs and articles, set about frantically to get the book off the press before Commencement. Owen Reeves, Jr., a bank clerk in Bloomington, who had a flair for cartooning, was inveigled into supplying the comic touch and the black and white pen drawings that were characteristic of school annuals of the period.[24]

The great Columbian Exposition about to open in Chicago kept students and faculty in a fever of excitement and anticipation throughout the school year 1892–1893. President Cook, Henry McCormick, and Thomas Metcalf recalled the exhibit that the Normal University had sent to the Exposition in Philadelphia in 1876. The Chicago exhibit must be larger and better. It must depict the growth that the school had made in the past seventeen years and properly indicate its prestige among the teacher training institutions of the nation. The State of Illinois, in a great burst of pride, had appropriated funds to construct a beautiful neo-classic edifice of stone, lath and plaster to house exhibits from its fields, factories, and schools. Two thousand dollars was allocated to Illinois State Normal University to finance its exhibit, and an area 27 by 29 feet was set aside for it in the east wing of the Illinois Building. Each department was instructed to prepare a display of

[24] *Index* 1892; *ibid.,* 1926 p. 220; *Vidette,* April 1892.

its best work depicting subject matter and method. When the exhibit was finally assembled, it filled eight glass cases. There were experimental projects in science, maps in geography, chronological tables and essays in history and pedagogy, and examples of student art. There were photographs of the building and classrooms showing teachers and students at their work. In an adjoining section there was a similar exhibit from the Southern Normal School at Carbondale. Normal University had been frugal in its expenditures, spending only about $1250 on its exhibit. With the remainder of its funds, a young student, John Keith, was hired to greet the visitors, explain the exhibit, answer questions and hand out leaflets on the school.[25] Here friends gathered, registered, talked over old times and rested between visits to the Court of Honor, the Palace of Art, Machinery Hall, the Pigmy Village or other unique attractions of the highly publicized Midway Plaisance.

What fine reports came from the campus, the new training building, the repairs on the "old" building, as the original structure was now so often called. That very summer A. T. Fagerburg was painting the brick red again and lining the mortar and trim in white.[26]

For visitors inquiring about former teachers, there was news that Dr. Frank McMurry and John Hall of the grammar school were going abroad to study and that Dr. Charles McMurry was coming from the Minnesota State Normal School at Winona to take over his brother's work in pedagogy and be assistant in the training school. Miss June Rose Colby, the first woman to receive a Doctor of Philosophy degree from the University of Michigan, was the new preceptress and professor of literature. Miss Colby was a most unusual person. She was an ardent feminist. Regardless of fashion she always had pockets in her skirts, insisting that pockets were as useful to women as to men. She entered into the teaching of Shakespeare with her whole soul. No one would ever forget the way she read poetry. She made her students love literature and she did not believe in examinations.[27] Despite heavy

[25] *Proceedings of the Board of Education* (Normal) December 21, 1892, pp. 8–9.

[26] Considering current prices, the Fagerburg contract of $760 for painting the exterior and lining the mortar seems fabulously cheap. *Ibid.,* December 20, 1893, p. 15.

[27] Harry J. Owens, "Great Personalities at ISNU," *Alumni Quarterly,* February 1954, p. 5.

demands on Dr. Cook as president, he still continued to teach as many as fifteen hours each week. Dr. Henry McCormick was named vice-president and now helped with the work of administration.[28] What a gain since the days of Edwards and Hewett, when the president not only taught, supervised, and personally attended to the school's records but carried on the school's extensive correspondence in long hand. Each year Flora Dodge and the "typing machine" were becoming more indispensable.

The YMCA and the YWCA were flourishing. That year each of the organizations through dint of self-sacrifice and a variety of fund-raising schemes was contributing five hundred dollars for the support of six native missionaries in China, India, and Armenia.[29] In November the state organization of the YWCA would hold its annual meeting on the campus. The Union Sunday afternoon meeting of the "Y's" was well attended, and as the winter season advanced and the boarding house parlors became crowded, an increasing number of young couples were seen at evening services of Normal's four churches.

Alumni stopping at the Normal University's exhibit at the Exposition invariably inquired about the boarding clubs, the Hitchcock, the Misses Shinn, the Jones, the Giddings, the Durham, and Clark's O.N.T. It had often been months before the new student learned that the letters O.N.T. were only the girls' facetious reference to a popular brand of cotton thread. Some of the old grads were as loyal to their boarding clubs as if they had been fraternities. They solicited patronage of young friends about to enter Normal University and in turn wrote letters in their behalf. A visit to the campus always meant a call at the old club and if possible a meal in the dining room. The price of board remained about the same, $1.75 to $2.07 a week. Few students had meals in private homes, and none boarded at restaurants. In a private home, board and room, exclusive of fuel, lights and laundry, was between three and four dollars a week. It was cheaper to "light housekeep," but to take one's meals at a club was ever so much more enjoyable. Would one ever forget the good-natured arguments, the heated discussions, the pranks, the

[28] *Ibid.,* December 5, 1894, p. 8: June 22, 1892, p. 18.
[29] *Index,* 1893, p. 74.

budding romances, and the inevitable oyster soup on Friday night?[30]

As often as President Cook could get away, he came up to the Fair to greet visitors at the Normal University's exhibit and inform them of the distinguished place the school was coming to have as a leader in teacher education. He spoke of the graduates who had gone abroad to study and returned to make a contribution to American educational thought. He was especially pleased with the part the graduates of Illinois State Normal University had had in the formation of the Herbart Club the year before, at the meeting of the National Education Association in Saratoga, New York. Yes, Rosenkranz was still being used as a text, but it was supplemented by a new book, *Introduction to Education,* by John Dewey, a promising young professor at the University of Chicago.[31]

Nothing delighted President Cook more on these trips to Chicago than meeting fellow normal school administrators. In a secluded corner away from the noisy midway and the milling crowds, the educators talked shop. They used such terms as "perception" and "apperception," "concentration," "correlation" and "coordination." To the uninitiated it was a bewildering jargon, but to consecrated Herbartians, seeking to develop a science of education, terminology, and procedures were all important. Common understandings were essential to common goals. Cook enjoyed telling how things were being done at Normal University. One of his earliest accomplishments as president was lengthening the courses in psychology and pedagogy. Another was the reorganizing of the elementary courses in the Model School along Herbartian lines. The application of the principal of apperception required a carefully worked-out course of study with continuity, and the work of each grade was planned to give pupils experiences and understanding that could be utilized in later years.[32]

---

[30] List of clubs compiled from advertisements in the *Vidette* and the *Index* 1893, and the prices of board and lodgings from catalogs, diaries, and letters of the era.

[31] Henry Hugh Edmunds, "History of the Herbartian Movement in the United States and Its Relation to Present Trends in Education" (Unpublished manuscript, 1929) Milner Library, p. 5.

[32] Dorothy McMurry, *Herbartian Contributions to History Instruction in American Elementary Schools.* ("Teachers College Contributions to Education" No. 920; New York: Teachers College, Columbia, 1929), p. 74.

In this connection Cook often cited the work being done in the training school by Charles McMurry, with the assistance of two critic teachers and a number of paid students. To interested listeners he would explain how the culture epoch could be used to correlate the work in history, geography, science, arithmetic, and language. McMurry would teach an epoch only one time and then it would be done thoroughly. For example, in the fifth grade at Normal University the story of Captain John Smith would be read in history. At the same time, in geography the class would investigate the Chesapeake area, its climate, soil and products, such as clams, oysters, fruit, and tobacco. In science the tobacco plant, oyster, and other products would be studied. In arithmetic there would be statistics on amount of tobacco produced, exported, and consumed. The findings in these various areas would be carefully recorded and thus serve the purposes of language composition in narration, description, and exposition. To McMurry and his fellow Herbartians, history was very important in the elementary curriculum.[33]

Correlation and integration as practiced in the training department at Normal University, said Cook, was natural, logical, and extremely practical. A central topic of interest motivated all activities and commanded the use of all basic skills. President Cook was becoming an authority on training techniques, and when he spoke an ever-increasing audience listened. Normal University was assuming a leadership in its new approach to education. Members of the faculty found time to write, and their books were eagerly read. In 1892 Charles McMurry published *Elements of General Method Based on Principles of Herbart*.[34] In 1890 he had published *How to Conduct the Recitation,* and in clear concise terms outlined the five formal steps of procedure: preparation, presentation, comparison, generalization, and application.[35] Both of these early publications were widely read and acclaimed. The title page of the 1901 edition of *The Elements of General Method* noted that it was part of the ninth edition, forty-second thousand.

[33] *Ibid.,* pp. 94, 146.
[34] Charles A. McMurry, *Elements of General Method Based on Principles of Herbart* (Bloomington: Public School Publishing Company, 1892)
[35] Dorothy McMurry, *op. cit.,* p. 107; Charles McMurry, *How to Conduct the Recitation* (Chicago: A. Flanagan, 1890)

The Method of the Recitation, in which McMurry and his younger brother Frank collaborated, sold over thirty-six thousand copies. Charles McMurry sought to implement his philosophy by preparing a *Course of Study for the Eight Grades of the Common School* and a handbook for teachers which he published in 1895.[36] In 1893 Charles McMurry published *Special Method for Literature and History in Common Schools,* which was to go through two editions. To facilitate the teaching of history in the elementary grades, a matter which had been greatly neglected before 1890, he prepared a series of books on American Pioneers on various grade levels.[37] His sister-in-law, Lida Brown McMurry, was working out a plan along Herbartian lines for teaching science in the primary grades, and with Mary Hall Husted, a former critic, she was adapting the story of Robinson Crusoe for young children. Mrs. McMurry was also writing stories and poems which she would publish later. C. C. Van Liew, Ph. D. (Jena), of St. Cloud, Minnesota, who joined the faculty when Rudolph Reeder left the University to enter business, was also a confirmed Herbartian.[38] An article by him on "Culture Epochs" appeared in the *First Yearbook of the Herbart Society for the Scientific Study of Education.* In 1893 he published his translation of *Life of Herbart and the Development of His Pedagogical Doctrines.* Charles DeGarmo's *Essentials of Method,* published in 1889, continued to identify him with Normal University long after he had gone on to Swarthmore College. The *Yearbooks of the Herbartian Society* and George P. Brown's *Public School Journal* at times seemed to be the mouthpieces of Normal University, so consistently did its faculty and graduates contribute articles. It was indeed gratifying to Cook to see his school "on the map," but he was never sure whether he was a true Herbartian or not. In some respects he was greatly influenced by Herbart's ideas, in other directions he found himself not aroused at all. He could never

[36] Charles A. McMurry, *A Course of Study for the Eight Grades of the Common School,* including a Handbook of Practical Suggestions to Teachers (Bloomington: Public School Publishing Company, 1895)

[37] Charles McMurry Pioneer series included *Pioneer History Series for Third and Fourth Grade* (1891), *Pioneers on Land and Sea* (1904), *Pioneers of the Mississippi Valley* (1904), and *Pioneers of the Rocky Mountains and the West* (1904) (New York: Macmillan, 1891–1904)

[38] Charles C. Van Liew had worked under Dr. Rien in his Practice School at Jena. *Proceedings of the Board of Education* (Normal) December 20, 1893, pp. 7–8.

ity could be of help to teachers in service would be through
summer courses on campus with the regular faculty and an oc-

go along with such an extremist as W. P. Burris of Bluffton,
Indiana, who declared Herbartian pedagogy to be "the angel to
roll away the stone from the sepulchre of formalism in which
the schools of America have been entombed." [39]

Cook's open-mindedness, along with his determination not to
become over-balanced about any particular system, kept the
Normal University on an even keel, and his ability as a moderator
and parliamentarian did much to keep discussions at meetings of
the Faculty Club from going too far afield. Interest in philosophy
and education by such men as George P. Brown and Richard
Edwards led the staff to grant the privilege of membership to
persons off campus. Through the facilities of Brown's *Public
School Journal,* the faculty hoped to extend the influence of the
club beyond the institution. Non-residents were invited to participate in the deliberations by correspondence, by submitting papers
to be read before the club, articles for the *Journal* or critical comment in its columns. In 1890 eight of the older more mature men
students had organized themselves into a Philosophy Club, and
under the direction of Professor Reeder spent an hour and a half
each week studying and discussing William Torrey Harris'
Introduction to Philosophy. The following year the four men left
in the club began the vigorous study of Schwegler's *History of
Philosophy.*[40] The more advanced and interested students were
admitted to membership in the reorganized Pedagogical Club, as
President Cook often referred to the study group. The first project
undertaken by the club was the arrangement of a course in science
teaching adapted to all the grades of the public school.[41]

Cook always liked to think of normal schools as service institutions. He believed that one very good way in which Normal University could be of help to teachers in service would be through
summer courses on campus with the regular faculty and an occasional visiting lecturer in charge. The staff was in sympathy

[39] First supplement to the *First Yearbook of the Herbart Society for the Study of
Education.* Quoted, Dorothy McMurry, *op. cit.,* p. 50.
[40] *Index,* 1892, n.p.
[41] At the outset of the Cook administration regular monthly faculty meetings were
held and two evenings were set aside for "discussing ways and means to promote the
general welfare of the school, and especially to formulate a distinct body of educational
doctrines that may be kept before our classes and illustrated in the ordinary work of
instruction." *Proceedings of the Board of Education* (Normal) December 9, 1891, p. 9;
December 20, 1893, p. 10.

with the idea, especially since it offered the prospect of eventual paid summer employment. When President Cook recommended that a teachers' institute be held in University Hall for a term of three weeks beginning May 21, 1894, the Board approved with the terse qualification that the instructors should be members of the Normal faculty who should serve "without extra pay." [42] Most of the rural and city schools were out by that time so that the institute was concurrent with the ninth, tenth, and eleventh weeks of the spring term. The course of instruction arranged by Henry Raab, the State Superintendent of Public Instruction, and President Cook provided for observation of the regular work of the normal school, observation of the practice school including teachers' meetings, attendance at a course of daily lectures by members of the faculty, and a series of round table discussions conducted by Professors Colton, McCormick, Van Liew, and McMurry. Elmer Cavins, teacher of spelling and penmanship, gave one lecture on penmanship. Miss Colby spoke on "Literature for High Schools," Professor Manchester discussed "Methods in Latin," Miss Milner gave a "Talk About Libraries," the venerable Professor Metcalf, about to retire at the end of the year, called his lecture "Hints from a Teacher's Notebook." Dr. Van Liew lectured on "Herbart," Miss Ela talked of "Methods in Drawing," Miss Lucas, the new reading teacher, spoke on "Physical Culture in Connection with Reading." President Cook reserved for himself the final lectures, speaking one day on "Feelings and the Will" and the last on "The History of Education."

To the surprise of President Cook, the Board, and the faculty, 161 teachers from forty-two counties and one other state enrolled. At the last session it was resolved that the institute be held annually.[43] The large enrollment was particularly gratifying because the panic had brought about a decline in attendance at all colleges and normal schools during the year 1893–1894. Summer institutes of three weeks were again conducted in 1895 and 1896. In 1896 the attendance was 120 teachers. A poll of the teachers revealed opinion that the institute came too early and that a summer term when other classes were not in session would more

[42] *Ibid.*, p. 16.
[43] *Ibid.*, June 20, 1894, p. 11.

nearly serve the needs of teachers in the field. To meet this demand such a three-week session was held in 1897 and tuition charged to defray the cost of operation. Meanwhile President Cook tried to convince the Board that the appropriations should cover a forty-eight week year, as was currently being done at the University of Chicago.[44] One hundred attended the summer term in 1897, but the financial return to the faculty was so low that few were willing to undertake another summer. President Cook was compelled to abandon the project for the summer of 1898 but repeated his request to the Board for at least an additional five thousand dollars to be allocated for a summer session. The request fell upon deaf ears, and for the next few years potential summer students gravitated toward the University of Chicago, other colleges, and county institutes that were providing special courses for public school teachers. The faculty at Normal University eagerly sought employment in county institutes or used the long summer vacation to advance their own training by taking work in the summer schools.

The depression brought a sharp decline in attendance in the spring of 1893, especially in the Model School, but by fall there was an encouraging upswing in enrollment. Meanwhile the Legislature, with a weather eye on state income, called for retrenchment in all departments. It was futile to ask for new buildings at this juncture. President Cook tried to pinch pennies where he could, hiring new teachers at much lower salaries than had been paid their predecessors, and doling out supplies with a careful hand. Repairs on the furnace and an iron fence around the campus to keep out stray teams were necessities.[45]

Two other matters threatened the peace and progress of the school. The Bakewell Claims Case was being renewed, and there was severe criticism of the high school. The panic of 1893 had brought distress to the aging Bakewells, who had deeded forty acres to the University in 1858, and despite a decision of the Supreme Court in 1887[46] and his failure to get an injunction against the school, Bakewell was once more trying to recover the tract. The Board reviewed the matter of the missing subscription

[44] *Ibid.*, June 23, 1897, p. 12.
[45] *Ibid.*, December 20, 1893, pp. 7–15.
[46] *Board of Education v. Julia A. Bakewell* 122 Ill. 339 (1887).

paper wherein Bakewell alleged he had made his donation contingent on the teaching of agricultural chemistry, and the warranty deed which he and his wife signed, conditional only upon the Normal University's remaining where it was then located. Again the Board rejected Bakewell's petition, little dreaming that the case would ever rise again, and eventually lend shape and substance to the curriculum.[47]

Since 1862 the high school had been an integral part of the Normal University's program. Its graduates had received diplomas and participated in the festivities of Commencement. To attract students to the normal department, President Cook had instituted a two-year course open to high school graduates. In 1895 a four-year course was set up with Latin and German for students who were anticipating further work in college. Soon attendance in the high school greatly exceeded the primary, intermediate, and grammar departments of the Model School. The record of University High School graduates at Harvard, Yale, and Princeton, where the wealthier citizens of Bloomington were wont to send their sons, spoke well for their training, but the high school itself was of little direct service to the normal department. Occasionally a student graduated from both the high school and the normal department and received two diplomas at the same Commencement, and sometimes after graduating from the normal department a student would return and take courses in the high school. Some normal students of their own choosing took Latin, Greek and German in the high school classes. In fact, the revenue from the tuition of high school students exceeded the salaries paid the three high school teachers whose time was chiefly given to teaching languages. On the other hand, forty-four percent of the total instruction received by the high school students was given by the regular normal department teachers, whose classes were already overcrowded. Many felt that their classes suffered from the presence of so many "juveniles."

In 1891 the Board limited the enrollment in the high school to 160 and raised the tuition to thirty-nine dollars. President Cook discussed the matter of the high school with Governor Altgeld when he laid before him the school's proposed budget for 1895-

[47] *Proceedings of the Board of Education* (Normal) December 5, 1894, p. 13.

1897. Altgeld was favorable to the request for a gymnasium but insisted that the Normal University have only two classes of people in it, young men and women who would agree to teach, and those children necessary to make up a model school. He would permit no children in the institution who were not absolutely essential for that purpose.[48]

Governor Altgeld did not attend the meeting of the Board, but the letter he sent made clear his position.

It is not the business of the state to run neighborhood high schools. What the state does want at Normal is the very highest grade of a Normal University that can be established. To accomplish this it is necessary to concentrate. Only in this way can the highest point of excellence be achieved. Teach everything it is necessary to be taught in a perfect Normal University.

As you are aware, this is not a new idea, but has been the policy of this administration from the beginning and I shall now have to insist upon its being carried out and that without any attempt to compromise.[49]

By vote of seven to six the Board concurred with the governor and the high school was abolished.

It had long been a rumor that Governor Altgeld was going to do away with the high school, but it was not a rumor that students or alumni wanted to believe. They thought the high school a well-established institution and were proud of its graduates. Charles Capen, member of the first graduating class in 1865, had gone to Harvard, where he had taken both a bachelor's and a master's degree, then studied law at Wesleyan and was now on the Normal School Board. Arthur Edwards, class of 1869, had taken bachelor's and master's degrees from Princeton and was now teaching English literature. William Bury and William Duff Haynie, class of 1871, had both graduated from Harvard and were now practicing law in Chicago. Edmund Janes James, a graduate of 1873, who had taken a Ph. D. from Halle in Germany, was Director of the Wharton School of Finance at the University of Pennsylvania. Frank Hall Thorp, class of 1883, had taken a Ph. D., cum laude, from the University of Heidelburg and returned to

[48] Governor John P. Altgeld to John W. Cook, Springfield, June 1, 1895. *Ibid.*, June 19, 1895, p. 11.
[49] *Ibid.*

teach chemistry at Massachusetts Institute of Technology. Dr. Charles McMurry, currently a member of the Normal University faculty, had graduated from University High School before going on to Germany for advanced study. A roster of successful Bloomington businessmen included graduates of University High School, Dickey Templeton, banker and civic leader, Jacob Bohrer, lawyer, and Nelson McCormick, physician.[50]

It did not seem possible that anything so "catastrophic" could happen. In the 1895 *Index* the author of the high school editorial had facetiously posed the question, "What would the normal students do if there were not high school classes in Latin, Greek, and German for them to enter?" Political economy taught by Professors Manchester and Felmley was likewise attracting many of the "pedagogs."

The governor's ruling evoked much comment. The *Daily Pantagraph* in a long editorial commended the faculty on the fine work it had done in the University High School and regretted its closing. Former President Richard Edwards regarded the closing of the school as a calamity to the entire community. B. E. Smith, superintendent of schools for the town of Normal, said that the town would now be compelled to build its own high school. David Felmley, while regretting the closing of the school, justified the governor's action on grounds of economy. He said that despite the tuition paid by the students the high school had never paid its way. Salaries paid to teachers always exceeded the amount paid in tuition, and the presence of the high school students had contributed greatly to the overcrowded conditions.

The students pondered the matter. They determined to let the public know how they felt about it. Carefully a group began to lay plans for a demonstration to be staged the night before Commencement. The *Pantagraph* reported that "at midnight the quiet town of Normal was thrown into a fever of excitement unparalleled in history." There was "a gruesome scene full of spectral horrors," not unlike the "horrible ghost scene in Hamlet." At 11:30 p.m. about fifty students assembled on the south side of

[50] Reminiscenses of Dr. Ralph Peairs, graduate from University High School, 1897; *Daily Pantagraph*, June 20, 1895, June 21, 1895.

town where they dressed themselves in black shrouds and masks. Soon a procession of dark figures bearing torches, picks, and shovels began moving to the sound of muffled drums broken now and then by the shrill blast of a bugle. Four silent figures carried a coffin, and four others bore a straw stuffed image of Governor John Peter Altgeld astride a rail. The procession proceeded north on Broadway past Professor Manchester's and Professor Felmley's homes and over to the campus. Curious faces peered from behind the curtains, and some of the more venturesome dressed and headed for the campus, where they knew some mischief was afoot. The electric current had been shut off. At one o'clock the bell on Old Main broke the silence. Slowly it tolled as the weird procession formed a circle at the south entrance of the building. Two figures solemnly dug a shallow grave and the coffin was deposited. A masked orator stepped forward and delivered an eulogy on University High School. He assailed John "Pardon" Altgeld, Governor of Illinois, as the assassin. Someone pointed to the figure of Altgeld. Cries rang out. "Hang him!" "Burn him!" The dummy was soon hanging from a nearby tree. Loud cheers and hisses rang out. As the flames lighted up the scene and revealed a gathering crowd of townspeople, the masked figures quickly dispersed in the darkness.

The fury of the students must have calmed considerably by 1896, as the *Index* for that year was discreetly dedicated to "The Honorable John P. Altgeld, A Friend of Education." If the University High School was abolished in name, it was not abolished in fact. Students who wished to continue their studies were permitted to take courses in the normal department's enriched curriculum and amass credits if not a diploma. Few students in the normal department availed themselves of the opportunity to take Latin, Greek, and economics or mathematics beyond arithmetic, and instruction remained on the high school level. The school was no longer advertised as a preparatory school whose graduates were readily accepted by eastern colleges. The catalog now merely stated that the practice department, a necessary adjunct of the normal department, consisted of twelve grades. Thus, says Professor Charles Harper in the *Development of the Teachers College,* the high school became a functional part of the practice school,[51] and with the increased demands for high school teachers, the Normal University began to place an emphasis on practice teaching on the high school level.

At the turn of the century more and more of Normal University's graduates went on to the great universities and colleges. In his lectures to the student body President Cook was constantly urging the students upon their graduation to take college training. To interest students in higher education, he conducted for several years a spring field trip to the University of Illinois. The students and their faculty chaperons made the trip by train and streetcar, carrying box lunches. They visited classes, listened to a specially arranged lecture, and made a tour of the campus.[52] Distinguished graduates of years past acted as lodestones, and soon little colonies of Normal University graduates were found at Harvard, Michigan, and Swarthmore. In 1896 five graduates of Normal University were attending Harvard, and when Charles DeGarmo became president of Swarthmore, graduates of Normal University followed him. Frank G. Blair, later state superintendent of public instruction, and another of Cook's innumerable protegés, was among the number. When he won the Pennsylvania Inter-Collegiate Oratorical Contest in 1896 as much joy and excitement pervaded the Normal University as if "Old Normal" had won the honors. These fine scholars paved the way for further recognition of Normal University graduates. Through Professor Edmund Janes James arrangements were made by which Normal University graduates might go to the University of Pennsylvania and after two years receive the degree of Bachelor of Philosophy.[53] By 1897 it was possible for graduates of Normal University to enter junior classes at the University of Illinois. Graduates of the four-year normal course or the two-year course for high school graduates could obtain bachelor's degrees at the end of two years, while graduates of the three-year normal course could obtain the Bachelor of Science in two years.[54]

When the General Assembly appropriated $40,000 for a fire-

[51] *Vidette,* April 1890, p. 21; *Catalog, Illinois State Normal University* 1897–1898, p. 7; Harper, *Development of the Teachers College,* p. 191.
[52] *Index,* 1896, pp. 134–135.
[53] *Vidette,* March 1892, p. 17.
[54] *Catalog Illinois State Normal University,* 1897, p. 71.

proof gymnasium in 1895, the societies believed that their dream of "more stately mansions" would be soon realized, but after a conference with Governor Altgeld, the Building Committee of the Board ruled otherwise, explaining that it was folly to leave the University's valuable library and museum to the mercy of a fire. Perhaps the removal of the museum, the library and the laboratories would afford more ample quarters for the ever-expanding societies. A delay came when the Governor disapproved the architect's plan for the new building. He thought since the building was to be situated on a beautiful campus, the ornamentation should be at the top. Personally he favored the turreted castles of his home Rhineland. What a beautiful picture they made silhouetted against the setting sun! [55]

The prospect of a gymnasium brought an upsurge in all things athletic, and plans were made for the use of the new building. President Cook was positive of one thing, classes in physical culture for young women. In the fall of 1890, when Miss Ruth Morris, the new preceptress and teacher of grammar learned how desirous President Cook was of providing the young women with instruction in the Del Sarte system of physical training, she employed a competent instructor to give part-time instruction during the winter term, and paid her from her own salary.[56] President Cook was so delighted with the experiment he resolved to employ a permanent teacher. In the fall of 1891 Miss Lucia Raines, of Memphis, Tennessee, was engaged to teach elocution and gymnastics. When she resigned after a year to be married, Cook told the Board, "She has established the work of physical culture" and "I am confident we shall be slow to abandon it. Its admirable results are manifested in a great variety of ways." [57] Miss Amelia Lucas, a graduate of the Emerson School of Oratory in Boston, was next employed as a teacher of reading and gymnastics. She gave instruction in the latter to both men and women students until 1896 when Frank Dillon was employed for three hours a day at

[55] *Vidette,* October 1895, p. 12.

The Index 1896 has a caricature of Governor Altgeld dressed in medieval costume with armour, buckler, and sword, surrounded by drawings of castles and sketches of the state penitentiary and mental hospital. It bears the caption "Our governor has decided ideas on architecture." p. 87.

[56] *Proceedings of the Board of Education* (Normal) June 24, 1891, p. 11.

[57] *Ibid.,* June 22, 1892, p. 9.

$25 a month to assist with the gymnastic work.[58] He soon became known as "Coach." Two years before, a group of men had organized the Normal Cadet Corps and their officers had asked the Board to apply to the United States government for the detail of a drillmaster and requisite stands of arms. The Board got no further than appointing a committee to investigate, and with the new interest in sports, the desire for military drill subsided.[59] Meanwhile indoor classes for both men and women were held in basement rooms formerly occupied by the janitor and the heating plant. There were no dressing rooms or lockers and no standard uniforms. Cook thought at least $750 might be spent for equipment even before moving into the building.

Baseball had long been popular on campus. The event that launched the closing exercises of the school year was the baseball game with the faculty. Early issues of the *Index* note that Normal's "White Stockings" played baseball with Wesleyan, Eureka College, Lincoln University, and Minonk. Football came to the campus in the early 1890's. In 1893 games were played with Wesleyan, Peoria, Eureka, and Gibson City. It was a rough and serious game to spectators as well as players.[60]

When Normal University's football team played at Gibson City in 1894, it was insulted by the crowd. Normal protested and Gibson City refused to give a return game. When Eureka played Normal University a return game at Wesleyan's ball park, the decision of Eureka's umpire was regarded as "so unfair that Normal refused to play the game to a finish." [61]

Basketball was introduced to the campus about 1895. Girls were initiated into the game in September 1896. The first girls' team organized was known as the Pioneer Team. During the first year that the girls played basketball twenty teams were organized. Toward the end of the winter term there was a contest for the school championship. The "Red and White" team (so-called from the ribbons they wore) won over the Pioneers.[62]

The first annual field day was held on Saturday, June 8, 1895.

---

[58] *Ibid.*, December 2, 1896, p. 60.
[59] *Ibid.*, December 5, 1894, p. 12.
[60] *Index* 1894, pp. 105–106.
[61] *Ibid.*, p. 86.
[62] *Ibid.*, 1897, p. 90.

Sixty-five dollars' worth of prizes had been solicited from the businessmen of Normal and Bloomington. Events included foot races, pole vault, discus throw, hammer throw, shot-put, kicking, jumping, tennis, bicycle races, and the less spectacular sack and potato races. Little time had been spent in training, but the *Index* proudly boasted that "Athletics now seem to have taken firm root in the school and by the aid of a new gymnasium building we hope in a few years to see Illinois State Normal University second to none in athletics and field sports." [63]

A campus athletic association was organized in 1897, and the president, Ferd McCormick, represented Normal University at the Illinois Inter-Collegiate Football Association, and was elected its treasurer. [64]

In 1897 B. C. Edwards, graduate of Boston School of Oratory was employed as teacher of reading and gymnastics. Whether the emphasis on sports had become too great is not known, but President Cook explained that he had employed Edwards because of his different outlook on physical culture. "My purpose," Cook said, "has been to use the gymnasium for training that should tell directly upon physical expression. . . . It is not to be forgotten that one great purpose of our gymnasium is to prepare teachers for giving to boys and girls in ordinary schoolrooms that mastery over their bodies which is so essential to health and grace." [65]

President Cook wanted to see the students have every opportunity to grow culturally and socially as well as physically and academically. He watched with interest the work of the old societies, Wrightonia and Philadelphia, the Philosophy Club, Political Economy Club so assiduously studying Henry George under the direction of Professor Manchester, and the new Sappho and Ciceronian societies, the former providing for the young women a varied study program of travel, history and art, and the latter giving men practical experience in public speaking and parliamentary procedures. [66] He gave every encouragement possible to the sporadic and struggling musical organizations that

[63] *Ibid.*, 1895, p. 83.
[64] *Ibid.*, p. 86.
[65] *Proceedings of the Board of Education* (Normal) December 8, 1897, p. 8.
[66] The Sapphonian Society was organized in the fall of 1887 under the guidance of the preceptress, Miss Flora Pennell. The Ciceronian Society developed from the Edwards Debating Club about 1879.

appeared on campus, the five or six piece orchestras, the quartets, and the bands that flourished from time to time. He hoped that it would soon be possible to employ a full-time music teacher.

The lecture course had been started the year before Cook became president. Originally it was voted to have only lectures and no musical or other entertainment, but in 1892 the constitution was revised and the attractions expanded. The Lecture Board was composed of twenty-five members, later reduced to fifteen, who pledged themselves to share the loss if the course failed to pay expenses. Any surplus was to be given to the president of the University to be held for the next year's treasurer. For their labors (and risks) the board members received two tickets, and the treasurer was allowed $7.50. In 1894 the course had six numbers —three lectures, two musical programs, and an interpretative reader. Among the distinguished numbers that appeared in Normal Hall during the Cook Era were the Old Boston Quartette; Kate Field, who presented "An Evening with Dickens"; Russell H. Conwell, famous Baptist preacher of Philadelphia, who spoke on "The Silver Crown or Born a King"; Maud Powell's Concert Company; Henry Watterson, who lectured on "Lincoln"; The New York Philharmonic; Professor Edmund Janes James, who spoke on "Bismarck"; and Francis Hopkinson Smith, who gave a program of readings. No number cost less than one hundred dollars and none over two hundred.[67]

Although Wrightonia and Philadelphia early added variety to their programs by the use of dialogs and dramatic skits, it was not until the 1890's that the true impact of "A play's the thing" was felt on campus. Traveling stock companies had early visited Bloomington and Dr. Henry Schroeder's Opera House; The Chatterton and the Durley Theatre had brought to their boards such actors as Joe Jefferson, Edwin Booth, Julia Marlowe, Lillian Russell, and the community's own opera star, Marie von Elsner or "Litta" as she was known in Paris, New York, and Chicago. Many students had never attended a real theatre before coming to Normal University. Rachel Crothers, daughter of a Bloomington physician, and an 1890 graduate of University High School was one of those upon whom the local billings made a deep im-

[67] *Index* 1894, pp. 88–89; 1895, pp. 70–71; 1896, p. 147; 1897, p. 129.

pression. She was fired with a desire to act, to write, and to produce. No longer content to write plays to be acted by her friends
in the front parlor of her home, she joined some other theatre-
minded young persons in organizing a dramatic club that dared
to rent lodge halls and charge admisison to their plays.

Inspired by these Bloomington players, Philadelphian and
Wrightonian joined as one in a dramatic club, and in Normal
Hall on June 19, 1892, under the direction of Professor Reeder,
presented Shakespeare's *Merchant of Venice*. On November 24,
1894, the Philadelphian Society presented Shakespeare's *As You
Like It,* and on June 8, 1895, Wrightonia played *Twelfth Night or
What You Will*. It was as good as plays went in Normal Hall, but
not even the most loyal Wrightonian would say it approached
Julia Marlowe's production in Bloomington the previous season.[68]
It is a matter of conjecture whether Shakespeare's plays were
selected because the students had come to know them through
Miss Colby's classes, or because Shakespeare was currently enjoy-
ing a revival among Eastern "highbrows" and the societies desired
to keep Normal University in the vanguard of good taste, or
simply because his plays no longer required royalty. The highlight of the 1897 Commencement was the production of Gilbert
and Sullivan's *H.M.S. Pinafore*.

As President Cook looked at the student body each morning
in General Exercises, he often thought of his own youth. Now a
polished, well-groomed, self-made man, he remembered the days
when he too felt self-conscious, awkward, and uncertain as to
soical amenities. He still winced at the word "clod-hopper." In
his appeal for the gymnasium he had stressed the importance of
posture and good carriage in the schoolroom. In one of his keying
up talks in the fall of 1897 he had advised the students to learn
to dance. Some were a bit surprised at the suggestion. Others
promptly took it up, and with President Cook's blessing the
Fortnightly Dancing Club was organized. Its membership was
limited to thirty gentlemen of the school who were free to invite
any of their "lady" friends to meetings on alternate Friday
evenings at the Normal Opera House. Later the club held its
fortnightly party in Trimmer's Hall, where there was music by

[68] *Ibid.,* 1892, n.p.; 1895, pp. 98, 103.

Ashton's Orchestra.[69] Cook thought school dances might be one of the uses of the new gymnasium, but when Charles Capen, alumnus and local Board member, proposed that the president be authorized to permit the occasional use of the gym for dancing if it involved no expense, the vote was a resounding "No." [70]

Not all of the daily General Exercises were given over to Scripture reading, "keying up" talks, professional homilies, and community singing, but occasionally there were special features, such as lectures by visiting professors or returned missionaries who spoke engagingly of life in distant lands. Among President Cook's papers is a letter which tells its own story of how he sought to bring novelty and variety to General Exercises.

Bloomington, March 25, 1897

(President Cook)

Kind friend: When I met you in this city and made arrangements with you to come out to the University and give an entertainment with my Graphophone I told you I would come for three dollars. Of course I want to make you rates as cheap as possible but I went to the extream by saying I would come for three $.

I expect to give your school a first class entertainment and as my pieces each cost me one dollar each, I think that five dollars is cheap enough. Please let me know as soon as possible the day and date that you want me to come so that I will know just what arrangements to make.

Yours truly

John K. H——— [71]

Increased costs of labor, materials and change of plans delayed completion of the gymnasium and hindered for a time the expansion of the physical training program. In 1897 the General Assembly voted an additional $16,000 and the building was ready for occupancy in the fall of 1898. To those who liked the cold gray stone of medieval castle and mongrel Renaissance the building was a joy to behold. It was located one hundred fifty feet south of the Main building, faced the east, and as a contemporary wrote "could easily be seen from the streetcar station and North

[69] *Ibid.*, 1898, p. 42; 1902, p. 145.
[70] *Proceedings of the Board of Education* (Normal) June 28, 1898, p. 15.
[71] *Cook Papers.* Milner Library.

Street." [72] The gymnasium proper was 40 by 90 feet and 22 feet in height. A gallery provided seats for spectators. Adjoining it was a three-story wing, the lower floor to be used for dressing rooms, baths, toilets, and storage; the second floor to be used as a library; and the third floor given over to science, biological and physical, with classrooms and laboratories. The original plans called for a basement and sub-basement, where an indoor swimming pool would be located. Expense made the pool prohibitive at the time and later developments proved the location undesirable. To those who were disappointed President Cook counseled patience. It had been thirty-three years since President Edwards had first gone before the General Assembly and asked for a gymnasium.

The new gymnasium boasted the popular equipment of the era—ropes, ladders, rings, slippery pole, parallel bars, turning, huge leather horses, and racks of Indian clubs and dumbbells. There was an alley for bowling but it was not yet outfitted. The students, generally speaking, took to physical training classes with much enthusiasm. Basketball was now an indoor sport, and competition between teams, societies and clubs took on a new emphasis. Wrightonians met Philadelphians on the basketball court as well as in forensics. The young women were quite as active as the young men in scheduling match games, and learning to use the new equipment. At last there were dressing rooms and a place to leave one's athletic gear. In the women's section might be seen rows of dark serge suits, long ample bloomers, and blouses with close necks and full three-quarter sleeves. [73]

Carter Harris, the janitor at the Training School, was transferred to the new gymnasium. This gentle son of a slave mother regarded the new post as a promotion, a reward, and a sacred trust. For over forty years he swept the building and locked the doors, and performed the humblest tasks with dignity. He preferred to be thought of as a custodian, not a mere janitor. Late evenings about his work he sometimes softly whistled or hummed

[72] *Index* 1896, p. 58.
[73] Four yards of fifty-four inch serge was required for the average girl's gym suit which was usually made at home from a pattern supplied by the instructor. The girl who complained of the weight of the suit might be reminded by her mother that at least it was modest.

the hymns and spirituals he had sung in his own college days at Fisk University. He became deeply attached to the boys who came out for sports. He cheered the teams to victory and consoled them in defeat. He lived frugally; in his off hours he and his wife worked as caterers, saving their money and investing it wisely. Often when a boy was discouraged, hungry and about to quit school, a word and a loan from Carter Harris would tide him over to receive his diploma.[74]

In the winter of 1887–1888 Charles Beach, a student, organized an all-school oratorical contest which for several years was a red letter event. Two prizes were offered by the Oratorical Board, and Wrightonia and Philadelphia each offered fifteen dollars to its member receiving the highest mark but not for winning first or second prize.[75] When smaller audiences and scantier door receipts almost smothered the enthusiasm of the faithful few who labored to maintain the oratorical contest, Mr. Beach, now a prosperous businessman, came to the rescue. In 1896 he began offering an annual cash prize of one hundred dollars, and a gold medal to the winner. That same year at the instance of President Reynolds Taylor of the Kansas State Normal School at Emporia, a league of Normal School Oratoricals was formed. Schools in Kansas, Iowa, Missouri, Wisconsin, and Illinois were invited to join. President Cook was quick to see the value of the league, and Illinois State Normal University promptly joined. In the first Inter-State Contest held in Warrensburg, Missouri, the winner of the Beach Medal took third place.[76]

On May 6, 1898, Normal University was host to the third Inter-State Oratorical Contest. There were seventy off-campus delegates. The presidents of four normal schools along with one or

[74] Unpublished MS. by Manfred J. Holmes. "A toast to have been given at a dinner honoring Carter Harris' retirement."

Carter Harris (1856–1944) was of mixed white, Negro and Indian parentage. A bright and capable youth, he exchanged manual labor with a legal firm for schooling. After two years in Fisk he organized plantation schools in Mississippi. For a time he was a tobacco tester and ran a grocery.

A Negro girl whom he later married had come north and was employed by Professor Metcalf. She encouraged him to come to Normal where he found work as a jack-of-all-trades. In 1892 he became janitor of the new Training School at a salary of $480 per year. He remained on the staff forty-eight years.

Harris was highly respected as a citizen, a Bible scholar, and a director of the Normal Building and Loan Association.

[75] *Index* 1892 n.p.

[76] *Proceedings of the Board of Education* (Normal) June 17, 1896, p. 47.

more faculty members accompanied their "entries." A delegation of fifty came from Kansas State and thrilled to see their orator win first place for fifty dollars and a gold medal. Normal's orator ranked fifth in the contest but the *Index* for 1898 took care to explain that he had had a very bad cold.[77]

The General Assembly that made the original appropriation for the gymnasium at Normal University, also passed "surprise" legislation creating two new normal schools. President Cook, Charles McMurry, and other educators had been advocating the move for several years. Cook felt that Illinois had lagged behind the other states in providing both normal schools and extension work. Massachusetts now had nine normal schools, Pennsylvania had fourteen and New York had twelve normals and the state was supplementing their work by supporting more than a hundred training classes in connection with high schools and colleges. While the General Assembly was deliberating, Cook helped to organize county Committees on Educational Progress, with the avowed purpose of creating sentiment in favor of normal schools.[78]

Another person very active in securing the new schools was Clinton Rosette, of DeKalb, a former schoolmaster who had been appointed to the State Board of Education by Governor Altgeld. While serving in his new capacity, Rosette began to speculate on what a similar institution might do for his community. He approached his fellow townsmen Joseph F. Glidden, Jacob Haisch, and Isaac L. Ellwood, who had made fortunes in barbed wire, about donations to secure the location of a normal school. Glidden offered a tract of land adjoining the city as a site, and Haisch subscribed $10,000 for a library. Politicians in the eastern part of the state were likewise interested in benefits for their section. Rockford, Oregon, Polo, and DeKalb were the chief competitors for the northern school, but the generosity of Rosette's friends enabled DeKalb to secure the location. Similar competition between Charleston and Mattoon resulted in the location of the Eastern Normal School at Charleston.[79] Subsequently plans were drawn and appropriations made. In September 1899 both schools

[77] *Index* 1898, p. 49.
[78] Harper, *Development of the Teachers College,* p. 177.
[79] Cook, *Educational History of Illinois,* pp. 244–254; Charles H. Coleman, *Eastern*

were ready to start classes, each with a massive greystone building reminiscent of castles on the Rhine.

In June 1897, Illinois State Normal University celebrated its fortieth anniversary. Present together for the last time on the rostrum of Normal Hall were the three former presidents, General Charles E. Hovey, Dr. Richard Edwards, and Dr. Edwin Hewett. Hundreds of alumni came for the two-day observance. Charles DeGarmo, President of Swarthmore, returned to speak on "The Normal School and President Edwards." Enoch Gastman, Superintendent of the Decatur Public Schools and a member of the first graduating class, spoke on "Early Teachers in the Normal School." Dr. Edwards, second president, spoke on "Nicholas Tillinghast and the Bridgewater Normal School." General Hovey, sick and scarcely able to travel, recalled "The Beginnings of the Normal School." The Honorable S. W. Moulton of Shelbyville, first president of the Board of Education, told of "The Normal School and the General Assembly of 1857." Mrs. Sarah Raymond Fitzwilliam appropriately talked on "Women of the Normal School." [80]

There had been many changes. There were new buildings, new students, new faculty. They missed the old teachers. The gentle, lovable Mr. Metcalf, who liked to have his name pronounced "Metcaulf" had died three years before, but the training building of which he had dreamed so long was now a reality.

From the balcony atop the south porch the four presidents looked across the campus. Hovey, resting on the arm of President Cook, noted the carefully laid out streets, the jangling little street car, and the many, many trees where once there had been only a cornfield. Cook told him of the terrible storm in June 1892, the wind, the lightning, and the rain. The roof had been torn off Old Main, eleven of her sixteen chimneys demolished, water had stood four inches deep in the study hall floor. He showed him the Lincoln tree that had been broken in half. It had taken six weeks to clear the campus and the town.[81] Hewett, still wearing a tall hat and the gold watch and chain that the students had given

---

Illinois State College Fifty Years of Service (Charleston: Eastern State College, 1950), pp. 9–25.
[80] *Index* 1897, p. 145.
[81] *Ibid.,* 1892, p. 28.

him so many years before and carrying his short little cane, stood apart with Edwards and pointed to the unfinished gymnasium. Edwards smiled and shook his head. It had been thirty-five years since he had broached the matter to the Legislature. He had also asked for a dormitory. When would that be forthcoming? President Cook called their attention to the new well,[82] the iron fence, the carriage gates, the tennis courts, and the lily pond. It was a pleasing sight. The old men smiled. John Cook was a worthy successor.

When the final day had come to a close and the last guest and graduate departed, General Hovey—pale, wan, and weak—turned to his brother-in-law. "John," he said, "I'm very tired." He spent the remainder of that sweltering summer at Cook's home in Normal. After a hundred days he summoned strength enough to return to his home in Washington, D. C. On November 17 he died.[83] He was buried with full military honors in the National Cemetery at nearby Arlington.

In visiting other schools, President Cook found Normal University was behind in facilities for music and kindergarten training. He believed that it was important for normal schools to prepare teachers who could give instruction in vocal music in the public schools and that there should be a well-graded course of music organized in the Practice School. As he talked with Ella Flagg Young, John Dewey, Francis Parker, Elizabeth Harrison, and other educators, he was convinced that Normal University had also neglected the kindergarten. "Very few normals of the age and rank of ours," he told the Board, "have neglected the kindergarten as we have done." A room in the training school had been set aside originally for a kindergarten, but it had never been equipped for that purpose. Cook now asked authorization to employ a kindergartner at a salary not exceeding $1,000 the first year. The Board generously voted approval of both a kindergarten and a music teacher, but it soon developed that sufficient funds were not available. The closing of the high school had shut off a source of income, and when three of the University's best teachers,

[82] The new well, 218 feet deep with 120 feet of water in it, cost $213.42. *Proceedings of the Board of Education* (Normal) December 8, 1897, p. 9.
[83] John W. Cook "General Charles E. Hovey," Memorial in *Twenty-second Biennial Report of the Superintendent of Public Instruction* (Springfield, 1898), p. LXXIV.

Charles Van Liew, Louis Galbreath, and Irving Reed,[84] were enticed to better paying positions, Cook knew that he could not employ a director of physical education, which the new gymnasium necessitated, and replace these men at lower salaries. Galbreath, an alumnus of 1885, who had taken a degree at Cornell, was valued not only for his teaching of pedagogy but for his ability and willingness to coach various sports in which the students were increasingly interested. Dr. Van Liew had come to Normal in 1894 to teach reading and pedagogy and in the absence of Dr. Charles McMurry had supervised student teaching. Van Liew wrote and spoke well, had been prominent in the Illinois Society for Child Study, and was largely responsible for the society going "Herbartian" rather than along lines advocated by G. Stanley Hall.[85] Fortunately Charles McMurry, on leave at the University of Chicago, and Mary Potter, teacher of foreign languages were returning, and Cook was able to secure in Van Liew's place Manfred J. Holmes of the Minnesota State Normal School, a graduate of Cornell University.

Although Cook wanted a kindergarten, music, manual training, a print shop, and a summer school, he would not jeopardize old departments by instituting new ones. Bravely he waived his dreams and recommended instead that salaries of the librarian and the assistant training teachers be raised from $800 to $900, that of the teacher of penmanship from $650 to $750, and that of the professor of mental science and didactics from $1,800 to $2,000.[86]

Cook believed in the purpose and destiny of the Normal University. He fought for good salaries for good men. As Professor Harper wrote in his *Development of the Teachers College* Cook was willing to participate in any fight if he thought there was danger of an educational position being filled on any other basis than merit.[87] He bristled at the faintest suggestion of outside in-

[84] Charles Van Liew was widely known for his contributions to American and German educational magazines. He was president of the State Normal School, Chico, California, 1899–1910.

[85] The Illinois Society for Child Study was organized in Champaign in May 1894 for the purpose of making known to parents and teachers the fundamental principles of child growth and development. Subsequently societies were organized in other states and eventually a national organization was effected.

[86] *Proceedings of the Board of Education* (Normal) June 28, 1898, p. 15.

[87] Harper, *Development of the Teachers College*, p. 176.

fluence or pressure in the affairs of the school. He was determined to keep his school and other schools free from nepotism and political interference. He refused to employ a niece of the president of the Board for a position in which there was no vacancy. He respected Governor Altgeld as a friend of the public schools and a believer in education as the great hope of democracy and social justice, but he would not consent to the Governor's removal of David Felmley from the faculty because he was a Democrat and had been active in the campaign in 1896. When the McLean County Republican Chairman, confronted with the matter of a campaign chest in 1892, wrote President Cook advising him that the amount to be contributed by his staff had been set at $400, one-half of which should be paid very soon, Cook's anger knew only decent restraint. He promptly replied in words whose meaning was unmistakable.

This institution is not in any sense a political institution under control of the Republican party. If it were ever so understood by the General Assembly of the state, it would never receive another appropriation. When the time comes that this institution must depend upon any one political party for its support, it will have a very short lease of life.

I wish to say most unequivocally, that I cannot submit to any suggestion from any person as to the amount of money that I shall contribute to a political campaign. This is an impertinence I cannot allow. If that is a condition to my present position, I shall certainly leave it. I shall doubtless make contributions, as I always have; doubtless others of the teachers will do the same but it must be upon their own motion, I certainly shall not suggest it to them.

He warned that if it became known that the Republican party, through its official committees was attempting to place educational institutions—institutions thus far free from suspicion—in the category of political machines operated in the interests of a particular political party, there would be a mighty cry of indignation throughout the state. He defied anyone to subject the Normal University to such criticism and place its faculty in such a dilemma while he had anything to say about it.[88]

Cook's frankness, honesty, sense of fair play, and straight for-

[88] John W. Cook to Calvin Rayburn, Treasurer, McLean County Central Committee. Normal, September 13, 1892. *Cook Papers.*

Olive Lillian Barton, a sweet girl graduate of 1899, taught mathematics, 1906–1911, and was dean of women, 1911–1940.

O. L. Manchester, who taught Latin and economics from 1890 to 1928, found time from his duties as dean to be mayor of Normal.

Henry McCormick, alumnus of 1868, on faculty, 1869–1918.

Carter Harris, beloved janitor, resigned in 1940 after forty-eight years of devoted service.

David Felmley succeeded John Cook as professor of mathematics and was president from 1900 to 1930.

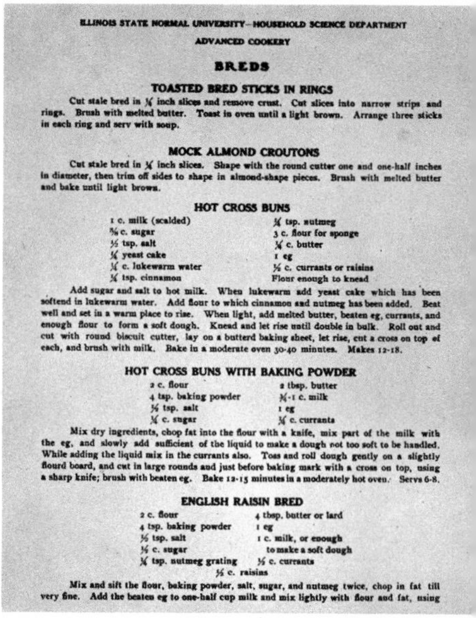

ILLINOIS STATE NORMAL UNIVERSITY—HOUSEHOLD SCIENCE DEPARTMENT

ADVANCED COOKERY

BREDS

TOASTED BRED STICKS IN RINGS

Cut stale bred in ¼ inch slices and remove crust. Cut slices into narrow strips and rings. Brush with melted butter. Toast in oven until a light brown. Arrange three sticks in each ring and serv with soup.

MOCK ALMOND CROUTONS

Cut stale bred in ¼ inch slices. Shape with the round cutter one and one-half inches in diameter, then trim off sides to shape in almond-shape pieces. Brush with melted butter and bake until light brown.

HOT CROSS BUNS

1 c. milk (scalded)	¼ tsp. nutmeg
⅝ c. sugar	3 c. flour for sponge
½ tsp. salt	¼ c. butter
¼ yeast cake	1 eg
¼ c. lukewarm water	½ c. currants or raisins
¼ tsp. cinnamon	Flour enough to knead

Add sugar and salt to hot milk. When lukewarm add yeast cake which has been softend in lukewarm water. Add flour to which cinnamon and nutmeg has been added. Beat well and set in a warm place to rise. When light, add melted butter, beaten eg, currants, and enough flour to form a soft dough. Knead and let rise until double in bulk. Roll out and cut with round biscuit cutter, lay on a butterd baking sheet, let rise, cut a cross on top of each, and brush with milk. Bake in a moderate oven 30-40 minutes. Makes 12-18.

HOT CROSS BUNS WITH BAKING POWDER

2 c. flour	2 tbsp. butter
4 tsp. baking powder	¾-1 c. milk
½ tsp. salt	1 eg
¼ c. sugar	¼ c. currants

Mix dry ingredients, chop fat into the flour with a knife, mix part of the milk with the eg, and slowly add sufficient of the liquid to make a dough not too soft to be handled. While adding the liquid mix in the currants also. Toss and roll dough gently on a slightly flourd board, and cut in large rounds and just before baking mark with a cross on top, using a sharp knife; brush with beaten eg. Bake 12-15 minutes in a moderately hot oven. Servs 6-8.

ENGLISH RAISIN BRED

2 c. flour	4 tbsp. butter or lard
4 tsp. baking powder	1 eg
½ tsp. salt	1 c. milk, or enough to make a soft dough
½ c. sugar	
¼ tsp. nutmeg grating	½ c. currants
½ c. raisins	

Mix and sift the flour, baking powder, salt, sugar, and nutmeg twice, chop in fat till very fine. Add the beaten eg to one-half cup milk and mix lightly with flour and fat, using

President Felmley was a firm believer in simplified spelling. Carrie Lyford's cookbook was published with the new spelling.

The last Happy Birthday for President Felmley, 1929.

President Felmley's office and the reception room featuring
"the new Oliver typing machine."

During World War I, Ange. V. Milner, librarian 1890–1927, wrote eight hundred letters
to soldiers and former students.

A science class, about 1911.

Frank Westhoff, director of music, 1901–1935 and an early orchestra.

Douglas Ridgley, professor of geography, 1903–1922, popularized field trips.
Summer students in his class visit a waterfall near Starved Rock.

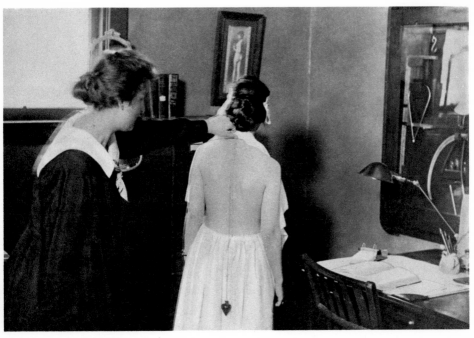

Early physical examination: curvatures ascertained by a plumb line...

Dancing on the green, from an early May fete.

Scene from "The Piper," presented by the Senior Class in 1921.

Scene in training school: those exciting stereopticon views.

Dr. Harvey Peterson and two students experiment in testing.

The old summer trolley.

A student prepares his meal in his room, 1908.

wardness enabled him to deal successfully with the General Assembly as well as faculty and students. When he appeared before the Legislature he got what he asked for. Not once during his administration had his requests for general expenses ever been cut and two new buildings had been secured. For the decade prior to 1890 the average annual appropriation was $28,930.60, while the average during the decade 1890 to 1900 was $42,807.50.[89]

No educator in the state had looked with greater favor upon the creation of the two new normal schools than Cook. He saw in the new schools great opportunity for leadership untrammeled by tradition. The Charleston Board selected for its president State Superintendent of Public Instruction Samuel M. Inglis of Greenville, Illinois, who had not intended to be a candidate for re-election. Before assuming his new duties he died, June 1898, and the Board turned to candidates outside the state and selected Livingston C. Lord, president of the Minnesota State Normal.[90]

When it became apparent in the spring of 1899 that the building at DeKalb would be ready for occupancy in September, the Board of the new school approached President John W. Cook of Normal. He was known in DeKalb, having spoken at the laying of the cornerstone. He was admired and respected. Cook hesitated. He had spent thirty-nine years of his life in Normal, as a student, teacher, administrator. The board painted a glowing future for the school and offered him unlimited authority in the selection of his faculty. He was offered an annual salary of $5,000, and Colonel Ellwood offered to pay out of his funds an additional sum of $1,000. To the latter President Cook shook his head. The one consideration that would influence him to accept the position would be greater opportunity to be of service to the cause of education and to shape the course of the new institution.

As soon as it became known that Cook was being considered for the DeKalb position, his friends in Normal became worried. The *Vidette* in May reported that ever since President Cook had gone to DeKalb in April to confer with the Board of Education in charge of the new normal school there had been much speculation as to whether he would accept the offer. "In behalf of the stu-

[89] *Index* 1904, p. 21.
[90] Coleman, *op. cit.*, pp. 33–34.

dents of this school," the editor wrote, "we sincerely hope he may not leave us." [91]

When Cook announced his decision to accept the DeKalb offer and to present his formal resignation to the Board when it met in June, the *Vidette* staff made elaborate plans for its Commencement issue. It would feature a symposium of parting tributes to President Cook. The editor of the *Vidette* would speak for the student body on Cook as a teacher and friend. Cook's good friend George P. Brown would evaluate his work as an educator, Charles McMurry would praise him as an administrator, and Richard Edwards, as a man of affairs.

While Cook prepared his baccalaureate sermon and began rounding out his affairs in Normal and lining up a faculty for the new school, the Committee on Teachers was busy looking for a successor. Some consideration was given to President Richard G. Boone of Ypsilanti, Michigan, but the three favored candidates were Henry McCormick, Rudolph Reeder, and Arnold Tompkins of the University of Illinois.[92]

When the Board met, President Cook modestly reviewed the nine years of his administration. In 1890, there was yet no regular librarian; the reference library was in the end of a narrow hall on the second floor, and the small circulating library was open half an hour on Friday afternoons. Ange. Milner was soon employed to assemble and catalog the books in the various collections about the school and the old reception room was converted into a library. When the Practice Building was completed, the library was moved to more commodious quarters in the Main Building, and with the completion of the gymnasium and classrooms, it had been moved there. The Practice School in 1890 was also located in the original building; two critic teachers supervised the student teachers who heard classes in the halls, in the basement and under the stairs. In 1891 the General Assembly appropriated $24,000 for the building, which currently was adequate to the needs of the practice school. The 1895 appropriation of $40,000 and the supplementary appropriation of $16,000 in 1897 had made possible the new gymnasium. (Bowling alleys were still uncon-

[91] *Vidette*, May 1899, p. 182.
[92] *Daily Pantagraph*, June 23, 1899; *Proceedings of the Board of Education* (Normal) June 21, 1899, p. 15.

structed.)[93] A heating plant had been built. Attendance in the normal department increased from 464 in 1890 to 840 in the school year 1898–1899.

The course of study, Cook said, had been altered "almost as materially as the physical plant." The changes in professional courses had been made in an effort to conform to modern trends in education. Cook had labored hard to maintain the purpose and spirit of the school as conceived by the founders and its early leaders.

Ella Flagg Young moved that Cook be commended for his services as a student, teacher, and president in advancing his alma mater to high rank among the normal schools, and that it take cognizance of the "immense intellectual and moral force" which would be withdrawn from the Normal University upon his departure. Later in the afternoon the Committee on Teachers and Salaries presented the name of Arnold Tompkins, Professor of Pedagogy at the University of Illinois, as its choice for president.

A vote was taken and there was a hurried call to Professor Tompkins. Would he please come to Normal at once.[94]

[93] The bowling alleys were installed later but the construction of the pool in the basement was abandoned.

[94] Two other candidates were nominated from the floor but Tompkins received twice as many votes as the others and was declared elected. *Proceedings of the Board of Education* (Normal) June 21, 1899, p. 17.

CHAPTER IX

The Year of Arnold Tompkins

As ARNOLD TOMPKINS sat beside President Cook at the Fortieth Commencement, he made a good impression. He was tall and large of frame, smooth shaven, and almost jovial in appearance. He was alert and interested, and his blue eyes twinkled when he smiled. He had been making friends ever since he arrived in Normal the evening before. He had hurried over from Champaign to attend the banquet honoring President Cook and had not had time to change to formal dress. When introduced, he made an amusing apology and charmed the guests with his humor, poise, and sincerity. Here was a man large of mind and large of heart. He beamed affectionately on President Cook as townspeople and faculty paid him tribute and the students presented a parting gift of a handsome gold watch and chain.[1]

Cook had confidence in the man who had been chosen his successor. He described Arnold Tompkins as "poet, philosopher, seer, and prophet all in one." As the procession of sixty-five graduates, the women in long white dresses of silk and organdy and the men in dark suits and stiff high collars, filed across the stage to receive their diplomas, they bowed respectfully to the new president. The next year's seniors, sitting down in front, took him to their hearts at once. For them the year to follow would be rich and joyous, long to be remembered.

Arnold Tompkins was born on his father's farm eight miles south of Paris, Illinois, on September 10, 1849. His first schooling was obtained at "Possum Kingdom," a rural school near his home. At the age of fifteen he walked three miles to attend another country school where a college-trained man enriched the curriculum for the older pupils by teaching geometry and algebra. This teacher inspired young Tompkins to go on to college. At the age of seventeen he taught a term of rural school and attended

[1] *Daily Pantagraph,* June 23, 1899.

the high school in Paris for two or three months. Then he returned to rural teaching and saved his money for college.

In 1869 Tompkins entered Indiana University but dropped out before the end of the year because of overwork. The following September he entered Butler University, but was again forced to leave on account of illness.

While principal of a two-room school at Grand View, Illinois, he married Jennie Snyder, his associate teacher. For several years they alternately taught and attended school, usually teaching through the winter and attending school in the spring. Both entered Indiana State Normal School at Terre Haute in the spring of 1875. Tompkins' work with William A. Jones, first president of the school, aroused his interest in organic thinking. Tompkins and his wife graduated in 1880, and for the next two years they taught at Worthington, Indiana. In the fall of 1882 he became superintendent of schools at Franklin, Indiana. Here he began his real work in organizing schools on a philosophical basis. At the conclusion of his first year he published *A Graded Course of Study for the Franklin Public School,* a book of 240 pages, based on psychological factors in education. In this beginning work he was far in advance of the general school thought.[2]

Tompkins became head of the English department of the normal school of DePauw University, Greencastle, Indiana, in 1885 and was made dean of the school in 1889. That same year he took his Bachelor's degree from Indiana University, just twenty years after his matriculation. Two years later he received his Master's from the same institution.

In 1890 the normal school was abandoned at DePauw and Tompkins accepted an offer to become head of the English department of the Indiana State Normal School at Terre Haute. After two years he entered the graduate school of the University of Chicago, where he studied for two years. In 1895 he received a doctorate from the University of Ohio. That fall he accepted the chair of pedagogy at the University of Illinois.

He had already achieved recognition as a writer and lecturer. His well-received text on composition, *The Science of Discourse,*

[2] "Arnold Tompkins, A Memorial," Chicago Normal School, November 5, 1905, pp. 3-4.

had been published in 1889 while he was at DePauw. *The Philosophy of Teaching* and a reprint of *The Science of Discourse* appeared in 1893, and in 1895, while he was still a student at the University of Chicago, his *Philosophy of School Management* was published. Shorter articles appeared from time to time in the *Indiana School Journal* and other educational magazines. While superintendent at Franklin, he began lecturing before teachers' institutes. He was as dynamic as a speaker as he was powerful in the classroom.

As professor of pedagogy at the University of Illinois, Tompkins was often called upon to speak at county institutes, state teachers' meetings, and national associations. He had always kept in close touch with the common schools, and was unusually sympathetic with normal schools. He believed a full-fledged practice school at the University would be an adjunct to the department of pedagogy, but this idea was far too advanced for its governing board. Few teachers at the University at the time were so vitally concerned as he with influencing teachers of the state.[3]

Tompkins was an idealist, and one of the early educators who could lay a distinct claim to having developed a real philosophy of education. Alfred Bayliss, State Superintendent of Public Instruction, said of him, "In the power of vivid presentation of educational doctrines and ideas Arnold Tompkins had few equals in the United States. He could make the commonest of us feel that the whole sky of truth bends over each recitation; and the teacher needs but climb Sinai to receive the divine law." [4]

A few months before accepting the presidency of Normal University he had made an address before the National Superintendents Association in Columbus in which he brought together what he considered the fundamental precepts of education. He called it *The Implications and Applications of the Principle of Self-Activity in Education:*

The impressive lesson from the history of thought is that the human mind can find no peace except in search for ultimate unity and reality of the Universe. This unity, as discerned from afar by the eye of faith in religion, and established by reason in art, science and philosophy, is the

[3] Harper, *Development of the Teachers College,* pp. 249–250.
[4] "Arnold Tompkins, A Memorial," p. 23.

ultimate goal of man's earthly endeavor. All processes of thought, from sense perception to reason, are but modes of satisfying the craving of the soul for touch with ultimate reality, with the life that binds the seemingly chaotic world into orderly system.

It is little wonder that John Cook called him "a poet, a prophet, and seer."

"All educational discussions," Tompkins continued, "are based on the assumption and prompted by the faith that there is a unifying principle which organizes and systematizes the distracting variety of details in the process of education." Although education made use of logic, ethics, psychology, and the other sciences he maintained that "the science of education went forth in its own right and organized all the sciences from its own creative center. The central principle which ordered all the details of the complex process of education in a unified harmonious whole was the principle of self-activity." [5]

To Tompkins this principle manifested itself primarily as a tension between the real and the ideal. He saw man in a "seeking, searching, surging world, constantly striving." The following aphorisms illustrate the character of his thought:

Coming to consciousness of the better self is the second birth of the soul.

At every stroke of the teacher some present stress must be released, and some new ideal born; some new stress set up.

To educate is to move the life onward and upward under the stress of ideals.

Secondly he saw the principle of self-activity assuming a form of tension between subject and object: "Whenever teaching is found to be dead, it is because the teacher tries to induce action from without, instead of utilizing the self-activity of the pupil." To Tompkins the subjects of the curriculum were but so many avenues to the enlargement of the self. History, language, mathematics, science were taught that the pupil "might have life and have it more abundantly." The precept, the concept, the judgment, and the syllogism were but processes in the unity of subject and object.

Lastly he envisaged the tension between the universal and the

[5] *Ibid.*, pp. 6–7.

individual, creative energy and its object. These tensions Tompkins believed should determine the methods, construct the course of study, organize and manage the school. Following this principle of self-activity would bring all school work into conscious and organic relation to every other educational force—the church, the state, the home. "All move," he concluded, "under the same principle to the same end—the full realization of all the beauty and worth implicit in human nature." [6]

The applause at Columbus had hardly died away when Tompkins accepted the presidency of Normal University. Here was the great opportunity to blueprint the principle, draft it into the curriculum, to implement the idea into reality. Tompkins lost no time. He seemed to have no time to lose. With his warmth and depth of human understanding, transparent honesty and passion for beauty and perfection he easily won over his faculty. He so completely identified himself with his beliefs that he seemed to be the living embodiment of his philosophy of life. The students were captivated and inspired. [7]

Cook had taken with him to DeKalb two outstanding members of the Normal University faculty—Charles McMurry, Professor of Pedagogy, and Miss Mary Potter, Professor of Ancient and Modern Languages. John J. Wilkinson, a graduate of 1885 who had studied at Jena and Berlin and recently taken a Ph. D. from Leipsig was selected by the Board to fill McMurry's place. He was considered well qualified to carry on the Herbartian tradition at Normal. The possibility of a decline in enrollment because of the opening of the two new normals relieved the Board of the necessity of immediately hiring a new language teacher.

When school opened in September 1899, there were 490 students enrolled in the normal department, 219 fewer students than there had been the previous September. Tompkins was not disconcerted. He heartily favored additional normal schools and felt confident that the need for qualified teachers was so great that in a few years a fifth normal school would be established. In the interim much work needed to be done.

[6] "Address of Arnold Tompkins before the National Superintendents Association, Columbus, Ohio, February 23, 1899." Quoted, *Ibid.*, pp. 6–14.
[7] Interviews, Mrs. Florence Sample Fleming, Class of 1900, June 6, 1953; C. W. Whitten, Class of 1900, July 5, 1953.

David Felmley asserted later that no year in the preceding thirty years had seen so much change as Tompkins wrought in 1899–1900. There were radical changes in the organization, administration, and spirit of the school.[8] Everywhere there was "new freedom in school life, less pressure, and more spontaneity." Attendance was now required only in the classes and at General Exercises. The rigid spelling standards that had sorely vexed the students since the days of President Edwards were relaxed. A flexible course of study was drawn up to serve the varying needs of students.

By December, the Tompkins' blueprint was ready. He had gone carefully over the structure with his faculty. His first recommendation was for four sessions a year of twelve weeks each as soon as the requisite appropriations could be obtained. Meanwhile he proposed the school year be divided into three terms of twelve weeks, and a summer term of six weeks, thus lengthening the school year from thirty-nine to forty-three weeks. A tuition of six dollars would be collected from the summer students to defray expenses and the faculty donate their services as far as necessary.

That Tompkins regarded the presidency as involving his personal, if not arbitrary, leadership is shown in his forthright preliminary statement to his plan for reorganization of the faculty. "I consider it my specific function to direct the thought movement of the school as a whole, to control the normal school process as a whole as indicated in the 'Logical View of the Course of Study'." That the mere external details of administration would claim as little of his attention as was consistent with the "thought movement" of the school, he delegated the bookkeeping to Mr. Elmer Cavins and employed a messenger boy. Flora Dodge continued to serve as clerk as she had done under Hewett and Cook, taking dictation, typing letters, mailing out catalogs, and keeping records of the faculty and graduates, but she no longer found time to reimburse the state by giving lessons in shorthand and typewriting.[9]

Tompkins in his reorganization plan differentiated between the "Faculty in Theory" and the "Faculty in Practice." Under the

[8] David Felmley in "Arnold Tompkins, A Memorial," pp. 22–23.
[9] In ten years Flora P. Dodge's salary as secretary increased from seven dollars a week to $480 a year.

"Faculty in Theory" were grouped the department of Philosophy of Education, General Method, involving what he liked to term "the logical and psychological movement of thought," Special Methods, and Science and the Art of Instruction. The "Faculty in Practice" embraced the Model School faculty from kindergarten through high school and the supervising teachers, or as he styled them, "the faculty of criticism." In the Model School, "master" teachers taught to illustrate theory and to make the ideal appear in the real, while in the Practice School the pupil-teachers taught to develop skill.[10]

As Tompkins viewed the situation, the Practice School was the weakest part of the University. "The model aspects of it," he said, "are almost wholly wanting." He believed much could be learned from "scientific" observation of master teachers and much was to be gained from careful counseling and criticism of pupil-teachers. Under the existing set-up he did not think it possible to turn out the carefully trained graduates that were needed in the schools of Illinois. He thought the departments of reading and gymnastics, for example, should be separated and asked for additional teachers in the Model School.[11]

The high school, which had been officially abolished upon the order of Governor Altgeld in 1895, had been quietly functioning as a preparatory department giving pre-normal work. Tompkins resolved to bring it out in the open again as a rightful part of the Practice School. The Herbartians had regarded the elementary school and the training of elementary teachers the chief concern of the normal school. "The normal school," said Tompkins, "must exhibit work, and an opportunity for practice, throughout the public school system of the state." High schools were increasing in number throughout the state, but there was no school in Illinois outside the normal schools offering the necessary preparation for high school teaching. In 1899 there were but two years of high school represented in the Model School. President Tompkins sought to extend this to four. He was careful to explain that what

[10] *Proceedings of the Board of Education* (Normal) December 6, 1899, pp. 10–13.

[11] The board approved the separation of reading and gymnastics, with B. C. Edwards as teacher of gymnastics, and Miss Amelia F. Lucas, teacher of reading; thereupon the University entered a new era in physical education. Soon the emphasis on sports took the place of physical exercise for body-building and personal development. *Ibid.*, December 6, 1899, p. 15.

he wanted was a high school having definite connection with the Practice School and not simply one having an administrative connection with the normal school. In this regard he hearkened back to the philosophy of Hovey and Edwards. "The normal school must prepare teachers for all the schools." Coming as he did from the State University with a growing department of pedagogy, he clearly realized that the normal school must strengthen its offerings and lengthen its line of defense if it would be the agency for training high school teachers.

In defense of the new Course of Study he explained that it had not been made by following tradition and patching together courses of study from other normal schools. "It is the result of an attempt to construct originally from the central idea of a normal school working under the environment in which our school is placed." The main effort in revising the course was to secure a high degree of organic unity from a strictly professional standpoint. Class periods were lengthened twenty minutes. The number of courses that a student could take was now reduced to four, with each class meeting daily. Formerly a student might have as many as thirty-one recitation periods in a week. Electives provided for the needs of individual teachers, but there was no other deviation from the standard course, which required twenty-four credits for graduation.

Dr. Tompkins inspired the same confidence among members of the Board as among the faculty and students. When he presented an idea the Board listened and almost invariably voted to consider it. Often the chairman of a committee, noting the nods of approval among the members, would propose immediate action. For the first time in the Board's forty-two years the president of the University was added to the Committee on Textbooks and Course of Instruction.[12]

In developing the new course of study, Tompkins had brought to the Faculty Club educators of the calibre of Ella Flagg Young, now Professor of Education at the University of Chicago and soon to earn a Ph. D. under John Dewey, Superintendent Enoch Gastman of Decatur, and Superintendent Peleg R. Walker of Rockford.

[12] *Ibid.*

Tompkins believed that the curriculum should be profession-
alized and also flexible. To him every normal school teacher was
a professor of pedagogy. There were no strictly academic teachers.
He would reduce the hours in pedagogy but not the emphasis.[13]
This the faculty could not see. He told Mrs. Young that the faculty generally believed that it was "the chief business of the
school to give good academic instruction to those people who have
failed to receive such in their home school." He was sympathetic
when the faculty found it difficult to go along with some of the
more radical changes that he hoped to effect. "I could not expect
them to understand suddenly that which I have spent years on,"
he wrote Alfred Bayliss, State Superintendent of Public Instruction. "From the first it has been to me a most interesting study to
watch the working in the minds of the different members of the
faculty. They were accustomed to think in terms of mathematics
and mechanism and not in terms of spiritual organism. This is a
matter of growth and their own personal development." [14]

Like Cook he too wanted a kindergarten and training in music
but he thought it best to wait until other departments already a
part of the school organization were built up and sufficient funds
were available to set up the proper equipment and pay qualified
teachers.

The matter of the Practice School concerned him most. In
January he circularized the Board relative to a plan of cooperating
with the local school board whereby students in the Normal University could have wider experience in teaching, but nothing came
out of it.[15] When he presented his second report in June he
reiterated the three points of weakness in the Practice School, the
scarcity of pupils, the scarcity of critic teachers, and the lack of
unity and organic life in the school as a whole and especially between the Practice School and the normal school proper.[16] To
meet the problem of scarcity of pupils President Tompkins recommended that a flat rate of one dollar be charged per pupil in
the elementary grades and six dollars per pupil in the high school

[13] Arnold Tompkins to Ella F. Young, Normal, December 13, 1899. Tompkins
Letterbook, pp. 134–135.
[14] Arnold Tompkins to Alfred Bayliss, Normal, December 12, 1899. *Ibid.*, p. 128.
[15] Arnold Tompkins to Judge William H. Green of Cairo, Illinois. Normal, January 19,
1900. *Ibid.*, p. 179.
[16] *Proceedings of the Board of Education* (Normal) June 19, 1900, p. 12.

instead of the former rates of $4.50 in the first six grades and $7.75 for all above. The resignations of two of the higher salaried teachers in the Practice School—Maud Valentine, who left for further study at Columbia, and Mrs. Lida Brown McMurry, who joined President Cook and her brother-in-law, Charles McMurry, at DeKalb—provided some money with which to angle for a large staff, but it would not stretch far enough. The Board must seek larger appropriations from the next General Assembly.[17]

Tompkins also wanted to beautify the campus with more trees, shrubs, and flowers. He was grateful to Mrs. John W. Cook for planting ivy around the gymnasium and the Practice Building before moving to DeKalb. He wanted to do away with the ugly cinder paths that marred the campus. He thought a covered connection between the buildings might add to their usefulness and be attractive as well. The library might be used more in bad weather if it were more accessible from the classrooms. He also wanted beauty brought into the classrooms through pictures and objects of art. He wanted the halls and corridors to be attractive with pictures and not to be mere passageways.

While President Tompkins labored over the curriculum and the budget, the faculty tried to implement the new guiding philosophy in their classes. In grading, there was less emphasis placed on arbitrary percentages. Under the old system anyone receiving a mark of ninety percent was on the verge of perfection, while seventy percent was passing and one point less was failure. Tompkins took over the classes that Cook had formerly taught, and was regarded as somewhat negligent in the matter of checking attendance and grades. It was what the student learned and not what he failed to learn that concerned the new president. Seniors in his philosophy class loved the genial teacher who would not only laugh with them but would take them soaring to the heights.

Student life went on much as it had before.[18] The Wrightonian, Philadelphian, Sapphonian, Ciceronian societies, the YMCA and the YWCA, and the Fortnightly Dancing Club held their scheduled meetings, exchanged programs, and joined forces in en-

[17] *Ibid.*
[18] Interview, C. W. Whitten, July 5, 1953.

couraging local entrants in the Inter-Collegiate Forensic Contests. They marched in a body to the train to give the Normal representatives to the annual contests a rousing send-off. They sat up late to get telegraphic returns and again turned out at the station to welcome them home.

Wrightonia and Philadelphia caught the spirit of the Tompkins' clean-up, brighten-up campaign and remodeled their halls. The two societies spent $600 each in flooring and frescoing their spacious halls and providing new stage decorations and furnishing. Wrightonian raised its floor two feet in the rear to slope down to the stage. New open seats were purchased, and the aisles carpeted. The 1899 *Index* describes the arch over the stage as very beautiful. "Round pillars with their capitals and footlights make the stage very pretty indeed." New curtains were placed at the windows. All manner of fund-raising devices were employed, and many a senior pledged a large part of his first month's wages to "dear old" Philadelphia or Wrightonia.

The Inter-Society Contest was the high mark of the year. Seven Wrightonians competed against seven Philadelphians in oratory, debate, declamation, essay, piano solo, and vocal solo. Weeks of preparation went into the contests. There was a task for every society member. Skilled artists of Chicago, Bloomington, and St. Louis might be employed to coach the contestants. Always there were the tryouts and selection of contestants within the societies, the joint meeting of officers to draw up and amend the rules, the winner of the previous contest always having preferred status. Then there was the night of the contest with every loyal Wright and Phil sitting on the edge of his seat, listening, applauding, and almost prayerfully waiting the judges' decision. Next there was the banquet, the celebration or the consolation, and after that plans for the next year's contest—thus ran the cycle of the societies.

Nor were the YMCA and the YWCA to be outdone by the societies. Delegates were sent to the annual conferences at Lake Geneva, and The Universal Day of Prayer was observed by sunrise prayer meetings. Both organizations lent their support to the great temperance movement in Bloomington which collapsed in its efforts to vote liquor out of the city. In the winter term 1899–

1900 seventeen young women were studying missions with the thought of eventually becoming foreign missionaries. That same fall the young women's organization felt it should play a larger role in the social life of the school and rented rooms in the home of Mrs. John S. Ball, 320 North Street. Here study groups met, teas and socials were held. Joint YWCA and YMCA functions were held in the gymnasium, the only place on the campus large enough to accommodate the student body.

The boarding clubs continued as popular social rendevous, and each year the rivalry between the respective clubs grew keener. Stewards were no longer content to greet students at the station in Normal, grab the nervous young co-ed's valise and politely offer to conduct her to lodgings, but they often walked to Hudson or Towanda, boarded trains, and solicited patronage for their respective clubs. Cleanliness, variety of meals, excellence of cooking, generous portions, good fellowship, access to rooming houses and the campus were points stressed by the energetic, ambitious young stewards. After 1898 men and women were no longer permitted to room in the same houses, but they could take their meals at the same boarding clubs.

In sports, tennis, bicycling, and skating in season continued to be popular, although the *Index* for 1899 averred, "Basketball is pre-eminently the game for the Normal Schools. It provides delightful recreation for a large number of persons. Twelve to sixteen teams may use one field. The game is easily learned." The enthusiastic reporter admitted that there were a few casualties but these were not too severe. To prove it he cited the list of injuries incurred by players during the past season—one knee gashed against a radiator, one dislocated finger, one strained shoulder, one sprained wrist, and two blackened eyes. The new game, he said, "cultivates courage, alertness, and subordination." [19]

After the University of Illinois Men's Glee Club presented a concert in the community in the fall of 1898, the men at Normal University took stock of their voices and decided that their school too should have a glee club. In January the singers organized and prevailed on Mary Hartmann, teacher of mathematics, and Elizabeth Mavity, teacher of grammar, to serve as directors. A few

[19] *Index*, 1899, p. 107.

weeks later the women of the school organized a glee club. On March 17, 1899, the men presented their first concert.

Students of this era never despaired for lack of training, and they were loath for any other school to surpass them in extracurricular activities. They rallied round their debaters and orators with the same enthusiasm that later generations gave to intercollegiate sports. As boldly as they had undertaken Shakespearian plays in the early nineties, they took to opera in the late nineties. With only the help of some of the more musically inclined members of the faculty, the senior class of 1899 dared to present the opera *Castanea* as a feature of Commencement Week. So well was the innovation received that for a time opera "threatened" to become a commencement tradition.

Arnold Tompkins had arrived on campus only the day before school began in September 1899, but in the ten months that followed he had wrought a revolution. He had won over the conservative, Herbartian-minded faculty, and on Wednesday before school closed in June the Board reluctantly but without dissent approved his plan for reorganizing the faculty and the curriculum and reducing tuition. It did not seem possible so much could be done in so short a time.

The students who sat starry-eyed listening to President Arnold Tompkins deliver the baccalaureate address that warm Sunday in June, 1900, little dreamed that they were listening to a valedictory. Perhaps he was not aware of it himself.

In the little school house by the road, without noise of drum or trumpet, without bluster of eloquence or spectacular display are the victories for humanity won. No work more humble or self-sacrificing. You will cast your bread upon the waters believing it will return in a higher order of humanity.[20]

In less than a week after Commencement the community was agog with rumors. Chicago papers reported that the Chicago Normal School Board had selected Arnold Tompkins for president and David Felmley, as professor of mathematics. Tompkins would receive $5,000 and Felmley $3,000. It was well-known that Felmley had been offered the vice-presidency of the Chicago

[20] Arnold Tompkins, "Baccalaureate Sermon, June 17, 1900," *Daily Pantagraph* June 18, 1900.

Normal School but that he had declined because the salary was not enough. The present offer was $750 more than he was receiving at Normal as professor of mathematics. The *Daily Pantagraph* on June 28, under a Chicago date line, carried the news that Tompkins' election had been confirmed and that it was understood that Felmley and Tompkins would accept.[21] When interviewed by the *Pantagraph* reporter that afternoon, Tompkins said he would accept, but Felmley was still undecided, and said that the statement that Tompkins would not go without him was unauthorized.

On Saturday morning June 30, President Tompkins sent identical letters to members of the Board:

You have a right to know my reasons . . . the Chicago school has so much more adequate equipment to carry out the plans I have projected here. Chicago has double the faculty for the same number of students; and a large practice school well organized. We have no kindergartener, Chicago has four and one of them is Elizabeth Harrison. They have two teachers in music; we can have none. They pay, when necessary $3,000 salaries. They will soon have a new building. Briefly I would say that equipment and opportunity to carry out my plans is my reason . . .[22]

Professor Harper maintains that Tompkins was aware that

Stern battles would have to be fought before the legislature if the Normal University were to maintain an important place in the educational system of Illinois or in the reputation of educators. His nature rebelled against that long fight as he realized how heavy were the odds and how unequal the struggle.[23]

Jennie Tompkins, however, knew the real reason for her husband's seemingly sudden decision to leave Normal. Working by his side and knowing him as she had known him for a quarter of a century, she could not but approve. To be president of the Chicago Normal School and follow in the footsteps of Colonel Francis Parker was to Arnold Tompkins ambition fulfilled.[24]

---

[21] *Ibid.*, June 27, 1900; June 28, 1900.
[22] *Proceedings of the Board of Education* (Normal) July 31, 1900, p. 7.
[23] Harper, *Development of the Teachers College*, p. 259.
[24] "Arnold Tompkins, A Memorial," p. 3.
Arnold Tompkins spent five stormy years as head of the Chicago Normal School. His faculty was too devoted to Colonel Francis Parker to welcome change and the Chicago Normal's Board was too economy-minded to carry out his program. He contracted typhoid fever and died at his country home near Menlo, Georgia, August 12, 1905.

CHAPTER X

The Unforgettable Mr. Felmley

IT WAS A dismayed and disgruntled Board that assembled in a special session in the president's office in Normal on July 31. It had met to take formal action on Arnold Tompkins' resignation and to name his successor. The Committee on Teachers and Salaries recommended that Tompkins' resignation, to become effective September 4, be accepted, but State Superintendent Alfred Bayliss, who had expected much from Tompkins and was indignant at his leaving, quickly moved "that the resignation not be accepted"; however, Enoch Gastman's substitute motion "that it be accepted" prevailed. The members agreed that Tompkins' successor must be willing to realize the full compass of his ambitions at Normal University, for a decent period at least, and give assurance that he had no intention of using the position as a stepping stone to one more lucrative and influential.[1]

David Felmley, who had been privately interviewed, sat in an adjoining room. He was well-liked and respected by faculty, students, and townspeople. He had been thinking long and seriously about the future, his own and that of the school. He was ready to cast his lot with the University.

The vote for David Felmley was unanimous. Introduced a few minutes later, he assured the Board he "had no ambition beyond the presidency of Illinois State Normal University: and that he "was willing to limit his career to the opportunities for service and achievements that the position afforded." [2] It was a pledge solemnly made and solemnly kept.

David Felmley, sixth president of Illinois State Normal University, was born near Somerville, New Jersey, April 24, 1857. His father, John S. Felmley, was of German descent and his mother, Ellen Voorhees, Dutch. The father died when David was three.

[1] *Proceedings of the Board of Education* (Normal) July 31, 1900, p. 8.
[2] David Felmley to Francis G. Blair, October 23, 1892. Quoted. *Ibid.*, (Carbondale) November 4, 1929, p. 13.

His earliest education was in the village school at Somerville. In 1868 the family moved to a farm near Perry, in Pike County, Illinois. His boyhood was spent in a home well provided with books and periodicals. He enjoyed reading. A farm hand interested him in natural science and started him in a study of botany and zoology by the rational method. Joseph Dobbins, a former student at Normal University, interested him in mathematics and literature. In 1873 he enrolled in Blackburn College, Carlinville, Illinois. After studying the classics there for three years, he entered the University of Michigan, at the age of nineteen. After studying at Michigan two years, he dropped out to teach, the first year in a rural school near Virden, Illinois, and the second at Carrollton, Illinois. He returned to Ann Arbor in the fall of 1880, and took his baccalaureate degree the following year. At the University of Michigan, young Felmley distinguished himself as a student, a debater, and a politician. He attained the highest scholastic rating that had ever been given to a graduate of the institution, and when he took his teacher's examination in Illinois he received the highest rating ever given from the office of the state superintendent.[3]

In the fall of 1881 Felmley became superintendent of schools at Carrollton, Illinois. Six years later he was married to Auta Stout.[4]

In 1890 Felmley came to Normal to take charge of the work in mathematics. Three years before he had declined Hewett's offer of a position in English. Cook had made for the mathematics department a reputation that was a challenge to his successor. The fact that Cook had searched far and wide for a worthy man gave Felmley a certain prestige among the faculty.[5]

Felmley soon ranked as one of the best teachers in the Normal University. With President Cook he prepared the work in arithmetic in the State Course of Study for sixth, seventh, and eighth grades. He was quick and accurate in his thinking and as a mathematician, he was clear, logical, and thorough. He was a forceful speaker and was in demand at institutes throughout the

[3] *Vidette*, September 1890, p. 2.
[4] Three children were born to David and Auta Felmley, Ruth, Mildred Helen, and John Benjamin.
[5] Harper, *Development of the Teachers College*, p. 262.

state. He had an almost uncanny memory for facts and names. Students and faculty marveled at his wide range of interests and his vast store of information. He was as much at home with the Astronomy Club studying Orion, Venus, and Mars as he was with the Economics Club struggling with the single tax theories of Henry George in the Saturday morning discussions of *Progress and Poverty*. He followed closely the work of the *Popular Science Monthly* in focusing attention on the need of scientific education. He came to the conclusion that the study of science was more pertinent to an understanding of the modern age than the study of the classics in which he had been so well trained.

He believed deeply in personal liberty and resented the injustice of outmoded institutions. He supported the Granger Movement, announced himself a "free-trader," a single taxer, and a silver Democrat. He dared incur the wrath of Governor Altgeld by writing and speaking in behalf of William Jennings Bryan in the campaign of 1896.

In the spring of 1897 it looked for a time as though new appointments to the Board might be conditional on willingness to dismiss the "unpolitic" young professor. President Cook wrote William Green, "It is quite clear that a fight is on against Mr. Felmley. It has been on in fact for over three months. . . . If it should happen that the politicians are really to come into our school and determine our teachers on the basis of their connection with political parties it will be the most lamentable thing this institution has ever encountered." [6] The incident stood between Felmley and the presidency in 1899. Cook did not think it wise at that time to nominate as his successor a man who incurred the ill will of politicians in Springfield.[7] By July 1900 tensions had eased, and Cook was relieved and pleased when Felmley was made president.

Fortunately for the school Felmley had cooperated faithfully and enthusiastically with Arnold Tompkins in the reorganization plan. The faculty breathed a sigh of relief; with David Felmley as president the work of the past year would not have to be done over. What a dither and whirlwind of faculty meetings the re-

[6] John W. Cook to Honorable William H. Green, Normal, April 26, 1897. Quoted. *Ibid.*, p. 264.
[7] John W. Cook, "Our Guest of Honor," *Alumni Quarterly*, III (August 1914), p. 4.

organization had entailed! Clarissa Ela wondered if now she might find a little leisure to pursue her art. J. Rose Colby resolved that if she had any time to be spared from the English poets and the grading of themes she would devote it to the cause of woman suffrage. Professor Manchester, who was becoming more and more interested in economics and political science, had plans for serious professional reading. Henry McCormick was beginning to talk of retirement. Ange. Milner agreed it was comfortable to have some one whom they all knew as president. But if the members of the faculty thought they could placidly return to their classrooms and the *status quo* they would be sadly mistaken. Stagnation would not be possible under David Felmley.

Attendance at the summer school in 1900 was 469. The teachers, who came largely from city schools, were enthusiastic over their work and wanted to return. President Felmley announced the summer school would be a regular part of the Normal University. How to pay the faculty was the immediate problem. A fee of six dollars was charged those who attended and the total amount pro-rated among the teachers but this plan had its disadvantages and Felmley knew that faculty altruism and professional zeal could not be capitalized or imposed upon year after year. He proposed that teachers be employed for forty-two weeks instead of thirty-nine and that whenever a faculty member chose not to teach in the summer school, one-thirteenth of his salary would be deducted. The Board acquiesced, provided the revenues of the summer school justified the additional compensation. A half-loaf was better than no loaf, and Felmley began thinking of how he could best use the one hundred dollars allocated for advertising the next summer school.[8]

Something had to be done about the situation in the Practice School. There were not enough rooms and not enough pupils to provide proper teaching experience for the practice teachers. In 1900 there were only 251 pupils distributed through twelve grades. Twelve classes were taught by critics or regular teachers for purposes of observation while for practice eighty-two student teachers each taught two consecutive classes. A new building on the campus was desirable, but when the low tuition rate of only a

[8] *Proceedings of the Board of Education* (Normal) December 5, 1900, pp. 16, 24.

dollar failed to bring in enough pupils, the structure could not be justified.[9]

In 1901 a contract was made with the local public school board by which as many grades as were needed were placed at the disposal of the University, a plan being pursued in a number of the normal schools. Tuition was free to residents of Normal. The public school buildings were close to the campus, and certain grades were taught in the Model School building and others in the town buildings. The Model High School was discontinued, and all high school work was done in the high school building on Ash Street, where the University provided teachers for six high school classes. The city superintendent reviewed lesson plans and supervised the high school, while supervision and direction of the grade school work was conducted by the University. Teachers in the public schools to whose rooms practice teachers were assigned were given additional compensation by the University. Facilities of the University in art, music, and physical education were made available to the pupils of the public schools. Felmley realized that there were many imperfections in the plan, but it was the best that could be done. A reassuring clause in the contract provided that either the University or the public school could terminate the arrangement any year by giving written notice prior to June 30.[10]

The Board was in sympathy with plans to beautify the campus, but no financial support was forthcoming until after the great storm of June 10, 1902, had left the campus in a state of shambles and ruin. As well as wrecking trees and shrubs, much damage was done to the buildings. The following year after the buildings were repaired, and the wreckage cleared away, John L. Gregory was employed to take charge of the grounds and school garden. In three months he planted 350 trees of seventy-four varieties, 254 flowering shrubs of sixty-nine varieties, and 113 climbing vines of twenty-seven varieties. Felmley urged the planting of nut-bearing trees. He had in mind not only a beautiful campus for students but a preserve for squirrels and birds. In 1904 Bruno Nehrling, a graduate in landscape and ornamental gardening

[9] *Ibid.*, p. 15.
[10] *Ibid.*, (Normal) July 31, 1901, pp. 10–12.

from the Missouri Botanical Gardens, Washington University, St. Louis, was engaged to take over the planting and gardening. There was no greenhouse, so classrooms, sunny basement windows, and the heating plant had to double for cutting, storage, and workrooms.[11]

When Felmley became president he selected George H. Howe, Ph. D., a graduate of the Oswego Normal School, to take over his own work in mathematics. The employment of Frank W. Westhoff, supervisor in music in the Decatur schools, as a full-time music teacher was considered by the new president as one of his first real achievements. Professor Westhoff directed the entire school in singing for twenty minutes each day during the period of General Exercises, held regular classes in the afternoon, and also directed the glee clubs. The handsome and dignified professor had a love for music that was infectious, and presently President Felmley was commenting that "music seems the most popular study today in the Normal School." Frank Westhoff was to remain on the faculty for over thirty years and number among the thousands the students whom he taught to sing.[12]

Another victory was won when a free kindergarten was made an integral part of the Practice School. In September of 1902 Caroleen Robinson, of Saginaw, Michigan, began her work as the school's first kindergarten teacher at a salary of sixty dollars a month. Thirty-four pupils were enrolled but only twenty-nine were regular in attendance and paid requisite fees. Upon President Felmley's recommendation the Board voted to eliminate the fees and to restrict the enrollment to forty pupils. Miss Robinson also taught a course in the philosophy and methods of the kindergarten which was set up as an elective in place of one of the regular courses in pedagogy.[13]

President Felmley's long range plans for an enriched curric-

---

[11] Of the 2500 trees planted in 1867 after the original Saunders plan, only eight hundred trees and forty-two varieties survived to 1902. *Index* 1902, p. 13.

[12] *Proceedings of the Board of Education* (Normal) December 18, 1901, p. 9. Frank W. Westhoff (1863–1938) was in charge of music at Illinois State Normal University from 1901 to 1934. He began the study of music at the age of eight under an uncle who had taught music in Germany. At fourteen he studied organ and piano, and at sixteen was director of a church choir. Meanwhile he had studied orchestra, coronet, and clarinet. In 1884 he taught piano and organ privately. In 1892 he took over vocal music in the Decatur schools.

[13] *Ibid.*, (Normal) December 19, 1902, pp. 7–8.

ulum included training in manual arts, household arts, and dramatics, as well as in music. He also wanted improvements in physical education and in the library. Courses in these fields could not be offered to any extent without new buildings.

In 1903 the northwest room in the basement of the Main Building was outfitted for shop work, and twelve Tole benches were installed. William T. Bawden of Buffalo, New York, a graduate of Denison University who had done additional work in the Mechanics Institute at Rochester and Teachers College, Columbia, was employed as teacher of manual training. He was also to do some work in men's athletics.[14]

Fifteen hours a week in manual training were given to normal classes, seven hours to grammar grade classes, and five hours to high school. Thursday evenings and Saturday forenoons he taught classes for teachers currently employed in the public schools. The first term that work was offered sixteen Normal students enrolled; the second term there were three times as many. An extra class was formed to meet after school and a number of applicants had to be turned away. The following year eight more benches were added, but again the equipment was inadequate to the demand.

In 1904 President Felmley broached the matter of a department of domestic science. Throughout the nation, women's clubs and farmers institutes were urging that schools provide training in household arts, and that teachers be given special training in these fields.[15] However, west of Indiana few normal schools had as yet provided such instruction. Here was an opportunity for Illinois State Normal University to blaze a trail. The Forty-fourth General Assembly voted an appropriation of $75,000 for a Manual Training Building designed to accommodate the departments of art, manual training and domestic science, offices for instructors, and an auditorium, but Governor Deneen vetoed the bill. Two years later an omnibus bill carrying an appropriation of $110,000 for a

[14] *Ibid.*, (Normal) June 2, 1903, pp. 10, 21; (Normal) December 16, 1903, p. 7.

[15] During the first term of the summer session of 1904 the Parents Club of Normal maintained a school of domestic science in one of the public school buildings. These classes were open to students of Normal University without cost. Twenty-four women and forty-eight girls of grammar school age enrolled.

manual arts building and other improvements won the approval of the governor.[16]

Prior to 1904 no regular work in public speaking was required of students. Philadelphian, Wrightonian, Sapphonian, Ciceronian, the Girls' Debating Club, and the Young Men's and the Young Women's Christian Associations, together with the annual February contests in oratory and declamation, the annual debates with the State Normal at Oshkosh, and the speeches at Commencement were expected to provide ample training in forensics. An investigation revealed that a large percentage of the students graduated without having availed themselves of educational experiences and training that these voluntary organizations afforded. Alarmed and disturbed by the facts, the faculty requested that some rhetorical work be required of all students either in the volunteer student societies or in regular classes organized for this purpose, and that three exercises, speeches, or public appearances be required each term.

Beginning with the year 1904–1905 rhetoricals were regularly required of all students, and the work distributed among the faculty. Assignments were made after consulting the students' preferences. It was a favorite joke with President Felmley that few students chose his section.

The rhetoricals, which substituted for General Exercises on Tuesday and lasted for forty-five minutes, varied with the instructor. Some emphasized oratory, some interpretative reading. Miss Colby and her pupils read poetry.[17] They were fascinated as they listened. Miss Colby neither read nor sang; she seemed to chant, withal capturing the innermost thought of the poet and recreating anew the scene. As she read, Banquo's ghost seemed suddenly near, another day Lear's grief might be as their own. Not all the rhetoricals were quite so inspirational. Those who were so naive or daring as to select the president's section testify it was a rigorous experience, one they would neither forget nor care to repeat. Regardless of the section, rhetoricals required preparation and before long the societies were complaining that

[16] Francis G. Blair to David Felmley, Springfield, May 20, 1907. *Felmley Papers; Index* 1907, p. 164.
[17] Interview, Lela Winegarner, June 5, 1953.

the new rhetorical system was making inroads on attendance.[18] Rhetoricals continued for over twenty years. At home nothing may have been "as sure as death and taxes," but at Normal it was "rhetoricals and senior themes." [19]

While the students groaned beneath their load and openly voiced complaint in the columns of the *Vidette* and in *Index* cartoons and editorials, the faculty were wont to shake their heads and sigh privately. The "critique," wherein a faculty member taught a model class before the student body and then later sat through a criticism of it by other members of the staff, abandoned when Arnold Tompkins became president, was revived under President Felmley.[20]

The union of training school and public school seemed to work very well at first. Seventy percent of the 661 citizens who had voted favored the arrangement. The union cost to the public school board was a little over $2,100, mostly in salaries for the critic teachers. In turn the children in the public school were given art, music, physical training, and privileges of the library, campus, and gymnasium. A minority of the townspeople were never reconciled to the idea and in the fall of 1903 began to agitate for a dissolution of the union. The school board of Normal, believing that most of the parents were pleased with the training that their children were receiving, declined to submit the question to a vote. Andrew Lindblad then applied to the Circuit Court of McLean County for an injunction to keep the school board from paying salaries of the critic teachers; he also instituted suits against the members of the board for the recovery of such salaries as had been paid. In December at an election called by Lindblad and his friends, a vote of 459 was cast for dissolution of the union, the friends of the union generally abstaining from voting. The next day the school board yielded to this sudden show of strength and notified President Felmley that the union would terminate June 30, 1904.

[18] *Index* 1912, p. 86.
[19] In December 1922 President Felmley reported there were forty-one rhetorical classes meeting each Tuesday for forty-five minutes. Students who showed proficiency in public speaking if elected to active membership in the literary societies were "excused" from rhetoricals. *Proceedings of the Board of Education* (DeKalb) December 6, 1922, p. 25.
The Board had voted December 12, 1921 to eliminate the graduating theme.
[20] *Ibid.*, (Normal) December 18, 1901, p. 8; *Index* 1902, p. 102.

When Lindblad proceeded with his suits against the school board, the members became indignant and the notice sent to President Felmley was recalled, pending the action of the Circuit Court. The decision denied the petition for an injunction and upheld the right of the school board to contract with the State Board of Education.

Lindblad took the case to the Appellate Court and on to the Supreme Court. Meanwhile there was school as usual. Members elected to the local board in 1905 and 1906 favored the union and it seemed the matter was settled. Plans went forward to strengthen the relationship and add to the efficiency of the training department. On April 18, 1906, the Supreme Court handed down its fateful decision that the union was unlawful by three counts: first, because the board of education of the town of Normal had delegated a portion of its powers to the Normal University; second, because public school funds were paid to critic teachers whose job it was, not to train children but Normal students in the art of teaching; and third, because children, when taught by student teachers, were taught by persons not legally qualified through a teacher's certificate. It looked as though the University's training program had been dealt a hard blow.

Upon hearing of the decision Enoch Gastman hurried over from Decatur and conferred with President Felmley, Charles Capen, and F. D. Marquis. On April 27, Gastman advised the town school board that Normal University was withdrawing its eighty-four student teachers from the public school but that the town board would be permitted to re-employ the critic teachers as regular teachers for the rest of the year. Thirty-seven of the student teachers quickly obtained certificates from County Superintendent Wren and were employed as assistant teachers for the rest of the year, while the other forty-seven continued as "observers."

It was gratifying to the Normal University that in May 1906, when the local board requested the parents of children attending the elementary schools to state whether they preferred to send their children to the public school or to the University Model School, of the 449 children in attendance, parents of 245 voted in favor of the University, the parents of 121 children for the public

school, and those of 83 children failed to report.[21] A majority of
the parents did not feel their children were injured by being "practiced upon" by student teachers. There was no doubt whether
there would be sufficient pupils to operate a model school successfully. The problem henceforth would be a matter of selection.

While the battle of the Model School was being fought on the
home front the University of Illinois took cognizance of David
Felmley's work and conferred upon him the honorary degree of
Doctor of Laws at its convocation in 1906.[22]

The Model School was reorganized and tailored to the limi-
tations of space. Seven grades and the kindergarten were housed
in the Training Building, and the eighth grade was brought into
the old high school room in the Main Building. A training school
building adequate for the Normal University's program to prepare teachers for the common schools was a matter of urgent
need, but a manual training building and auditorium should
come first. It was not a good idea to abandon one building in
favor of another and scarcely politic to ask for two buildings in a
single appropriation. But no sooner did the General Assembly
vote favorably on the manual arts building than plans were laid
to ask for a new training building.

The Lindly Act, passed by the General Assembly in 1905, provided for one free scholarship per township upon competitive
examination of eighth grade graduates. President Felmley believed this would bring more students to Normal University and
that the high school department should be built up to meet their
need. The severance of the union with the Normal public schools
made this more imperative. Since many of the eighth grade
graduates were under sixteen and entrance requirements to the
normal schools were still sixteen, the development of a high
school program was more important than ever. The increase in
the number of students attending high school in the state would
soon be placing a new emphasis on training teachers beyond the
common branches and needs of elementary principals.

Normal University needed to be prepared to meet the new
challenge. So President Felmley told the faculty as they pre-

[21] David Felmley to Alfred Bayliss, Normal, May 1, 1906. *Felmley Papers. Proceedings
of the Board of Education* (Normal) June 6, 1906, pp. 8–9.
[22] Harper, *Development of the Teachers College,* p. 276.

pared to celebrate the first fifty years of the history of Normal University. A backward glance and a flush of pride were not ill-becoming. Illinois State Normal University was known throughout the length and breadth of the land. Six Filipino students on campus, as beneficiaries of the Congressional Act of July 1903, bore living testimony to the high regard in which the Federal Commissioner of Education held the institution.[23] Like the Bridgewater Normal of an earlier era, Illinois State Normal University had contributed so many graduates to presidencies and faculties of other normals that it was often spoken of as the Mother of Western Normals. Educational literature had been enriched by the writings of the McMurrys, Edmund James, Charles DeGarmo, John Keith, and other graduates. As director of the Wharton School of Finance at the University of Pennsylvania, Edmund James first showed an American university how to educate business leaders.

To mark the passing of the years, members of the faculty under the direction of Professor O. L. Manchester and Professor John A. H. Keith prepared a Semi-Centennial History together with an Alumni, Faculty, and Board Register.[24]

Meanwhile the social life of the school centered in the gymnasium, Normal Hall, and the Wrightonian and Philadelphian societies. Though not averse to inter-scholastic athletics President Felmley believed that the students should share in the responsibility of managing athletic events, and in 1901 an Athletic Association was formed and the supervision of sports delegated to a Board of Control consisting of three students and two faculty members. The personnel changed each quarter. The emphasis around the turn of the century was in intramural contests, tennis, and basketball, but with the new interest in football, students and players looked beyond the campus for competition worthy of their prowess.

Girls played inter-scholastic games in basketball with Wesleyan, Eureka, and nearby high schools. They wore pleated bloomers bloused below the knee, high-ribbed stockings, high-necked waists

[23] *Index* 1905, pp. 131–132.
[24] Twelve hundred copies of the Semi-Centennial History were printed at a cost of $900. The book sold for one dollar. *Proceedings of the Board of Education* (Normal) June 5, 1907, p. 12.

with long sleeves, middy collars, and dickeys, and their hair was held secure with ribbons and bows. For the boys' basketball it was an era of turtle-neck sweaters and knee trousers.[25] Lawn tennis was played in the short grass until about 1901, when devotees Professor Manchester and student Thomas Barger set a new fashion by having a good clay court built.

By 1906 season tickets were being sold to athletic events, and the new speech teacher, Howard Spencer Woodward, organized a yelling section. Rowdiness and poor sportsmanship were not unusual. The *Index* of 1902 explained that the University's poor luck in football the past season was due among other things to poor coaching. In 1905 Normal University's team objected to the refereeing at Jacksonville and left the field after sixteen minutes of play in the second half, asserting that "leaving the field" was a prerogative to get "decent refereeing" and for the preservation of the sport.

Such conduct led to considerable opposition to football from some of the faculty and students. President Felmley spoke sarcastically of the game two or three times a week in General Exercises, and after announcing a forthcoming game in a colorless way would say, "I hope many of you will see fit to attend this game." [26] Intramural contests were looked upon with greater favor by most of the faculty. However, these contests were "not without incident." One of the devices to arouse interest before an inter-society athletic or forensic event was a "color rush." There was a mad and excited scramble to see which society would succeed in flying its colors high above the gymnasium or from the cupola of the Main Building. Fighting sometimes followed, as in 1901, when window panes were broken. During the melee President Felmley appeared, seized several of the culprits, and later assessed damages against the societies. Another time banisters were broken during a junior-senior color rush preceding a basketball game.[27]

A coach was hired in 1908 to take over training for athletic contests,[28] but a campus row in the winter of 1909–1910 led the

[25] *Index* 1902, p. 92.
[26] *Ibid.*, 1906, p. 96.
[27] *Ibid.*, pp. 54–55.
[28] Willfred George Binneweis, A.B. (DePauw) was the popular coach at Shurtleff

faculty to suspend inter-scholastic games in baseball and foot-ball.[29] No baseball was played in 1910, but the game was resumed in 1911.[30]

The inter-society forensic contests that had excited rivalry and attracted townspeople for over fifty years, commencement exercises, the entertainment series, and the daily General Exercises were held on the third floor of the Main Building. School parties, receptions, and banquets were held in the gymnasium. The Fortnightly Club, encouraged by President Felmley, succeeded in getting the Board to open the gymnasium for dancing in September 1903. When the teacher of gymnastics forbade the waxing of the floor the students parafined their shoes. After each dance a committee scrubbed the floors.[31]

The Junior-Senior banquet was the great social climax of the year. Class officers and faculty received the guests in the library on the second floor of the gymnasium building. The somber book-lined shelves were enlivened by potted palms and large baskets of spring flowers. Tables were set up in the gymnasium on the first floor. The bleak walls and gallery were masked and transformed into a "fairyland of crepe paper streamers, green boughs and flowers." The caterers took over the dressing rooms. Here Carter Harris and his wife and their helpers busied themselves with borrowed silver and china, and tried their best to keep the hot foods warm and the iced foods from melting. Each junior class fondly hoped it would be entertained in the new building.

It was 1909 before the new manual arts building was completed. The lowest bid had been $30,000 over the amount appropriated, and new plans had to be drawn. Room sizes were cut and tile floor and marble base gave way to hard maple and other economies that were later regretted.[32] The bridge connecting the two buildings, a suggestion of Ella Flagg Young, happily was not one of the items that had to be sacrificed.

College, Alton. When Shurtleff students collected $300 to induce him to remain, President Felmley countered by increasing Normal University's offer $300. Binneweis assisted in German while on the faculty 1908–1910.

[29] In 1908 "N" sweaters were awarded to men who played in three games. *Index* 1908, p. 47.

[30] *Ibid.*, 1911, p. 118.

[31] *Ibid.*, 1904, p. 115.

[32] *Proceedings of the Board of Education* (Normal) December 18, 1907, pp. 23–24.

The opening program held in the auditorium later named in honor of resident Board member, Charles L. Capen, was the debate with Oshkosh Normal on Friday, May 21, 1909. Normal won a unanimous decision on the subject of the "Commission Plan of Government for Cities over 25,000." Elaborate plans for the visitors from Oshkosh included a drive about Bloomington on Saturday morning. At noon the Domestic Science Department served a luncheon for the Oratorical Board, the guests from Oshkosh, the Normal debaters, and a few of the faculty. So royally were the guests entertained that they missed their train.[33]

In 1901 as the result of a class vote, the seniors petitioned the Board for a special Commencement speaker instead of the seven class speakers, the expedient used after the classes became too large to permit each member to present an essay or oration, but the proposition was voted down as being undesirable at the time "to change the established custom of the school." Succeeding classes made similar appeals, and in 1915 it was left to the faculty to decide whether there would be seven class speakers or one eminent outsider.

While the students resolved to spell progress on the campus by outlawing old customs and establishing new precedents, President Felmley quietly, but no less determinedly, pursued a reform of his own. It was simplified spelling. David Felmley believed that every teacher should be a good speller and throughout his long administration every candidate for a diploma had to pass a qualifying test in spelling. Prospective teachers not only had to be able to spell but they had to know all the rules of spelling. As rules for sports were revised from time to time and the game improved, so President Felmley believed spelling reform would do service to the language.

To David Felmley silent letters were an abomination. Why a final *e* if it were not pronounced? What was the virtue of a double letter, the second of which was never pronounced? What justification was there for such antiquated combinations of unsounded letters as "ough"? It is not known when President Felmley developed his convictions on spelling, but it was reassuring to him to learn of the organization of the Simplified Spelling Board in

[33] *Index* 1909, p. 102.

New York on January 13, 1906.[34] He was by no means blazing a trail. He found himself in such illustrious company as David Starr Jordan, President of the University of California; William T. Harris, United States Commissioner of Education; Theodore Roosevelt, President of the United States; Mark Twain; and Richard Watson Gilder of *Century Magazine.*

Shortly thereafter letterheads from the office of the president of Illinois State Normal University carried the legend "The spellings recommended by the Simplified Spelling Board are used in the correspondence of this office." Flora Dodge, the secretary, painstakingly learned the new system and noted when and to whom to use the conventional spelling and to whom to use the reformed. Whenever President Felmley attended a meeting of the Simplified Spelling Board or received an annual report she expected to have to revise her spellings.

Not every one connected with the Normal University shared President Felmley's enthusiasm for simplified spelling. Ella Flagg Young, principal of the Chicago Normal School and long a member of the State Board of Education, could not accept the new reform. The use of "ar," "sho," "nite," and "rite" annoyed Mrs. Young. She could not understand why David Felmley could subscribe to such unconventional practices, and she often chided him about his hobby. On May 1, 1909, she replied to one of his letters:

My dear Mr. Felmley:

After careful and painful effort I have succeeded in translating your deformed spelling into my own vernacular. I make out that the world looks pretty fair at Normal . . . you are to be congratulated.[35]

At institutes and other educational meetings President Felmley spoke in behalf of simplified spelling. The Simplified Spelling Board took cognizance of his efforts and invited him to membership.

Students were enthusiastic until they learned that President Felmley's case for simplified spelling did not "make every man his own spelling authority" and that the SSB only substituted new and more numerous rules for spelling.

[34] Helen E. Marshall, "Simplified Spelling—And David Felmley," *Alumni Quarterly* (May 1954), pp. 8–9.
[35] Ella Flagg Young to David Felmley, Chicago, May 1, 1909. *Felmley Papers.*

Aside from catalogs, board reports, and University bulletins, the most significant piece of printing employing simplified spelling to come from Normal University during the Felmley regime was a cookbook. When Miss Carrie Alberta Lyford came to Normal University in 1908 as its first home economics teacher, she not only had some very definite ideas about household science but she was aware of the scarcity of good textbooks. Continually besieged for copies of her choice recipes, she longed to commit them to print and posterity. She told President Felmley that she would like to prepare a cookbook for her advanced class if the University would arrange for its publication. Outside sales, she added, might provide some much needed equipment. President Felmley agreed to undertake publication only if the book were written in simplified spelling. In glee he told Carrie Lyford that her *Advanced Cookery* would probably be America's first cookbook to use simplified spelling. Little did Miss Lyford realize the mutilation to which her precious recipes would be subjected. Date buns and English muffins came to rest under "Breds." Eggs lost a "g" and mouthwatering meringues seemed less mouthwatering deprived of their useless "ue." Parsley was now "chopt" not "chopped"; onions were "minst" although pies remained the traditional "minced." Braised tongue emerging as "tung" was more suggestive of fresh paint than food. "Doughnuts" mysteriously escaped President Felmley's creative genius and he can be given no credit for the current popular "do-nut." [36]

When educational foundations were no longer interested in underwriting the activities of the Simplified Spelling Board, the organization fell apart. In his personal correspondence President Felmley never deviated, although in his later years there was greater conformity to conventional spelling in printed materials sent out from the Normal University.

The installation of a pipe organ in the new auditorium was a great delight to President Felmley. To his surprise it had not been cut from the appropriation for the new auditorium. Mrs. Young had forewarned him that he had had more courage than she to

[36] Page one of Carrie Lyford's *Advanced Cookery* brings the interesting information that in her day and that of David Felmley "Cocktails are of two classes, fish cocktails and fruit cocktails."

ask for it.[37] Felmley knew nothing about pipe organs, but he welcomed the opportunity to learn something new and off his beaten track. He consulted Frank Westhoff, Professor of Music, William T. Bawden of the Manual Training Department, and local organists. After zealously studying various makes, models and qualities of organs, he announced he was ready to let the contract. The organ was built by Hillgreen, Lane, and Company of Alliance, Ohio, at a cost of $6,400. It had a three-manual console with thirty-four registers, and 2,184 pipes, couplers, combinations and accessories. The Board of Education thought an expert should test the organ before final payment was made. President Felmley insisted that a hundred dollars for this service was reckless extravagance. He said he would read up on organs and do the testing himself. The Board hired the expert but Felmley checked the work. While the organ was being installed, President Felmley was constantly at the heels of the workmen asking questions about the pipes, the wiring, and the console. When the students assembled each day for "Gen. Ex." and beheld the pipe strewn stage he passed along to them the knowledge he had so recently acquired. Later he had much satisfaction in showing prospective teachers of music the organ, asking them questions they had never expected, and then telling them things they never expected a college president to tell them.[38]

The interviews to which he subjected applicants live long in the memories of those who successfully answered his scrutinizing questions and became members of his faculty. David Felmley had little use for timid vacillating souls. He respected the teacher who had opinions and the courage to defend them, but he resented arrogance and willful display. If a teacher failed to give satisfaction, he had no hesitancy in suggesting, even demanding, a resignation. Those who met his standards and continued on the staff became for the most part his devoted friends. They marveled at his vast knowledge of so many things, and reveled in his quick repartee. They accepted his judgment and his leadership, arbitrary though it may have seemed at times.

[37] Ella Flagg Young to David Felmley, Chicago, February 13, 1909. *Felmley Papers.*
[38] Interview, Miss Ruth Stroud, Normal, Illinois, June 2, 1954.

A man of less fortitude and vision might have given up in the face of dwindling enrollments and a penurious Legislature and succumbed to more tempting offers.

David Felmley was born to fight. He stayed on.[39]

[39] Although the enrollment in May 1906 was ninety-five percent higher than in May 1924, it was twenty-one percent less than in 1901, the first year of David Felmley's administration. *Index* 1906, p. 7. *Illinois School Reports* 1902, 1904, 1906, 1908.

CHAPTER XI

From Normal School to Teachers College

IN THE PARADOX of decreased enrollment in the normal schools and the increased number of high schools, President Felmley saw the handwriting on the wall. Teacher training was being siphoned away from the normal schools by high schools, four-year colleges and the state university. A diploma from a normal school did not constitute a certificate to teach.[1] Although the Normal University had been a professional school from the beginning, it did not have authority to license those who completed its course. It was assumed that its function was to train every kind of teacher needed in the public schools, from first grade through high school.[2] In the late 1880's midwestern universities became aware of the phenomenal growth of high schools and the need for adequately prepared secondary teachers. Inspired by the University of Michigan, other universities began a movement to standardize and accredit high schools. They insisted upon graduation from a recognized college as a prerequisite for high school teaching. Chairs of pedagogy, later departments of education, and finally schools of education were established by the universities. This new aggressiveness on the part of the universities all too often relegated the normal schools to "step-child" status with the sole function of preparing teachers for the elementary schools.

Illinois State Normal University, says Professor Harper, had from its beginning "certain ideals, concepts and practices, characteristic of an institution of higher education." It was compelled to compromise with educational situations as they existed, but its

---

[1] Under the antiquated certification laws all teachers in order to receive salaries from public funds were required to pass county superintendent examinations. The marks received determined whether the certificate was first, second, or third grade.

[2] David Felmley to F. W. Shepardson, Normal, December 7, 1918. *Felmley Papers.*

ultimate goal was the training of teachers for all the schools. In 1859 Charles Hovey, first principal, a Dartmouth graduate, in speaking before the first Normal School Convention said,

If it be attempted to prepare fully for high schools and similar institutions, I do not see how to avoid the ordinary four-year college courses, with all that is necessary as a preparation, and the professional courses besides. If the pupils were taken from the best of the grammar schools, the work here indicated would require at least eight years of time.[3]

Richard Edwards, who succeeded Hovey, believed that normal schools should confer a professional degree to indicate the profession of teaching and to give "distinctness, dignity, and influence" to teaching and "place it along side the other professions where for usefulness and worthiness it justly belongs." The Normal University curriculum in the 1870's included advanced work in mathematics, natural science, Latin, Greek, German, and French, and an extensive course in English. In order to complete the optional studies a student found it necessary to lengthen his term of study to four years. Graduates of the Normal University were in such demand prior to 1910 that more men secured employment as administrators and high school teachers than as elementary teachers.[4] Although in the early years the high school was not an integral part of the practice school, some student teaching was done in its classes; when the high school was restored after its official discontinuance under Governor Altgeld, it was recognized as a bona fide practice department.

President Felmley regarded with concern the sudden leadership assumed by the universities. The normal schools were under attack: they were accused of being shallow, of being out of touch with the educational life of the state, and of making no contribution to the science of education. Felmley bluntly declared the first two accusations were untrue and that the third was an affront. Was not the Normal University the cradle of the great Herbartian Movement?

[3] Charles E. Hovey, *Proceedings of the First Normal School Convention* 1859, pp. 81–82. Quoted, Harper, *Development of the Teachers College*, p. 308.
[4] David Felmley, "The Expansion of the Normal School," *Educational Review*, XIV (April 1913) p. 410.

As Felmley accompanied the Normal University's students to the annual debate and oratorical contests in Oshkosh, Emporia, Kirksville, or Cedar Falls, he talked with other normal school presidents. Their problems were much the same. In order to have more opportunity for discussion and exchange of information on teacher education, Felmley and his friends organized the North Central Council of State Normal Schools in 1902. A Department of Normal Schools had been created within the National Education Association in 1870, but the new Council composed of presidents and principals of public-supported institutions, which met separately and inaugurated special studies, better served their needs. In 1917 the North Central Council expanded into a national association; a year later the degree-granting western schools desiring a more aggressive organization formed the American Association of Teachers Colleges. It published its first yearbook in 1922. In 1936 the North Central Association joined the American Association of Teachers Colleges under the name of the latter. Two years later it replaced the department of normal schools within the National Education Association. Subsequently it became known as the American Association of Colleges for Teacher Education.[5] It has worked consistently for higher standards in teacher training.

While the question as to whether normal schools or colleges should train high school teachers was being threshed out in the annual meetings of the National Education Association 1900–1920, leadership in behalf of normal schools was taken by President Felmley, Homer Seerley, president of Iowa State Teachers College, Cedar Falls, and John Kirk, president of the Normal School, Kirksville, Missouri.[6] They insisted that the colleges, in ignoring courses in method and educational psychology, did not turn out good teachers, that it was unwise to train high school teachers apart from elementary teachers, that the essential outlook could not be obtained in the colleges and universities, and that the colleges and universities could not alone supply the number

[5] Donald P. Cottrell, *Teacher Education for a Free People* (Oneonta, New York: American Association of Colleges for Teacher Education, 1956), pp. 31–32.

[6] Felmley paid tribute to John Kirk on his twenty-fifth anniversary, calling him "the resolute champion of the teachers college against the Brahminical pundits of the traditional college and the arrogance of the university." David Felmley to John Kirk, Normal, October 30, 1923. *Felmley Papers.*

of high school teachers that were needed.[7] On one occasion
Felmley declared,

Any rule of the North Central Association that confirms the tendency to
educate elementary teachers in one kind of an institution and high
school teachers in a different institution with different traditions,
methods, standards and ideals, drives a wedge horizontally through our
public school system. There is already too great a separation between the
pedagogical aristocracy of the high school and the commonalty of the
grades, too little appreciation of their common problems where mutual
understanding and cooperation are vital to the best interests of the
school.[8]

He questioned the merits of some of the accrediting agencies
and doubted if the quality of high school teaching had improved
merely by the requirement of a degree. He thought that teachers
should know how to teach and he told the N. E. A. in 1902 that
too much attention was paid to degrees. "A degree," he said, "is
not a sacrament. It is not the outward and visible sign of an invisible and inward spiritual grace." He was often sarcastic about
the quality of university teaching.

The controversy not only put the normal schools on the de-
fensive but it forced them to take careful stock of their offerings.
Their curriculums had to be revised if they were to command the
respect of the universities and accrediting agencies. Shortly after
becoming president, Felmley began to agitate for legislative permission to grant a professional degree. Iowa State Normal inaugurated a four-year college curriculum leading to the degree of
Bachelor of Arts in 1904.[9]

In December 1906 President Felmley advised the Board that
the course of study had been developed to a point where it justified asking the General Assembly for authority to confer degrees
on persons who had completed two years of work beyond that
prescribed for the diploma.[10] The presidents of the other four

---

[7] David Felmley, "The Educational Progress of a Quarter Century" *Normal School
Quarterly* (April, 1909), p. 17.

[8] David Felmley "In Defense of Our Senior College" *Alumni Quarterly* (May, 1912),
p. 13.

[9] The name of Iowa State Normal was changed to Iowa State Teachers College April 5,
1909. Irving H. Hart, *The First Seventy-five Years,* (Cedar Falls: Iowa State Teachers
College, 1951), pp. 16–18.

[10] *Proceedings of the Board of Education* (Normal) December 19, 1906, p. 10.

normal schools promptly sought degree-granting status for their institutions and four similar bills were introduced. Strong opposition came from the small colleges. President Chamberlin of McKendree College wrote Governor Charles Deneen that the normal school degree bill was "another attempt to put the razor to the throat of our private institutions." [11]

President Felmley reassured the college presidents that the normals had no desire to invade the domain of the liberal arts college or proselyte for students. They were only trying to do their own work better and the degree to be conferred would not be a Bachelor of Arts, a Bachelor of Science or a Bachelor of Philosophy, but a strictly professional degree.[12] The fury temporarily subsided, and the General Assembly before adjourning in 1907 conferred the right to grant degrees not only to Normal University, but also to the normal schools at Carbondale, DeKalb and Charleston.[13]

In June 1908 two students, Alma Mary Hamilton and Lillie R. Palsley, had completed requirements at Normal University and were awarded the degree of Bachelor of Education.

The small colleges were appeased, but there remained the threat of the ever-expanding state university. Through its inspection and accrediting of high schools it might discredit the teachers college degree and discourage prospective high school teachers from attending teachers colleges. It might refuse to honor at face value credits of students transferring from normal schools to the undergraduate school or those who wished to take advanced degrees. Furthermore by obtaining huge appropriations at the expense of the teachers colleges, the university could cripple their programs for expansion. President Felmley became apprehensive in the fall of 1910, when the university began a pre-legislative campaign for $250,000 for a School of Education Building. When a resolution urging the appropriation was adopted by the High School Conference, Felmley bristled. This one building would cost more than the state had expended for all the buildings at Normal University!

[11] Quoted, Francis G. Blair to David Felmley, Springfield, April 20, 1907. *Felmley Papers.*
[12] David Felmley to Francis G. Blair, Normal, April 30, 1907. *Felmley Papers.*
[13] The privilege of granting a degree was extended to Macomb in 1917.

In somewhat restrained simplified spelling Felmley directed a ten-page letter to Edmund James, president of the University of Illinois, copies of which were sent to the Board and to the press. Felmley was indignant that the Legislature had denied the normal schools' appeal for larger appropriations to provide for increased enrollment and expanded programs because the state university was asking so much. He had made no protest when a department of education had been set up as a part of the university's graduate school, but now that the university projected a school of education that appeared to compete with the normal schools, he was furious.[14]

The move on the part of the University of Illinois to undertake the training of principals, superintendents, high school and special teachers had especially tragic overtones for Normal University because Edmund James, president of the University of Illinois, was a graduate of the Normal University High School in 1873 and had been its principal from 1879 to 1883. Peleg Walker, a graduate of Normal University and a member of the Board, agreed with Felmley but he was more pessimistic as to the outcome, "I believe the chains are now forged and we are beaten." [15]

Charles Capen, local Board member, supported Felmley. "My own opinion," he said, "is the Normal schools should lock horns on this issue with the state university." [16]

Neither President Cook of DeKalb nor President Lord of Charleston was quite as disturbed over the prospects for the future of the normal schools. President Bayliss of Macomb was non-committal.[17] President Parkinson of Carbondale saw possibilities of compromise by which both the normal schools and the university might profit.[18]

President James in his reply to President Felmley, reiterated his belief "that there should be no feeling of competition between the state university and the normal schools." He suggested a meeting of the presidents of the schools and some of the leading

[14] David Felmley to Edmund J. James, Normal, November 21, 1910. *Felmley Papers.*
[15] Peleg R. Walker to David Felmley, Rockford, November 28, 1910. *Felmley Papers.*
[16] Charles L. Capen to David Felmley, Bloomington, November 28, 1910. *Felmley Papers.*
[17] L. C. Lord to David Felmley, Charleston, November 21, 1910; John W. Cook to David Felmley, DeKalb, November 28, 1910; Alfred Bayliss to David Felmley, Macomb, December 5, 1910. *Felmley Papers.*
[18] D. B. Parkinson to David Felmley, Carbondale, December 3, 1910. *Felmley Papers.*

educational men of the state to talk over their common problems.[19]

Meanwhile the Illinois State Normal University Club at the University of Illinois adopted resolutions favoring the state university's program for a practice school, expressing the opinion that Felmley's attack on the University of Illinois would only react against the normal school, and urging all loyal alumni to use their influence to persuade the president to withdraw his opposition.[20] Copies were circulated among the alumni and educators of the state.

In an effort to thresh out matters in advance of the State Teachers Meeting, Francis G. Blair asked the presidents of the University of Illinois and the normal schools to come to Normal on December 19. James had a previous engagement and sent Professor William C. Bagley to present the university's position;[21] Parkinson of Southern missed his train.[22] After a long and serious talk, the small group that attended decided it unwise to fight the proposed appropriation for the university. Instead it should be endorsed along with a highly expanded program for the normal schools. In the end David Felmley, who had fought so hard against the university, helped to write the resolutions to be brought before the State Teachers Meeting the following week. When they were presented he rose and publicly seconded the motion to approve.[23]

The normal schools doubtless made gains by the compromise, but not all apprehension of the so-called "Colossus of education" was allayed. Particularly irritating to President Felmley was the state university's unwillingness to accept reports and recommendations of the high school inspector from the office of the State Superintendent of Public Instruction. The university employed its own high school visitor to inspect and accredit the high schools of the state. Felmley believed that in the smaller high schools of the state the visitor exercised strong pressure upon school boards

[19] Edmund J. James to David Felmley, Urbana-Champaign, November 23, 1910. *Felmley Papers.*
[20] David Felmley to Edmund J. James, Normal, December 24, 1910. (Mimeographed) *Felmley Papers.*
[21] Edmund J. James to David Felmley, Urbana-Champaign, December 21, 1910. *Felmley Papers.*
[22] D. B. Parkinson to David Felmley, Carbondale, December 21, 1910. *Felmley Papers.*
[23] *Journal of the Proceedings of the Illinois State Teachers Association,* 1910, pp. 14–15.

to employ teachers who were graduates of the University of Illinois rather than the normal schools or other colleges, and that the majority of young persons who planned to become high school teachers were thus lured away from the normal schools.[24]

The university was also reluctant to grant full credit for work done in the new teachers colleges, and graduates who wished to do advanced study at the university were confronted by considerable loss in credit. A ruling of the American Association of State Universities provided that the rating accorded any school or college by its own state university would be accepted as the same by all other state universities. Graduates of normal schools of Iowa and Kansas, where universities and teachers colleges were administered by the same board and enjoyed full exchange of credit, might enter the University of Illinois without loss of credit.

Felmley was determined that Normal University should be a teachers college in the best sense of the word. A circular broadcast the school's progress in meeting the challenge of the times through the establishment of special departments to prepare teachers in the fields of music, domestic science, manual training, and nature study with special emphasis on the elements of agriculture. In order that the school might "move forward in its legitimate and larger field, its present resources required a new model school building costing not less than $110,000, a rural school department to keep in touch with rural schools and provide the best preparation for rural teachers, increased library facilities, an expanded curriculum for the training and preparation of high school teachers, and a larger teaching force." [25]

It was a masterly campaign, and in June 1911 Felmley was able to report, "The Forty-seventh General Assembly has dealt more liberally with this institution than has any other Legislature in the history of the state." [26]

The new training school building, for which it appropriated funds, although not entirely completed, was opened for use in the fall of 1913 and made possible an expanded program in teacher

[24] David Felmley to Francis W. Shepardson, Normal, December 7, 1908. *Felmley Papers.*
[25] David Felmley, Circular letter, Normal, December 17, 1910. (Mimeographed) *Felmley Papers.*
[26] *Proceedings of the Board of Education* (Normal) June 7, 1911, p. 12.

training. This three-story brick building, 96 by 216 feet, costing approximately $140,000, was situated east of the Main Building and connected to it by a bridge corresponding to the one between the Main Building and the Manual Arts Building. This building which was to be the home of the kindergarten, the elementary school, and the high school for more than forty years, was named for Thomas Metcalf, one of the early and best loved training teachers.

In 1916 an arrangement with the Illinois Soldiers Orphans Home [27] whereby the University assumed responsibility for the educational program of the institution further extended opportunity for student teaching and observation.[28]

The old training school building was converted now into a library, and part of the lower floors provided classroom space for what Miss Milner described as "the more quiet departments such as geography." The space released in the Castle, as the classroom wing of the gymnasium was known, made room for a new commercial department. Business courses were being established in high schools of the state, but as yet no institution had set up courses to give special training for high school teachers of commercial subjects. As early as December 1912 President Felmley asked for two teachers "to start the ball rolling," and place Normal University among the first to recognize the need for training teachers in this special field. One teacher would have classes in typing and stenography, and the other, classes in bookkeeping, business methods, and commercial law.[29]

In the summer of 1914 Arthur R. Williams, A. B. and M. A., Kenyon College, was employed to teach commercial subjects. To attract publicity to the University's program in training commercial teachers, Professor Williams arranged a statewide contest in shorthand and typing to be held in Normal, May 22, 1915. Sixty-eight contestants from thirteen high schools sat for the test.[30] The following fall twenty-two students enrolled in the commercial courses in the normal department and twenty-three in the high school. The second state-wide contest attracted 185

[27] Later known as Illinois Soldiers and Sailors Childrens School.
[28] *Proceedings of the Board of Education* (Normal) June 7, 1916, p. 12.
[29] *Ibid.*, (Normal) December 18, 1912, p. 10.
[30] *Ibid.*, (Normal) June 9, 1915, p. 13.

contestants from twenty-seven high schools. A second teacher was employed, and another new department was securely launched.[31]

In 1911 Illinois led the list of states in the number of one-room rural schools.[32] To serve more effectively the needs of rural schools, a country school department was authorized by the Board. Many prospective rural teachers came from urban communities and knew nothing of rural life. Two programs were outlined, a two-year course for students who had finished the eighth grade and a one-year course for students who had had at least two years of high school. For the director of the new department President Felmley selected Miss Mabel Carney, a vigorous and enthusiastic young woman from the country school department of Washington State Normal School at Cheney. Miss Carney was a graduate of the Northern State Normal School at DeKalb and had already had teaching experience in Illinois rural and normal schools. She had a national reputation as a speaker on rural life. She agreed with President Felmley that the country school department must take into account that young teachers could not be expected to apply general principles and methods to the particular conditions of the one-room rural school without observation and supervision. A course was needed for not only town-bred teachers but for young teachers who had grown up in badly-managed country schools.[33]

An arrangement was made in 1913 with the directors of the Walker School, south of Bloomington, by which advanced students in the country school department could come there for observation. Miss Eula Atkinson, a graduate of the State Normal School at Florence, Alabama, who had studied at Teachers College, Columbia University and had been a rural supervisor under the Peabody Fund, was employed as teacher at the Walker School.[34] Normal University students traveled back and forth on the trolley cars to observe teaching in this model rural school. In the three years that Mabel Carney was in charge of the department she not only aroused students to the peculiar needs of

[31] *Ibid.*, (Normal) June 3, 1914, p. 13.
[32] Stanley Brown to David Felmley, DeKalb, June 6, 1926. *Felmley Papers.*
[33] David Felmley, *Annual Report to State Superintendent for the Year Ending* June 30, 1912. (Typescript n.p.)
[34] *Proceedings of the Board of Education* (Normal) December 17, 1913, p. 9.

rural schools, but as a speaker at farmers' institutes she did much to convince rural folk of the necessity of providing better educational opportunities for their children.[35] When she suddenly resigned to become Supervisor of the Training Departments for Country Teachers in the High Schools of Minnesota, President Felmley was dubious about the future of Normal's country school department [36] and affiliation with the Walker School was temporarily suspended. However, his fears as to the future of the department were groundless, a remarkable *esprit de corps* had been built up. Students in the department became veritable crusaders in behalf of better country schools. "The Pioneers," as the alumni of the department styled themselves, returned each year to meet with those finishing the course and to share experiences at a banquet and reunion.[37]

At the same time Mabel Carney was appointed teacher of rural school management, Irwin Arthur Madden was appointed professor of agriculture. His appointment marked the inauguration of a department of agriculture,[38] which opened with seven normal students and twenty-two high school students. With agitation on the part of farmers' institutes for practical work in agriculture in the schools, Professor Madden, energetic and far-sighted, longed to see more constructive use made of the Bakewell tract, which had figured in so much litigation in times past.

In 1903 when President Felmley asked an appropriation for a greenhouse he had called attention to the need of developing teachers of agriculture. He noted that European schools had gardens. Teachers in the training school and their pupils were soon cultivating small tracts set aside at the University farm. The Act of 1857, which established the Normal University, stipulated that instruction should be given in agricultural chemistry, "animal and vegetable physiology." How literally the obligation had been followed in the past was open to question, but Felmley determined it should be observed to the letter. For fifty years the land had

[35] During Mabel Carney's first year at Normal, she made ninety-eight addresses in eighty-three different localities. *Ibid.,* (Normal) June 5, 1912, p. 12.

[36] David Felmley to Francis G. Blair, Normal, March 31, 1914; Francis G. Blair to David Felmley, Springfield, April 6, 1914. *Felmley Papers.*

[37] Edgar Packard succeeded Mabel Carney as head of the country school department. *Index* 1913, p. 75.

[38] *Proceedings of the Board of Education* (Normal) June 7, 1911, p. 25.

been rented to nurseries for a low annual fee. When the Augustine contract expired December 1, 1909, it was rented for crops. The Farmers Institute of the Seventeenth District sought ways and means by which at least a portion of the tract might be transferred to the University of Illinois as an experiment station.[39] To this proposal President Felmley would not consent.

Meanwhile consolidated schools were calling for teachers of agriculture and offering as much as $100 per month for young men able to teach agriculture in the high school grades. "This situation," said Felmley, "imposes upon the normal schools a new duty to prepare teachers for the widening fields of rural education. . . . Any plan for the training of teachers must include use of the University farm. No instruction can be of lasting value unless exemplified by actual farm conditions."

No sooner had Madden arrived on campus and outlined the courses in agriculture than he began laying plans for the organization of the farm and the construction of the necessary farm buildings. By spring 1914 the farm house, a barn, and a silo were completed, construction of hog and chicken houses and a dairy barn begun, and a farm manager was employed.

By the end of the year President Felmley was able to point out to any returning Bakewell heirs or alumni the University's model farm. The house cost $7,760, including window screens, interior shades, furnace, cistern, and soft water supply as well as city water in every part of the house. As a final flourish there were other "conveniences that will lighten the labor of the farmer's wife."[40] Four Percheron mares, two of which were imported, were purchased at a cost of $1,630.55. Twenty Holstein cows, a bull, eleven Duroc Jersey hogs, and seventy-one Plymouth Rock chickens constituted the original livestock. Before President Felmley realized it, Normal University was in the dairy business. A bottling machine was installed and a milk route was established. Soon one hundred sixty families were being supplied with milk from the University's choice herd, bottled in its "spotless" dairy house.[41] By June 1915 it was impossible to cover the milk route with one

[39] Resolutions adopted by Farmers Institute, Seventeenth Congressional District, 1909. Quoted, *Ibid.*, (Normal) June 2, 1909, pp. 23–24.
[40] *Ibid.*, (Normal) June 3, 1914; (Normal) December 16, 1914, p. 12.
[41] *Ibid.*, (Normal) December 16, 1914, p. 12.

or even two horses, and a Ford car was purchased to care for the eighteen-dollar-a-day sales.[42]

The reputation of the new agriculture department and the model farm became widely known, and high schools were soon asking for more teachers of agriculture than the Normal University was able to supply. It became necessary to employ an assistant to Mr. Madden. The Smith-Lever Act of 1914 for extension work in agriculture and home economics focused attention on the need of scientific training in agriculture. When the Smith-Hughes Act for vocational agriculture was passed in 1917, there were high hopes that Normal University would be in on the "ground floor." Little did President Felmley dream that for the next forty years, Smith-Hughes recognition would harass the administration at Normal University.

For sixty-five years one of the needs of the school had been dormitories. In 1915 the Forty-ninth General Assembly was asked for an appropriation of $150,000 for a women's building which would serve as a women's dormitory and social center for the University, but only $95,000 was granted. Upon the advice of the state architect, plans were drawn for a building with its equipment to cost $150,000 as originally proposed, such portions of the building to be constructed as the funds available would permit. The old lily pond and aquatic garden in the grove south of the gymnasium was chosen for the site. The new dormitory was to be known as Fell Hall in honor of Jesse Fell, early friend of the school. Again contractors defaulted, and it was late spring 1918 before the building was ready for occupancy.[43] There was not enough money to provide walks and approaches, and for months cinder paths had to suffice. It was thirty years before funds were appropriated to complete the south wing, and ninety years since President Edwards had first sought funds for a dormitory.

Students and faculty were often disappointed by the scant appropriations, but they did not despair. More and more the school was taking on the semblance of a real college. Conveniences and improvements were being slowly added. A new $30,000 heating

[42] *Ibid.,* (Normal) June 9, 1915, p. 14.
[43] *Ibid.,* (Normal) December 20, 1916, p. 22. Board and room was $6.50 a week at the new dormitory. Miss Eleanor Sheldon, M.A., teacher of English and dean of women, 1917–1920, was the first resident director of Fell Hall.

plant completed in 1916 gave more even heat and comfort in classrooms. On the campus south of North Street, a waiting station had been built by the Bloomington and Normal Railway and Light Company. Its ample porches and heated waiting room provided shelter for streetcar patrons and at the store inside one might buy stationery, school supplies, ice cream and candy.[44]

At the east entrance to the campus drive an imposing gray sandstone Fell Memorial Gateway, erected by the Women's Improvement League and the heirs of Jesse Fell in 1914, lent a gracious dignity and friendliness that was never attained by the old wooden gate with its overhead admonition "For Carriages Only."

Each year more students returned to take work beyond the two-year diploma. More teachers attended summer school to meet increased certification requirements and accumulated credits toward a diploma or degree. Commencement took on a university atmosphere. No longer did the graduating class elect speakers. The address was given by a distinguished outsider. The four-year graduates in 1917 for the first time posed for *Index* pictures in cap and gown.[45] Although some students and faculty looked favorably upon a commencement procession with staff as well as graduates in academic costume, President Felmley was adamant in his opposition. As late as 1926 he wrote a prospective faculty member:

We have not yet indulged in an academic procession at Commencement, or at any other time for a display of academic millinery. Some of our seniors have rented caps and gowns; there was some little talk of a "procession" as a feature of our Commencement. The other members of our faculty are inflexibly opposed to this innovation. They think it detracts from the real dignity and significance of the occasion. . . .

I trust it will be a long day before you will need a master's regalia at Normal.

Cordially yours,
David Felmley [46]

With the expansion of Curriculum K, as the four-year course

[44] The waiting station 25 feet by 57 feet had an enclosed portion 16 feet by 40 feet which contained an office, waiting room and store. It was built in 1910 at a cost of $1,800. No tobacco was sold and none could be used inside the waiting room. The President had authority to inspect and rule on the deportment of students at all times. David Felmley to Peleg R. Walker, Normal, September 28, 1910. *Felmley Papers.*

[45] When the graduating class of 1896 discussed wearing caps and gowns, the men favored the idea but were outvoted by the women. *Index,* 1896, p. 54.

[46] David Felmley to Esther Vinson, Tucson, Arizona, April 5, 1926. *Index,* 1917.

for secondary teachers was called, numerous departmental clubs sprang up, some of which still exist.[47] Others languished after a few terms, and later were reactivated or disbanded. The Story Telling League organized by Miss Frances E. Foote, "an artistic story teller of much renown" who joined the faculty in 1911 as third grade critic, was one for which enthusiasm skyrocketed and then dropped when its sponsor moved to another position three years later.[48] The Dramatics Club was first organized through the efforts of Grace Arlington Owen, teacher of reading in 1909. In 1913 President Felmley's daughter, Mildred, who had just graduated from the University of Illinois, entered the normal school, and through her efforts the old Dramatics Club was reorganized into the Jesters.[49] The Country Life Club was composed of students in the country school curriculum and a few others whose rural background inspired an interest in its program. A Social Science Club was organized in 1916. Seventy students under the leadership of Professor Manchester [50] closely followed the political events of that election year and trends for several years thereafter.[51] The old long-established literary societies, Wrightonian and Philadelphian, felt competition from the new specialized clubs and the new emphasis on athletics, but they continued their periodic meetings and the inter-society contests. The Sapphonian Society succumbed in 1913 after a quarter of a century, but the Ciceronian lingered on to become a casualty of the First World War. The Index of 1919 lamented:

> Lead out the pageant: sad and low
> As fits an universal woe
> The last great Ciceronian is gone.[52]

The Nature Study Club under the guidance of Alice Jean Patterson, teacher of nature study with her interest in gardens, became

---

[47] *The Alumni Quarterly,* May 1916, noted thirty-five student organizations.
[48] *Index* 1911, p. 100; *Ibid.,* 1913, p. 131.
[49] The Jesters' first play was *Green Stockings,* March 5, 1914. *Ibid.,* 1915, p. 139.
[50] Professor Manchester was long remembered for his famous "fish problem," a device involving a skill in mathematics as well as an understanding of the operation of certain economic laws. The variables were changed from time to time and the student who could work the fish problem on the final examination was sure to pass the course.
[51] The present Social Science Club was organized in 1935 under the direction of Dr. Lucy Lucile Tasher, professor of American history.
[52] *Index* 1919, p. 205.

the pattern and parent of hundreds of other nature study clubs throughout Illinois schools.

Alumni were brought up to date on happenings at their alma mater through the *Alumni Quarterly* which appeared in February 1912, as the outgrowth of action taken at the alumni meeting during Commencement of the previous year. By June of 1912, the *Quarterly* had three hundred subscribers.

Since 1909, Founders Day, February 18, had been an occasion for reunion and reminiscence. A feature at the first annual banquet was an address by Captain John H. Burnham of the Class of 1861, who told of the founding of the school.[53] At the second Founders Day observance, members of the Class of 1900 presented a portrait of President Arnold Tompkins.[54] In 1913 a reception with addresses rather than a banquet paid tribute to the University's first president, Charles E. Hovey. A portrait of Hovey in the uniform of a Union general, painted by Clarence Messer, was presented by the ISNU Club of New York City.[55] Honoring the occasion, Mrs. Hovey sent along to the school her husband's dress sword and scabbard, his field sword which showed usage, his general's yellow sash, his colonel's red sash, epaulets and minor military relics together with the first battle flag of the Normal Regiment.[56] In a few years the portraits of all former presidents of the University, its benign founder, Jesse Fell, and the beloved teacher, Thomas Metcalf, would look down from the walls of the reception room in Old Main.

When other colleges and universities began laying plans for commemorating the three hundredth anniversary of the death of Shakespeare, Professor June Rose Colby decided this was an event which Normal University should not overlook. She envisaged it as a wonderful opportunity for the departments of English, speech, physical education, art and music to work together on a pageant portraying "The Evolution of the Drama." Grace Arlington Owen, imaginative and energetic teacher of reading, who five

[53] *Ibid.*, 1909, p. 115.
[54] *Ibid.*, 1910, p. 118.
[55] E. C. Messer who painted the Hovey portrait taught music and art privately in Bloomington and Normal during the Civil War. In 1863 he lived at the Hovey home. Later he was associated with the Corcoran Gallery in Washington, D. C.
[56] Harriette F. Hovey to David Felmley, Washington, D. C., January 15, 1913. *Felmley Papers.*

years before had written and staged a remarkable masque "Judgment of the Ages," was enthusiastic over the idea. Soon the pageant assumed community proportions with a cast of 2,000 persons. Bloomington High School, the Normal Public School, the Soldiers Orphans Home and the Wesleyan College of Music joined forces with the University. In six colorful episodes, the story of drama was projected, from wandering troubadors, miracle and morality plays, folk dances and music, to the Court of Queen Elizabeth with a Bacchanalia, the great bard and characters from his plays. The scene was set on the south campus among the trees and shrubbery near the old lily pool that was soon to be drained for the site of the dormitory. Bleachers were set up and tickets sold for the greatest dramatic event in the history of the school. No one seemed to reckon with the possibility of summer showers. Thunder clouds appeared a week before the performance was scheduled and for ten days there was rain. Commencement came, and the students went home. The rented costumes were returned. An abridged performance during the summer term honored the memory of William Shakespeare, but it failed to erase the deficit.[57]

The new certification laws had the effect of bringing enrollment in the summer school of 1916 to a record-breaking 2,285, despite auxiliary schools at Carlinville, Danville, Spring Valley, Canton, and Kewanee. Additional teachers had to be employed, and rooms in the Normal public school were used for the overflow of classes. Rooming houses and boarding clubs were filled, and the restaurants in Normal found it difficult to feed the hungry hordes that descended upon them at noon time. Students from Bloomington brought their lunches and ate under the trees.

In response to the many requests of teachers who wished to improve their professional status, an extension service was inaugurated in 1913. Professor E. A. Turner taught Principles of Teaching at Joliet, and Professor Douglas Ridgley had a geography class in Springfield. These were ninety-minute thirty-week courses. Soon Professor Herman Schroeder had three classes in

---

[57] *Index* 1916, pp. 98–99; *Alumni Quarterly*, August 1916, p. 31. An old program advised that box lunches could be obtained for fifteen cents and coffee, sandwiches, and ice cream for a nickel at the Metcalf Building. Marchpane, an Elizabethan sweetmeat, and Banbury tarts were to be sold by vendors.

Principles of Teaching at Pontiac, Dwight, and Joliet.[58] Two dollars was charged for the course, and one credit in each course
could be earned toward graduation. The extension idea took hold
quickly. For the school year 1914–1915 forty-seven students were
registered in four centers. A special director of extension was employed in 1915, and in the following year 474 persons were enrolled in twenty-one classes at sixteen centers. The fourth year
saw an enrollment of 639, with eight teachers conducting classes
in twenty centers. Correspondence courses begun in 1916 together
with the war precipitated an abrupt decline in extension and by
the year 1921–1922, there was only one off-campus course with an
enrollment of nine persons.[59]

World War I made a heavy impact on the Normal University.
The new program with its completely reorganized curriculum
and allocation of special authority to the heads of the twenty departments was just getting under way when the war came.[60] War
was declared just three weeks after the spring term began and
three weeks before the special midterm was scheduled to start. A
movement was started to introduce military training in the school.
Two hours of daily drill was offered to all men who cared to
take it, but there was no equipment, and enthusiasm for broom-
stick parades soon waned. Many men left school, some to enlist,
some to join units of the Students Army Training Corps on other
campuses, and others to return to the farm. By June 1917, seventy-
two young men had left the school—one-fourth to enlist, the
others to farm.[61] The Normal School Board permitted seniors
who were making passing marks at the time they enlisted to substitute military service for the remaining credits, and their
diplomas were conferred *in absentia.*[62] Students who left Normal

---

[58] *Proceedings of the Board of Education* (Normal) December 17, 1913, p. 11.

[59] *Statistics,* Division of Field Services, 1915.

[60] The departments as set up in 1916 were education, mathematics, physical science,
biological science, geography, history and political science, economics and sociology,
literature and composition, reading and public speaking, music, art and design, manual
training, household science, household art, agriculture, commerce, the training school
with divisions of elementary, high school and Soldiers Orphans Home, country school
department, normal school extension, and physical education.

[61] *Index* 1917, p. 93; *Proceedings of the Board of Education* (Normal) June 6, 1917, p. 11.

[62] *Ibid.,* (Carbondale) January 21, 1918, p. 4. Under the Civil Administrative Code,
the separate boards of trustees for the five normal schools were replaced July 1, 1917
by the Normal School Board, consisting of nine members appointed by the governor and
two ex-officio members—the Director of the Department of Registration and Education

University to perform service on farms were granted credit for the courses they were taking upon statements that they had completed assignments in their spare time and had kept a diary of their agricultural work.[63] In 1916 there were 2,285 enrolled for the first term of summer school; in 1917 there were 1,823, of whom only 100 were men. Enrollment in the normal and college department declined from 834 for the fall term 1916 to 605 in 1917. Each succeeding term saw a decline in attendance.

On September 18, 1918, President Felmley wrote Superintendent Blair that enrollment in the normal and college department was 362, of whom twelve were men. This was forty percent less than the number in September 1917 and less than half of the fall term in 1916.

It is evident the normal schools ar going to hav hard sledding this fall. Our senior class numbers only a little more than a hundred. We shal not hav students enuf properly to care for classes in the Soldiers Orphans Home, in Normal University High School and Elementary Training School. . . . Our faculty is needlessly large (seventy-two) . . . all our teachers but three or four are underworkt.

The "underworkt" teachers, he said, were free to start correspondence courses, and already members of the staff were preparing to offer correspondence work in geography, history, civil government, economics, ethics, history of education, psychology, teaching of high school biology, nature study, English grammar, advanced composition, English literature, teaching of reading in both upper and lower grades, elementary drawing, mechanical drawing, accounting, typewriting, and Gregg shorthand.[64] A month later he reported that correspondence courses were being conducted in twenty-two subjects with from one to three persons enrolled in each course. The charge for the course was one dollar, with the student paying all postage.[65]

Administratively the war years were difficult years. The Fiftieth General Assembly, in session at the time of the declaration of war, was reluctant to increase appropriations. The situation under the

---

who served as chairman, and the Superintendent who served as secretary. No less than five meetings were to be held annually.

[63] Many of these letters and diaries are among the *Felmley Papers*.

[64] David Felmley to Francis G. Blair, Normal, September 18, 1918. *Felmley Papers*.

[65] *Proceedings of the Normal School Board* (Springfield) October 15, 1918, p. 18.

new Civil Code was frustrating. No longer were the presidents of the normal schools able to operate as the letter of the law and their consciences dictated, now the final arbiter was Francis Shepardson, Director of Registration and Education, who was vigorously trying to bring order and uniformity into the administration of a large and unwieldy department. Under the old system the Auditor had permitted the presidents to treat the entire appropriation for salaries and wages as a single fund from which faculty and other employees were paid. The appropriations bill in 1917 had itemized salaries and wages for the various teachers and other employees for the biennium. It was no longer possible to raise the salary of a good teacher to hold him through the saving that accrued in employing a new and younger teacher in some other vacant position. Furthermore the new Civil Code required that tuition fees and other receipts be turned in to the State Treasury. Additional staff could be employed and paid from the Reserve and Contingencies Fund up to the amount each school had turned in to the Treasury, but none of this money could be used to augment slender salaries. It took rare juggling ability on the part of a normal school president to shift a teacher from a position paid out of the salaries and wages appropriation to one paid out of the Reserve and Contingencies Fund. Salary checks were now issued from the office of the Director of Registration and Education and not from the offices of the respective normal school presidents.[66]

As prices skyrocketed, the teaching, clerical and maintenance personnel suffered. The maintenance staff, noting an increase in commodities from fifty to one hundred percent, petitioned for an increase of forty percent in wages, similar to that being given in other fields of labor. Good teachers were enticed to better paying positions. A few asked for leaves of absence to enter military service or take up war work. Women whose salaries averaged seven hundred dollars below those of men were especially hard hit by the rising prices. Spreading the annual salary over thirty-six week school year instead of thirty-nine additional compensation for summer school, and distributing funds from unfilled vacancies and military leaves, provided scant relief. Many persons remained

[66] *Ibid.*, (Normal) December 11, 1917, p. 22.

on the staff because they had property or families in Normal, many because of their loyalty to the institution and to President Felmley who was making every effort to improve salaries. The Board voted favorably on a $1,000 increase for the presidents and a twenty-five percent increase for other staff members, although the governor and Director of Finance approved only a ten percent increase for the faculty. President Felmley wrote Francis Shepardson, Director of Registration and Education, that he did not think any of the presidents would be willing to accept an additional $1,000 if the over all faculty increase was only ten percent. Shepardson replied that the normal school seemed to doubt the integrity of the governor and the Budget Commission and that, through the action of the Normal School Board, his department had been the only one to oppose the administration but added that a faculty committee could still go to the governor and talk it over.[67] And they did! A shortage of coal, a flu epidemic that closed the school for three weeks, and a smallpox scare were among the other worries of the war years.

Except for the high school and the training school the campus took on the semblance of being largely a woman's world. When the number of men in the normal and college department dropped to twelve, girls were encouraged to take up manual training and meet the teacher demand in that field.[68] In addition to classes, the campus hummed with war-time activities. Early in April 1917 a Red Cross auxiliary was organized, and Miss Colby, who normally prided herself on not being domestic, urged girls and faculty women to join the unit and spend their spare time sewing, making surgical dressings, and rolling bandages in the faculty women's cloakroom, which had been outfitted as a sewing room. Courses in home economics were fitted to war-time needs with special courses in food conservation. On May 9, 1917, the *Vidette* issued a special Red Cross number. Young women brought their sewing to the rhetorical section of Miss O. Lillian Barton, Dean of Women, and in General Exercises knitting needles clicked as Professor Westhoff led the singing of "Over There" and "Keep the Home Fires Burning." Wrightonia, the

[67] David Felmley to Francis Shepardson, Normal, November 26, 1918; Francis Shepardson to David Felmley, December 31, 1918. *Felmley Papers.*
[68] David Felmley to Livingston C. Lord, Normal, September 18, 1918. *Felmley Papers.*

YW, and the Science Club rented plots of ground and started gardens in the southwest part of town. The gospel of thrift, saving, and giving permeated Normal University from kindergarten through college. Peach, apricot, and cherry stones were brought to school and sent away to be used in gas masks. Trench candles were made of old newspapers, melted paraffin and wax. Thrift stamps were sold by the secretary in the president's office.[69] Rhetoricals took on the zest and force of a crusade as kits of speeches for "Four Minute Men" arrived from the Office of War Information. The war gave new motivation to what had often been a burdensome performance. Now the appeal for funds in a rhetorical might be so dramatic and compelling that then and there a collection would be taken and a drive begun.

The University participated in the Student Friendship Fund,[70] the YMCA War Emergency Fund, Fatherless Children of France Campaign,[71] the various war loan drives, and the United War Work Campaign. A War Service Commission was set up to coordinate war-time activities. It conducted a column in the *Vidette* with a message from a faculty member in each issue and mailed copies to the men and women in service. It also maintained a service flag and prepared a roster and a permanent file of those in service. Each faculty member considered himself a member of a committee on correspondence and after the war when Ange. Milner counted up the letters she had received, she found she had written over eight hundred.

The news of the Armistice came out just after the "flu recess" and before all the students had returned to the campus, but those present joined with the community in celebrating "peace and victory." In a few weeks the war-time activities began closing up their work and compiling records. At the final count the service flag bore 626 stars, fourteen of them gold ones. On Arbor Day in 1919 a group of ex-service men planted a tree to honor Normal University's "fallen heroes who died for democracy." By the spring term a number of veterans were back in school, and for

[69] *Index*, 1919, pp. 112, 109.
[70] *Ibid.*, 1918, p. 67.
[71] For the "Fatherless Children of France" the French government gave ten cents a day and a donor in the United States gave ten cents a day or $36.50 a year. Twenty-four adoptions were made by student organizations and faculty members. *Index* 1919, pp. 105, 107.

the first time Commencement featured an original production "And They Did Come Back, A War Time Revue," with songs, dances and music, as the program announced, "Written, directed and produced by them." [72]

There was little doubt that the enrollment in the college and normal department, which had dropped to 350 the past winter, would soon increase and that the limited facilities of the school would soon be sorely felt. President Felmley believed that all too long the Normal University had been the Cinderella of the state's educational institutions.[73] In league with the other state normal school presidents, he drafted a budget that would include an extensive building program and a substantial increase in teachers' salaries. He had always been sensitive about his own $6,000 salary when there were teachers on his staff who were receiving as little as $850 for thirty-six weeks and no guarantee of summer employment. Boldly he asked for a fifty percent increase in salaries. After twenty-two teachers had resigned because of low salaries, President Felmley told Professor Manchester and Professor John L. Pricer, teacher of biology, who had directed a faculty study on salaries to feel free to go ahead as they saw fit to publicize the need of salary increases. He told the Board in September 1920 that he had spent a large part of his time that summer "trying to capture a $2,000 teacher with a $400 salary." [74]

Meanwhile Dean Manchester, with his characteristic vigor, prepared a "brief" for salary increases. He reduced the matter to an economic formula, using data from Dunn, Bradstreet, the Annalist, and the Bureau of Statistics. He compared the salaries of teachers in twenty-seven leading normal schools. He noted that salaries at the University of Illinois had increased from seventy-five to one hundred percent, but even then President James said they did not keep pace with the increase in the cost of living. Manchester asserted that the faculty at Normal would have to ask a seventy-five percent increase to put them on a level with the University of Illinois. "Penuriousness in pay," he warned, "will

[72] *Ibid.*, p. 114.
[73] On October 30, 1916 Felmley wrote Governor Dunne, "The University of Illinois with its $900,000 per annum for building purposes may build as it pleases, consequently it builds in marble and furnishes in mahogany, while we are obliged to build with common brick at $10 per M and furnish in oak, pine, and poplar. . . ." *Felmley Papers.*
[74] *Proceedings of the Normal School Board* (Carbondale) September 24, 1920, p. 29.

be followed by strained relations, fleeting attachments, penuriousness in service. . . . Teachers should stay in the Normal, not because they cannot get out, but because it profits them to stay." [75]

Despite the warning of Shepardson that the Budget Committee
would consider only those buildings that were absolutely necessary, Felmley drew up both long range and immediate building
plans and stated his case for each. He listed first a $225,000 gym-
nasium. The old one had been in use for twenty-three years. By
law, pupils in schools of the state were required to have one hour
of physical education each week, and so many students desired
to become special teachers or supervisors that a special curriculum
for such training was being offered. [76] He asked for a gymnasium
with parallel basketball courts, with arrangements for seating
1,500 spectators, and with a swimming pool, requisite locker-
rooms, showers, and a club room for men.

President Felmley's other askings looked forward both in curriculum and in housing. Realizing that a new building was necessary if the Normal University were to continue its pioneer work
in nature study and science, he asked for a $250,000 science build-
ing. In 1918 the Normal University had been designated a teacher
training institution in home economics and agriculture under the
provisions of the Smith-Hughes Act. One requirement was a
house and furnishings where the young women could have
practical experience in household management through cooperative housekeeping. Two thousand dollars had been appropriated
in 1919 for renting and furnishing a house, but when President
Felmley tried to find a suitable house none was available. He now
renewed the request and sought an appropriation for a house. He
further asked for the rebuilding of the greenhouse and toolhouse,
the completion of the south wing of Fell Hall, which he thought
could be done for $75,000, a fine arts building, a second dormitory
for women, and a house for the president. Reluctantly he had
joined the other presidents in asking the state to provide homes
for the normal school presidents. A home had been built for the

[75] Orson L. Manchester "Work and Pay of the Normal School Teacher." (Mimeographed) *Manchester Papers.*
[76] In 1916 President Felmley had asked the Board to include a science building and a
gymnasium in the 1917 budget but the coming of the war dashed all hopes of new
buildings.

president of the University of Illinois twenty-five years before.[77] Felmley was growing weary of all the petty economies that he had been practicing and forcing upon students and faculty through all the years—the cheap stationery, writing on both sides of the paper, the low grade of chalk, and the homemade erasers.[78] Perhaps one way to stop the General Assembly from looking upon teacher training institutions as educational step-children would be for their presidents to make their "askings" comparable to those of the University of Illinois.[79]

To the economy-minded legislators, the requests were fantastic. Although the case for salary increases could not be ignored, there would be no money for new buildings, and repairs on old ones were to be kept at a minimum.

Felmley resolved to renew his requests. By hammering away, year after year, from one session to the next he might obtain some of the badly needed buildings. In 1923, the $250,000 request for a new gymnasium had been whittled down to $150,000. Felmley determined the original plan would be carried out as far as the $150,000 grant would permit, even though some features such as the swimming pool and the running track would have to be left out.[80] Two years later appropriations were made for a hall of science. The other buildings might not come in his time, but he would keep on asking.[81]

True to Felmley's predictions the enrollment took a sharp turn upward after the war. By December 1925 there were 1,300 students in the college department, and the first summer term in 1924 saw 2,726 students on campus and 1,090 the second term. Every available room in Normal and Bloomington was rented, and many students commuted from nearby towns on the Illinois Terminal.[82] After 1921 it had been necessary to open a cafeteria in the boys' playroom in the Metcalf Building and take over the

[77] *Proceedings of the Normal School Board* (Springfield) November 8, 1920, p. 15.
[78] When a passenger train was wrecked near Normal President Felmley obtained permission to have the plush ripped off the broken seats, and had the manual training students nail layers of the plush on blocks of wood and thereby save the price of new felt erasers. As late as 1936 some of these erasers were still in use in Old Main.
[79] David Felmley to Francis Shepardson, Normal, December 5, 1918. *Felmley Papers.*
[80] *Proceedings of the Normal School Board* (Macomb) September 25, 1923, p. 19.
[81] Felmley in 1920 estimated the total value of the university plant including the land, buildings, and equipment of the farm, at $1,000,054.00. David Felmley to Francis Shepardson, Normal, October 2, 1920. *Felmley Papers.*
[82] *Proceedings of the Normal School Board* (Chicago) October 13, 1924, pp. 21–22.

home economics room across the hall as a kitchen. Additional teachers were employed in summer and the heavy student load in the regular year curtailed the extension and correspondence work that had formerly attracted many teachers.[83] In 1926 to provide adequate teaching experiences and observation for students in rural and special curricula as art, music, and physical education, an affiliation was made with two rural schools, the Price and later the Houghton, and by 1928 the Little Brick School and the Rose Hill School were added to the list. A base salary paid by the district to the supervising teacher was supplemented by the University. Transportation of student teachers was provided by the University.[84]

The health of the students had long been a concern of the faculty and administration, and in September 1923, Florence Ames, M. D., took up her work as the Normal University's first physician. Dr. Ames taught seven classes in personal hygiene each week, examined all women on admission to the school and all men on athletic teams, and daily inspected the rooms of the training school. She engaged in no private practice and collected no fees but was available for consultation and administered medication for minor ailments.[85]

The increased attendance of the 1920's brought about many changes in the social and cultural life of the school. The governing bodies had never looked with favor on social fraternities and sororities, and none was ever established. Filling their place on the campus was a multiplicity of clubs, organizations, and other extra-curricular activities. In 1920 a student council, composed of a representative of each club, was set up to coordinate student activities and to assist new students in adjusting to college life. In 1921 it published a Students' Hand Book offering sage advice. Students were admonished not to use ink in the study hall except in fountain pens; for best home study conditions, sixty-eight degree temperature and a forty to sixty watt light bulb were suggested; and three baths a week were recommended.

In addition to the time-honored Wrightonian and Philadel-

[83] *Ibid.*, (Carbondale) September 24, 1920, p. 32.
[84] Affiliated schools in 1928 were Soldiers Orphans Home, Price, Houghton, Little Brick, and Rose Hill.
[85] *Proceedings of the Normal School Board* (Macomb) September 25, 1923, p. 20.

phian societies, the YWCA, the reactivated YMCA, the Women's Athletic Association, Jesters, the Kindergarten Club, the Latin Club, and the Nature Study Club—all of which antedated and survived the war, there were the various musical organizations such as the glee clubs, chorus, orchestra, and bands that had maintained a certain continuity through the years. The Lowell Mason Club for music majors, sponsored by Professor Frank Westhoff, came into being in 1922. A Varsity Club for men was organized in 1919, and a Women's League "to assist the Dean of Women" was organized in 1926. An Art Club was formed in 1920. Majors in agriculture organized the Hopkins Agriculture Club in 1922, and a year later majors in industrial arts formed their Manual Arts Club. The more strictly professional Hieronymus Club developed out of the Country Life Association, and before long the Women's Athletic Association was spawning its Orchesis and the Women's League its League of Women Voters; and the Varsity Club and Men's Athletic Association were sponsoring the N Club, where membership was conferred on men who had earned letters in sports, and later the Gamma Phi, a physical education fraternity soon to be noted for its annual circus. Mathematics majors were organized into a "Euclidean Circle" in 1927 as the French majors had been in Le Circle Francais in 1924 and the Spanish majors in El Circulo Espanol in 1926. The German Club, Der Bildungsverein, had become one of the war casualties when German had been dropped from the curriculum. In the midst of the curricular clubs, national Greek letter honor societies appeared and neophytes learned the ancient alphabet. The first of these, Kappa Delta Pi, education society, received its charter in 1922. Pi Kappa Delta, forensic organization, in 1923 afforded membership for students who had done distinguished work in the field of oratory and debate. Theta Alpha Phi, national dramatic organization, installed Delta chapter in 1926. In 1928 Theta chapter of Pi Omega Pi was installed for the recognition of commerce majors. There was no national organization for geography majors and on May 15, 1928, the faculty granted permission to the ambitious Geography Club to organize a fraternity under the sponsorship of Dr. R. G. Buzzard, head of the department of geography, and to expand its scope nationally if the work of the organization warranted, and thus Alpha chapter of Gamma Theta Upsilon was begun.

Coeducational religious clubs made their appearance—the Newman Club for Catholic students in 1924 and the Lutheran Club in 1926. With the coming of other religious organizations, participation in the activities of the YM and YW declined and their quarters were moved from their rooms on North Street back to the campus. Wrightonia and Philadelphia lingered on for another generation. Each of the "modern" organizations, as a veteran faculty member described the newer clubs, sponsored a variety of social events, picnics, skating parties, dances, and banquets and gave new tone to the programs in the daily General Exercises. The *Index* each year beneath the name and picture of each graduate listed his distinctions and memberships. Some of the faculty were wont to shake their heads: the school was becoming a university of joiners.[86]

An innovation after the war was the Homecoming each fall sponsored jointly by the student body and the Alumni Association. On a visit to the East during the winter of 1920–1921 President Felmley was impressed by the "Homecoming Trend" in eastern schools. He thought such an event on campus might help dispel "popular feeling that the Normal School was not progressing." Annabelle Harper and Annette Cooper, members of the faculty and graduates of the Normal University, asked President Felmley to approve one for the school. He promptly named them to a committee, added the name of Harrison Russell, the football coach, and allowed $75 for expenses. Students and faculty were at the trains on November 4–5, 1921, to meet returning alumni. Guests registered in the Main Office, were given a souvenir booklet, a badge and a bunch of wahoo berries. By noon on Saturday seven hundred had registered. On Friday night there was the Jester play and an Auld Lang Syne party afterward. On Saturday morning the girls in the domestic science class served a waffle breakfast, and Miss Milner held open house in the library. At one-thirty there was a parade from Old Main to the football field. The Wrights and Phils met in their halls at seven and ad-

---

[86] Data on student organizations has been obtained from club records, files of *Vidette* and *Index*.

journed for a party in Fell Hall and the dance in the gymnasium.[87]

So successful was the affair that it became an annual event, and with slight modification the first Homecoming has been the model for subsequent celebrations. In 1923 a Hobo parade through the streets of downtown Normal was sponsored by the Hopkins Agriculture Club. When the new gymnasium was opened for inspection in 1925, extra streetcars had to be switched to the Park Street line to care for the crowds. Houses were decorated for the first time in 1927.[88]

In 1925 David Felmley rounded out his twenty-fifth year as president, and his thirty-fifth on the campus. He found it difficult to believe he was growing old, although each year since 1906 the students had been celebrating his birthday, April 24, in one way or another. Sometimes there were surprise programs in General Exercises, songs and tributes from the classes. Always there was a basket of flowers, a rose or a carnation for each year of his busy life. Although President Felmley prided himself on being a busy man, he found time to know students. He made a point of remembering names, curriculums and home towns. Students could have loved him for this trait alone. He was touched by these birthday demonstrations and for the time being dropped off a bit of what those who did not know him well described as "crustiness." Privately he recapitulated, noting things accomplished and things yet to be done. Someday he would retire but not yet. He would spare himself a bit, perhaps take longer and more frequent vacations, find more time for bridge, which he enjoyed and played so well, often to the discomfiture of many of his faculty competitors. He would let one of the younger men climb to the tower and oil the clock. He was not ready to leave. For one thing, there was the matter of rating and recognition. In 1920 when the University of Illinois had sent six faculty members to the Normal University to examine the library, catalog, and faculty credentials to see if its graduates should be admitted to the graduate school at Urbana, they had reported Illinois State Normal University not qualified. At the invitation of the registrar Felmley had taken

---

[87] *Index* 1922, p. 18; *Alumni Quarterly* (November 1925), p. 14.
[88] An unidentified clipping says the first parade "reeked with originality." In the walking entries were such popular characters as "Andy and Min," "Uncle Walt," "Skeezix," and "The Old Woman Who Lived in a Shoe."

three of his staff to Urbana and gone over the report. The University had then given the Normal University "B" rating, which meant that four-year graduates were admitted with eight to sixteen hours "on condition." It could be scaled down for good work and entirely canceled for the superior student. He wanted to live to see the Normal University accorded an "A" rating.[89]

There were so many things he wanted for the school, things for which he had long been agitating—greater selectivity in admissions so that ultimately a better product could be returned to the classrooms,[90] improved standards of certification that would raise the level of teaching in the high schools of the state,[91] a positive assurance that the normal schools would be permitted to go on training teachers for the secondary schools,[92] opportunity to develop the program of visual aids in which Douglas Ridgley had pioneered some years before.[93] He wanted to be able to encourage more pioneering in the various departments, such as Professor Buzzard had been doing with the geography tours. He wanted to see an adequate salary and retirement system that would attract good teachers. It was hard to be always trying to hire good teachers at low salaries, and harder still to see good teachers leaving for better paying positions. He wanted means for helping gifted but financially poor students to attend teachers college. The Lindly scholarships and a student loan fund dating from 1902 supported by plays and benefits, and the Faculty Women's Club Loan Fund established in 1916 helped, but these did not meet

[89] David Felmley to Stanley Brown, Normal, May 26, 1920; David Felmley to Francis Shepardson, Normal, May 26, 1920. *Felmley Papers. Proceedings of the Normal School Board* (Springfield) June 21, 1920, p. 21.
[90] David Felmley to Francis G. Blair, Normal, January 25, 1921. *Felmley Papers.*
[91] David Felmley to Livingston C. Lord, Normal, December 16, 1924. *Felmley Papers.*
[92] *Proceedings of the Normal School Board* (Chicago) May 7, 1923, p. 4.
[93] Douglas Ridgley worked with the Keystone Company in preparing geographic slides for stereopticon news, and later slides for classroom use. As early as 1911 Mabel Carney asked the Board to allow $180 for a "lantern" to take to institutes. In 1920 Felmley asked Shepardson to get permission from the governor for Ridgley to attend a conference on visual aids in Madison. His reasons for the trip were that Normal University was making extensive use of moving picture films in educational work, and that the school has been a distributing point for films prepared by the United States government during and after the war. Felmley wanted to spend $500 for photographic equipment to be used by the agriculture teacher who was an expert photographer but Shepardson said it was providing "busy work." This angered Felmley who replied, "We can get along without it, just as people can get along without many things that add to the pleasure and dignity of life." For fifteen years Felmley wanted to have photography taught in the school. David Felmley to Francis Shepardson, Normal, August 24, 1920. *Felmley Papers.*

the need. He admitted quite frankly that he had not worked out solutions to all these problems, but he wanted to try a little while longer.

He had not asked much for himself. He had had offers to go elsewhere, but he considered the pledge he made when he accepted the presidency as a thing inviolate. He was repeatedly asked to run for state superintendent, but his only venture in politics was when he considered becoming a delegate to a Constitutional Convention. A frown of disapproval from the Board brought him back on his academic heels but not without a pronouncement that politically he stood for the utmost freedom of discussion on all social and political reform.[94] The Board had been generous in the matter of salary for the five normal school presidents. Sometimes Felmley felt embarrassed at his own $7,500 when members of his faculty, some of them more highly trained, were receiving so much less. He had his own ideas of how the Board could be organized to function more effectively.

The physical condition that had been harassing President Felmley for several months got the upper hand in the late summer of 1929. He was unable to attend the Board meeting in Springfield in August and had his report read by Herman H. Schroeder, who had been serving as dean since O. L. Manchester's sudden death in June 1928. He did not improve, but he managed to arrange student programs in September, employ teachers, make out reports and attend to correspondence from his bed at his home near the campus. Finally he began to allocate to others, one by one, the duties he had so zealously performed for over thirty years. Randolph D. Marsh came in as the newly appointed business manager on November 15 and relieved him of many time-consuming details that had hitherto always been a part of the president's job.[95]

When President Felmley prepared his fall report, he also dictated a letter which he asked Dean Schroeder to read to the Board. It was his valedictory, forthright and unadorned. Without vainglory he reviewed the nearly thirty years that he had served as president. He was grateful for the confidence and co-

[94] David Felmley to Francis Shepardson, Normal, January 3, 1920, and July 10, 1919. *Felmley Papers.*
[95] *Proceedings of the Normal School Board* (Springfield) January 16, 1930, p. 9.

operation that he had been given. There was no hope of recovery. Perhaps the Board might feel that the interests of the Normal University required an able-bodied man at its head. In that event he was ready to accept emeritus rating under the plan adopted the previous year.

A few hours later Francis Blair dispatched the Board's reply. Felmley should continue as president until such continuance interfered with his own peace and happiness. The same mail brought word that the new science building would be known as Felmley Hall of Science and that a different name would be given the gymnasium.[96] Both letters pleased the ailing president. He had never been particularly happy over the naming of the gymnasium in his honor. Science, rather than athletics, had been his abiding interest.

Close by his side those long months was his wife, Jennie Green, to whom he had been married only a little over a year. The day after Christmas he dictated his letter of resignation, but before it reached the Board he had lapsed into a coma. On January 24, 1930, he died at his home on School Street.[97]

[96] *Ibid.*, (Carbondale) November 4, 1929, pp. 14–16.
[97] *Ibid.*, (Macomb) April 28, 1930, p. 31; *The Normalite*, January 24, 1930.

CHAPTER XII

The Era of Uncertainty

HERMAN HENRY SCHROEDER, professor of education and psychology since 1913 and dean of the Normal University since June 1929, was named acting president.[1] He was thorough, methodical, well-informed, and possessed of many of the qualities for which President Felmley had been noted. He prided himself on his virtues of thrift, promptness, and accuracy. It embarrassed him to make mistakes. He was willing to work long hours, and he stood adamant on any point he regarded as a matter of principle. He had not been on campus long when President Felmley met him in the hall on the way to a class. He inquired how things were going. Professor Schroeder did not stop, but taking out his watch, called back, "I have never been late to a class, Sir, and I will not begin now." Felmley turned to some students who were standing nearby, "Great fellow, Schroeder."

By the time Dean Schroeder was given full authority as acting president, a committee from the Board had already been appointed to select Felmley's successor and had reviewed thirty-two applications and interviewed several candidates. Meanwhile Manfred J. Holmes temporarily took over the work of dean, and Dean Schroeder bent his efforts toward keeping affairs of the school running smoothly and carrying out the policies of his predecessor. Staff members found him approachable and willing to listen. Students found him fair-minded and firm but not insensible to tears. His judgments were generally respected, and some persons hoped the Board would select him as president.[2]

[1] When President Felmley became very ill Superintendent Blair, as secretary of the Board, authorized Dean Schroeder to assume the duties of the president. In April 1930, the Board confirmed his appointment as acting president at the regular salary of $7,500 and made it retroactive to February 1, 1930. *Proceedings of the Normal School Board* (Macomb) April 28, 1930, p. 67.

[2] Thirty-six candidates sought the position; ten were from Illinois, three from the faculty—all Illinois men off the faculty were receiving more money. The best qualified man who could come without personal sacrifice was the president of Wisconsin State Teachers College at Oshkosh. He and his wife went to Charleston and were interviewed by the Board. *Ibid.*, (Charleston) May 26, 1930, pp. 5–6.

Late in May the news was released that Dr. Harry Alvin Brown, president of Wisconsin Teachers College, Oshkosh, had been named president of the Normal University. The selection was heralded as a wise one. Dr. Brown had wide experience as a teacher and administrator. Since 1917 he had been president of the Wisconsin State Teachers College at Oshkosh. He had brought that school from a two-year course to full college level, with a four-year curriculum and a degree that was recognized by the North Central Association of Colleges and Secondary Schools. He had organized the college into divisions each with a director and divisions into departments with a specially trained head. Members of the faculty had been urged to get additional training and courses had been reorganized.[3]

After publishing a provocative article in the *Elementary School Journal,* November 1924, on "Standards for Teachers Colleges," Harry Brown was named chairman of a Committee on Standards set up by the American Association of Teachers Colleges. After visiting every teacher training institution in the country, he prepared a set of standards which was adopted by the Association. It was regarded the most significant forward step in the history of the Association. In 1926 Dr. Brown reported his findings to the National Education Association in an address, "On What Should State Teachers Colleges Place Chief Emphasis in Developing Higher Standards." [4] President Felmley had known Dr. Brown through the American Association of Teachers Colleges. They had occasionally exchanged letters, and Felmley had been impressed by the constructive work being done by Brown of Oshkosh.

Harry Alvin Brown was fifty-one years of age when he became president of Illinois State Normal University. He was tall, well-built, carefully groomed, and distinguished in appearance. His dark hair, Van Dyke beard and closely cropped mustache set him apart in any gathering. He was not as approachable as Dean Schroeder or President Felmley, and there was something about him that suggested "stranger" rather than "home folk." Despite living in Wisconsin for thirteen years, his speech bore the unmis-

---

[3] *Teachers College Advance,* Oshkosh. Quoted, *Vidette,* June 2, 1930.
[4] *Vidette,* May 26, 1930; *Alumni Quarterly,* August 1930, p. 7.

takable accent of an Easterner. Frequent nostalgic references to Maine woods and New Hampshire hills betrayed an origin not of the Midwest.

Harry Brown was the son of Alonzo Allen and Caroline Knowlton Brown. He was born in Liberty, Maine, August 19, 1879. He taught rural schools in Maine while working for his bachelor's degree at Bates College in Lewiston. After receiving his degree in 1903, he served as supervising principal and district superintendent for schools in Maine and New Hampshire for four years. In 1907 he took a master's degree from the University of Colorado, and after two years as superintendent of schools in Glasgow, Montana, he returned to New Hampshire. At Christmas time in 1908 he had been married to Florence Maria Sever of Keene, New Hampshire. In the summer of 1912 he taught psychology and education at the State Normal School at Plymouth, New Hampshire and the following year he joined the staff of the New Hampshire Superintendent of Public Instruction as Director of the Bureau of Educational Research. In the summers he taught courses in psychology and education in the State Normal School at Keene, New Hampshire. In 1917 he became president at Oshkosh. Ten years later he published a study "Latin in the Secondary Schools."[5] He received the honorary degree of Ed. D. in 1925 from both Bates College and Miami University.

Dr. Brown visited Normal on June 24, and Dean Schroeder presented him to the summer school students in General Exercises. He pledged his loyalty to the school. "My main purpose," he said, "in existing as president is the upbuilding of the school. I shall strive to make this the outstanding teachers college in the United States. It has the background and the setting to be that." A week later he returned and settled himself to the task that lay ahead. Dean Schroeder, in charge of the summer school, was told to remain the president's office in Old Main and President Brown took temporary quarters on the second floor of the new science building. It was quiet there, and he had much work to do. Later, he decided that he preferred the location, and a suite of rooms was outfitted as a permanent office.

President Brown's immediate concern was the revision of the

[5] *Who's Who In Education* 1929–1930, p. 119.

curriculum and teacher load—conditions responsible for the dropping of the institution from the North Central Association's "A" rating. Many teachers at Normal University taught twenty classes a week rather than the prescribed maximum of sixteen. President Brown discussed with Dean Schroeder recommendations which the faculty had drawn up previously and held group meetings with staff members.

The catalog for 1931–1932 contained no material changes in courses and curricula except that the curricula were organized under thirteen divisional headings corresponding to the different types of teachers which the school prepared. Code letters for curricula were abandoned, and no longer were the courses for prospective high school teachers listed under K, commerce under J, and music under D. Each curriculum provided for the completion of four years of work, instead of two or three as previously indicated.[6]

In March 1931 the North Central Association restored the Normal University to "A" rating, but the American Association of Teachers Colleges placed the school in "A" classification with a deficiency under Standard IV, which related to the staff of the training School. Under Standard XIV no school having a deficiency would be given an "A" rating in 1932. The staff at Normal was considerably less than standard requirement for the number of student teachers to be supervised each year. To prevent the Normal University from being relegated to a "B" rating, President Brown secured approval to employ a dean or director for all the training schools, and three additional staff members who were to serve as part-time supervisors in the training schools and as part-time instructors in the college, thus "unifying instruction in method and practice in teaching."[7]

The coming of a director of training schools and three new supervisors necessitated the shifting about of some of the old faculty, a considerable amount of which was being done without consent or consultation with teachers who had established reputations in certain fields and courses. These changes made deep wounds which were slow to heal. Meanwhile some of the faculty

[6] *Catalog,* Illinois State Normal University, 1931–1932. *Proceedings of the Normal School Board* (Charleston) May 11, 1931, p. 53.
[7] *Ibid.,* p. 55.

learned from professional associates at Oshkosh, a number of whom were graduates of Normal University, that all had not gone well for Dr. Brown at Oshkosh.[8] It was reported that he had had "favorites" at Oshkosh and that eventually he would probably place them on his faculty at Normal. When the first Oshkosh teacher came to Normal at the beginning of the second term in December, one or two persons were apprehensive, but when the appointee displayed unusual ability, their fears were temporarily allayed. However, before long it became apparent that the positions of at least two of the older staff members were in jeopardy.[9]

Those faculty members unaware of the undercurrents were loyal and appreciative of the consideration President Brown had shown in providing office space and desks for study and conferences when classes were not in session. No longer were the wide window sills cluttered with the books and papers of faculty members who had no other place to put them. The rickety table back stage in Capen Auditorium, which had for years been the dramatics coach's professional hide-out, was consigned to the kindling pile.

President Brown neither courted nor excited popularity among the students. Most of them stood somewhat in awe of the bearded president in the oak paneled office in the Science Building. They were far more inclined to take their problems to Dean Schroeder, to Miss Barton, the Dean of Women, to "Doc" Linkins, Dean of Men, or to one of the coaches. However, they went along enthusiastically with some of the "reforms." A weekly assembly was greatly to be praised over a daily period of General Exercises. A freshly painted and refurbished lounge for girls in the basement of Old Main added to the comfort of the women students.

Most of the students were pleased over the new placement system. In February 1932 President Brown employed Miss Hester Hood, formerly with the American College Bureau, to organize a bureau of appointments on the campus.[10] The matter of recommending graduates for positions had come to be largely the pre-

[8] R. G. Buzzard to Helen E. Marshall, Charleston, February 22, 1956. *Marshall Papers.*
[9] Only fragments of President Brown's papers are extant. Details of his administration have been obtained from interviews and correspondence with members of his faculty, newspapers, Board reports and miscellaneous notes and papers in Milner Library.
[10] *Proceedings of the Normal School Board* (Charleston) April 4, 1932, p. 26.

rogative of Professor E. A. Turner, who directed student teaching and carried names of seniors and prospective teachers, their curriculums and qualifications carefully coded in a little black book. Occasionally senior classes had set up their own placement committee for locating vacancies, and the faculty wrote recommendations directly to school boards and superintendents. In a few months Miss Hood had set up a complete, orderly, and efficient system of records.[11]

The new president extended cordial good wishes to the success of the athletic teams but said he would be too busy to attend many of the games. Like President Felmley he regretted colleges tended to limit their recreational programs to the few men who participated in major sports. He thought all men in college should build strong bodies and participate in the recreational and health values of sports and exercise. He believed they should get a training that would enable them to be leaders of high school boys in wholesome recreation and healthful living, and through their influence be builders of right-minded citizens.[12] When the basketball team won the Little Nineteen championship, he assured the student body that he too rejoiced. The 1931 *Index* was prudently if not affectionately dedicated to the new president in appreciation of his interest, the things he had accomplished in one year and the great things planned.[13]

The *Vidette* predicted:

Even now one can safely say that when the Centennial history of Old Normal is written twenty-six years hence the year just drawing to a close will be considered a milestone. The year 1930–1931 has been one of reorganization, achievement, and of the infusion of new blood. . . . With the high quality of President Brown's leadership and the continued faith on the part of the students and faculty in the future of this school, Old Normal will be one of the institutions that will lead in making of teaching a real profession.[14]

At Homecoming in the fall of 1930 President Brown had greeted alumni and taken an active part in the dedication of

[11] Interview, Mrs. Lorene Meeker, Secretary in Office of Bureau of Appointments since 1932, January 12, 1956.
[12] An interview with President Harry A. Brown in the *Vidette*, Summer 1931. Quoted *Alumni Quarterly*, November 1931, p. 14.
[13] *Index* 1931, p. 23.
[14] *Vidette*, June 1931.

Felmley Hall of Science and the renaming of the gymnasium in honor of Professor Henry McCormick, who had given forty-three years of service to Normal University. The new president had his dreams of buildings too—a new library, a new classroom building, a manual arts building, but this was hardly the time to project a building program. As he looked toward Old Main, however, he could see the tower leaning dangerously to one side after the manner of Pisa. The roof was sagging and the walls and floors were beginning to show the effects of wind and weight and time. Something would have to be done about it before another year. Meanwhile he would confine his proposals to the internal development of the institution.[15]

A few months after the existing curricula had been regrouped in divisions and printed in the catalog for 1931-1932, President Brown sought the authorization of an entirely new curriculum. Illinois schools were coming rapidly to provide learning opportunities for every child. Several cities had separate classes or schools for crippled children and provided special instruction for children with defective vision or who were blind and for children with defective hearing or who were deaf. Other cities had made provision for so-called subnormal children. One city in Illinois had set up special classes for gifted children.

President Brown believed that provisions for groups of non-typical children had gone far enough to justify a teachers college in establishing some courses for teachers of such children. He wanted to see the Normal University introduce a curriculum designed to prepare teachers of atypical children of different kinds. It would be an expensive program and he did not think it possible to offer a complete program at once, but he thought that in the near future several courses might be offered as electives which would represent the beginnings of a definite curriculum and give teachers some preparation for this special work in Illinois schools. He further stressed the idea that progress made with atypical children in public schools would be affected by the availability of teachers. Eventually, he believed, special training should be given in a study of the problems of the gifted, the crippled, the mentally

[15] Harry A. Brown to Governor Louis Emmerson, *Fifteenth Annual Report*, Department of Registration and Education, p. 15.

deficient, the incorrigibles and truants, and those with specific defects in speech, hearing, and sight. The Board listened to his plea for an expansion of the curriculum of Normal University to provide for exceptional children and referred the matter to the Council of Presidents of the five teachers colleges for further consideration.[16] In April 1932, President Brown, recently honored by election to the presidency of the American Association of Teachers Colleges, again brought up the matter, and once more it was postponed.[17]

By this time the nation was in the throes of a depression. Illinois fared no better than the rest of the country. There were hundreds of persons in the bread lines in cities such as Chicago, Rockford, Rock Island, Moline, Peoria, and East St. Louis. In Cook County alone 135,000 families were being cared for by relief agencies, and over 18,000 unemployed and unattached persons were being cared for in shelters.[18] President Brown's plans for special education and new buildings had to be abandoned. When it was discovered that the floor in the corridor of the second story of the Old Main had dropped about three inches overnight, a call to Springfield released funds appropriated by the Fifty-seventh General Assembly, for the repair of the tower. During Easter vacation 1932, steel supports were placed from foundation to clock tower, bisecting the large study hall on the second floor. The leaning tower was straightened and the upper part of the structure preserved for a few more years.[19]

Despite hard times enrollment in teachers colleges increased. Many young people gravitated toward teachers colleges because of the low tuition and the declining opportunities in industry. A large percentage of the students hoped to work their way through school. Some did well to raise enough money for tuition. Many worked for board and room. Some brought food from home and lived in the cheapest of furnished rooms, cooking their meals on gas burners in basements or on single electric plates in their rooms. Their clothing was often shabby and worn. Patched blue

[16] *Proceedings of the Normal School Board* (De Kalb) November 9, 1931, pp. 52–53, 55.
[17] *Ibid.*, (Charleston) April 4, 1932, p. 46.
[18] *First Annual Report of the Illinois Emergency Relief Commission* (July 27, 1932–February 5, 1933) Chicago: 1933, pp. 59, 75.
[19] *Index* 1932, p. 236.

jeans were not uncommon, and sox were saved for special oc-
casions. Haircuts were luxuries and often a boy had to borrow
money for a suit to wear on an interview for a position. The Faculty Women's Club gave benefits to provide scholarships and
loans to needy students.[20] There were more requests for loans than
could be granted.

Nor were faculty members immune from fear. Their salaries
were low. The General Assembly, facing the growing depression,
had granted only an eighteen percent increase in appropriations,
and the faculty had asked for sixty percent.[21] New appointments
had been managed out of economies such as savings on salaries
of teachers on leave for advanced study whose vacancies were
filled at lower figures, and an occasional resort to the revolving
fund. Instructors received as little as $1,700, assistant librarians,
$1,200. The highest paid professor received $4,230, while the average received $3,500. No associate professor received over $3,400.
Many teachers shared their meager salaries with less fortunate
relatives. Demands for retrenchment were incessant. There were
rumors that the faculty might have to be employed on a month-
to-month basis, and salaries be subjected to cuts as the finances of
the state dictated. Many school districts throughout the state were
unable to pay their teachers except in script, which was heavily
discounted by local banks. Would a similar situation confront the
faculty in teachers colleges? President Brown and the teachers
college presidents stood adamant on the matter of salaries. They
would reduce other expenditures but they would oppose any re-
duction of teachers' salaries until it was necessary to cut the wages
of all state employees. President Brown in the interest of economy
dropped the Home Study Department, which had enrolled 333
persons in 1930. Supplies were doled out with a meager hand. In
March 1933 the cut came. All salaries over $100 per month were
reduced ten percent. Most of the faculty accepted the cut stoically:
at least they had employment and, being state employees, their
credit was good.

On other scores there was murmuring among the faculty. As
the months went on and President Brown advanced more and

[20] The Faculty Women's Club was organized in 1916.
[21] *Alumni Quarterly*, August 1931, p. 16.

more changes in the school, questions arose as to the wisdom, method, and purpose of his procedures. Dr. Brown had worked rapidly and intensely, vamping and revamping the curriculum. Not since the days of Arnold Tompkins had the course of study been subjected to such fury. Brown wanted to see his ideas crystallized, but he did not take the faculty as a group into his confidence. They missed the give-and-take of President Felmley's wide open faculty meetings, where every staff member was free to speak until interrupted and "outspoken" by another. Dr. Brown did not have President Felmley's gift of being able to direct faculty debate; in fact he found it distasteful. He ignored the "elder statesmen" of the faculty, preferring to counsel with his own appointees. There were rumors of discriminations in salary. President Brown was accused of being aloof and unsocial, of withdrawing to his paneled office and trying to avoid commitments and conferences that savored of anything that might be unpleasant and embarrassing. He preferred to write notes or send bulletins to staff members. Privately there came to be considerable headshaking, name-calling, and suspicion. To some persons the president was arbitrary and dictatorial; to others he was "cowardly" and "spineless." When the controversial head of the training school, one of President Brown's own appointees, was abruptly dismissed for reasons not generally regarded as justifiable, even those who disliked him were moved to sympathy.

Discontent grew with the passing months. A few were beginning to fear that peace and security and progress would never come as long as Harry A. Brown remained president. In some small groups the president's failings and faults were grimly recounted. Instances were cited where he seemed to have no business sense, where he exercised poor judgment, had been inconsistent and unfair, extravagant in personal expenditures and in the outfitting of his office, and where he failed to keep appointments.[22] Could nothing be done to restore peace and equanimity?

About a year after President Brown came it was learned quite by accident that he intended to replace one of the older men in a very responsible position by a younger new appointee with a

[22] "Reasons Why the President's Office Should Terminate, July 1, 1933." (Manuscript) Milner Library.

Ph. D. If displaced in these days of economic stringency, the older man would find it difficult to secure a position. A small group of young professors who were aware of the charges of favoritism, highhandedness, and duplicity leveled at Dr. Brown at Oshkosh were indignant but bided their time. Wisconsin friends had said that if a critical situation ever developed at Normal they were willing to present factual evidence which might be of service. In the spring of 1933 the older professor was advised that he was being replaced, and another professor who had been promised in writing that he would be permitted to teach certain courses in which he enjoyed a wide and favorable reputation was told that his courses were being dropped. Both had rendered years of valued service to the school. It was too late for either of these men to begin work for doctorates, and the chances were that neither could secure a position as good as that held at Normal. Their younger colleagues now went into action. Securing the confidence and advice of a member of the Board, they proceeded to send for the Wisconsin evidence. They were well aware that if it were not what its sponsors claimed, President Brown might charge them with insubordination, in which case, they would resign. Believing they could find positions more easily than the older men, the younger men assumed the burden of proof. The evidence which came confidentially from Wisconsin was startling.

During an executive meeting at the Normal School Board in the Administrative Building of the World's Fair in Chicago on June 3, 1933, several members reported that criticism had come to them relative to administrative action at Normal. A committee was appointed to visit the institution, investigate, and report at the meeting in Springfield on June 26. The seven men who constituted the self-appointed faculty committee kept careful watch for visitors to the campus, and when Saturday, June 24, came and it seemed no one from the Board had appeared, a spokesman telephoned C. M. Bardwell, chairman of the Board's investigating committee, and asked if they might come to Aurora that afternoon and talk with him. Bardwell received them graciously and explained that he had been to Normal early in the week, had lunch with President Brown at his home, and been assured that everything was going well at the school. A few faculty members were disconcerted over changes in professional supervision, but it was nothing to be alarmed about. Bardwell said he had already sent a report to Secretary Blair exonerating President Brown.

A theoretical question was then put to Bardwell. As a superintendent of schools, what would he do if he found he had employed a teacher whose credentials were spurious? Without hesitation Bardwell answered that he would dismiss anyone who was dishonest in stating credentials. He was asked to read three letters and a telegram. They related to a transcript of sixty-four hours of college credit which President Brown had sent from the Teachers College, Oshkosh, to Columbia Teachers College for a teacher now on the staff at Normal. The letters stated there was no record of the person ever having enrolled at Oshkosh in any class at any time. The telegram from New York confirmed the signature on the transcript as that of President Brown rather than that of the registrar.

Bardwell was then informed that if the Teachers College Board had not discharged President Brown by Monday afternoon or he had not resigned, the group would give the whole story to the Associated Press and ask the teaching profession of Illinois to protest to the Board. The threat of publicity carried with it political implications. Bardwell asked the men to appear before the Board on Monday. When they replied they could not be absent from duty without President Brown's permission, he wrote an order for each of the seven men to meet him and members of the Board in Springfield on Monday, June 26, an hour before the Board was scheduled to meet in Superintendent Blair's office.

When summoned before the Board, they presented the single charge against President Brown: he had recommended for employment by the Normal School Board in December 1930, and repeated this recommendation each succeeding year, a person whose credentials he knew were spurious in that they were secured through unethical or forged credit. As evidence the three letters from Oshkosh and the telegram from Columbia were submitted. The faculty spokesman told the Board that unless Brown were dismissed, the whole story would be given to the Associated Press.

Harry A. Brown, president, 1930–1933, undertook an academic revolution during an economic depression.

Raymond W. Fairchild, president, 1933–1954.

Arthur H. Larsen, acting president, 1954–1956.

Robert G. Bone, ninth president, 1956.

Draft horses at the farm were the special pride of the "Ag" boys.

"Anchors Aweigh!" Sixth graduation class U. S. Naval V-12 Unit. June, 1945.

Teachers from foreign lands arrive to study teacher training at Normal, 1956.

Dr. Arthur Watterson, professor of geography, takes his European field trip by air, 1954.

The Edna Gueffroy doll collection in Milner Library has a never failing interest for young visitors.

Homecoming parade moves east on Beaufort Street.

Story time with a student teacher.

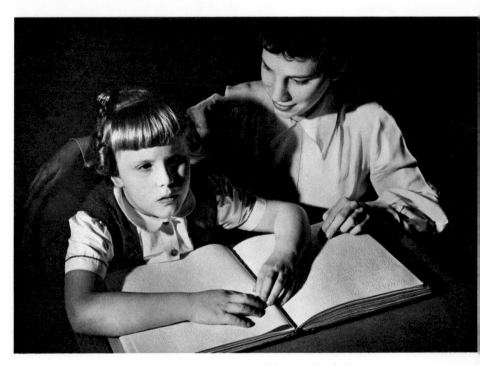

Special education: learning to read by the Touch System.

Catalog room, Milner Library.

Creative art is a serious matter.

Home Economics Department, 1956: foods in the modern manner.

A class in modern office practice.

The play's the thing—"Ethan Frome," 1955.

The Gamma Phi Circus, since 1928 a spring highlight in entertainment.

Aerial view, 1955.
Illinois State Normal University

1. Milner Library
2. Student Union Building
3. Administration Building
4. Thomas Metcalf Building
5. Old Main
6. David Felmley Hall of Science
7. North Hall
8. Site of Schroeder Hall
   (New Classroom Building)
9. Heating Plant
10. Industrial Arts Annex
11. Industrial Arts Building
12. John W. Cook Hall
13. Greenhouse
14. Music Building
15. Rambo Home Management House
16. Fell Hall (Women's Residence)
17. Federal Buildings
18. McCormick Gymnasium
19. Intramural Building
20. Carpenter Shop
21. Dunn Hall (Men's Residence)
22. Barton Hall (Women's Residence)
23. Walker Hall (Women's Residence)
24. Fairchild Hall of Special Education
25. Health Service
26. Site of New Elementary School

A few minutes after the interview terminated, President Brown was called in, confronted with the charges and the evidence, and advised to prepare his resignation in writing. There was no alternative.

After routine business the Board again went into executive session. President Brown was called in and told that his resignation had been accepted, that he would be given a leave of absence with pay for July and August and that Dean H. H. Schroeder would assume the duties of acting president on July 1, 1933. Subsequently, Dean Schroeder was called in and informed he had been made acting president, and invested with authority to dismiss such of the new appointees as he thought the interests of the school demanded.[23]

It was an unhappy incident, one that neither the school nor the Board wished to publicize or ever see happen again. The press was merely informed that Harry A. Brown, president of Illinois State Normal University since 1930, had resigned. Not until August 15 did the *Daily Pantagraph* mention the nature of the difficulties north of Sugar Creek.[24] Harry Alvin Brown returned from Springfield, cleared out his files and packed his goods, and he and his wife left Normal, never to return.[25]

[23] *Proceedings of the Normal School Board* (Springfield) June 25, 1933, p. 25.
[24] *Daily Pantagraph*, August 15, 1933; September 23, 1933.
[25] After leaving Normal, Harry A. Brown took graduate work in Teachers College, Columbia University and was awarded the degree of Doctor of Education. He served as a successful superintendent of schools in a suburb of Boston for several years before his death on July 8, 1949.

CHAPTER XIII

R.W.F. : Architect and Builder

THE SUMMER and early fall of 1933 were filled with anxiety and suspense for the University and townspeople. Never before in the long life of the school was it so generally felt that the future and prestige of the institution rested upon the choice made by the eleven members of the Board. Meanwhile Dean Schroeder, who had effectively held the school together during President Felmley's illness and death, undertook to reassure the student body and faculty alike and to put matters in order for the fall term and the new president. He took great care in selecting persons to fill vacancies. He scrutinized credentials and made sure that applicants were not only qualified by training and experience but were professionally minded and devoted to the cause of teacher education. Herman Schroeder put his whole soul into the task that had fallen to his lot for the second time. He was the first to arrive at Old Main in the morning and the last to leave at night. It might be that he would be asked to continue as president. Both the *Pantagraph* and the *Normalite* had editorially placed their stamp of approval upon him as a candidate.[1]

On Monday, October 9, the Board announced its decision. Raymond Wilber Fairchild, Professor, School of Education, Northwestern University, was named president. Two days later the newly elected president visited Normal. When he arrived at the office of William Bach, resident Board member, he found a *Pantagraph* reporter waiting to take a photograph and secure a statement for the press. Bach hurriedly brought the new president to the campus, where the faculty had been assembled in Capen Auditorium. Mr. Bach paid high tribute to Dean Schroeder and then presented Dr. Fairchild. The new president had not planned to make an address, but he quickly sensed the spirit of the occasion, expressed appreciation for Dean Schroeder's work, and

[1] *Daily Pantagraph*, September 20, 23, 1933. *Normalite*, September 8, 15, 22, 1933.

292

set the tone that was to dominate his administration for the next twenty years.

I came with no preconceived ideas of teacher training as applies to this or any other institution. An administration of this school is a purely co-operative enterprise. I shall maintain an open attitude and my office door shall always be open. This policy I intend to maintain. Not revolution but evolution will be the policy of progress at the University. . . . I hope to take up my duties here without factional feelings, to make a new start, without reference to past difficulties.[2]

In Old Main, the University farm manager, a paper in hand, sat anxiously awaiting Dr. Fairchild's appearance. Would the president authorize the exchanging of seventeen pigs for five calves? Unless a direct trade could be made, it would be necessary to advertise a sale and have the livestock checked by the Department of Agriculture. In that length of time the pigs would probably be hogs and the calves would have reached the butcher's block. President Fairchild smiled and reached for a pen. Within an hour he had met the faculty, made a speech, and performed his first official act.[3]

Raymond W. Fairchild was forty-four years of age, the father of two sons, Ralph Bronson and Robert Eugene, and was in his prime at the time he came to the presidency of Illinois State Normal University. He had the clean vigorous look of an athlete, and there was warmth and strength in his firm handclasp. He was smooth shaven, his light brown hair was carefully groomed, and his blue eyes were friendly and kind and fun-loving. He stood six feet four, broad-shouldered and straight. A small boy at the Soldiers and Sailors Childrens School seeing him for the first time asked, "Are you really a giant?"

President Fairchild was a midwesterner of native stock. He was born in Bismarck, Illinois, September 9, 1889, the son of Wilber Daniel and Serena Mattie Johnson Fairchild. His father was a Methodist minister, a brilliant and scholarly man and erstwhile professor at Illinois Wesleyan. The two Fairchild sons, Raymond and Donald Hurlstone, attended public schools in the towns where their father held pastorates. After high school Ray-

---

[2] *Vidette,* October 13, 1933.
[3] Interview, R. W. Fairchild, Normal, January 2, 1956.

mond attended the University of Illinois and Illinois Wesleyan, where he held an assistantship, majored in biology, and earned a letter in track. He decided not to take his degree at Illinois because he wished to study with a famous bacteriologist at the University of Michigan.

He taught biology and social studies, coached football, and acted as assistant principal of the high school in Vandalia, 1909–1910. From 1910 to 1914, he held a similar position at the Moline High School. On June 25, 1913, he was married to Nellie Bronson. He studied summers at the University of Michigan, and in 1914 was awarded a Bachelor of Arts degree in bacteriology. He was dean of men at Wisconsin Teachers College, Stevens Point, from 1914 to 1920. He continued his summer study at the University of Michigan and was granted a Master of Arts in 1919. He was superintendent of schools, Fond du Lac, Wisconsin, 1920–1923, and superintendent of schools at Elgin, Illinois from 1923 to 1930. He then began graduate study in education and administration at Northwestern University. While completing the work for his doctor's degree in 1930–1932, he taught classes in the School of Education at Northwestern.

Walter Dill Scott, president of Northwestern, believed there should be special training for teachers college administrators, and that this was a field in which his university might well pioneer. He selected Professor Fairchild with his background of liberal arts, public school, and teachers college experience, as the man most able to assist in the development of such a program. He wanted first of all a survey of administrative practices and procedures in the teachers colleges of the United States. Dr. Fairchild was teaching mostly graduate classes, so it was possible for him to be away from the campus for as long as two weeks at a time. He traveled over 25,000 miles and visited seventy teachers colleges in forty-three states. He was "saturated" with teachers college work. These visitations served as a basis for his doctoral dissertation, "The Improvement of Teacher Education." As a consequence President Fairchild came to Normal prepared for teachers college administration as were few men at that time.

Carter Harris, the beloved "custodian" of Old Castle as the University High School gymnasium was then known, watched the new president as he went from building to building, acquainting himself with the plant, talking with employees, and pausing to watch the boys at football practice. Harris was glad the president's office was being set up in Old Main again. After hearing Dr. Fairchild speak, he confided to his friend Manfred Holmes that he was afraid the new president would not stay, that the school would not be big enough.[4]

As a school superintendent he had seen shortcomings in the preparation of teachers. He was now in a position to work out ideas. He had his own theories but he also wanted to know what others were thinking. After all he had promised progress, service, evolution, not revolution. There was a feeling abroad that teachers colleges had walls around them and operated without regard to the public schools whose teachers they supplied. President Fairchild invited the principals and superintendents of twenty-seven counties served by the Normal University to come to the campus on the first Saturday of December and talk things over. After a keynote speech the crowd would break up into small groups, and discuss phases of the topic, "What's wrong with teachers colleges and Illinois State Normal University?" At noon they would be guests at a luncheon in Fell Hall. From a popular song of the day, the meeting was styled "The First Round-up of Superintendents and Principals." President Fairchild hoped that the "First Round-up" would not be the last.

Never before had the public school administrators of Illinois been invited to participate in such a conference. Some came out of curiosity, a few to voice grievances, and others to meet friends. The faculty were asked to attend, to listen, and to learn. The University promised to do something about the complaints and report progress at a similar meeting a year hence if the administrators approved. The schoolmen liked the idea, and the University gained from the frank exchange of opinion, and the Roundup became an annual affair.[5]

There was also the matter of acquainting the faculty with what was going on in the public schools. The new president urged his teachers to take visiting days to observe teaching as it was done

[4] Manfred J. Holmes, "Carter Harris," *Holmes Papers*.
[5] As this Centennial History leaves the press, preparations are under way for the twenty-four annual Round-up.

in rural, elementary, and secondary schools. A county contact system, later to become effective in recruiting students, was set up to acquaint the schools with the offerings of the Normal University and to bring back to the campus written reports of the teaching in the schools. President Fairchild used every opportunity to bring teacher education and Illinois State Normal University to the attention of the public. From October 11, 1933, to May 8, 1934, he made seventy-eight speeches.[6]

For some time there had been no regular faculty meetings. The new president promptly set up the second Tuesday of each month for faculty meetings. The first year's meetings were devoted to faculty relations—with each other, to students, to the community, to the school territory served, and to the training profession. President Fairchild accepted the divisional and departmental organization set up by President Brown without making any immediate changes. However, in April 1935, he organized a University Senate, composed of the directors of divisions, departmental heads, deans, the registrar, and other administrative officers, for the purpose of initiating and furthering administrative policies and obtaining a wide range of ideas and reactions. This new body promptly began discussion of a new grading system, selective admission, the school calendar, class attendance and absences.[7] Three years later an Administrative Council composed of the deans and other administrative officers for purpose of assisting in matters of discipline and other important decisions was effected.[8]

When President Fairchild came to Normal University in 1933, twenty-six percent of the faculty had less than master's degrees, and only thirteen persons had doctorates. He began immediately to work for improvement of faculty qualifications. He advised against employing persons who did not have at least a master's degree and those having five years of teaching experience were preferred. Within two years, the number of doctorates increased to thirty and there were only one or two staff members who had not yet completed work for the master's degree.[9] Within the first five years of his administration 87 percent of the faculty had

[6] *Proceedings of the Normal School Board* (Springfield) May 15, 1934, p. 51.
[7] *Index* 1936, p. 24.
[8] *Ibid.*, 1942, p. 18.
[9] *Proceedings of the Board of Education* (Carbondale) October 7, 1935, p. 140.

taken graduate work through leaves of absence, summer courses, or extension work. By 1938 thirty-four percent of the staff held doctorates and the remainder master's degrees. In the five-year period fourteen books and ninety-six articles were published by members of the faculty.[10] At the same time that President Fairchild encouraged his faculty to undertake advanced studies, he made efforts to get the ten percent salary cuts restored and a salary schedule set up.

He saw the same need for buildings that his predecessors had seen. A poll of the faculty confirmed his own belief that the library was the school's most critical need. Next to that was perhaps a center where students could gather between classes. But with fifteen percent of the state's population on relief in 1933, it was difficult to see how any of the state's revenues could be diverted into buildings.[11] Although the library would have to wait, it was possible to do something about a student social center. Fell Hall still served admirably for formal all-school receptions and other functions, but a place was needed for club meetings and where students could go between classes for a social hour with friends. Through the Civil Works Administration funds for labor and the University's resources for materials, a lounge was set up in the southeast corner of the basement of Old Main in what had been originally the living quarters of the janitor and more recently a scene shop for classes in dramatic production and a convenient catchall for broken and discarded furniture and janitor's supplies. The Student Council, with the aid of numerous clubs and a generous faculty, raised $1,200 to furnish it. The lounge opened officially April 6, 1934.[12] A student union building would not be lost sight of, although for the time being, three large rooms and a kitchenette would have to suffice for dancing, cards, club functions, and teas.

In the days of economic depression students had little money to spend on necessities, to say nothing of the pleasures of college life. Since 1915 an activity fee had been charged each student to cover cost of the *Vidette,* lecture course, oratorical and musical events, and literary and athletic contests. The fee had gradually

[10] R. W. Fairchild, "Five Years in Retrospect," 1938. MS *Fairchild Papers.*
[11] *Statistical Abstract,* State of Illinois 1937–1938, p. 327.
[12] *Proceedings of the Board of Education* (Springfield) May 15, 1934, p. 50.

increased from $1.25 to $3.00 a quarter.[13] The fund thus obtained was apportioned among various organizations and activities by a board of faculty, students, and administration. During the school year 1933–1934, for the first time free movies—and according to the *Index* "good ones at that"—were provided for the students.[14] In 1935 the fee was increased to cover cost of the *Index,* class dues, organizations which provided entertainment and services for the entire student body, health service, and hospitalization. Fell Hall had long served as a residence and social center for women, but there was no comparable dormitory or center for men. In 1934 the University Club, under the sponsorship of Ralph H. Linkins, Dean of Men, leased the large home of Colonel Dudley C. Smith on University Street opposite the South Campus and provided residence for thirty-two men.[15]

On May 21, 1934, the University held open house for the community. Townspeople and alumni were invited to visit the campus, inspect the buildings, witness demonstrations and exhibits in the various areas and departments. Despite threatening skies 3,000 came. They wandered through the buildings, saw musical organizations and a play in rehearsal, observed spectacular experiments in science. Student guides and "barkers" outside the various exhibits gave a touch of carnival atmosphere to the miniature century of progess.[16] The visitors found a friendly welcome, intriguing displays and went away pleased. President Fairchild in addressing the Normal Chamber of Commerce in March had been presented as the man who had taken down the iron fence around the University and brought school and community together. The open house was further proof.

Commencement 1934 was highlighted by a full dress academic procession. This year for the first time the graduating exercises were held out-of-doors in a grove of trees which had come to be known as Sherwood Forest. The two-year graduates in their blue robes, led by marshals in bright red robes with white velvet sleeve

[13] *Ibid.,* (Normal) November 16, 1914, p. 28; David Felmley to Livingston C. Lord, Normal June 16, 1919. *Felmley Papers.*
[14] *Index* 1934, p. 4.
[15] Smith Hall was purchased in 1941 at a cost of $25,000. *Proceedings of the Teachers College Board* (formerly Board of Education, Normal School Board) December 15, 1941, p. 211.
[16] *Vidette,* May 18, 1915; May 23, 1915.

bars and white tassels on their mortarboards and carrying white batons headed the procession. They were followed by the four-year graduates in black baccalaureate gowns, and the faculty and administration in black relieved by velvet sleeve bars and facings and the bright satin chevrons on their academic hoods, with here and there the sparkle of a fresh gold tassel. As the double line moved slowly from Old Main across the campus to the strains of "Pomp and Circumstance," parents waited in the improvised bleachers, but undergraduates and alumni loitered along the line of march, cameras in hand, snapping pictures of favorite professors or graduating friends in their academic regalia.[17]

The summer session of 1934 witnessed two more innovations that were to become annual events, an Educational Conference at which leading educators of the nation were invited to speak and an Educational Exhibit to which representatives of school supply houses were invited to set up displays of their respective wares. Principals, superintendents, teachers, members of school boards throughout the area, faculty and students assembled in Capen Auditorium for morning and afternoon sessions on the pertinent topic of "Readjustment in Education." They listened to addresses in the morning and panel discussions in the afternoon, and then they asked questions. Before, after, and between the sessions they visited the exhibits set up in McCormick Gymnasium.[18] Publishers sent copies of their standard and latest texts, maps, workbooks, and other classroom aids. Seating companies displayed the newest in tables, chairs, and desks. Other firms exhibited modern equipment for shopwork, for physics and chemistry and business machines, typewriters and comptometers. There were demonstrations in the teaching of handwriting, in arts and crafts, and in the use of audio-visual aids. The first year forty firms exhibited, and two thousand persons registered as visitors. Four years later 120 firms were listed and there were more than four thousand visitors.[19]

The vigorous young president was reaching out and bringing people to the campus. In the summer handwriting clinics, reading clinics, and parent-teacher workshops brought hundreds of other

[17] *Ibid.*, June 5, 1934.
[18] *Ibid.*, June 21, 1934.
[19] Fairchild, "Five Years in Retrospect" MS.

persons to the University for one or two weeks to avail themselves of instruction under specialists. President Fairchild wanted
the school to be recognized as a service institution. In 1935 extension classes were resumed in five centers with ten classes and
an enrollment of 196. Two years later thirty-six classes were being
taught in twenty-one centers with 1089 persons enrolled.[20] A
publicity office was established to serve as a clearing house for
university news, to issue certain university publications, and to
carry on public relations projects.

The financial situation of the Normal University in 1932 rendered it impractical to attempt any extensive observation of the
seventy-fifth anniversary of the founding of the school. Professor
Charles A. Harper had written a volume tracing the history of
the Normal University in relation to the development of the
teachers college in the United States, but there were no funds to
publish it. Economic conditions were somewhat improved by
1935, and the faculty voted to commemorate the Diamond Jubilee
of the first graduating class. Professor Harper's book was published and twice during commencement week a pageant, *The
Lighter of Flames,* was presented in front of Old Main.

The pageant based on Professor Harper's book was the most
ambitious and elaborate dramatic presentation attempted on the
campus since the ill-fated Shakespearean production nearly
twenty years before. This time the cast had only five hundred
persons, but the weather was favorable and more than four
thousand witnessed the two performances. *The Lighter of Flames,*
like its predecessor, was a cooperative enterprise. Miss Mabel Clare
Allen, director of dramatics, was general chairman and staged
the production, while numerous committees of faculty, faculty
wives and students worked on script, costumes, properties, music,
publicity, finance, and seating. In music, color, action, and song,
the story of seventy-five years unfolded, showing the position of
dignity which the school had had from the beginning and the
efforts of its administrators to justify the faith of its founders in
its role of educational leadership. By 1870 it had been the largest
and most respected normal school in America. Its graduates not

[20] "Summary of Extension Program September 1913 to June 1, 1955" Division of
Field Services, Illinois State Normal University. MS.

only had taught in Illinois schools but some had gone out to establish other normals. As Bridgewater was the inspiration of eastern normals, so Illinois State Normal University was the model for western normals.[21] After the final scene depicting the years of expansion under President Felmley, came the epilogue:

Three quarters of a century have now been recorded. Illinois State Normal University enters upon a new phase of her existence. A new leader is upon her campus. A new hand takes up the pen to write a future record significant as the past. . . .[22]

Already there was evidence of the new leadership. Student assemblies were revived on a weekly rather than a daily basis. A board of students and faculty planned programs designed both to entertain and to widen the horizon of the members of the university community, and to build school spirit, loyalty, and professionalism. The president used time in assembly as well as monthly faculty meetings to acquaint his audience with needs and progress of the school, always stressing the importance of cooperative effort. Faculty committees undertook surveys on subjects ranging from the curriculum to buildings, and studies on professional growth and welfare. Broadcasts from the Tower Studios in Cook Hall, through the facilities of Bloomington's new radio station, WJBC, brought special programs and news of the campus to alumni and friends of the University.

By the summer of 1935 a number of significant developments had taken place in the curriculum. Psychology was separated from education and organized as a special department. The offerings of other departments were expanded, notably in music education, art education, physical education, visual education, and journalism. An increase in number of affiliated schools offered greater opportunities for observation and student teaching. The catalog for 1935–1936 announced that beginning in September the Normal University would operate on a semester basis and that in

---

[21] Lyman B. Kellogg, Class of 1864, was made president of Kansas State Normal, Emporia, Kansas, in 1864. In 1875 Henry Norton, Class of 1861, who had gone to Emporia with Kellogg pioneered in California as vice-principal of the Normal School at San Jose. President Edwards often visited the school at Emporia and sent his best graduates to Kellogg.

[22] Program, "The Lighter of Flames" a pageant commemorating the Seventy-fifth Anniversary of the first graduating class of Illinois State Normal University, 1860–1935. June 7, 8, 1935, p. 10.

place of the traditional percentage system of grades, there would be one of letters and honor points. By 1936 Dr. Fairchild was talking in terms of work beyond the bachelor's degree and was selecting faculty who were qualified by training and experience to teach courses on a graduate level.[23]

The new president quickly made use of federal funds under the CWA, the WPA, and the NYA to improve the general appearance of the campus, in the construction of walks, drives, tennis courts and playing fields, and explored the possibilities of PWA grants for the construction of buildings. From the million-dollar state appropriation Governor Horner released $18,500 which permitted some badly needed painting and rewiring of Old Main and other buildings. Federal funds for labor helped stretch the slender resources of the school, and by excavating here and partitioning there in various buildings, twenty-four additional classrooms and offices for thirty-two more teachers were made available. A lounge for faculty women was provided in the basement of Old Main, and a room 30 feet by 80 feet excavated beneath the Old Castle was made into a music rehearsal hall.[24]

The General Assembly sent a Committee to visit Educational Institutions in the spring of 1935. The chairman, Senator T. V. Smith, made a scintillating report, and although it produced no marked increase in appropriations it was nevertheless a vote of confidence. The state, he concluded

... *can not afford not to support substantial education for all its children.* To provide instruments for this substantial education is the prime duty of the normal colleges. This provided, other departments of the state that have achieved the same efficiency of economy may then be allowed the luxury of paying patronage with remaining surplus funds of the state. Put first things first by reversing *the places now occupied by patronage and principle, and we shall soon enough see how much easier it is to afford education, from normal college to one-room school, than it is to afford public officials who mince every educational appropriation like a miser but play the patron to many a lesser need. Only pudgy politicians will treat like a stepmother, this fine mother of all our stoutest virtues, the educational system of Illinois.*[25]

[23] *Proceedings of the Teachers College Board* (Formerly Normal School Board) (Springfield) May 25, 1936, p. 43.
[24] Fairchild, "Five Years in Retrospect," 1938 MS.
[25] T. V. Smith and W. E. C. Clifford, *Senate Committee Report on the Normal Colleges, State of Illinois,* 1935 (DeKalb: Northern State Teachers College Press, 1936) p. 12.

Salary cuts were restored for the other teachers colleges in 1935,[26] but it was 1937 before the restoration came to Normal University. Until faculty salaries were improved, President Fairchild would not press the case for badly needed buildings. He asked only for some costly repairs that were urged by the office of Architecture and Engineering. New roofs on Old Castle, Old Main, McCormick Gymnasium, and parts of the library and the strengthening of the smoke-stack at the heating plant were imperative. The greenhouse, for which state and federal funds had been made available, was completed in the summer of 1937. In view of steadily increasing enrollment, President Fairchild asked the Board to approve a program of selective admission and a limitation of 1850 on the student body until classroom and other housing facilities could be expanded. This request was approved, October 7, 1935, and was operative for four years.[27]

In 1937 the Budget Committee of the Normal School Board recommended the construction of three buildings at Normal University—a library, an auditorium-music-speech-administration building, and a home management house. However the General Assembly did not appropriate sufficient funds to satisfy all the building needs at the various teachers colleges and under a rotation system funds were released to Normal University in October for the construction of a home management house costing $34,800, of which $20,000 was provided by the state and the remainder from federal funds.[28] The following March work began on the $556,000 library. The home management house, known as Jessie E. Rambo Home, was occupied in September 1939, and the library with a capacity of half a million books named in honor of Ange. V. Milner, although not entirely completed, was dedicated during Commencement Week, June 1940.[29] An art gallery and four museum rooms afforded space for temporary exhibits and permanent collections relating to the history of the University, natural science, agriculture, and a remarkable doll collection given to the school by Dr. Edna Gueffroy, of the geography department. Carter Harris, aging janitor of Cook Hall, as Old Castle was now

[26] *Proceedings of the Normal School Board* (Chicago) February 18, 1935, p. 20.
[27] *Ibid.*, (Springfield) February 19, 1940, p. 24. Limits were removed, June 19, 1939.
[28] *Ibid.*, (Springfield) November 14, 1938, p. 157.
[29] Dedication brochure "Milner Library" June 10, 1940. (n.p.)

called, trudged over to inspect the beautiful red brick Georgian building with its sandstone columns. As he stood inside the grey marble foyer looking at the handsome balustrade and double winding stairs, he remembered what he had said to Manfred Holmes five years before. "I was wrong," he mused, "Instead of leaving because the school is too small, President Fairchild is staying on and building it to his own size." [30]

In an article, "Approaching the Century Mark," in the *Alumni Quarterly,* May 1940, President Fairchild shared his plans with the alumni. As for buildings they included the speech-art-music-auditorium and administration building, a high school building, improvements at the University farm, a swimming pool, the completion of the south wing to Fell Hall, and a student union which he hoped could be begun that very fall.[31]

The General Assembly in 1941 acted favorably upon the proposals to complete the gymnasium and the entrance to Fell Hall, but while the Division of Architecture and Engineering was drawing plans, ominous events were taking place. As the war in Europe progressed the United States embarked upon an all-out defense program. By the summer of 1941 the government demands for structural steel forced the suspension of plans for non-essential buildings. Facilities of Normal University were placed at the disposal of the federal government, and certain departmental courses were geared to the national emergency.

With community cooperation and federal funds allocated through the State Board of Vocational Education, the University facilities were used intensively in national defense. The Industrial Arts Department in six-hour shifts gave round-the-clock instruction in machine tool work, sheet metal, welding, polishing, and blueprint reading. Over seven hundred persons received training in this program under the director, Professor Ray Stombaugh.[32] When the National Youth Agricultural-Industrial Project was discontinued in December by federal order, a new emphasis was placed on preparing workers for the heavier defense industries.

---

[30] Holmes, "Carter Harris." *Holmes Papers*

[31] R. W. Fairchild, "Approaching the Century Mark," *Alumni Quarterly,* May 1940, p. 3.

[32] Gertrude M. Hall, "Defense Classes at State Normal," *Alumni Quarterly,* February 1942, p. 16; *Proceedings of the Teachers College Board* (Carbondale) May 19, 1941, p. 72.

However, a short intensive course for training farm workers was given in the spring of 1943, and from it 175 men were placed on Illinois farms. A civilian pilot training program was begun as a non-credit course in the summer of 1940, with a junked airplane stored at the University farm serving as a laboratory piece. Professors Clarence Cross, Harry Lathrop, and Howard Adams gave nine weeks' instruction in the principles of navigation, meteorology, and mechanics; Art Carnahan of the Bloomington Airport and two other pilot teachers gave flight training. In the first two years the program was in operation over 110 students received their wings.[33] In the spring of 1943 Normal University was designated as a center for training of high school instructors in pre-flight aeronautics.

In July 1942 the Civilian Pilot Training program was changed to a War Training Service program, and twenty army flyers were assigned to Normal University for an intensive eight-weeks course. The army program continued until January 1943, when navy flyers replaced the army under the Navy V-5 program.[34]

Meanwhile the regular enrollment took a sharp decline. The number of students in the college for the first semester 1940–1941 was 1820, for the same period, 1941–1942 it was 1621, and in the fall following the attack on Pearl Harbor it had dropped to 1067. Only 779 civilian students were enrolled in the college during the first semester 1943–1944, and fifty fewer students during the second semester.[35] During the second semester 1943–1944 the number of civilian men in the college dropped to fifty-six. Emergency teaching positions, war work, armed services, early marriages and lucrative jobs in industry took toll of college women as well as men. Nor was the faculty unaffected. Numerous leaves were granted to teachers who served in the armed forces or who were "loaned" to defense work.

As classes became smaller and the ratio of teachers per students became disproportionate, many of the faculty were troubled lest they find themselves without employment. President Fairchild remained ever hopeful and encouraging. No new teachers would be employed, but he would keep a place for all who wished to re-

[33] *Index* 1942, pp. 120–121.
[34] *Proceedings of the Teachers College Board* (Chicago) May 17, 1943, p. 60.
[35] *Ibid.*, (Chicago) April 3, 1944, p. 36.

main on the staff and find constructive work for them to do. There would be an upsurge in enrollment after the war, and it would not be easy to build up a strong faculty. He encouraged those who did not have doctorates to take advantage of the decline in enrollment and engage in advanced study. Extension courses were offered in as many centers as public transportation and the restrictions on gasoline and tires permitted. First aid courses were taught by Professor Clifford Horton and other members of the health and physical education staff, and Red Cross certificates as well as college credit were earned by students completing the courses. Professor Leslie Holmes taught short courses in map-reading, and the home economics staff offered their talents widely in developing healthful meals within the restrictions of sugar and red and blue ration coupons.

A War Service Council was set up to coordinate different areas of student and faculty war-time activities. The War Funds Board supervised drives for funds, the War Records Board gathered data on university personnel in service, the War Literature Board collected literature, photographs, and phonograph records, the Student Activities Board sponsored a multiplicity of projects from making surgical dressings to serving in Red Cross canteens and mailing copies of the *Vidette* to camps where former students were based; a Government Relations and Americanism Board cooperated with the American Legion, the DAR and the Red Cross, while the Community War Service Board did its share to build up morale and patriotism.[36]

Dwindling enrollments and vanishing man power cast a shadow of apprehension and gloom over the school. The great lift to the general morale of the school came with the announcement from Washington in the spring of 1943 that the University would receive a unit of from two hundred sixty to three hundred men in the Navy V-12 program.[37] On July 1 a contingent of 291 men arrived at Fell Hall and with the Commanding Officer, Meldrim F. Burrill, were inducted into the Unit.[38] They came

[36] *Index* 1942, p. 179.
[37] *Proceedings of the Teachers College Board* (Chicago) May 17, 1943, p. 61.
[38] Other officers of the Navy V-12 Unit were Lt. (j.g.) Eugene W. Bowman, executive officer, Lt. (j.g.) Edwin A. Busse, and Lt. (j.g.) Merrill W. Rusher, medical officer. A ship's company of five enlisted men served as athletic specialists, yeoman, storekeeper and pharmacist's mate.

from thirty-one midwestern colleges and universities. A few had seen active duty and one bore the purple heart. Four-fifths of the men were quartered in Fell Hall, the Unit's headquarters, and the others in Smith Hall. Three sixteen-week terms a year were set up, and the length of time the men spent on campus depended on their previous college work. Regular staff members taught courses in physics, English, advanced mathematics, chemistry, engineering, history, United States naval history, economics, and foreign languages. Upon completion of their college work the students with good records went on to midshipmen schools, from which they were commissioned as ensigns; those who failed in their work were dispatched to boot camp or the fleet.[39]

On the whole the V-12 boys were a superior lot. When their close and full schedules permitted, they participated in university extracurricular activities, music, sports, and dramatics. In their trim uniforms of winter blue and summer white they added color and life to a campus that deplored complete feminization.

The south reserve room at Milner Library was set aside for "naval personnel only." Weekday bounds were from Beaufort to Willow and from Main to Fell, and often at closing time a co-ed walked her seaman from the library to his dormitory, bade him a fond goodnight, and scurried home alone.

Saturday reviews on McCormick Field and morning inspection in front of Old Main ending with a salute to the flag attracted much attention, and an invitation to the Navy V-12 semester's formal dance was esteemed by many co-eds as next to making the academic honor roll; others secretly rated the honors in the reverse order.

The second V-12 term had barely begun when the continuance of the Unit was threatened. About noon on November 9, the community was startled by the shriek of fire sirens, the clanging of the fire trucks, the odor of burning timbers and the heavy pall of smoke that quickly enveloped the campus. Fell Hall, the navy ship, was on fire! The town's volunteer fire fighting equipment rushed to the scene. Additional fire trucks came from Bloomington and the Soldiers and Sailors Childrens School to help battle the flames. The navy men had already rescued most of the valu-

[39] Gertrude M. Hall, "The Fleet's In," *Alumni Quarterly*, August 1943, pp. 2–3.

ables in the hall. Damage by fire was confined entirely to the attic and the roof, but water damaged other parts of the building.

While the faculty and women students speculated on the outcome of the fire, the townspeople, the commanding officer, and President Fairchild were busy. Dr. Fairchild telephoned Springfield, and Lieutenant Burrill telephoned Washington. Priorities on repair materials were granted immediately, and by the middle of the afternoon the State Architect was on the grounds initiating steps for repairs. The people of Normal offered food and lodgings but by night the seamen had temporary beds neatly arranged on the floor of McCormick Gymnasium. Within twenty-four hours the kitchen and dining room were again in operation and less than half a day was lost from classes.[40]

Six hundred four seamen were trained at Normal University before the V-12 Unit was disbanded in June 1945. At a final convocation on June 16, the Commanding Officer, Lieutenant Meldrim F. Burrill, presented President Fairchild with a citation of appreciation and commendation from Secretary of the Navy James Forestal, together with the battalion flag and the United States flag of the Unit, to be placed in Milner Library as a remembrance of "service beyond the call of duty." [41]

For some time prior to the disbanding of the Navy Unit the University began making plans for "reconversion" to the needs of a post-war era. It was expected that there would be a sharp uptrend in enrollment. During the war, the University inaugurated an extensive adult education program in which evening classes were taught by members of the staff. Despite restrictions on gasoline and tires, the classes, especially those in typing, arts and crafts, were well attended. Eventually the program was turned over to the Bloomington Public School system, one of the best in the area. Public school adult programs are now well-established with a part-time coordinator in the office of the State Superintendent of Public Instruction.

[40] *Proceedings of the Teachers College Board* (Chicago) December 18, 1943, pp. 279–280.
[41] Meldrim F. Burrill, "Brief History of the Officer Training Navy V-12 Unit, Illinois State Normal University.

The U. S. Navy paid a total of $380,498.08 to Normal University for use of plant and teaching personnel for the V-12 program; of this $69,000 was available for rehabilitating Fell Hall and Smith Hall. *Proceedings of the Teachers College Board* (Springfield) October 15, 1945, p. 61.

Graduate work, with Dr. Chris A. DeYoung as the first graduate Dean, was inaugurated at the inter-session and summer session of 1944.[42] The first summer thirty-eight students were enrolled in five qualified departments. In order to qualify for offering graduate work, fifty percent of the department's staff had to have doctoral degrees, and graduate courses were taught only by persons who held such degrees. Thirty-two semester hours of graduate study was required for the degree of Master of Science in Education. No graduate courses were offered by extension, and no graduate courses were open to seniors except to those within seven hours of graduation and then only with special permission. A thesis or equivalent was required.[43] During the first year ninety-four persons availed themselves of the program. Courses held in late afternoon, evenings, and Saturdays were attractive to teachers in service. On June 4, 1945, the first degree of Master of Science in Education was granted to Charlotte Elizabeth Wilcox in biological science. The subject of her thesis was "Rapid Methods for Health Teachers and Health Educators to Use in Spotting Stream Pollution." [44] From June 1944 to June 1956, 1481 students have been enrolled in graduate courses at Illinois State Normal University, and degrees have been conferred on 478 persons.

The University also cooperated closely with the federal government in providing counseling and testing services for veterans as well as special training facilities. In the spring of 1945 Normal University became one of the five counseling and testing centers in the state of Illinois. Two Veterans Administration representatives and a secretary were assigned to the campus to handle administrative details, and five members of the psychology department gave counseling services. From September 1945 to June 1, 1947, a School for Veterans taught by members of the regular staff of teachers and graduate assistants enabled ex-service men

[42] A Graduate Council consisting of the President, the Dean, the Director of Admissions, the Director of Research, the Director of Student Teaching, Head of the Department of Education, and Coordinator of Curricular Activities and one member from each of the departments approved for graduate study, was organized in 1943 to develop the graduate program. *Ibid.*, (Chicago) September 7, 1943, p. 183.
[43] *Ibid.*, (Chicago) January 26, 1944, p. 9.
[44] Subsequently Charlotte Wilcox took a M.S. in Public Health, University of North Carolina and D.Ed. in Health Education, University of Illinois. She is co-author of ten textbooks in health for elementary grades (*Health Action Series,* Chicago: Beckley-Cardy Company, 1952–1955). Since 1948 she has been a member of the Normal University staff.

to complete high school work. Veterans could enter at any time, and courses were geared to needs, interest, and abilities of the individual student. Of the 186 persons enrolled, varying in age from eighteen to forty-five years, 122 passed the G.E.D. test (high school level), five failed, and thirty-one withdrew before completing their work. The Veterans Guidance and Counseling Center, which was closed June 30, 1947, had given tests and counsel to 832 persons.[45] Those with special aptitude for teaching were encouraged to take further work in the university.

Outstanding among the developments of the post-war years has been the Division of Special Education with curricula for training teachers of exceptional children. In July 1943 at a meeting to discuss future plans for the teachers colleges, President Fairchild suggested that some school should do something for the handicapped. The previous January, Irving Pearson, secretary of the Illinois Education Association, had written him that the Illinois Commission for Handicapped Children, Director Rodney H. Brandon of the Welfare Department, and "a host of others" were interested in setting up at an early date child study bureaus in the various teacher-training institutions that would provide teachers and prospective teachers with general training in diagnosis and treatment of atypical children, physically or mentally handicapped.[46] Superintendent of Public Instruction Vernon Nickell was also in sympathy with such a program. Since 1923 the state had been extending financial assistance to school units to provide educational facilities first for crippled children, then for children with defective vision and impaired hearing, until study, experimentation, and public interest led to the passage of a law in 1943 which provided special education for all types of physically handicapped. In 1942 there had been 3,723 children in special classes in Illinois, ninety percent of these in Chicago. Few trained teachers were available.[47] The Board immediately seemed interested in such a program. President Buzzard believed Normal University was the place for carrying on

[45] *Proceedings of the Teachers College Board* (Macomb) June 14, 1947, pp. 189–190.
[46] Irving Pearson to R. W. Fairchild, Springfield, January 16, 1943. *Fairchild Papers.*
[47] In 1911 state aid was made available for providing education of children declared delinquent by the courts. The state of Illinois appropriated $1,717,500 for special education 1941–1943. Ray Graham, "History of Special Education in Illinois." Dedicatory brochure, Special Education Building, Illinois State Normal University, March 2, 1951.

the work. President Fairchild was advised to include such a proposal in his next Board Report.[48]

On September 27, the organization of a Division of Special Education at Normal University received formal approval. To head the new division President Fairchild recommended Dr. Rose E. Parker, who was acting as Director of the Division of Rural Education. Not only did Miss Parker have ability as an administrator, but she was peculiarly fitted to organize curricula in the new field. Since 1932 she had been teaching courses dealing with exceptional children, such as "The Psychology of the Maladjusted School Child," and "Diagnosis and Remedial Teaching." She had also cooperated with Dr. Chris DeYoung, then head of the Department of Education, in the organization of two courses, "Behavior Problems in the Elementary Schools," and "The Education of Exceptional Children."

A Committee of Thirteen, from administration and special fields of health, science, speech, and education and psychology, began a study of the problem. Conferences were held with Ray Graham, newly appointed State Director of Education for Exceptional Children; Lawrence J. Linck, Secretary of the Illinois Commission for Handicapped Children; and Edward H. Stullken, principal of the Montefiore Special School in Chicago. The eleventh annual Administrative Round-up in December 1943 was given over to the consideration of "The Education of Special Children in Illinois." Returning from one of these conferences, Mr. Graham wrote President Fairchild:

Your conference yesterday has not adjourned. The sessions continued all the way home and so far as my mental processes are concerned, it is still going on. I think you should know that the group spoke very warmly of your fine concept and vision in regard to this problem . . . . It gives . . . a great feeling of elation to note the sanity and breadth of vision which you have concerning this problem.[49]

By September 1944 complete curricula were offered leading to the degree of Bachelor of Science in Special Education in given areas such as the socially maladjusted, partially sighted, mentally subnormal, and speech correction. Subsequently the training was

[48] R. W. Fairchild, Interview, January 2, 1956; *Proceedings of the Teachers College Board* (Chicago) September 27, 1943, p. 141, 188.
[49] Ray Graham to R. W. Fairchild, Springfield, November 18, 1943. *Fairchild Papers.*

added in the areas of the deaf and hard of hearing, the blind, and the physically handicapped. A fifth year of work leading to Master of Science in Special Education began in 1945. Three students were enrolled in the curricula in 1944; the number had risen to 225 in 1955.

From its inception at Normal University, the basic principles of the work in special education have been that every child has a right to the education he can use to advantage, that exceptional children are like normal children in many ways, that teachers in the usual classrooms should share responsibility for some handicapped children, and that teachers should regard their work an integral and not a segregated part of the school system.[50]

In 1945 the General Assembly appropriated $976,000 for a Special Education Building and authorized the purchase of property adjacent to the campus as a site for it and other contemplated buildings. The amount appropriated for the Special Education Building was not adequate to build the type of structure demanded by the program, and two years later the Legislature reappropriated the same amount and added to it funds originally allocated to other buildings at Normal, thus making a total of $1,900,000 available for a building to serve as a Special Education Center. Rising construction costs made it necessary to call upon the Legislature in 1949 for $740,000 to complete the building and $215,000 to equip it. Built of red brick and white stone in modified Georgian architecture, the block-long, three-story building with its solarium and deck is an imposing structure. The east wing, housing the University Health Center, provides convenient access to its services.

When the building was dedicated on March 2, 1951, thirty-five hundred persons filed through its halls, admiring its spaciousness, its beauty, and the purposeful planning that had gone into it. Nowhere was there a building like it, and the architects had had to be guided solely by the composite thinking of those who were responsible for the program. Uppermost had always been the need of the children requiring special services—the hard of hearing, the deaf, those with defective vision and defective speech, the

[50] Rose E. Parker, "Special Education—A New Division." *Alumni Quarterly,* February 1, 1944, p. 3.

blind, the palsied, and the cardiac cases. The special services required meant special equipment with provision for testing, counseling, and therapy, and facilities for play and exercise, music, and art.

Nor were these exceptional children to be segregated into a world apart. They were to have varied contacts and experiences with other children in regular classrooms from the kindergarten through the elementary school. To achieve these ends, specially trained teachers share responsibility for many exceptional children. Dr. Parker, commenting on "The Program of Teacher Education for Exceptional Children," said at the dedication of the building:

For ninety-four years Illinois State Normal University has been dedicated to the preparation of teachers. This latest assignment, growing out of an extension of services in the public schools of the state, places on this University the obligation to prepare teachers for exceptional children; teachers with sound mental health, common sense, ability to enjoy work and play with children and to cooperate with people, an unfailing sense of humor, and an abundant capacity for hard work . . . . The new obligation has been accepted in the spirit which has characterized this University from the beginning, to the end that teachers of courage, devotion and intelligence may go forth "gladly to lerne and gladly teche" the exceptional child of Illinois.[51]

While the staff was engrossed in plans for the Special Education Building, the Administrative Unit of what was originally planned to be an administration, music, art, and auditorium building, and a pair of self-liquidating dormitories, calamity fell upon the school. President Fairchild enroute to Cleveland to speak at the American Association of Colleges for Teacher Education was called to Springfield on Thursday, February 21, 1946, to hear a report from the Division of Architecture and Engineering. Old Main had been examined and found unsafe. That afternoon the faculty was summoned to Capen Auditorium. Only a few persons knew the reason for the president's unexpected return. Standing tall and pale, his voice somewhat affected by the gravity of the occasion, Dr. Fairchild spoke briefly. The condition of Old Main was dangerous, the tower was leaning and the

[51] Rose E. Parker, "Program of Teacher Education for Exceptional Children at Illinois State Normal University." Dedicatory brochure, March 2, 1951.

third floor was unsafe. All offices and classrooms above the first floor would have to be evacuated within forty-eight hours. Temporary quarters would have to be found in churches and buildings about town. An assembly of students was called Friday morning, and on Monday there were padlocked gates on all stairs leading up from the first floor of Old Main.[52] Never again would Wrights and Phils assemble in the old hall.

On May 22, the bell tolled for the last time from what was once a majestic tower. Classes were dismissed and faculty and students stood mutely by as a giant crane lifted the great dome from its resting place and lowered it slowly to the earth. By the end of the summer, memories were all that remained of the old landmark and the third story with its halls sacred to Wrightonia and Philadelphia. A flat roof and steel reinforcements again made twelve classrooms and a number of offices available. In September 1950 administrative offices were moved into the new Administration Building, and only faculty offices and classes remained within the venerable and decaying walls. To thousands of alumni the spot where once Old Main stood in all her glory is hallowed ground, and her tower forever the symbol of Normal University.

As government defense plants and war installations were dismantled after the war, President Fairchild was successful in obtaining considerable surplus property in machine tools and a number of barracks. These temporary structures provided classrooms and rehearsal halls for the ever-increasing bands and orchestras. Twenty-seven units located on the south side of the farm and known as Cardinal Court furnished accommodations for eighty-five married veterans and ninety-six unmarried veterans.

The upsurge in enrollment had only begun. Each year scarcity of desirable rooms and eating places became more critical. The deans of men and women and the housing director conducted a door-to-door survey in their search for rooms. The week after the Navy V-12 Unit departed, a cafeteria was opened in Fell Hall. Smith Hall and Fell Hall were crowded beyond their capacity. Meanwhile building costs rose, and the Budget Director took a

[52] *Vidette*, February 22, 1946; R. W. Fairchild, "The Sad Plight of Old Main," *Alumni Quarterly*, November 1949, pp. 2–3.

gloomy view of the teachers colleges' demands for additional housing.

In 1947 Richard Dunn, resident Board member and alumnus of Illinois State Normal University, drafted a bill authorizing the construction of self-liquidating projects on the Illinois teachers college campuses. When it was enacted in law, the way was opened whereby housing facilities could be obtained at no expense to the state and at lower figures than under state contract. Two dormitories built under this program were ready for occupancy in the fall of 1951. The residence for men was named Dunn Hall in honor of Mr. Dunn, and the residence for women was named Barton Hall in honor of Olive Lillian Barton, alumna and long the beloved dean of women. About the same time the south wing to Fell Hall was completed after thirty-five years. A third self-liquidating residence hall with facilities for 410 young women was opened in September 1955 and named Walker Hall in honor of Lewis Walker, chairman of the Teachers College Board and an alumnus of Normal University.

A student union was not overlooked in the planning of new buildings. Increased enrollments made a social and recreational center more imperative. A rustic building was proposed first, and later a Georgian structure costing about $40,000 had been suggested for the South Campus, but the matter of financing had held back construction. President Fairchild had hoped for something better and more substantial. Through his efforts and those of the other college presidents and the approval of the Board, legislation was passed making it possible for the teachers colleges to set up foundations and accept gifts. With the self-liquidating measure enacted in 1947, it was now possible to combine gifts and loans and proceed with the construction of a union adequate to the needs of the student body. To undertake such a project would require the assessing of fees and pledges of gifts from faculty, alumni, and business men before a bonding company would advance funds. The Student Council presented the matter before the student body, and of the 1305 who voted on May 14, 1953, only twenty-eight opposed the levying of a ten dollar union fee. Dr. Harold Gibson, Director of the Bureau of Appointments, who had had phenomenal success in fund drives elsewhere was given the task of directing a campaign to raise $150,000.[53] The funds were raised, plans approved, contracts let, and construction begun.

The modern structure of brick and plate glass, with its lounges, dining halls, cafeteria, snack bar, game and conference rooms, and alumni headquarters differs greatly from the plans for the Society Hall, the turreted monstrosity projected by Wrightonia and Philadelphia in the 1890's,[54] and the rustic retreat envisaged in the 1930's or the Georgian edifice proposed in the 1940's. The new union building, completed in 1956, is more in keeping with the activities and philosophy of the University's second century than any of the previous plans.[55]

As Dr. Fairchild approached his twentieth year as president he could well be proud of the growth the University had made. In two decades new buildings on the campus and at the university farm stood as monuments to his labors. The enrollment had almost doubled, the number and qualifications of the staff had been greatly strengthened and faculty salaries increased; student entrance qualifications were raised; the curriculum and off-campus services had been expanded; a graduate school and a Division of Special Education had been offered and a junior college projected; off-campus student teaching facilities had been expanded; there was wider faculty participation in policy-making through the elected University Council.

President Fairchild was especially gratified over developments in certain training areas such as music and art. In 1933 there had been four teachers in music and fifteen majors; by 1954 the Division had a staff of fifteen and enrolled 140 students. The course offerings had been expanded from a single sequence of thirty-two semester hours with major emphasis on basic fundamentals and methods to a series of sequences ranging from forty-three to sixty semester hours, including many phases of music and music education. An extensive music library, an ample supply of instru-

[53] *Proceedings of the Teachers College Board* (Normal) February 21, 1954, p. 342; *Vidette* May 5, 1954.
[54] The Wrightonian and Philadelphian societies succumbed to the pressures of the extracurricular clubs, organized forensics, dramatics and honor societies and were formally disbanded in 1952 after ninety-five years of continuous operation.
[55] The students wished to name the union in honor of President Fairchild but he demurred saying he wished to be remembered for his academic work. In 1954 the Board designated the Special Education Building as Fairchild Hall.

ments, and a well-equipped technological laboratory had been acquired, and graduate work had been initiated.

Similar advance had been made in art. Monthly senior art shows on the bridge between Old Main and Industrial Arts Building acquainted the passerby as well as the major with the work being done in art. "Art for the individual" rather than the training of the professional craftsman was the new emphasis of the art curriculum. The completion of Milner Library with its art gallery made it possible for temporary exhibits from the leading galleries to be brought to the campus. In 1953 a Radio Arts Class for Grades Three to Eight was begun. The response was enthusiastic, and it has been estimated that 12,000 children participated in the programs broadcast over stations in Bloomington, Danville, and Ottawa.

The matter of approval of graduates in agriculture for Smith-Hughes positions was however the most frustrating problem during President Fairchild's entire administration. The education of men to become teachers of vocational agriculture began at Normal University in 1922. Graduates of the two-year course in agriculture had been accepted as teachers of vocational agriculture in high schools of the state for a period of four years. In 1926 the State Vocational Board raised the standards and required the satisfactory completion of a four-year course. By the fall of 1929 Normal University had a four-year curriculum in agriculture. From 1922 to 1938 graduates of the Normal University agriculture curriculum were recognized by the State Board for Vocational Education, but after 1938 they secured positions only on an emergency basis. Legislation enacted in 1937 made it necessary for teacher training institutions offering work in vocational agriculture to be approved by the U. S. Office of Education. Normal University's request for approval in 1937 was denied on the grounds that its facilities were inadequate.[56] Governor Henry Horner promptly released $10,000 to repair farm buildings and construct a stock-judging pavilion. Additional stock and farm equipment were purchased and certain experimental work begun. On June 22, 1938, President Fairchild conferred with the Federal

[56] Ralph A. Benton, "The Ag Department Looks Ahead," *Alumni Quarterly,* May 1950, p. 6.

Board in Washington and learned to his surprise that the State
Vocational Board had a larger voice in the destiny of agriculture
at Normal University than the federal office. A week later when
the State Board approved the June graduates, President Fairchild
was assured that if standards were met, an amendment would be
presented to the Federal Board to include Normal University in
the five-year plan as a regular Smith-Hughes training institution.
But no action was forthcoming.[57]

During World War II few men were enrolled in the agriculture
curriculum, but in 1947 the Normal University renewed its request for Smith-Hughes approval. This time the State Board
approved the application, but before action had been taken in
Washington, a letter of protest was issued by Dr. George W.
Stoddard, President of the University of Illinois, declaring that
the State University had a priority in training teachers for vocational agriculture, that its facilities were adequate for training all
agricultural teachers needed in the state and that approval of
graduates from the agricultural departments of the state teacher
training institutions would be an unnecessary expense.[58] The fact
remained that despite facilities at the State University not enough
men were trained to meet the demand. Meanwhile the Normal
University improved its plant and increased its staff. Some of the
faculty already employed engaged in advanced study. In 1949
application for recognition in the 1947–1952 plan was again made.
The Board for Vocational Education sent a committee to Normal
to evaluate facilities and personnel, and on April 28, 1950, the
State Board voted 8 to 1 in favor of approving the Normal University. With high hopes the request was referred to Washington. Again the reply from the Assistant Commissioner on
Vocational Education was "Recommend disapproval." Throughout the long struggle President Fairchild remained resolute. He
personally checked inventories, facilities, and personnel against
standards. If a cow barn or sheep barn or a hog shed was needed,
it was built. He urged the professors of agriculture to complete
their doctorates and add more academic lustre to the milking
parlor and the poultry house. There were times when it seemed

[57] *Proceedings of the Teachers College Board* (Springfield) November 14, 1938, p. 90.
[58] *Ibid.*, (Macomb) July 14, 1947, p. 145.

that the purchase of a tractor or a Guernsey bull took precedence over a piano or a curtain for the stage in Capen Auditorium.

On April 30, 1954 the Illinois Board for Vocational Education in considering Normal University's most recent petition voted to delay approval until a survey "to secure the latest data available upon which to base their judgment" was made.[59] Notwithstanding, young men continue to enroll in agriculture hopeful that before their course is half completed the division will be approved and they can remain at Normal and graduate fully qualified for Smith-Hughes positions.

The changes that took place at Illinois State Normal University during Dr. Fairchild's persidency were by no means solely the work of its capable administrator. Although the Board held the college presidents strictly accountable and charged them with the responsibility of seeing that the teachers colleges kept pace with educational trends as well as providing leadership in the general field of public education, the faculty played a substantial role in advancing programs and implementing those proposed by the administrators.

In the early years of the institution the role of the president was arbitrary, and the faculty had small voice in deciding such matters as curriculum, admissions, student welfare, and public relations. Hovey had discussed some matters with Ira Moore, and Edwards had consulted with Hewett, Metcalf, and Sewall, but in the main the presidents had made their own decisions. Hewett and Cook were more inclined to take the entire faculty into their confidence and relied especially on the bright young men who had returned to teach at their alma mater after a sojourn in European universities. During the Herbartian era the Faculty Club had much to do with the shaping of University policy, but the system of standing committees seems to have been a twentieth-century development. The catalog did not list committees until 1911 but the fact that twenty-nine were listed for that year indicates the system doubtless had been in existence for some time. The catalog for 1915 listed thirty-eight committees, and the catalog for 1923 listed thirty-nine. Between 1924 and 1930 there was

[59] Vernon L. Nickell to R. W. Fairchild, May 5, 1954. Quoted, "An Inventory of the Facilities of Illinois State Normal University to Meet the Evaluative Criteria for Teacher Training Institutions for Vocational Agriculture." (Typescript) 1956. *Fairchild Papers*.

some reorganization, and by the time of President Brown the number of committees had been reduced to twenty-three.

The expansion of the University in the middle thirties resulted in the creation of many new committees with some overlapping of areas and duplication of effort. A few of the faculty served on as many as six committees. After two years of study a Committee on Committees was ready to report. On September 25, 1942, the faculty went into a two-day retreat at East Bay Camp, Lake Bloomington, to take action upon the matter of areas and committee loads. An unprecedented and heavy snowfall the first afternoon sent cars back to town for blankets and winter coats. The next morning as the odor of mothballs mingled with that of pine burning in the great fireplace, the shivering faculty set to work in all seriousness to reduce the burden of committees. Instead of twenty-two committees the day ended with thirty assigned to five areas with a coordinator for each area. The number of committees on which a staff member might serve was limited.[60]

The role of the faculty in administration, which had been extended first through the Senate in 1935 and then the Administrative Council in 1938, was further extended in 1951 when the Board authorized the formation of an elective university council at each of the teachers colleges to make recommendations on curriculum, campus planning, scholarship, the budget, and the appointment, promotion, and tenure of staff members. Since the formation of this representative body special studies have been made of travel funds, methods of choosing department heads, retirement, loyalty oaths, scholastic standards, credit unions, the junior high school, faculty committees, and the improvement of college teaching.[61] Faculty forums held under the auspices of the Professional Affairs Committee have afforded opportunity for the exchange of opinion and the crystallization of policy. Since 1942 an Advisory Council of twenty or more persons from the community including the mayors of the two towns, local members of the state legislature, and representatives of civic organizations such as the chambers of commerce and the press, have rendered

[60] *Catalogs*, Illinois State Normal University 1942–1943 and 1944–1945.
[61] *Minutes of the University Council*, 1951–1956.

valuable service in interpreting the University to the public, in suggesting ways for mutual help, and in acting as a sounding board for school policy on such matters as housing, recreation, and campus expansion.[62]

To relieve the president of certain routine responsibilities, the position of Administrative Assistant to the President was created in 1941, and Dr. Chris DeYoung, Head of the Education Department, filled the post until 1943, when he became Dean of the University upon the retirement of Dean Schroeder. Dr. Leslie Holmes of the Geography Department then became the Administrative Assistant to the President. When Dr. Holmes resigned to become president of Northern State Teachers College, DeKalb, Dr. Bjarne Ullsvik, Professor of Mathematics, became assistant to President Fairchild. Meanwhile Dr. Arthur Hoff Larsen became Assistant Dean of the University in 1944. Dr. DeYoung voluntarily resigned the deanship in 1949 in order to devote more time to classroom teaching, writing, lecturing, and educational work of an international character.[63] Dr. Larsen then became Dean of the University.

In the post war years the reputation of the school again spread abroad through members of the staff on leave as exchange professors, Fulbright scholars, and consultants on education to foreign governments. Teachers and administrators from England, Germany, Sweden, South America, Thailand, Pakistan, and India came to study and observe.

In October 1953, as Dr. Fairchild rounded out his twentieth year as president, the faculty wished to honor him for his services. Although he would be eligible for retirement in 1956, it was known that he did not intend to retire until after the Centennial. The faculty wished to show appreciation to the man who had done so much for the University and who at the same time could be first to congratulate a staff member upon receiving an advanced degree, the publication of a book, or the arrival of a new baby, and the first to offer sympathy in bereavement. He did not

[62] In 1954 the Advisory Council undertook as a Centennial project the raising of funds for the portrait of President Fairchild.

[63] In 1947 Dr. De Young served as educational consultant with the U. S. Army. His *Introduction to American Public Education,* first published in 1942 is regarded as standard text in the history of American education and has been translated for use in Italy.

take kindly to the idea of public recognition. "My work is not done," he said. It was known that Eastern State College was honoring President Buzzard on the completion of his twentieth year with a special convocation at which President Fairchild was asked to make the address. Finally Dr. Fairchild consented to a family party at Normal. "No fanfare," he cautioned. "No fulsome praise, no distinguished guests, no long speeches." And so it was. The Jesters were repeating his favorite comedy, *Seven Keys to Baldpate,* at Homecoming, and from it the speakers took their cue. His own purloined key ring provided the motivation for a gay and spirited review of his twenty years at Normal. Given back all of his keys save one, he responded with an appreciation of his loyal faculty and his hopes for the future growth of the school. The seventh key represented a gift from the faculty, a television set, given in appreciation and in the hope that he would spend more of his evening hours away from his office.

Ever working long hours, going over committee reports, carrying on an extensive correspondence, making public addresses, attending educational conferences, participating in surveys and studies, serving on church and civic committees, counseling with students and faculty, and at the same time managing to attend many of the school functions, plays, musicals, concerts, and sports events, President Fairchild's health began to break. In 1950 he was given a temporary sick leave, and Dean Larsen was authorized to act in Dr. Fairchild's absence.[64]

After three and one-half months' rest, President Fairchild returned to his office. Soon he was working as hard as ever, meeting with committees, studying architect's designs for dormitories, classroom buildings, a new high school, and an elementary school, striving for Smith-Hughes approval and for continued recognition by the American Association of University Women, arranging for the Visitation Committee of the American Association of Colleges for Teacher Education, and feverishly planning for a greater university. Above everything he considered the laboratory school essential to rounding out his concept of teacher education at Normal University. He never missed an alumni meeting if it was

[64] *Proceedings of the Teachers College Board* (Macomb) March 27, 1950, p. 177; (Springfield) July 21, 1950, pp. 353-354.

possible for him to attend. He enjoyed meeting the former students, and they regarded the president's remarks almost as good as a visit to the campus. He always spoke graphically of the changes, the improvements. He shared his dreams for the future and his conviction that Normal University must ever remain a professional school, a teacher training institution. Of late years he liked to tell of the fine new snack bar in the new wing of Fell Hall, the large attractive room with a sun porch where young people could linger long over a coke or quickly devour a hamburger. He wished he had time to drop in more often for a "malted" and visit with the students. He was especially pleased over the prospects of a Student Union, a project he had had in mind ever since his first official visit to the campus on that memorable day in October 1933.

On May 24, 1954, upon returning from a trip to Springfield to see what could be done about the Smith-Hughes situation, President Fairchild was in such excruciating pain that he had to be taken to the hospital. On June 22 he underwent surgery, having his right leg above the knee removed. The operation was successful and Dr. Fairchild planned to return to the campus in September, but he was slow in regaining his strength. When he realized that his recovery would require more time than he had anticipated, he asked the Board on August 15, 1955, to take steps to secure his successor.[65]

Like President Hewett many years before, President Fairchild would resign, but Normal would remain his home.[66] Others would grasp his vision, carry out his plans.

[65] *Daily Pantagraph,* August 15, 1955.
[66] President Fairchild died June 12, 1956. As he lay in state in Capen Auditorium where he had presided over countless student assemblies, faculty meetings, and public gatherings, hundreds came to pay tribute—members of the Teachers College Board, educational leaders, former students, faculty, townspeople, and friends. Messages poured in from over the nation.

CHAPTER XIV

Prologue to the Second Century

WHEN President Fairchild resigned, Dr. Arthur Hoff Larsen, Dean of the University, was asked to continue as acting president until a worthy successor to Dr. Fairchild could be found. As Dean of the University since 1949, Dr. Larsen had worked closely with President Fairchild. He knew what Dr. Fairchild had projected for the University. During Dr. Fairchild's first illness he had performed his duties as acting president with directness, insight, and humility. It was natural for the Board to turn to him when the president again became ill.

A member of the faculty since 1935, first as teacher of mathematics in the University High School, and later as Professor of Education and head of the Department of Education, Dean Larsen had witnessed most of the growth that had taken place under the administration of President Fairchild.[1] He now took up the unfinished business of the construction of the Student Union, the matter of the laboratory school, so dear to President Fairchild, and for which money for plans had been appropriated in 1951, and again in 1953, a classroom building, some curricular reorganization, and further plans for the Centennial.

With 3,059 students enrolled in September 1955, the matter of additional classrooms became a pressing issue. A building for college classes and enlarged facilities and another to house a combination elementary and junior high school unit of the laboratory school would release rooms in Metcalf for high school use and rooms in other buildings used by the high school could revert to college use. Dunn, Barton, and Walker halls had been built under self-liquidating programs, and except for the extension to Fell Hall granted by the Sixty-seventh General Assembly, the

---

[1] Arthur Hoff Larsen, of Danish parentage, was born in Boston, Massachusetts in 1907. He received his B. Ed. from Wisconsin State Teachers College, Superior, and both his Ph.M. and his Ph.D. from the University of Wisconsin. He was married to Faith Herrick in 1933.

state had made no appropriation for major construction at Normal University since the Administration Building and the Special Education Building.[2]

The Advisory Council gave support to plans for the construction of a new classroom building and the laboratory unit of a combined elementary and junior high school. Among the voices strongly urging both projects were those of the *Daily Pantagraph's* editor, H. Clay Tate, and State Senator David Davis III. The editor of the *Pantagraph* kept in close touch with the area and knew well the paramount needs of the University. The senator as vice-chairman of the School Problems Commission had made a careful study of educational conditions throughout the state. The Davis family, moreover, from the time of Judge David Davis, had had first-hand knowledge of the school, many of its members having attended the University high school. To some of the Board and some of the faculty as well as many of the alumni, public school people, notably the Illinois Education Association and other friends of the school, the erection of a modern laboratory school meant giving to the University an opportunity to improve its major function, the preparation of teachers for Illinois schools.

When Acting President Larsen prepared the budget to go before the Sixty-ninth General Assembly in January 1955, he included these buildings in his request. Friends of Normal University had done their work well, and before the session closed, $1,900,000 had been appropriated for the laboratory school and $950,000 for a class-room building.[3] Plans for the classroom building to be located on Mulberry Street north and west of Old Main were drawn and approved, and construction on both buildings was begun in the spring and summer of 1956. The Board concurred with the wishes of the faculty in naming the new classroom building "Schroeder Hall" in memory of Herman Henry Schroeder, Dean of Normal University from 1929 to 1946.

Meanwhile the Board considered the appointment of a successor to Dr. Fairchild. On September 19, 1955, a resolution was passed

---

[2] The amount appropriated for Fell Hall addition was $717,420 for construction and $75,000 for furnishings. *Appropriations Regular Session Sixty-seventh General Assembly.* Compiled by the Department of Finance, Springfield 1953, p. 339.

[3] *Ibid.,* Sixty-ninth General Assembly 1955, pp. 159–160.

relative to the manner of selecting a new president. The faculty were invited to participate in the evaluation of candidates through an elective committee with one member each from the ranks of professor, associate professor, assistant professor, and instructor; the fifth member who was to act as chairman was the chairman of the University Council. Under a ruling of the Board, present staff members were not eligible for consideration for the presidency.

For six months a special committee of the Board and the faculty committee reviewed credentials and interviewed candidates.[4] On March 31 the Board announced that Dr. Robert Gehlmann Bone, assistant provost of the University of Illinois, had been named president.

Dr. Bone, for twenty-one years a member of the faculty of the University of Illinois, had rich training and experience to qualify him for the position. After completing his bachelor's degree at Wooster College in Ohio in 1928, he taught English and commercial law (French) in the American University of Alexandria in Egypt for three years, serving as acting director during his last year. He returned to the United States and took his M.A. in history from the University of Illinois the following year. From 1932 to 1934 he was professor of history and speech at Lincoln College, Lincoln, Illinois, where he was also dean for one year. In 1934 he was invited to teach ancient history at the University of Illinois while Professor J. Ward Swain was on leave; in 1937 after receiving his Ph.D. he joined the permanent staff. He was selected by the honor students in 1939 as one of the most effective teachers in the University.

During World War II Dr. Bone went through officers' training school in the Army Air Corps and for two years was assigned to cadet pilot training at San Antonio, Texas. In the fall of 1944 he was sent overseas as a member of the Headquarters Staff of the U. S. Forces in Europe. He helped to organize the American University at Schrivenham, England, and during its existence,

4 "Resolution Concerning the Election of the President of Illinois State Normal University" *Proceedings of the Teachers College Board* (Normal) September 19, 1955. (Reprint) Committee of the Board: Vernon L. Nickell, Clarence Ropp, William Reed, R. A. Stipes, Jr., J. A. Houle, Jr. Committee of the faculty: Burton O'Connor, chairman, Chris De Young, Howard Ivens, Howard Hancock, Margaret Westhoff.

was head of the history department. He was separated from the service as a major in July 1945.

He returned to the History Department and the Division of General Studies of the College of Liberal Arts and Sciences at the University of Illinois, in 1946 and was made director of the division. In 1947 he was named Director of the Division of Special Services, established in 1945 to set up special curricula for returning veterans. In 1952 he resigned from the Division of Special Services and returned to teaching history and administering the Division of General Studies. A few months later he was asked to serve as acting Dean of the College of Education, a position he held for a year until a new dean was selected. In October 1954 he became Assistant Provost of the University. Meanwhile he served in important committee posts and was a member of the Athletic Board of Control.[5]

Dr. Bone is of native Illinois stock. He was born in Springfield, Illinois, June 2, 1906, and attended the Springfield public schools. His father was the late Judge Eugene E. Bone. In 1944 Dr. Bone was married to Karin Levanius of Springfield, a graduate of the National College of Education. They have two sons, John L. and Robert G., Jr.

When Dr. Bone was asked what led him to accept the presidency of Normal University, his reply was brief and succinct, "The Challenge!" Then thoughtfully he added, "The challenge to build a great school into a greater one, to provide more and better teachers for the schools of Illinois." Almost immediately he set about saturating himself with the history and traditions of the institution whose second century he was to launch.

On May 8, when he was formally presented to the faculty by the Teachers College Board, he was thoroughly familiar with the many facets of Illinois State Normal University's program and the leadership and ambitions of the presidents who had preceded him.

Standing tall and straight in gray tweeds, his face somewhat pale beneath its summer tan, Dr. Bone seemed fully aware of the responsibility that rested upon him. He asked for time to study

[5] *Daily Pantagraph,* April 1, 1956. He and his wife have been active in the Parent Teacher Association, Cub Scouts, church and civic projects.

and to know the faculty and the school before embarking upon any sweeping changes. He spoke humbly and earnestly and in a manner that invoked confidence and good will. He concluded:

Ever mindful of the great history of the past ninety-eight years of Illinois State Normal University, it is essential that we look toward the future and develop this university so that it will be even greater in its second century.

A century ago, Jesse Fell, Newton Bateman, Jonathan B. Turner, Simeon Wright, Ninian Edwards, Samuel Moulton, and others of the founding fathers were carefully planning and working hard to create this university. They dreamed and hoped, and at times they were daring in their procedure. Their work and their dreams have obviously been continued through the decades. Teachers and administrators have come and gone, and each has contributed in the development of this institution. Their mantles have fallen upon us. We must dream and hope. We must plan and work. We must at times dare and try.

We must present our individual plans, our ideas, and our ideals. We must work out a common plan. It is essential that we realize that people, who have imaginations and who think, often feel strongly concerning their ideas and plans. We must discuss and study them. There will be disagreements. However, they may be healthy provided we have understanding and can agreeably disagree. In the end we must reach decisions; these may be compromises. In any case, when a decision is made in what is felt to be the best interests of this university, it is essential that we have a united front. As Jonathan B. Turner said on December 20, 1856, in a speech concerning the need for a normal school in Illinois, "Let us all take hold and strive toward the future, in such form as we think best."

Each member of the Board, each teacher and administrator of Illinois State Normal University must dedicate himself to that great principle so ably stated by President Richard Edwards in 1867 when he wrote, "The education of the children of the state is the grandest of enterprises." [6]

[6] Robert G. Bone, "Address to the Faculty, Illinois State Normal University," May 8, 1956. (Manuscript)

Bibliography

a. PRINTED MATERIALS

Books and Pamphlets

Anniversary Week in Bloomington. Chicago, 1860.

Arnold Tompkins: A Memorial. Chicago: Chicago Normal School, 1905.

Ballance, C. *History of Peoria, Illinois.* Peoria: N. C. Nason, 1870.

Brown, Harry Alvin. *Certain Basic Teacher Education Policies.* New York: Teachers College, Columbia, 1937.

Burnham, John Howard. *History of Bloomington and Normal.* Bloomington, 1879.

————. *History of McLean County, Illinois.* Chicago: William LeBaron, 1879.

————. *Some Influences Which Led to the Founding of Normal University.* Bloomington, 1909.

Carriel, Mary Turner. *Life of Jonathon B. Turner.* Jacksonville, Illinois: By the author, 1911.

Cole, Arthur Charles. *Era of the Civil War.* Springfield: Illinois Centennial Commission, 1919.

Coleman, Charles H. *Eastern State College, Fifty Years of Public Service.* Charleston: Eastern State College, 1950.

Cook, John Williston. *An Appreciation of Richard Edwards.* Privately printed, 1922.

————. *Educational History of Illinois.* Chicago: Henry O. Sheppard, 1912.

————. and McHugh, James V. *History of Illinois State Normal University, 1857–1882.* Normal: Pantagraph Printing Press, 1882.

Cottrell, Donald P. *Teacher Education for a Free People.* Oneonta, New York: American Association of Colleges for Teacher Education, 1956.

Darrah, William Culp. *Powell of the Colorado.* Princeton: Princeton University Press, 1951.

Darroch, Alexander. *Herbart and the Herbartian Theory of Education.* New York: Longmans, Green, 1903.

DeYoung, Chris A. *Introduction to American Public Education.* New York: McGraw-Hill, 1942.

Duis, E. *Good Old Times in McLean County.* Bloomington: Leader Publishing House, 1874.

Edwards, Richard. *Fifth Reader.* New York: Mason, 1866.

————. *Decennial Address,* Illinois State Normal University, June 27, 1882. Peoria: N. C. Nason, 1882.

————. *The Heritage of Culture,* An Address delivered before the Societies of Illinois State Normal University, at Bloomington, June 26, 1862. Bloomington: Daily Pantagraph Printing House, 1862.

————. *Life and Character of Abraham Lincoln,* An Address delivered in the hall of Normal University, April 19, 1865. Peoria: N. C. Nason, 1865.

————. *Memoir of Nicholas Tillinghast.* Boston: J. Robinson Company, 1857.

————. *Universal Education,* An Address before the St. Clair County Teachers Institute, Belleville, Illinois, April 15, 1863. Bloomington: Daily Pantagraph Book and Job Printing House, 1863.

————. and Warren, Mortimer A. *Analytical Speller.* Chicago: George Sherwood Company, 1871.

Edwards, Owenetta. *Early Schools and Teachers in McLean County.* Bloomington: Lang-Fuller, n.d.

Fairchild, Raymond W. *How Teacher Training Institutions May Produce a More Effective Type of Teacher.* Normal: Illinois State Normal University, 1934.

Felmley, David. *Elements of Efficiency or Some Essentials of Twentieth Century Ethics.* Normal: Illinois State Normal University, 1922.

————. *Our School Revenues.* Presidential address before the Central Illinois Teachers Association, Quincy, 1899. Jacksonville: Press of the State School for the Deaf, 1900.

————. *The Making of a Man.* Bloomington: Pantagraph Printing Company, 1904.

Gorky, John P. *Rise and Growth of the Normal School Idea in the United States.* Washington: Government Printing Office, 1891.

Gray, Miriam (Ed.) *A Century of Growth: The Historical Development of Physical Education for Women in Selected Colleges of Six Midwestern States.* Ann Arbor: Edward Brothers, 1951.

Harper, Charles A. *A Century of Teacher Education.* Washington: National Education Association, 1939.

————. *Development of the Teachers College in the United States With Special Reference to Illinois State Normal University.* Bloomington: McKnight and McKnight, 1935.

Hart, Irving H. *The First Seventy-five Years.* Cedar Falls: Iowa State Teachers College, 1951.

Hasbrouck, Jacob L. *History of McLean County, Illinois.* Topeka-Indianapolis: Historical Publishing Company, 1924.

Hewett, Edwin C. *Elements of Psychology.* Cincinnati: Van Antwerp, Bragg, 1889.

————. *Manual of Arithmetic.* Chicago: Rand McNally, 1896.

————. *Practical Arithmetic.* Chicago: Rand McNally, 1897.

————. *A Treatise on Pedagogy for Young Teachers.* New York: American Book Company, 1884.

Hurst, Homer. *Illinois State Normal University and the Public Normal School Movement.* Nashville: George Peabody College for Teachers, 1948.

Index. Yearbook, Illinois State Normal University, 1892–1956.

Keith, John A. H. (Ed.) *Semi-Centennial History of Illinois State Normal University.* Normal: 1907.

Lewis, Lloyd. *John S. Wright—Prophet of the Prairies.* Chicago: Prairie Farm Publishing Company, 1941.

Loomis, Burt Weed. *Educational Influence of Richard Edwards.* Nashville: George Peabody College for Teachers, 1932.

Lovinger, Warren C. *General Education in Teachers Colleges.* Oneonta, New York: American Association of Colleges for Teacher Education, 1948.

Lyford, Carrie Alberta. *Advanced Cookery.* Normal: Illinois State Normal University, n.d.

McMurry, Charles A. *A Course of Study for the Eight Grades of the Common Schools, Including a Handbook of Practical Suggestions to Teachers.* Bloomington: Public School Publishing Company, 1892.

————. *Elements of General Method Based on Principles of Herbart.* Bloomington: Public School Publishing Company, 1892.

————. *How to Conduct the Recitation.* Chicago: A. Flanagan, 1890.

McMurry, Dorothy. *Herbartian Contributions to History Instruction in American Elementary Schools.* New York: Teachers College, Columbia, 1946.

Manchester, Orson L. *The Normal School Crisis.* Springfield: Schnepp and Barnes, 1921.

Marshall, Albert O. *Army Life: From a Soldier's Journal.* Joliet: Printed by the author, 1883.

Morehouse, Frances Milton I. *Life of Jesse W. Fell.* University of Illinois Studies in Social Science Vol. V. No. 42, Urbana: University of Illinois, 1916.

Parker, Rose E. "Program of Teacher Education for Exceptional Children at Illinois State Normal University," Dedicatory Brochure, Special Education Building, (later named Fairchild Hall) March 2, 1951.

Pease, Theodore Calvin. *The Frontier State.* Springfield: Illinois Centennial Commission, 1918.

Rhodes, James Ford. *History of the Civil War.* New York: Macmillan, 1917.

Richardson, Harriet Fyffe, *Quaker Pioneers.* Milwaukee: Gillet and Co., 1940.

Russell, John Dale. *Report of the Study of the Structure of Tax-supported System of Higher Education of Illinois.* Springfield, 1950.

Schroeder, Herman Henry. *War, Peace and Education.* An Address delivered at the Eighty-fourth Annual Commencement, Illinois State Normal University, June 14, 1943. Normal: Illinois State Normal University, 1943.

Stegner, Wallace. *Beyond the Hundredth Meridian.* Boston: Houghton, Mifflin, 1954.

Watson, Elmo Scott. *The Illinois Wesleyan Story, 1850–1950.* Blooming-ton: Illinois Wesleyan Press, 1950.

Wells, H. W. *Schools and Teachers of Early Peoria.* Peoria: Jacquin and Company, 1900.

YWCA, 1872–1922. Normal, 1922.

YWCA: Recognition of Seventy-five Years. Normal: Illinois State Normal University, 1947.

PERIODICALS

Alumni Quarterly, Illinois State Normal University, (1912–1956).

"Alumni Register, Illinois State Normal University 1860–1927," *Normal School Quarterly,* XXII (July, 1927) 5–362.

Benton, Ralph A. "The Ag Department Looks Ahead," *Alumni Quarterly,* XXXIX (May, 1950), 5–7.

Browne, Richard G. "Let's Have an Autonomous Teachers College Board," *Alumni Quarterly,* XXXVIII (November, 1949) 5–8.

————. "The Quality of our Graduates," *Education Today,* XIII (March, 1954) 2–4.

Cook, John W. "Jesse Fell," *Alumni Quarterly,* V (August 1916), 7–16.

Education Today. Published by the Illinois State Teachers Colleges, 1941–1956.

Fairchild, Raymond W. "ISNU Approaches the Century Mark," *Alumni, Quarterly,* XXXVI (February, 1947), 3–4.

————. "The Sad Plight of Old Main," *Alumni Quarterly,* XXXVIII (November, 1949), 2–3.

Felmley, David. "Defense of Simplified Spelling," *Alumni Quarterly,* I (August, 1912) 11–14.

————. "Expansion of the Normal School," *Educational Review,* XLV (April, 1913), 409–415.

————. "Normal School and the Training School." National Education Association, *Journal of Proceedings and Addresses* (1911), 700–704.

————. "Reorganization of the Normal School Curriculum," National Education Association, *Journal of Proceedings and Addresses* (1914), 498–504.

Hall, Gertrude M. "The Fleet's In," *Alumni Quarterly,* XXXII (August, 1943), 2–4.

Hovey, Charles. "Who Shall be Principal of the Normal University?" *Illinois Teacher* III (March, 1857), 107.

Illinois School Journal, 1881–1889, known as *The Public School Journal,* 1889–1898, and as *School and Home Education,* 1898–1922.

Illinois Teacher, (1855–1860).

Marshall, Helen E. "Simplified Spelling—And David Felmley," *Alumni Quarterly,* XXXII (May, 1954), 8–10.

Parker, Rose E. "Open Letter to Administrators," *Education Today,* VII (December, 1948) 3.

————. "Progress Report on the Preparation of Teachers for Exceptional Children," *Education Today,* IV (December, 1945) 3.

————. "Special Education: A New Division," *Alumni Quarterly,* XXXIII (February 1944), 2–4.

Teacher Education, Field Service Bulletin of the Illinois State Normal University, issued four times a year, September, December, March, and June. 1938–1956.

DOCUMENTS

Illinois, Adjutant General, *Illinois 1861–1866* (revised) *Roster of Officers and Enlisted Men, 16–35* Vol. II, 1900.

Illinois, Board of Education of the State of Illinois, *Proceedings,* 1857–1917 continued as *Proceedings of the Normal School Board,* 1917–1941, and as *Proceedings of the Teachers College Board,* 1941–1956.

Illinois, Illinois State Normal University, *Catalogs,* 1860–1956.

Illinois, Illinois Emergency Relief Commission, *First Annual Report,* (July 27, 1932 to February 5, 1933) Chicago, 1933.

Illinois, State Superintendent of Public Instruction, *Biennial Reports,* 1855–1955.

U. S., Bureau of the Census, *Census of the United States: Population,* 1850, 1860, 1870.

NEWSPAPERS

Daily National Flag (Bloomington, Illinois), 1857–1858.

Daily Pantagraph (Bloomington, Illinois), 1853–1956.

Illinois State Journal (Springfield), 1853, 1857. (Daily)

Normalite (Normal, Illinois), 1920–1956. (Weekly)

Peoria Journal Transcript, 1937. (Daily)

Vidette (Illinois State Normal University student publication, currently issued once a week, was originally a monthly, and later a bi-weekly and a semi-weekly), 1888–1956.

Weekly Pantagraph (Bloomington, Illinois), 1857–1876.

b. UNPUBLISHED MATERIALS

MANUSCRIPTS

Barger, Thomas Morse. "Study of the Curricula Offered for the Preparation of High School Teachers in State Teachers Colleges of Illinois," Unpublished Master's thesis, University of Illinois, 1933.

Burrill, Meldrim F. "Brief History of the Officer Training Navy V-12 Unit, Illinois State Normal University." Marshall Papers.

Burrington, L. L. "Examination in Greek Conducted by the Principal of Illinois State Normal University High School Department," 1876. Milner Library.

Cook Papers. Fragmentary collection of letters to and from John W. Cook, President of Illinois State Normal University, 1890–1899. Milner Library.

Davis Papers. Letters of Judge David Davis and his family. Courtesy of Willard L. King, Chicago, Illinois.

Edmunds, Henry Hugh. "History of the Herbartian Movement in the United States and Its Relation to Present Trends in Education," 1929. (Typewritten) Milner Library.

Edwards, Betsey Samson. Letters to her husband, Richard Edwards, 1844–1900. Edwards Papers. Milner Library.

Edwards, Ellen. "Biography of Richard Edwards." (Typewritten) Ellen Edwards Collection, Milner Library.

————. Collection of letters exchanged by members of Richard Edwards family, also diaries, poems, and essays by Ellen Edwards. Milner Library.

Edwards, Richard. "Autobiography of Richard Edwards." (Typewritten) Edwards Papers. Milner Library.

Edwards Papers. Diaries, letters, sermons, and addresses by Richard Edwards, President of Illinois State Normal University, 1862–1876. Over one thousand items. (Manuscript and typed) Milner Library.

Fairchild, Raymond W. "Five Years in Retrospect, 1933–1938." (Typewritten) Fairchild Papers. Office of the President, Illinois State Normal University.

————. "Modern Trends in the Training of Secondary Teachers," An Address, Thirty-second annual meeting of the Federation of Illinois Colleges, Lake Forest, Illinois, February 14–15, 1936. (Typewritten) Fairchild Papers.

————. "Teaching Teachers to Teach," Address, College Alumni Club, April 18, 1952. (Typewritten) Fairchild Papers.

Fairchild Papers. Correspondence and miscellaneous notes of Raymond W. Fairchild, President of Illinois State Normal University, 1933–1955. Milner Library.

Fell Papers. Letters of Jesse W. Fell. Illinois Historical Survey. University of Illinois, Urbana.

Felmley, David. "The Great Delusion." (Typewritten) Milner Library.

Felmley Papers. Correspondence, notebooks, and manuscript writings of David Felmley, President of Illinois State Normal University, 1900–1929. Milner Library.

Gale Manuscripts. Papers relating to John W. Cook, collected by his daughter, Agnes Cook Gale. Chicago, Illinois.

Hanna, John C. "Early Days at Normal." (Typewritten) Milner Library.

Harper Papers. Notes assembled by Charles A. Harper in preparation of the seventy-fifth year history. Milner Library.

Hewett-Reeder Papers. Fragmentary collection of letters and papers of Edwin C. Hewett, President of Illinois State Normal University, 1876–1890. E. H. Reeder, Champaign, Illinois.

Holmes Papers. Letters and miscellaneous notes of Manfred J. Holmes. Mrs. Elizabeth Holmes Funk, Normal, Illinois.

"Inventory of the Facilities of Illinois State Normal University to Meet the Evaluation Criteria for Teacher Training Institutions for Vocational Agriculture," Illinois State Normal University, 1956. (Mimeographed)

"Lighter of Flames." A pageant commemorating the seventy-fifth anniversary of the first graduating class, 1860–1935, presented June 7, 8, 1935. (Mimeographed)

Marshall Papers. Letters to Helen E. Marshall from faculty, students, alumni and friends of the school, contributing historical data, memorabilia, and reminiscence. Milner Library.

Minutes, Faculty Meetings, 1935–1956.

Niess, Minnie. "George Bunsen." (Manuscript) Milner Library.

Pearson, Irving F. "History of the Illinois Education Association." Springfield: Illinois Education Association, 1953. (Mimeographed)

Pike, Meshack. "Will." McLean County Courthouse. Bloomington, Illinois.

Philadelphian Society Records. Milner Library.

Philadelphian-Wrightonian Joint Records. Milner Library.

"Summary of Extension Program, September 1913 to June 1, 1955." Division of Field Services, Illinois State Normal University. (Typewritten)

Thomasson, Arnold Lee. "A Half-century of Teacher Training in State Normal Schools and Teachers Colleges in the United States, 1890–1940." Unpublished Ph.D. thesis. University of Illinois, 1943. (Typewritten)

Tompkins, Arnold. Letterbook. Copies of letters written by Arnold Tompkins, President of Illinois State Normal University, 1899–1900. Milner Library.

University Council Minutes, 1951–1956. (Mimeographed)

Wakefield, Bandusia. "Examination of first six weeks work of a beginning class in syntax." 1876. (Manuscript)

Wrightonia Society Records. Milner Library.

SCRAPBOOKS

Burtis, Edwin. Programs, photographs, clippings and memorabilia relating to student days of the Burtis family at Illinois State Normal University. Edwin Burtis, El Paso, Texas.

Edwards, Florence. Clippings relative to the Richard Edwards family, Normal University, and the cultural life of Normal and Bloomington. Milner Library.

Gale, Agnes Cook. Volumes relating to John W. Cook while president of Illinois State Normal University and later as president of Northern State Normal School, DeKalb, Illinois. Mrs. Henry Gale, Chicago, Illinois.

Holmes, Manfred James. Photographs and clippings relating to Normal University. Mrs. Elizabeth Holmes Funk, Normal, Illinois.

Lindsay, Mrs. Vernon. Programs, clippings, and memorabilia of the Felmley era. Milner Library.

McLean County Historical Society. Newspaper files, miscellaneous collections.

Sanders, Sue Pike. A niece of Meshack Pike who donated the original campus. Volumes relating to cultural and civic affairs in Normal and Bloomington. Withers Library, Bloomington, Illinois.

Withers Clipping File. Withers Library.

OTHER SOURCES

Illinois State Normal University. Personal interviews with administrative officers, faculty, students, and alumni. 1953–1956. (See footnotes)

————. Office of the Registrar. Miscellaneous records, grades, tuition, attendance. 1857–1956.

Index

337